INEQUALITY, POWER, AND DEVELOPMENT

SECOND EDITION

INEQUALITY, POWER, AND DEVELOPMENT

ISSUES IN POLITICAL SOCIOLOGY

JERRY KLOBY

Humanity Books

an imprint of Prometheus Books
59 John Glenn Drive, Amherst, New York 14228-2119

Published 2004 by Humanity Books, an imprint of Prometheus Books

Inquiries should be addressed to
Humanity Books
59 John Glenn Drive
Amherst, New York 14228-2119
VOICE: 716–691–0133, ext. 210
FAX: 716–691-0137
WWW.PROMETHEUSBOOKS.COM

16 15 14 13   12 11 10 9

Library of Congress Cataloging-in-Publication Data

Kloby. Jerry. 1954–
    Inequality, power, and development : issues in political sociology / by Jerry
Kloby.—2nd ed.
        p. cm.
    Includes bibliographical references and index.
    ISBN 978–1–59102–103–2 (pbk. : alk. paper)
    1. Political sociology. 2. Political culture—United States. 3. Power (Social
sciences) I. Title.

JA76.K58 2003
306.2—dc21

                                                                2003010524

CONTENTS

ACKNOWLEDGMENTS

Knowledge is a social product and acknowledging the help of a few individuals risks doing a disservice to many people whose resources contributed to the publication of this book. Nevertheless, I want to state my gratitude to a number of individuals who were especially helpful.

Susan Gjenvick's assistance in the early stages of developing this manuscript was immensely valuable. She helped transform an early draft into a much more readable text. Her work was meticulous and helped me get over a major stumbling block in writing this new edition. Likewise, Ann O'Hear at Humanity Books made a commitment to this second edition early on, and was instrumental in bringing it to fruition. My colleagues at Montclair State University, Barbara Chasin and Dick Franke, both read selected chapters and helped me clarify my thoughts as well as the presentation. Julia DeGraf copyedited the manuscript. Susan Irby provided research assistance, helped construct the bibliography, and formatted some of the tables. Kathryn Hammond read portions of the manuscript and offered practical suggestions and encouragement. During the writing of this edition, my conversations with Steve Shalom were always helpful. And I want to thank Steve for all the arrangements he made to get us to the World Social Forum in 2003. Much appreciation also goes to Harold Simon for his intellectual support, sense of humor, and last-minute technical assistance.

I also want to thank Kevin Danaher of Global Exchange, Father Roy Bourgeois of the School of Americas Watch, and Mark Berenson for their encouraging comments. Thanks also to William Blum for providing me with his updated "hit list," which readers will find at the end of chapter 8. And thanks to John Cavanagh and the folks at the International Forum on Globalization for information they provided that I've included in chapters 4 and 10, and for all the work they do to expose the faults of corporate-led globalization and to create an alternative vision of the world's future based on justice and sustainability.

I also want to express my appreciation to Michael Burgoon, A. J. Faas, Lisa Scully, and Charles Nagy. Their deep interest in the issues helped motivate me to do a better job.

Finally, my students, especially those in Political Sociology and the Sociology of Rich and Poor Nations, contributed in many different ways. One learns a lot by teaching.

Jerry Kloby
December 2003

1 INTRODUCTION

The typical American lives a relatively secure life. The modern American home has a well-stocked refrigerator, central heating, electricity, modern plumbing, and a wide variety of modern appliances and gadgets. The United States has a very productive economy, but the fruits of this productivity don't reach everyone, and the costs of production take a toll on the people and the planet. The most difficult and dirtiest work is usually done by people who receive the lowest pay. Likewise, the poor often suffer from injuries and diseases that result from unsafe and unhealthy working conditions. And it's not just the working conditions that are unsafe; often it's the living conditions, too, with traffic, pollution, toxic wastes, and crime usually concentrated in or near poorer neighborhoods.

The existing system of production and distribution is not just a national system, it is a global one. This system generates inequality, not just domestically but throughout the world, and in the process it generates animosity and conflict. Contemporary world market trade is dominated by wealthy countries and large transnational corporations, and has displaced millions of people, immiserating them and sowing seeds of economic insecurity and violent social conflict. In addition, it is environmentally unsustainable. The wealthy nations consume a vastly disproportionate amount of the world's resources, particularly its energy supplies, and spew out much greater amounts of pollutants per person than the less-developed nations. To maintain their high rates of production, wealthy nations—the United States in particular—often ally themselves with disreputable governments, giving priority to "energy security" and similar issues over human rights, democracy, and environmental preservation. Global warming, brought about primarily as a result of the high consumption of fossil fuels, has caused large sections of both polar ice caps to melt away. The average temperature of Alaska has increased by 8 degrees over the past 30 years, causing permafrost to thaw, insects to breed at accelerated rates, and forests to die.[1] Great strides have been made in technology, some of which make life easier, better, longer, but perhaps some just make it easier and quicker for us to dig our own graves.

The rapid advances in communications and transportation technology that have taken place over the past few decades have connected the far reaches of the earth like never before and have given rise to the term *globalization*. Is there a special significance to this era? Could it be that by dwelling on the "newness" of the era we are overlooking some common threads that tie the present with the past, threads that should alert us to the continuing existence of age-old challenges that must be faced if humankind is ever truly to live in peace and prosperity?

In his 1964 book, *The Gutenberg Galaxy*, American media critic Marshall McLuhan coined the term "global village." The term was a romantic one that suggested the people of the world were being connected in new and meaningful ways. McLuhan's vision, shared by many, was that technological advances in communications would give us more control over our lives, they would increase democracy, and, simply put, make life better. But today there seems to be a growing fear of, or even resistance to, globalization, with even the elite beginning to question its virtue. Joseph Stiglitz, a Nobel Prize winner and former senior vice president and chief economist of the World Bank, for example, recognizes that the current mechanisms of globalization are deeply flawed and that "globalization today is not working for many of the world's poor. It is not working for much of the environment. It is not working for the stability of the global economy."[2]

What exactly is globalization? Generally, the term refers to increased communications and trade among nations, which in recent decades has accelerated due to advances in transportation and communications (including computers, the Internet, fax machines, fiber optics, satellites, cell phones, etc.), as well as to changes in organizational forms (the division of labor, management structure, organization of production, etc.). But in this shrinking world globalization is being reduced to a four-letter word.

Today, globalization is often seen as a contributor to inequality, a threat to traditional ways of living, a force that erodes highly valued communal bonds, a catalyst for a great deal of violent conflict throughout the world, a threat to the health of the planet, and a threat to privacy and civil liberties. Globalization, in its current form, is a primary cause of *polarization*—a growing division of the world in which income, wealth, and power are becoming more concentrated on one end of the scale and scarcer at the other end. As I will show (especially in chapter 3), a clear polarization of classes has been taking place in the United States for several decades. The same trend can be seen throughout much of the world. In 1979, per capita income in the rich nations of the world was forty-one times higher than that of the world's low-income countries, and by 1992 the gap had increased to fifty-seven times as much. To put this in a historical perspective, consider that two hundred years ago, before the era of intense colonization, the average per capita income in rich countries was only about one and one-half times higher than that of poor countries.[3] The gap between the rich and the middle-income countries has grown as well. These trends will be discussed in detail in the following chapters. Because of the heavily weighted influence of developed nations like the United States, many of the changes that are occurring in the world can be best understood as an extension of the dynamics at work in the developed nations. Understanding the internal economic and political dynamics aids our comprehension of the global ones. In addition, these are processes with deep historical roots. A good understanding of globalization and its accompanying increase in inequality of wealth and power requires an understanding of those roots.

World system theorists use the terms *core* and *periphery* when discussing international affairs, and these are very appropriate terms when talking about globalization. Cores have continuously expanded into peripheries, overrunning local indigenous societies (core nations, or regions, being the wealthy and expanding nations).

Modern globalization is the continuation of the process of core domination of the periphery. This is a process that reached global proportions about five hundred years ago. Early forms of conquest usually depended on brute force. More than five hundred years ago the British were destroying Scottish villages and brutally subduing and removing the population. The conquest of the Americas came about in part by brute force and in part due to the germs Europeans carried with them to which native populations lacked immunity. Likewise, the barbaric raids on Africa deprived that continent of tens of millions of people who played, or could have played, valuable roles in building African societies. In all of these cases, the root cause was economically motivated conquest and expansion, and the end result was the destruction of indigenous cultures—the destruction of traditional communities.

Today, the destruction of local social systems takes place occasionally via brute force but more often through a system that has been in existence for hundreds of years, although it has recently become more centrally coordinated and more efficient. I am referring to the global market. But the global market, too, has rules that can ultimately be enforced by the threat or actual use of brute force. Nations that seek to change the rules or withdraw from the game face severe punishment, as can be seen in the case of Cuba, Iraq, Nicaragua, Vietnam, and Yugoslavia, to name a few of the recent pariahs.

The world economic system, with its political and military support mechanisms, generates tremendous inequality. A study of seventy-seven countries found that between the 1950s and 1990s inequality rose in forty-five of them and fell in only sixteen.[4] Currently, it is estimated that the richest 10 percent of the world's people receive as much income as the poorest 57 percent. In the United States, the richest 10 percent (about 28 million people) have a combined income greater than that of the poorest 43 percent of the world's people (around 2 billion people).[5]

This inequality has created a world of contradictions and startling contrasts. So while the wealthy elite in California try to prevent common folk from accessing the beautiful beaches outside their multimillion dollar homes (one of them claimed the swimmers blocked his view), approximately 1.1 billion of the world's people lack access to adequate clean water; and the elite running some of the world's major transnational corporations have found new profit-making opportunities in the large-scale privatization of government-run water systems taking place in many nations. Dreaming of profitable opportunities, large corporations, such as Suez and Vivendi, have been buying up water supply systems, but no one seems very impressed with their ability to get water to the needy. The main effect of the privatization has not been greater access to clean water but rather higher prices leading to demonstrations and even riots in countries such as Bolivia, Ecuador, Peru, and South Africa.[6]

The world's failure to provide potable water to over a billion people is, in large part, the result of weak and unresponsive governments—governments that are unable or unwilling to mobilize the necessary resources. Private business interests often exploit such situations. They can raise the capital and they impress local leaders with their technological know-how. But their services often neglect the poor because the poor are unable to pay. The technological ability to provide clean water to the world's people exists, but the resources to do the task are not mobilized because it is not a priority of the rich and powerful. The same can be said for many of the other challenges the world faces.

Nearly two and a half billion of the world's people lack access to basic sanitation. Eleven million children under age five die each year from preventable causes—thirty thousand each day.[7] Many of these deaths are from tropical diseases, yet a 1999 study found that of the 1,223 medicines commercialized by multinational drug companies between 1975 and 1997, only thirteen were designed to treat tropical diseases.[8]

According to UNICEF, five thousand children die every day (over two million each year) because they are not immunized against preventable childhood diseases—specifically, measles, polio, tuberculosis, tetanus, whooping cough, and diphtheria. It costs only about seventeen dollars to immunize a child for life against all six of these diseases.

The world has made some significant strides forward over the past few decades. Average life expectancy, for example, has increased by eight years since 1970. The literacy rate has gone up from 47 percent to 73 percent. Infant mortality rates are, in most places, on the decline, and there has been significant progress toward gender equality in school enrollment.[9] Democracy, too, is on the rise, if one defines democracy rather narrowly as the percent of nations having multiparty elections. In 1974, only about 30 percent of all nations had multiparty elections, but by the end of the twentieth century more than 60 percent of the world's nations had multiparty elections.[10]

The downward slide into poverty continues, though, for many people in the nations formerly comprising the Soviet Union, as well as for the former Soviet bloc nations of Eastern Europe. Likewise, sub-Saharan Africa continues to be devastated by war, hunger, disease, and environmental degradation. There are about thirty-six million people in the world suffering from AIDS, 70 percent of them in sub-Saharan Africa.[11]

The 1990s, in spite of economic growth that added approximately $10 trillion per year to the global economy, left the number of people living in poverty basically unchanged at more than one billion.[12] One billion, two hundred million people live on less than one dollar a day; 2.8 billion live on less than $2 a day. And even in the most highly developed nations, more than 130 million people live in poverty.[13]

What is the place of sociology in promoting a better understanding of the many challenges facing the world today? I believe the field of political sociology has much to offer. In his 1979 book *Political Sociology*, Tom

Bottomore wrote: "The pre-eminent themes of political sociology in its formative period during the first half of the nineteenth century were the social consequences of the emergence of democracy as a form of government, and the political significance of the development of social classes on the basis of industrial capitalism."[14]

Today, the challenge to the field is to reevaluate the consequences for democracy in light of the entrenchment of ruling elites and the growth of corporate power, the near monopolization of the media by corporate interests, and the tremendous influence of the mass media on the exchange of ideas. In addition, political sociology needs to elucidate the political significance of the evolution of economic and social relationships in the present-day capitalist world economy, particularly in light of the development of powerful global institutions. Thus, it is necessary for us to update the themes of political sociology and ask: What are the consequences for the great masses of people as a result of the growth of modern transnational corporations, global financial and political institutions, and the extensive influence of modern mass media?

Of course, there is no single answer to this question. The consequences are very different for people in different parts of the world, and they vary according to one's social class. In addition, the question as posed is a very broad one that would take volumes to fully explore. What this book specifically intends to do is give some fairly general answers along with some particular illustrations. In the process the reader will be exposed to a great number of writings that have addressed issues related to the general themes presented here. Thus the book is meant to be useful on two levels: (1) as a general introduction to the issues of power, economic inequality, and global development; and (2) as a sourcebook with references that can be used as jumping-off points to a deeper examination of the issues.

UNDERSTANDING POWER

Some of the best insights into the nature of power in contemporary American society were provided by the sociologist C. Wright Mills (1916–1962). During the height of anticommunism in the 1950s, Mills was able to overcome the biases and fears that afflicted many of his colleagues and astutely analyze power in the United States. Mills recognized the connections among the upper echelons of government, the military, and the corporate world, and labeled this overlapping triangle of power the *power elite*. In

Mills's view the power elite decide national priorities and policies, and their power is reinforced and strengthened by other institutions, especially the mass media. In Mills's analysis of the media, he pointed out that "very little of what we think we know of the social realities of the world have we found out first-hand."[15] We rely on others for our information, hence the media is extremely important in shaping our worldview and our understanding of a wide variety of events. The media, in other words, plays a crucial role in shaping public opinion. In a democracy, the control of public opinion is a very important part of attaining power and holding on to it. Leaders cannot remain in power and have a difficult time instituting their programs if they run counter to public opinion. The exception to this is when the alternative candidates are seen as being as bad as or worse than the current leaders—an all too common occurrence nowadays. The point, however, is that the power elite are acutely aware of the importance of public opinion, which is why they work so hard at managing their image and shaping the public's worldview. As Mills stated, "Alongside or just below the elite, there is the propagandist, the publicity expert, the public-relations man, who would control the very formation of public opinion in order to be able to include it as one more pacified item in calculations of effective power, increased prestige, more secure wealth."[16]

Since the publication of *The Power Elite* in 1956, much work has been done analyzing the control and the content of the mass media, but sociology has not been leading the way. One could argue that sociology, for the most part, has failed to live up to the promise outlined by Mills in *The Sociological Imagination*. The promise of sociology, argued Mills, is to enable us to grasp the interrelationship of biography and history, to help us understand the "larger historical scene in terms of its meaning for the inner life and the external career of a variety of individuals."[17] Instead, much of sociology has focused on quantifiable minutia, almost as an exercise in some prescribed scientific method rather than an attempt to address social problems or to challenge the powers and structures that foster the problems that afflict the individual and society.

This book is an attempt to look at power in American society and the ways in which it extends beyond our borders, affecting individuals in what were once considered to be far-off lands. In the spirit of Mills, this text makes an effort to link the problems of individuals in many different circumstances and tries to understand the social, economic, and political structures that generate these problems. In doing so, I am attempting to do what Mills advised in *The Sociological Imagination*: "to turn personal troubles and concerns into social issues and problems open to public reason" and to combat forces "which are destroying genuine publics and creating a mass society," that is, to struggle against the forces that are creating a society, an entire world even, where people are molded by an extensive penetrating system of propaganda and manipulation.[18]

TYPES OF POWER

What is power? Essentially power is the ability to control other people's behavior with or without their consent. It is the ability to determine who gets what and how much, and it is the ability to attain one's own goals over the opposition of others. The German sociologist Max Weber (1864–1920) described power as "the chance of a man or of a number of men to realize their own will in a communal action even against the resistance of others who are participating in the action."[19] Most people would recognize that it is not always practical that everyone directly exercise power themselves in all situations. The notion that power cannot be equally distributed is reflected in such ageless popular expressions as "too many cooks spoil the broth" or "everybody on the ship can't be a captain." Therefore, power is often invested in certain positions or individuals. Sometimes we consider these power holders entitled to hold power, and sometimes we do not. The question of who is entitled to hold power in particular social institutions or in particular situations is dealt with by the sociological concepts of authority, legitimacy, coercion, and manipulation.

Authority

Authority is the form of power that people recognize as rightfully possessed by an individual, an institution, or a position within a social group. It is a form of power to which people willingly yield. Max Weber described three types of authority:

1. Traditional authority is established and maintained by the customs of a group. Tribal chiefs and feudal monarchs, for instance, based their authority on unwritten laws, birthright, and the general claim that "that's the way it's always been done." Much of everyday behavior falls under the rubric of traditional authority.
2. Legal-rational authority is outlined by clearly defined rules. These

rules are usually written, and they transcend any single individual. Usually these rules are established through a formal procedure by a group of people other than those who must live by them or enforce them. For instance, the laws governing our behavior are not established by the police but by various legislative bodies. Likewise, various regulatory agencies establish the regulations by which various organizations or industries are guided. At least in theory, these agencies are independent of the organizations they are regulating, and they establish their rules according to some objective criteria rather than based on narrow self-interests.

3. Charismatic authority is a type of authority in which power is legitimized by the unique and remarkable qualities that people attribute to a specific individual. The word *charisma* is from a Greek root meaning "the gift of grace."[20] A charismatic leader is often seen as a person of destiny whose mass appeal is fairly spontaneous and sometimes irrational. Charismatic leaders can be a very powerful force that threatens existing leaders and established systems of power.

Legitimacy

The concept of legitimacy can refer to an individual's right to hold power, but more often it refers to the right of a group of leaders or of whole institutions. In much of the discourse in sociology and political science, the term *legitimacy* is used to describe the generally held belief that a political system or economic system, or virtually any social institution, is valid and justified—that it has significant mass support. A *legitimation crisis* is said to occur when a significant number of people begin to question the validity or authority of a political system or of a particular group of leaders. This may go well beyond the point of merely questioning, to refusing to behave as the system of leadership requires, and even so far as setting up alternative institutions. One of the issues addressed in the later chapters of this book is the legitimacy of the new global institutions, such as the World Trade Organization, as well as some of the older ones; the UN, for instance.

Coercion

The term *coercion* refers to another key element of power. Coercion is the use of force, or the threat of force, to obtain a certain goal or to enforce certain patterns of behavior. Coercion can refer to force in the traditional military or police sense, but equally important, though often overlooked, is the notion of economic coercion. Economic coercion is the threat of deprivation and loss, the threat of poverty and hunger, that forces people to make certain decisions and take certain actions. For example, an all-volunteer army is not truly voluntary. The lack of economic opportunity or job training "forces" many young people to "choose" to join the armed forces. Likewise, an economic blockade may coerce a nation's people to elect a political party whose programs they do not agree with, in the hope that this will persuade the other nations to end the blockade. Although technically these people have made a free choice, in fact they have been coerced into making a particular choice.

Manipulation

Manipulation is an illegitimate use of power. It occurs when a group intends to conceal the true role it is playing in an attempt to bring about a desired goal. Mills defined manipulation as "the secret exercise of power, unknown to those who are influenced."[21] Manipulation exists when a person or group is able to set up a set of circumstances that appears genuine but is, in fact, designed to bring about a predetermined outcome, or an outcome favored by the concealed group. Staged events such as presidential press conferences may appear to the public to be an honest exchange between the audience and the president, but in many cases hostile reporters may be excluded and the questions and answers scripted ahead of time. Likewise, a nation might secretly fund opposition groups in a foreign country as a way of promoting a political party that it favors, without people knowing of its involvement.

SOME COMMENTS ON HUMAN NATURE

In discussions about the nature of power one is often confronted with dubious claims about human nature. Humans, some claim, are inherently selfish and aggressive, and they are therefore bound to seek power for themselves. Hence, the structure of society is a clear reflection of people's innate character. Arguments of this sort usually end up drawing one of two conclusions: (1) Since people are inherently selfish, violent, or aggressive, they are bound to create societies that concentrate power and resources in the hands of relatively few people. Systems of inequality are therefore inevitable. (2)

In 1991, at a closed-circuit broadcast to an audience in California, a White House microphone was left on and broadcasting continued after President George Bush had finished his public remarks. Mr. Bush was heard complaining that the questions he was asked were not given in the order in which his staff had prepared him to answer. "These questions! We've got to get this sorted out here. It happened last week, too. Something's going awry here," Bush said to one of his aides. When the questions came in the wrong order Bush appeared confused and told his audience that he could not hear the question.[22]

Society is always going to seem repressive because it needs to hold people's natural selfishness in check in order to keep their destructive nature from wreaking havoc. Systems of inequality and privilege, according to this view, are a small price to pay for maintaining social order.[23]

Both of these points of view tend to justify the existing order of things and dismiss attempts to redistribute power and wealth. However, they either rest on assumptions regarding human nature that are contrary to the anthropological evidence, or they make claims that are virtually impossible to prove or disprove. I believe that the available anthropological evidence shows that people and societies are extremely variable: Some are violent, some are peaceful, some are highly stratified, others are more egalitarian. In the long view of human history, the present era, which is characterized by great technological accomplishments coupled with tremendous social disasters, contains a variety of social structures that did not exist for most of human history. Today we are capable of accomplishing so much, but we have invested a great deal of our efforts in the forces of war and destruction. Is this an inevitable consequence of human nature? I believe the answer is no.

For the vast majority of human history, people lived in hunting and gathering societies, accumulating little in the way of material goods and sharing much of what they were able to produce. The great social inequality that we have today, the extremely complex division of labor, and the tremendously powerful state apparatus, are all relatively new on the scene of human history, and their appropriateness is constantly called into question by the vast scale of the social conflicts and social problems that are so common in the world today. There is a valuable lesson that anthropology is trying to teach us: In particular settings, people emphasize cooperation and sharing; and in other settings, competition and hostility are fostered.[24] This is also the lesson of numerous social-psychological experiments. Stanley Milgram's famous experiment on obedience to authority found that most of us are capable of a level of cruelty beyond what we would believe possible and that this capacity emerges from our conditioned obedience to authority and by our creation of both a physical and a social distance from our victims. His experiment also showed that the vast majority of his subjects were very uncomfortable administering shocks to their "victims" and that many of them would "cheat" in the absence of the authority figure.[25]

Similar lessons have been drawn from Bibb Latane and John Darley's experiments on bystander intervention.[26] Positive responses can be elicited from people when the situation is structured in an appropriate manner. This is true on the level of small groups, and it is true on the societal level. Unfortunately, many of our institutions, particularly on the broadest levels, are structured in ways that elicit destructive behavior. Regardless of one's view of human nature, it is hard to dispute the claim that different social structures bring out different qualities in people. Today, in the United States, there is a highly stratified society with great differences in income, wealth, power, status, and dignity, which are compounded by race, ethnicity, and gender. These differences create a low degree of social solidarity, which makes it easier for people to treat one another disrespectfully and without compassion. Of course, we could console ourselves with the thought that things could be a lot worse than they presently are, but that is not the task of sociology.

Oppressive social institutions and low levels of solidarity exist on the global level as well as on the national level. The world capitalist economy has penetrated into every part of the globe. It coerces people into making decisions that are often self-destructive. Peasants are forced to overfarm or overgraze land that quickly turns to desert, poor people have more children because children are their only hope for future economic security, local elites ruthlessly suppress incipient labor movements. All these are decisions made by individuals and groups who are compelled by external forces that they have not created—and that few people are in a position to even recognize. These are issues that this book hopes to illuminate, to link together, to make public, and to open to critical thinking.

To accomplish this, we need to look at the underlying structures of contemporary American society and grasp the historical forces that have brought us to this point. We also need to understand the influence the United States has on the rest of the world, because over the past fifty to one hundred years, it has exercised greater influence than any other nation in history. In the course of examining these structures and trends we will see that many of today's problems—war, hunger, poverty, underdevelopment, environmental destruction, and so on—have structural roots. The resolution of these problems can come about only through fundamental structural changes that involve a redistribution of power so that decision making will finally include those who have suffered at the hands of the elites around the world.

With this in mind, we ought to recognize that power today is so much greater than it was at the time when Weber wrote his treatise on power. In many ways Weber's concepts seem to be too weak and small in comparison to the modern institutions they are supposed to help us understand. In the twentieth century, 100 million people died in wars, and millions more were the victims of the ruthless pursuit of power and profit. Today, power means control over weapons of mass destruction, and control over billions of dollars of capital that can be used for a great variety of purposes, some that benefit the masses and some that benefit the elites. Power means being able to control international markets and domestic production, to move millions of people to make way for dams, hydroelectric projects, highways, agricultural projects, and the like. In the twenty-first century power means, more literally than ever before, control over the fate of the earth. Power in the twenty-first century is the power to control the media, to control the flow of information with the ultimate goal of controlling public opinion; indeed, controlling people's thoughts. In today's world, stories are leaked to the press, press conferences are orchestrated, the testimony of biased experts is trotted out for corroboration, phony human rights organizations are established to cover up the effects of government policies, dissident journalists are expelled, fired, or rendered speechless in more permanent ways. Power for the elite means demobilizing the masses, keeping them ill-informed or passive with a sense of hopelessness.

It is these aspects of power that this book aims to address, and it does so in two main sections. The first part of the text (chapters 2–5) deals with the development and present-day structure of social classes and political power in the United States; the second (chapters 6–10) deals with a broad spectrum of international issues and events that, in large part, are extensions of the internal political and economic structures of the United States. What I aim to show is that the contemporary period of intense globalization of economic, political, and cultural activity is highly connected to the issues of economic stagnation and growth in the United States, and to the current political climate that has weakened the working class and allowed significant cutbacks in the social-service functions of the state. Competition in a capitalist economic system forces corporations to attempt to increase the rate of exploitation domestically, while investors also search for more profitable capital outlets in other countries and put pressure on the government to pursue a variety of policies that further these two goals. Thus, the U.S. government, as well as many others, has moved to cut back many programs and agencies that serve the general public. This has the dual effect of further weakening the working class while also allowing the state to more efficiently serve the interests of the elite.

When power is held by a relatively small portion of the population, and that group—a political elite—is also the dominant economic class, then the ability to act for the good of broader interests is severely compromised. The perversion of national and international programs by the economic interests of a nation's upper class can lead to disaster. For that to be avoided we have to understand the consequences of U.S. power and the possibilities for transforming it.

NOTES

1. Timothy Egan, "Alaska, No Longer So Frigid, Starts to Crack, Burn and Sag," *New York Times*, June 16, 2002.

2. Joseph E. Stiglitz, *Globalization and Its Discontents* (New York: W. W. Norton, 2002), p. 214.

3. Takis Fotopoulos, "Development or Democracy," *Society and Nature* 3, no. 1, p. 59. See also L. S. Stavrianos, *Global Rift: The Third World Comes of Age* (New York: William Morrow and Company, 1981), p. 38. Stavrianos writes that the average per capita income in the First World in 1500 was three times higher than that of the Third World; by 1850 it was 5 to 1, in 1900 it was 6 to 1, in 1960 it was 10 to 1, and 14 to 1 in 1970.

4. United Nations, *Human Development Report, 2001* (New York: Oxford University Press, 2001), p. 17.

5. Ibid., p. 19.

6. Timothy Egan, "Owners of Malibu Mansions Cry, This Sand Is My Sand," *New York Times*, August 25, 2002. John Tagliabue, "As Multinationals Run the Taps, Anger Rises Over Water for Profit," *New York Times*, August 26, 2002.

7. Gary Gardner, "The Challenge for Johannesburg: Creating a More Secure World," Worldwatch Institute, *State of the World, 2002,* p. 7. See also the UN's *Human Development Report, 2001.*

8. Gardner, "The Challenge for Johannesburg," p. 13.

9. *Human Development Report, 2001,* pp. 9–10.

10. Ibid., p. 11.

11. Ibid., p. 13.

12. Christopher Flavin, preface to *State of the World, 2002.*

13. *Human Development Report, 2001,* pp. 9–10.

14. Tom Bottomore, *Political Sociology* (New York: Harper and Row, 1979), p. 22.

15. C. Wright Mills, *The Power Elite* (New York: Oxford University Press, 1956), p. 311.

16. Ibid., p. 315.

17. C. Wright Mills, *The Sociological Imagination* (New York: Oxford University Press, 1959), p. 5.

18. Ibid., p. 166.

19. Max Weber, "Class, Status, Party" in *From Max Weber: Essays in Sociology,* ed. H. H. Gerth and C. Wright Mills (New York: Oxford University Press), p. 180.

20. Ian Robertson, *Sociology,* 3d ed. (New York: Worth Publishers, 1987), p. 482.

21. Mills, *The Power Elite,* p. 316.

22. Situations such as these were common during the Reagan and Bush administrations. In this particular case the fuss came about because the questions were asked in the wrong order. Imagine if the president had been asked questions that were completely unexpected or that could be considered hostile. See Michael Wines, "Bush's Responses Come From Script," *New York Times,* November 26, 1991.

23. This is essentially Freud's argument in *Civilization and Its Discontents.*

24. One of the best overviews of anthropology's contribution to the understanding of human behavior and social organization is Peter Farb's *Humankind* (Boston: Houghton Mifflin Company, 1978).

25. Stanley Milgram, "Behavioral Study of Obedience," *Psychology and Society: Readings for General Psychology,* ed. Marvin Karlins (New York: John Wiley and Sons, Inc., 1971).

26. Bibb Latane and John Darley, "Bystander 'Apathy,'" in Marvin Karlins, *Psychology and Society* (New York: John Wiley and Sons, Inc., 1971).

2 POLITICAL ECONOMY

UNDERSTANDING THE COMPLEX WEB OF POLITICS, ECONOMY, AND HISTORY

I n the eighteenth and nineteenth centuries, the term *political economy* was commonly used by social theorists to emphasize the connection between the state and the economy. The term gradually fell into disuse partly as a result of the narrow specialization that developed in the social sciences, but also because of the triumph of a particular ideology that sought to obscure the true connections between politics and economics. It has become commonplace to view the economic system as something independent of society's power relationships, almost as if it were not a human creation but a natural entity with a life of its own. Politics, to further cloud reality, has been seen as an entity divorced from the economic system; but in truth, they are not two separate realities. I have chosen to use the term *political economy* here because it emphasizes the fact that politics and economics are closely intertwined, as will be illustrated in the following pages.

In this chapter, I examine the evolution of modern-day capitalism from its roots in feudal Europe to the rapid growth of industrialism and class divisions in the United States, and the transformation of leading industrial societies into imperial powers. This is not an attempt to tell the history of capitalist development in a few pages but, rather, to highlight some themes that may increase our understanding of the forces that have shaped the world into what it is today. For if it is true, as Karl Marx said, that "the tradition of all the dead generations weighs like a nightmare on the brain of the living," then to begin to understand ourselves today we must look at our past.[1]

> "Men make their own history, but they do not make it just as they please; they do not make it under circumstances chosen by themselves, but under circumstances directly found, given, and transmitted from the past. The tradition of all the dead generations weighs like a nightmare on the brain of the living."
>
> —Karl Marx

Chapter 3 continues exploring the relationship between economic and political power in the contemporary United States. In particular, it examines economic inequality and how differential access to economic resources is a form of power that is at least the equal of the various forms of power normally studied under the rubric of political power. In addition, chapter 3 will begin to elaborate how the two realms of power—economic and political—are interrelated and complementary, a theme that will continue throughout the book.

Although my major focus is on the United States, understanding the development of capitalism in Europe can help us to more fully understand capitalism as a whole and how people are affected by the broad sweep of history. There are significant differences between American and European history, especially since the "New World" was free of many of the entrenched institutions and traditions that existed in Europe. But there are similarities as well. Tracing the development of capitalism in Europe will help us understand our own history and, in addition, it will shed light on the impact of modern capitalism in the Third World today, an issue taken up in later chapters.

Historically, the United States has had a reputation as the land of opportunity. In the Americas, unlike Europe, there was no established system of feudal ranks and no historical memory of an aristocratic order of society. In short, the New World was relatively free of many institutions and traditions that could place restraints on its development or provide a model for a new but similar system of social inequality.

THE RISE OF CAPITALISM

In the 1700s and early 1800s, the United States was predominantly a nation of small farmers, small traders, and small businesspeople of various sorts. Ownership of property in the United States, as opposed to the European countries at that time, was quite widely distributed. In the early part of the nineteenth century, some 80 percent of the working population (excluding slaves) owned the means of production (the land, tools, and machines) with which they worked.[2] Since then the class character of the nation has changed dramatically. Today only about 7 to 8 percent of the population falls into the statistical category of "self-employed," and many of these people lack the independence of their predecessors. In fact, some estimate that as many as half of these workers are illegally classified as independent contractors so that employers can avoid paying Social Security taxes and other benefits.[3]

From its early form as a society of independent, small producers and plantation farms dependent on slave labor, the United States quickly developed great concentrations of wealth and a tendency toward monopolization on the one hand, and, on the other, a loss of property and the creation of a large working class almost entirely dependent on the forces of capital (the wealth-owning class).

The development of capitalism in Europe took a very different form than it did in the United States. Europe was a feudal society with long-standing obstacles to the growth of capitalism. In order for capitalism to fully develop, many aspects of politics and the economy had to change, and some of these changes took several centuries to evolve.

Capital

As the word implies, capitalism could not have developed without a certain accumulation of capital, particularly in the form of money. A combination of factors, such as the desire for wealth, population pressures, improvements in navigation, and quests for glory, caused a surge in trade between Europe and other parts of the world. This growth in trade was facilitated by the use of money as a means of exchange and had a significant impact on production. As trade became more widespread so did the switch from production for use to production for exchange, that is, the production of *commodities*. Thus trade, along with nascent small-scale manufacturing, was responsible for the development of the early stage of capitalism often called *mercantile capitalism*.

Labor

The growth of small-scale industry could not have taken place to any significant extent as long as the great masses of laborers were tied to the land as serfs. The quest for labor was one of capitalism's first major conflicts with the existing feudal system. Gradually throughout Europe, the battle for free labor was won as the serfs were freed in country after country. In England serfdom had already nearly disappeared by the late 1300s, but in Russia it continued as late as 1861 when twenty-three million serfs were finally granted their freedom by Czar Alexander II.[4] A similar battle over labor took place in the United States between northern industrialists and southern plantation owners, with slavery finally being abolished by the Thirteenth Amendment to the Constitution in 1865.

Land

The relationship of classes to one another and to the land also underwent great changes, and these changes illustrate the extent to which various social forms are dependent on one another. For instance, abolishing serfdom wasn't enough to gain the laborers needed for the newly developing industries. The peasantry had to be deprived of its right to work the land and make a subsistence from it. It is this element of development, if it can be called that, which remains one of the cruelest and most barbaric stages in the capitalist transformation. In addition to creating a class of potential wage laborers, driving the peasantry off the land gave manufacturers and large farmers access to new land that could be used for their own purposes. The transformation of arable land into pastures for sheep grazing, for example, was critical to wool manufacturing, one of the earliest industrial enterprises. This transformation often required the displacement of large numbers of people and cut into food production, adding to the poverty and misery of an already harsh time.

There was also the large-scale *spoliation* of church property. The Catholic Church was one of the major landowners throughout feudal Europe. In fourteenth-century England, the Church owned about one-third of all the land. It owned about one-third of the land in France, 21 percent in pre-Reformation Sweden, and up to 40 percent in parts of sixteenth-century Russia.[5] Gradually, the large estates owned by the Catholic Church were broken up and given away or sold very cheaply to various royal families and landlords. This spoliation was greatly aided by the Protestant Reformation's attacks on the Catholic Church and is a prime example of how ideological changes come about as a result of, and in support of, changes in the economic system.

There were also a whole series of *enclosure acts* passed by governments, or decreed by royalty, which deprived the peasantry of access to common lands. Typically, villages and towns in feudal societies had unoccupied lands within, or adjacent to, their borders. Villagers could cut down trees in the commons for firewood or building materials, or they could take their livestock there to graze. The common lands were a valuable resource that enabled people to supplement their income, in a manner of speaking. By closing off access to the common lands or making them private property, elites further deprived the rural peasantry of a right to earn a subsistence. They were denied the ability to work and produce for their own survival. The net effect of the enclosure acts was summed up neatly by Thomas Lupton when he wrote in 1622, "Enclosures make the herds fat and the poor people thin."[6]

All these changes put immense pressure on the rural populations of Europe and made it exceptionally difficult for people to remain in the countryside. And if these measures weren't enough to free up the land for landlords, there was always the forced wholesale clearing of estates such as Marx described in volume 1 of *Capital*. In one instance, the duchess of Sutherland (in Scotland) sought to clear 15,000 people from an area of land of nearly 800,000 acres. Marx writes:

> From 1814 to 1820 these 15,000 inhabitants, about 3,000 families, were systematically hunted and rooted out. All their villages were destroyed and burnt, all their fields turned into pasturage. British soldiers enforced this eviction, and came to blows with the inhabitants. . . . Thus this fine lady appropriated 794,000 acres of land that had from time immemorial belonged to the clan. She assigned to the expelled inhabitants about 6,000 acres on the sea shore—2 acres per family. . . . The whole of the stolen clan-land she divided into 29 great sheep farms, each inhabited by a single family, for the most part imported English farm-servants. In the year 1835 the 15,000 Gaels were already replaced by 131,000 sheep.[7]

Deprived of their land and their traditional means of support, the peasantry was transformed into a new class—the *proletariat*—people who must sell their labor to make a living. The displacement of the rural populations of Europe produced one of the greatest mass migrations in human history, what is often referred to as the great *urban implosion*. This dislocation produced a great mass of people who were in many ways superfluous to the new economic order.[8] It created a surplus population that flooded the cities looking for work and eventually crowded the ships headed for North and South America and the hope of a better life. In the Third World today a similar displacement has been occurring as agriculture becomes more mechanized and large landowners and foreign agribusiness push out families who have farmed their land for generations.

In Europe many people were either unable or unwilling to adapt themselves to their new circumstances. The industries in the urban centers had not grown enough to handle the great influx of "free" laborers. As Marx notes, "Great numbers of people were turned en masse into beggars, robbers, vagabonds, partly from inclination, but in most cases from stress of circumstances. . . . Legislation treated them as 'voluntary' criminals."[9]

The changes that took place in landownership and use were tightly interwoven with the form that labor took. In fact, the transformation of land use and ownership probably did more to "free" labor than did all the declarations of emancipation ever made.

It is generally agreed that the modern capitalist class in Europe did not grow out of the old feudal classes of aristocrats and nobles but, rather, out of the small class of merchants and traders that flourished in the spaces that feudal economies left open. But as this new class grew in wealth and stature, the feudal lords were compelled to exercise their authority and tax their way into the new profits.

Feudal Authority

At times the people of the new "middle" class (the *bourgeoisie*) were able to work hand in hand with the feudal nobility, but their overall position and well-being was hindered by the existence of a feudal authority that was able to regulate and tax them. Thus a political struggle was waged in which the system of feudal authority was attacked on ideological and economic grounds. The abolition of serfdom and the decline in the estate or manorial system of relations inevitably weakened feudal authority. The ultimate blow came in 1789 with the French Revolution.

Ideology

Human history has gone through a variety of economic stages. Each of these stages has its own corresponding ideology that serves as support for existing social and economic relationships. The dominant ideology of the feudal era looked at the world, both physical and social, as an immutable God-given arrangement. The condition of human life was to a great extent seen as inalterable and in some ways as payment for humanity's "original sin." Church and king were invested with supreme authority and seen essentially as God's representatives to his earthly kingdom.

As capitalist economic forms proliferated and feudal authority was challenged, the age of Enlightenment dawned upon Europe. The social and political world came to be seen as more and more controllable. Humanity, it was thought, could shape its own destiny guided by reason and determination. The Catholic Church and royalty were increasingly viewed as obstacles to the new order and as accomplices in an oppressive and exploitative feudal system. The staid power of the church and the dominant ideology of the time were challenged by advances in the physical sciences, especially those of Nicholas Copernicus, who put forth the heretical notion that the sun, not the earth, was the center of the solar system, and Galileo Galilei, who confirmed the new theory.

But the new ideology was biased in favor of the privileged and served to justify a new system of economic relations, exploitative and oppressive in its own way. Great masses of people had been deprived of their prior means of support, and the rising bourgeoisie did not want to accept the responsibility for this. Thus an ideology of individualism developed in which one's fate was seen as the result of one's own doing. If you were rich, it was because you worked hard and were skilled. If you were poor, it was due to laziness or perhaps some innate deficiency. The poverty stricken were seen as defective in some way. Their fate was regarded as unrelated to social structure and certainly disconnected from the good fortune of others.

The official treatment of the displaced peasantry and the nascent working class shows clearly that the ideology of the time suited the interests of the dominant class. This ideology took a long time to develop and was perhaps harshest in its earliest formations. In England during the 1500s, a variety of laws aimed at controlling the poor and setting an example for others were enacted. Many of these laws are powerfully described in volume 1 of Marx's *Capital*:

> Beggars old and unable to work receive a beggar's license. On the other hand, whipping and imprisonment for sturdy vagabonds. They are to be tied to the cart-tail and whipped until the blood streams from their bodies, then to swear an oath to go back to their birthplace or to where they have lived the last three years and to "put themselves to labor."
>
> For the second arrest for vagabondage the whipping is to be repeated and half the ear sliced off; but for the third relapse the offender is to be executed as a hardened criminal and enemy of the common weal. . . .
>
> If anyone refuses to work, he shall be condemned as a slave to the

person who has denounced him as an idler. The master shall feed his slave on bread and water, weak broth and such refuse meat as he thinks fit. He has the right to force him to do any work, no matter how disgusting, with whip and chains. If the slave is absent for a fortnight, he is condemned to slavery for life and is to be branded on forehead or back with the letter S; if he runs away thrice, he is to be executed as a felon. The master can sell him, bequeath him, let him out on hire as a slave, just as any other personal chattel or cattle. If the slaves attempt anything against the masters, they are also to be executed. Justices of the peace, on information, are to hunt the rascals down. If it happens that a vagabond has been idling about for three days, he is to be taken to his birthplace, branded with a red hot iron with the letter V on the breast and be set to work, in chains, in the streets or at some other labor. If the vagabond gives a false birthplace, he is then to become the slave for life of this place, of its inhabitants . . . and to be branded with an S. All persons have the right to take away the children of the vagabonds and to keep them as apprentices, the young men until the 24th year, the girls until the 20th. If they run away, they are to become up to this age the slaves of their masters, who can put them in irons, whip them, etc., if they like. Every master may put an iron ring round the neck, arms or legs of his slave, by which to know him more easily and to be more certain of him.[10]

Later laws under King James I were equally harsh. Royalty had little notion of how to handle the problem of rural displacement and urban poverty other than to punish the victims: "Whilst in prison they [rogues and vagabonds] are to be whipped as much and as often the justices of the peace think fit."[11] This "surplus population" became such a nuisance to King Henry VIII that his highness had 72,000 vagabonds hanged during his rule.[12]

Marx sums up the plight of the poor in the early years of capitalism: "Thus were the agricultural people, first forcibly expropriated from the soil, driven from their homes, turned into vagabonds, and then whipped, branded, tortured by laws grotesquely terrible, into the discipline necessary for the wage system."[13]

Gradually, the views of the upper class toward the poor changed as capitalism became more firmly entrenched. The poor came to be viewed in a somewhat kinder way, almost as though they were children who needed to be watched over. They were not regarded as fully capable adults. By the early years of the Industrial Revolution the "theory of dependence," as elaborated and advocated by philosophers such as John Stuart Mill, had become popular among members of the ruling classes: "According to this view the poor are children, who must be governed, who should not be allowed to think for themselves, who must perform their assigned tasks obediently and with alacrity, who must show deference to their superiors, and who—if they conduct themselves virtuously—will be protected by their betters against the vicissitudes of life."[14]

The transition from feudalism to capitalism was accomplished in fits and starts. There was no turning back, and its influence would eventually be felt in every corner of the world. The private ownership of property (including the *means of production*—land, tools, factories, money, etc.) had displaced virtually all forms of collective ownership. The exchange of commodities via a market system became critically important, and wage labor supplanted serfdom and various forms of slavery.

The classic statement of the principles of early capitalism was set forth by Adam Smith in his well-known book *The Wealth of Nations* (1776). Smith argued that each individual would work hard and produce as much as possible if he or she was allowed to work for personal profit. Smith felt that individual greed would be transformed into public good through the workings of the free market, regulated only by the forces of supply and demand. The profit motive, it was claimed, would drive manufacturers to supply goods that the public demands, and competition would ensure that the goods were reasonably priced. The market would regulate itself in the most efficient possible way, as though guided by an "invisible hand."

WEALTH AND POWER IN THE UNITED STATES

In the United States capitalist development was not constrained by feudal economics or firmly established aristocracies. In addition, it was a nation of great resources, eventually populated by a large pool of laborers, and it contained a vast, attractive frontier waiting to be exploited.[15] However, it was far from a classless, or even a fully democratic, society. From the birth of the nation rich and powerful men had a greater voice in determining the nation's course, and they attempted to exclude others from sharing in their power.

During the formation of the U.S. system of government, John Jay (a delegate to the first Continental Congress and the nation's first chief justice of the Supreme Court) declared that "the people who owned the country ought to govern it," and many of our nation's founders agreed with that sentiment.[16] Similar sentiments were expressed by such figures as Alexander Hamilton, the nation's first secretary of the treasury. According to Hamilton:

> All communities divide themselves into the few and the many. The first
> are the rich and the well-born, the other the mass of the people. . . . The
> people are turbulent and changing; they seldom judge or determine right.
> Give, therefore, to the first class a distinct, permanent share in the govern-
> ment. They will check the unsteadiness of the second, and as they cannot
> receive any advantage by a change, they therefore will ever maintain
> good government.[17]

In fact, at least twenty-one of the fifty-five delegates at the Constitutional
Convention favored some sort of monarchy.[18] Ultimately, the vast majority
of Americans were excluded from the right to vote because of their sex,
their skin color, or because they did not own sufficient property. Property
ownership was often a requirement to hold office as well. To be a member
of the New Jersey legislature, for example, one had to be worth at least one
thousand English pounds. In South Carolina, one had to possess an estate
worth at least seven thousand pounds. In Maryland, a candidate for governor had to be worth at least five thousand pounds.[19] Not surprisingly, the
policies of the government tended to favor the wealthy at the expense of
others. These policies helped to firmly establish an American upper class
that is highly exclusive and has vastly disproportionate power and wealth.

The United States has always indulged itself in a powerful myth of social
mobility, but entrance into the upper echelons of its society is very difficult.
This was true in the early years of our nation's history and it is true today.
Historian Howard Zinn, for instance, in his discussion of wealth and power
in the 1800s, points out that "a study of the origins of 303 textile, railroad,
and steel executives of the 1870s showed that 90 percent came from the
middle or upper class families. The Horatio Alger stories of 'rags to riches'
were true for a few men, but mostly a myth, and a useful myth for control."[20]

Building America's Fortunes

Much of the wealth of the early American upper class was derived from
trade within the new nation and also with the countries of Europe. Increasingly, cotton production and textile manufacturing became an important

---

"The necessity of civil government grows up with the acquisition of valuable
property. Till there be property there can be no government, the very end of
which is to secure wealth, and to defend the rich from the poor."

—Adam Smith[21]

part of the world trade system, a way for some to enrich themselves and a way into slavery for others. It has been said that in the eighteenth and nineteenth centuries cotton was to the world economy what oil would become in the twentieth century. Ultimately, the wealth of the plantation owners in the South, and the textile mill owners in the North, along with that of much of the merchant class, was based on the labor of slaves. It was supported by the labor of a people stolen from their homelands in Africa, forced to take a perilous journey across the ocean in ships packed with bodies under debilitating conditions, and finally, if they survived the journey, forced to labor under the cruel whip and harsh authority of the plantation overseer. Slavery was a system of brutal exploitation supported by the legal system and backed with the full force of the government until after the Civil War. Even after legal emancipation, blacks were not entirely free of slavery's effects as they faced discrimination and segregation and toiled under a different form of oppression called "free" labor, but which some referred to as "wage slavery."

The slave "trade" between Africa and Europe actually dates back to pre-Columbian times. The Portuguese started bringing slaves from Africa fifty years before Columbus "discovered" the New World. With the full blessings of the Catholic Church, the slave trade flourished. At first slaves taken from Africa were used as domestic help and as field hands in parts of Europe. Previously the slave trade had been conducted in the area around the Mediterranean Sea for centuries, and it did not have a significant racial character to it. One of the earliest steady supplies of slaves consisted of the people of Eastern Europe, the Slavs. In fact, the English word *slave* is derived from *Slav*.[22]

With the advent of European settlements in the New World and the development of the plantation system, Africans were enslaved in great numbers in order to ensure a steady supply of cheap labor. The majority of slaves were taken from West Africa. Some were taken by force directly by the Europeans, and many others were acquired through trade with coastal African rulers to whom the Europeans paid a rent for land on which to construct their trading posts.

The number of people taken from Africa is unknown. The most common estimates are in the range of forty to fifty million, with only ten to twelve million reaching their final destination alive. Many slaves died on the overland march through Africa to the coastal trading posts, and many more died on the overcrowded slave ships that typically took about five weeks (sometimes much longer) to complete the transatlantic journey. The

Guyanese scholar Walter Rodney (1942–1980) claims that the estimate of ten million Africans brought to the Americas still alive is too low a figure. Rodney also notes that the number has been commonly used by European scholars "who are apologists for the capitalist system. . . . In order to whitewash the European slave trade, they find it convenient to start by minimizing the numbers concerned."[23] Rodney states that "warfare was the principal means of obtaining captives" and that the slave trade, along with the resultant changeover to warlike activities and kidnaping, seriously disrupted Africa's social order and its development. He asks provocatively, "What would have been Britain's level of development had millions of them been put to work as slaves outside of their homelands over a period of four centuries?"[24] The effect of the slave trade on African development is something to keep in mind when reading chapter 7 herein, but our concern at this time is the development of the wealth and power structure of the United States.[25]

Many of the great American fortunes in existence today have their roots in the availability of low-wage labor and in the great land giveaways that followed the Civil War. The greatest of these involved the first transcontinental railroad that was built by the Central Pacific and the Union Pacific railroad companies. During the 1860s, the Central Pacific spent $200,000 on bribes for politicians and was rewarded with nine million acres of free land and $24 million in bonds, in addition to other benefits. The Union Pacific was given twelve million acres of land and $27 million in bonds and sold shares of the railroad to members of Congress for artificially low prices. These great giveaways helped well-known American tycoons such as Cornelius Vanderbilt and Jay ("I can hire half the working class to kill the other half ") Gould make their fortunes, and they were also instrumental to the Carnegies and the Rockefellers, who could now transport their coal, oil, steel, copper, iron ore, and other valuable materials more easily. John D. Rockefeller made secret agreements with the railroad companies that helped drive his competitors out of business and establish Standard Oil as one of the nation's richest and most powerful monopolies. Banking families such as the Drexels, the Morgans, and the Mellons, were also able to take part in the feast, enriching themselves rapidly and fortifying their privileged social positions.[26]

The Pacific Railway Act of 1862 gave the Central Pacific and the Union Pacific five square miles of land for every one mile of track laid. This ensured that the railroad companies would continue to profit as development occurred over the next few decades. Two years later, "after an amazing round of bribery," Congress granted an additional ten miles of land for each mile of track. Congress also decided to put additional cash into the hands of the railroad companies—up to $48,000 for each mile of track.[27] Meanwhile, laborers who built the railroad, mostly Chinese and Irish immigrants, worked for $1 or $2 a day, and railroad workers throughout the country were enduring intolerable conditions. By the mid-1870s, the country was suffering a major economic depression, and 1877 saw the outbreak of a great many strikes and other forms of protest by railroad workers. The owners and the government did not look kindly upon the strikers, and although the strikers ultimately won some concessions, they had to pay a heavy toll. By the end of 1877, 100,000 workers had participated in strikes, 100 people had died, and 1,000 had been imprisoned.[28] Nevertheless, railroad workers were still forced to toil under unfavorable conditions, and an average of ten per day died on their jobs. In 1889 alone an estimated 22,000 railroad workers were killed or injured.[29]

The nation's largest lumber companies also benefited from the government's generosity toward the railroads. When the Northern Pacific Railroad was chartered in 1864, it received a "checkerboard land grant of ten square miles for every mile of track completed in Oregon and Minnesota."[30] In the territory of Washington, the company received twice that amount. All together, the Northern Pacific was generously deeded 38.5 million acres of public land. The primary owner of the Northern Pacific was James Hill. In January of 1900, Hill sold 900,000 acres of Northern Pacific land to his neighbor, Frederick Weyerhauser, for a mere $6 per acre. The deal was the biggest sale of private land in the history of the nation up to that time. It enabled Weyerhauser to obtain a vast supply of resources for his lumber industry at an estimated price of $0.10 per thousand board feet for wood that today sells for an average of about $500 per thousand board feet.[31] What had once been public land or native land was turned into private property and an immensely profitable resource for a select few (reminiscent of the enclosure acts in Europe), while the masses were deprived of land and forced to take on low-paying, hazardous jobs with the railroad and lumber companies. According to author Timothy Egan, "Weyerhauser lumber camps were run like prison yards. No conversation was allowed at meal times, no booze, no women, and, for several bloody decades, no union. Until the labor revolts of 1917, the average pay was no more than two dollars for a ten-hour work day. Men were fired without prior warning. Pay was deducted for use of boots, blankets and bunkhouses, most of which were not heated."[32]

The railroads were not alone in the special treatment that many early

U.S. industries received from the government. The steel industry, for instance, benefited from tariffs imposed on foreign steel. This helped to stifle competition and was instrumental in building the great steel fortunes of the Carnegies and the Morgans. Also key was the exploitation of low-wage labor. At the turn of the century, approximately 200,000 men were employed by the steel industry, and they were often working twelve hours a day for an income that barely supported their families. Millions of workers were toiling to build America's great fortunes, but they reaped few of its benefits. It is estimated that by 1888, 100 workers a day, 35,000 per year, were being killed by the industrial system. From 1888 to 1908, more than 700,000 workers were killed in industrial accidents. In 1913, nearly one million workers suffered injuries on the job.[33] Their working conditions were maintained by a system of labor and other laws that restricted their right to organize, and gave preferential treatment to the owners of capital over the rights of workers. This situation existed not just in the steel industry or on the railroads but throughout the economic structure. Zinn sums up this era of fortune building and monopoly making: "And so it went, in industry after industry—shrewd, efficient businessmen building empires, keeping wages low, using government subsidies. These industries were the first beneficiaries of the 'welfare state.'"[34] Indeed, the state played a vital role in economic development and the accumulation of wealth among a small class of American citizens.

While capitalism was enriching the pockets of a select few, it also experienced major recessions that caused additional suffering and contributed to the development of monopolies. At times, even the wealthiest felt the sting of depression. Eventually, it became frightfully clear that Adam Smith's notion of the invisible hand was not an imaginative and appropriate metaphor but simply wishful thinking. Capitalism throughout the 1800s and 1900s experienced a variety of severe recessions and depressions, with twenty-two crises taking place between 1825 and 2000.[35] Even in good times capitalist societies characteristically have a great deal of poverty. The simple fact is that real demand does not always translate into effective demand. The term *effective demand* refers to demand created by people who have the ability to pay for a particular good or service. Many people, however, are deprived of sharing in society's production because they do not have the money to pay, and when there is no money there is no demand, at least in the strict economic sense. Furthermore, it has become painfully obvious that effective demand is an insufficient stimulus to bring about full production.

SURPLUS VALUE

The heart of the problem lies in what is often called the *crisis of overproduction*, or alternately, the *crisis of underconsumption*. Marx pointed out that since the system of capitalism is based on profit and profit is made by not paying workers the full value of their labor, it is not possible for them to buy back all they produce.

It is important to understand how profit is made. The capitalist purchases materials and labor to make something of value, which he or she sells at a higher cost than of its production. The difference is called *surplus value*. Surplus value is produced by labor. The sale of the product is often referred to as the *realization* of surplus value. This term indicates that there is no profit unless the goods are sold, and that there are whole sectors of workers not involved with production who are essential to the profit-making process, whose payment must ultimately come out of the surplus value when it is realized. Capitalism's basic flaw is the very fact that workers cannot afford to purchase all that they produce. Demand always falls short of production, hence there is a continual crisis of overproduction that periodically worsens and causes major depressions.

Some scholars (e.g., Samir Amin, John Bellamy Foster, Harry Magdoff, Paul Sweezy) have described the problems of contemporary capitalism in slightly different terms. They talk about the tendency of surplus to rise; that is, the productive capacity of modern capitalist societies and the money available for investment are increasing, but capitalists are having greater difficulty finding ways of investing this capital profitably or of putting the increased capacity to work. This is sometimes referred to as the "law of rising surplus" or the "problem of surplus absorption" or simply "overaccumulation." It results from a shortage of profitable investment opportunities and is seen as the primary cause of the periodic economic crisis occurring in world capitalism.[36]

IMPERIALISM

In any event, capitalism's periodic crises, the search for more markets and greater profits, the need for a release valve to relieve the pressure created by the unemployed and the poor all led to an increased tendency to take advantage of the less-developed nations of the world. This meant more than increased world trade; it meant the economic, military, and political domination of a wide variety of nations by the advanced capitalist ones. Such domination reached something of a peak in the late 1800s and early 1900s, a period that is often referred to as the "Age of Imperialism." Some social commentators and statesmen did not view imperialism as a system of exploitation; rather, they saw the colonial age as a time when great nations took a role in governing lesser ones for the good of the latter. Others were more keenly aware of the true purposes of acquiring colonies. English businessman and statesman Cecil Rhodes (1853–1902), who helped colonize southern Africa and made his fortune from Africa's diamonds and gold, saw the acquisition of colonies as a way of defusing social disorder in England. Rhodes, however, did not show a similar concern for the social disorder that white settlements would create in southern Africa, and he declared that he was in favor of "equal rights for every white man south of the Zambezi."[37] A glimpse into Rhodes's thinking, and the thinking of the British elite, is provided in the following statement that he made in 1895:

> I was in the East End of London yesterday and attended a meeting of the unemployed. I listened to the wild speeches, which were just a cry for "bread," "bread," "bread," and on my way home I pondered over the scene and I became more than ever convinced of the importance of imperialism. . . . My cherished idea is a solution for the social problem, i.e., in order to save the 40,000,000 inhabitants of the United Kingdom from a bloody civil war, we colonialist statesmen must acquire new lands to settle the surplus population, to provide new markets for the goods produced in the factories and the mines. The Empire, as I have always said, is a bread and butter question. If you want to avoid civil war, you must become imperialists.[38]

Rhodes is best known as the founder of the De Beers Mining Company and as the person for whom the southern African colonies of Northern Rhodesia (now Zambia) and Southern Rhodesia (now Zimbabwe) were named. His will established the Rhodes Scholarship at Oxford University to educate promising individuals from the British colonial empire, the United States, and Germany.[39]

In the United States the rationale for imperial conquest came from many sources, but the words of Senator Albert Beveridge, speaking in 1898, stand out for their clarity. Beveridge does not cloud the issue with any do-good rhetoric but gets straight to the heart of the matter:

> American factories are making more than the American people can use. American soil is producing more than they can consume. Fate has written

Figure 2.1. Colonialism in Africa, 1914

With the exception only of independent Ethiopia and Liberia,
the African continent was divided among seven European countries in 1914.

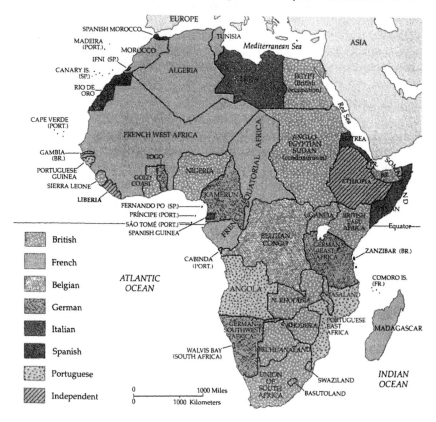

our policy for us; the trade of the world must and shall be ours. And we shall get it as our mother, England, has told us how. We will establish trading posts throughout the world as distributing posts for American products. We will cover the ocean with our merchant marine. We will build a navy to the measure of our greatness. Great colonies, governing themselves, flying our flag and trading with us, will grow about our posts of trade. Our institutions will follow our trade on the wings of our commerce. And American law, American order, American civilization, and the American flag will plant themselves on shores hitherto bloody and benighted, by those agencies of God henceforth made beautiful and bright.[40]

Woodrow Wilson, the twenty-third president of the United States (1913–1921), also spoke frankly about the "need" for imperialism. His words are particularly revealing since he openly admitted that one of the functions of government is to back up, with force, the concessions gained by private interests in other parts of the world and that these concessions are more important than national sovereignty:

Since trade ignores national boundaries and the manufacturer insists on having the world as a market, the flag of his nation must follow him, and the doors of the nations which are closed against him must be battered down. Concessions obtained by financiers must be safeguarded by ministers of state, even if the sovereignty of unwilling nations be outraged in the process. Colonies must be obtained or planted, in order that no useful corner of the world may be overlooked or left unused.[41]

Wilson's administration, as well as those of numerous other presidents, put that willingness to batter down the doors of other nations, sovereignty be damned, into practice many times, as we shall see in detail in chapters 8 and 9.

At times even people who had long careers in the military were willing to speak out to the American public concerning the role that the military often plays. The ability to make such statements requires that an individual break free from an ideology that has been an extremely powerful force, and it also requires the ability to step back and take a very broad view of things. Such an ability was shown by Major General Smedly D. Butler of the United States Marine Corps, who served a portion of his time while Wilson was president:

There isn't a trick in the racketeering bag that the military gang is blind to. . . .

It may seem odd for me, a military man, to adopt such a comparison. Truthfulness compels me to do so. I spent thirty-three years and four months in active military service. . . . And during that period I spent most of my time being a high-class muscle man for Big Business, for Wall Street and for the bankers. In short I was a racketeer, a gangster for capitalism.

I suspected I was just a part of a racket at the time. Now I am sure of it. Like all members of the military profession I never had an original thought until I left the service. My mental faculties remained in suspended animation while I obeyed the orders of the higher-ups. This is typical with everyone in the military service.

Thus I helped make Mexico and especially Tampico safe for American oil interests in 1914. I helped make Haiti and Cuba a decent place for the National City Bank boys to collect revenues in. I helped in the raping of half a dozen Central American republics for the benefit of Wall Street. The record of racketeering is long. I helped purify Nicaragua for the international banking house of Brown Brothers in 1902–12. I brought light to the Dominican Republic for the American sugar interests in 1916. In China in 1927 I helped see to it that Standard Oil went its way unmolested.

During those years, I had, as the boys in the back room would say, a swell racket. I was rewarded with honors, medals and promotion. Looking back on it, I feel I might have given Al Capone a few hints. The best he could do was to operate his racket in three city districts. I operated on three continents.[42]

Thus the major capitalist nations battered down the doors of all nations, demanding "free trade," forcibly annexing colonies, bribing government officials, and making crooked deals. By 1900, much of the world had been divided into colonies, and tensions between the colonial powers were growing, eventually exploding into the destructiveness of World War I. Gradually, the colonized nations obtained their independence, but many would remain beneath the yoke of *neocolonialism*, and others would be so devastated by the colonial experience that they will remain immiserated for many years to come. A further discussion of the full effects of colonialism will be taken up in chapters 7 and 8.

THE EXPANDED ROLE OF GOVERNMENT IN THE ECONOMY

Adam Smith's dreamworld of laissez-faire capitalism crumbled long ago in the face of the real world of economic crisis and political upheaval. In the period after the Great Depression of the 1930s, capitalist governments generally took the point of view that the free market is an inadequate force and therefore requires some government intervention or stimulus. The theorist most often credited with providing the intellectual underpinnings for the idea of government intervention is British economist John Maynard Keynes (1883–1946). Keynes advocated direct government intervention in the business cycle, particularly through control of the money supply, in order to keep up effective demand and avoid periodic crashes. In the United States his ideas heavily influenced the policies of Franklin Roosevelt as his administration struggled to free the nation from the Great Depression. The government practice of generating revenue through taxation and spending in order to stimulate the economy (or to provide services that the private sector has failed to provide) helps to keep the economy functioning. Nowadays the government often spends far more than it actually takes in through taxation, forcing it to borrow billions of dollars each year. The reasons for this go well beyond the single purpose of stimulating demand and will be discussed in chapter 5.

The growth of the federal government during the Great Depression and the various job programs created by Roosevelt did have an impact on the economy, but they were not enough to pull the country out of the Depression. As late as 1939, the United States was still suffering unemployment of over 17 percent.[43] It took a world war to create the kind of stimulus needed to fire up the economy, and after the war, the United States found itself in a uniquely beneficial position.

The United States emerged from World War II with its industrial system intact and working at full capacity. Its communication and transportation systems were in good shape, and the U.S. military was paramount. By contrast, its economic rivals were devastated by the war. European factories and infrastructures were greatly destroyed, and the nations of Europe had suffered tremendous loss of life.[44] This left the United States in a situation where it could expand its political and economic influence in the less-developed countries and also in Europe. France, England, and Holland, in particular, were unable to maintain their overseas colonies, and the vacuum was partly filled by the United States. In Europe, the United States, primarily through the Marshall Plan, made new inroads into the European economies. The United States provided grants and loans amounting to over $13 billion for the rebuilding of Europe. The plan was not purely an act of altruism. It was also a long-term investment that gave U.S. companies a share in Europe's profit making for the next couple of decades.

Table 2.1. Unemployment Rate 1929–1943

1929	3.2%
1930	8.9
1931	16.3
1932	24.1
1933	25.2
1934	22.0
1935	20.3
1936	17.0
1937	14.3
1938	19.1
1939	17.2
1940	14.6
1941	9.9
1942	4.7
1943	1.9

Meanwhile, consistently high levels of military spending provided a stimulus for the U.S. economy and supplied industries with expanding profits and a large reservoir of capital. American automobile companies flourished, and American oil companies enjoyed almost unlimited growth and unrestricted access to the world's oil supplies due to the defeat of their Japanese and German counterparts. The growth of government and corporations in the post–World War II period laid the foundation for prosperity and optimism in the following decades in the United States. However, it was a prosperity and optimism that not all shared, and in the end it proved temporary as worldwide stagnation took hold in the 1970s.

NOTES

1. Karl Marx, "The Eighteenth Brumaire of Louis Bonaparte" in *The Marx-Engels Reader*, ed. Robert C. Tucker (New York: W. W. Norton, 1972), p. 437.

2. Tom Bottomore, *Political Sociology* (New York: Harper and Row, 1979), p. 48.

3. Abby Scher et al., "Habitual Offenders," *Dollars and Sense*, September/October 1999, p. 29.

4. Karl Marx, *Capital* (New York: International Publishers, 1967), 1:717; and Louis L. Snyder, *The Making of Modern Man* (Princeton, N.J.: D. Van Nostrand Company, 1967), p. 453.

5. Harold R. Kerbo, *Social Stratification and Inequality* (New York: McGraw-Hill, 1991), pp. 74–75.

6. Michel Beaud, *A History of Capitalism, 1500–1980* (New York: Monthly Review Press, 1983), p. 31.

7. Marx, *Capital*, 1:729–30.

8. One researcher estimated that in 1788, in France, 10 percent of the rural population was reduced to begging because of land seizures (Kerbo, *Social Stratification and Inequality*, p. 77).

9. Marx, *Capital*, 1:734.

10. Ibid., 1:734–36.

11. Ibid.

12. Karl Marx, "The German Ideology" in *The Marx-Engels Reader*, ed. Robert C. Tucker (New York: W. W. Norton, 1972), p. 145.

13. Marx, *Capital*, 1:737.

14. Reinhard Bendix, *Work and Authority in Industry* (Berkeley: University of California Press, 1956), p. 435.

15. It was to the advantage of the settlers (and the colonial powers) to think of the "new world" as a frontier ripe for the taking, and much of American history has underplayed the extent to which the two continents were populated by established societies. The most recent estimates put the population of North and South America in the tens of millions and possibly over 100 million at the time Columbus made his first landing in the Caribbean. See Roxanne Dunbar Ortiz, "Aboriginal People and Imperialism in the Western Hemisphere," *Monthly Review* (September 1992); and also Hans Koning, *Columbus: His Enterprise* (New York: Monthly Review Press, 1976, 1991), and *The Conquest of America* (New York: Monthly Review Press, 1993).

16. Michael Parenti, *Democracy for the Few*, 5th ed. (New York: St. Martin's Press, 1988), p. 5.

17. Dennis Gilbert and Joseph A. Kahl, *The American Class Structure* (Homewood, Ill.: Dorsey Press, 1982), p. 2.

18. Parenti, *Democracy for the Few*, p. 67.

19. Ibid., chap. 4.

20. Howard Zinn, *A People's History of the United States* (New York: Harper and Row, 1980), p. 248.

21. Parenti, *Democracy for the Few*, p. 4.

22. Michael Parenti, *Against Empire* (San Francisco: City Lights Books, 1995), p. 2.

23. Walter Rodney, *How Europe Underdeveloped Africa* (Washington, D.C.: Howard University Press, 1974), p. 96.

24. Ibid., p. 101.

25. Information on the slave trade comes primarily from L. S. Stavrianos, *Global Rift: The Third World Comes of Age* (New York: William Morrow and Company, 1981), pp. 105–10. See also Basil Davidson, *The African Slave Trade*

(Boston: Little, Brown and Company, 1961). Davidson makes the point in regard to the loss of lives: "So far as the Atlantic slave trade is concerned, it appears reasonable to suggest that in one way or another, before and after embarkation it cost Africa at least fifty million souls. This estimate may be about one-fourth of Black Africa's approximate population today, and is certainly on the low side" (pp. 80–81).

26. Zinn, *A People's History*, p. 249. On the Rockefeller deals with the railroads, see p. 250; and Peter Collier and David Horowitz, *The Rockefellers* (New York: Signet, 1976), pp. 21–22.

27. Harvey Wasserman, *Harvey Wasserman's History of the United States* (New York: Harper and Row, 1972), p. 5.

28. Zinn, *A People's History*, p. 246.

29. Wasserman, *Harvey Wasserman's History*, p. 32; and Zinn, *A People's History*, p. 250.

30. Timothy Egan, *The Good Rain* (New York: Random House, 1990), p. 167. The land given to the Northern Pacific Railroad amounted to approximately sixty thousand square miles. By comparison, the state of Washington is about sixty-eight thousand square miles.

31. Ibid., pp. 167–68.

32. Ibid., p. 168.

33. Wasserman, *Harvey Wasserman's History*, p. 32.

34. Zinn, *A People's History*, p. 251.

35. Ernest Mandel, *The Place of Marxism in History* (Amherst, N.Y.: Humanity Books, 1994), p. 34.

36. For examples see Paul Baran and Paul M. Sweezy, *Monopoly Capital* (New York: Monthly Review Press, 1966), esp. p. 108; and John Bellamy Foster, *The Theory of Monopoly Capitalism* (New York: Monthly Review Press, 1986).

37. *Encyclopedia Britannica* (1985), vol. 10, p. 27.

38. Quoted in V. I. Lenin, *Imperialism, The Highest Stage of Capitalism* (New York: International Publishers, 1939), p. 79.

39. David Crystal, *The Cambridge Biographical Encyclopedia* (Cambridge: Cambridge University Press, 1994), pp. 794–75.

40. Felix Greene, *The Enemy: What Every American Should Know About Imperialism* (New York: Vintage, 1971), p. 105.

41. Parenti, *Against Empire*, p. 40.

42. Greene, *The Enemy*, pp. 106–107.

43. Depression-era unemployment rates are from Nancy E. Rose, *Put to Work* (New York: Monthly Review Press, 1994), p. 19.

44. An estimated nineteen million military personnel were killed in World War II, along with twenty million civilians. Most of the dead were Europeans, although the Chinese and Japanese suffered severe loss of life as well. In addition, the Nazis exterminated 5.1 million Jews, 2 million Poles, and 800,000 Gypsies. See Zbigniew Brzezinski, *Out of Control: Global Turmoil on the Eve of the Twenty-first*

Century (New York: Macmillan, 1993), pp. 9–10. See also Eric Hobsbawm, *The Age of Extremes: A History of the World, 1914–1991* (New York: Vintage Books, 1996), chap. 1.

Table 3.1. Income in Constant (1999) Dollars

Year	Median Family Income	Median Household Income
1973	42,536	37,104
1983	41,115	34,934
1993	42,612	36,019

single-parent households and nontraditional living arrangements. One byproduct of this has been the switch from "family" to "household" data by the Census Bureau, and other researchers and analysts, in order to more accurately depict trends in income and other indicators of well-being. (See "Note on Income Distribution" below and also Fig. 3.3.)

Both the family and household data show the same trend, however, and that is a serious dip in median income starting in 1974 and continuing, with minor fluctuations, for twenty years. Thus, in stark contrast to the steady and significant income growth the typical American household experienced from the end of World War II to the early 1970s, incomes barely changed from 1973 to 1993 (Table 3.1).

The slowdown in economic growth of most of the last quarter of the twentieth century put many people out of work and caused many others who might not have previously needed jobs to look for employment. Hence the unemployment rate paradoxically climbed at the same time that the labor force participation rate went up. During the 1960s, unemployment averaged

Note on Income Distribution: The differences between households and families is worth noting, especially as to how the two have changed over the last fifty years or so. According to the Census Bureau, a smaller percentage of people live in families now than in the 1940s. As a result the Bureau feels that income distribution by household is the more comprehensive unit of analysis. The Bureau started collecting income distribution data by household in 1967. Families are defined as two or more people living together who are related by blood, marriage, or adoption. Households include these criteria, as well as unrelated people living together, or people living alone.[1]

Note on data coding: Beginning with data collected for 1993, the survey permitted households to report up to $1 million in earnings, up from $300,000. The older survey artificially decreased income inequality. The new one is more accurate but it makes comparisons between different years more difficult. One analyst estimated that the change accounted for about one-third of the increase in inequality.[2]

3

ECONOMIC INEQUALITY IN THE UNITED STATES

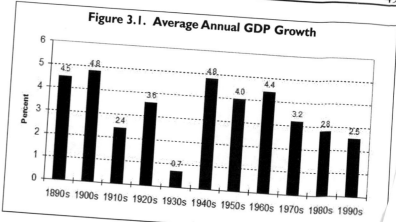

Figure 3.1. Average Annual GDP Growth

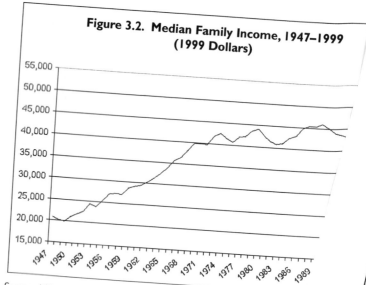

Figure 3.2. Median Family Income, 1947–1999 (1999 Dollars)

Source: U.S. Bureau of the Census

World War II left the United States in a unique position that boosted the economy for years to come with much of the population sharing in the benefits. As measured by the most commonly used indicator of economic strength, the Gross Domestic Product (GDP), the U.S. economy grew at an average annual rate of over 4 percent during the 1940s, 1950s, and 1960s (see Fig. 3.1). This economic growth was shared by much of the population, and median income grew accordingly (Fig. 3.2). During the 1950s real median family income increased 35 percent, and in the 1960s it increased 37 percent. Americans enjoyed economic prosperity and a feeling of optimism that came with the steady growth. But by the 1970s, the European and Japanese economies had been rebuilt into strong independent competitors, and since none of the long-term problems that accompany production for profit had been successfully addressed (specifically, the problem of surplus absorption), long-term economic stagnation set in. By the 1970s, growth had dropped to 3.2 percent per year and then 2.8 percent in the 1980s. The 1990s started off even slower. GDP growth in the first six years of the decade averaged just 1.8 percent, the lowest growth rate since the Great Depression. Three strong years to finish out the decade brought the average growth for the 1990s up to 2.5 percent annually.

As the U.S. economy slowed, more and more women entered the labor force. This provided some with a newfound economic independence, which, along with liberalization of divorce laws, set the stage for more

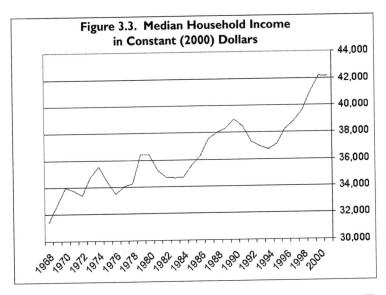

Figure 3.3. Median Household Income in Constant (2000) Dollars

4.4 percent per year. During the 1970s, the average rose to 6.2 percent. The rising trend continued in the 1980s as the average yearly unemployment rate climbed to 7.2 percent before it dropped back down to just below 6 percent in the 1990s. The contrast in unemployment rates between the 1960s and more recent years would be even greater if not for several revisions made by the federal government in the way the rate is calculated. All of the revisions resulted in a lower official unemployment rate (economist Michael Yates has pointed out that no change was ever made that increased it).[3]

Like the unemployment rate, the labor force participation rate, which measures the percent of the civilian noninstitutional population age sixteen and over who are either employed or actively looking for work, has risen significantly. In 1960, the labor force participation rate was 59.4 percent and by 1970 it had crept up to 60.4 percent. But as stagnation set in and incomes faltered, the labor force participation rate rose more dramatically. In 1980, 63.8 percent of the population age sixteen and up was in the labor force, and by the late 1990s, that number had climbed to over 67 percent, with most of the increase due to more women entering the labor force. In 1960, the labor force participation rate for women was 37.7 percent, but by 1990, it had grown to 57.5 percent.[4]

The basic fact is that income growth for typical American families and households nearly came to a halt after the mid-1970s, and this happened even though more people took on jobs. A look at Figure 3.2 shows that from 1950 to 1973, median family income more than doubled but from the mid-1970s to the mid-1990s, median family income increased only slightly. The labor force participation rate, on the other hand, increased only slightly from 1950 to 1973 (from 59.2 percent to 60.8 percent) but grew quite dramatically from 1973 to 1996 (from 60.8 to 66.8 percent).[5]

Median income figures don't tell the whole story, however. The median is a mathematical "middle" that doesn't give us much of a sense of overall

Who Counts in the Unemployment Rate?

The Bureau of Labor Statistics (BLS) calculates unemployment rates from a monthly sampling of approximately sixty thousand households. The BLS defines employment as full- or part-time work for pay, fifteen hours or more without pay in a family business, or unpaid leave because of illness, labor dispute, bad weather, or personal reasons. Persons in the sample are considered unemployed if they are jobless during the survey week, are available for work, and had made specific efforts to find work sometime during the past month—answering want ads, contacting an employment agency, and so forth. The BLS categorizes as out of the labor force, students, retirees, people at home because of long-term ill health or disabilities, homemakers, and those who have given up looking for work.

The BLS undercounts the unemployed in a number of ways. The most glaring exclusion is the category of "discouraged workers," those who say they want work but are no longer looking. The BLS calculated an average of 500,000 such "discouraged workers" in 1994.

Also omitted by the BLS were 1.3 million people who said they were available to work but were not currently looking due to family responsibilities, time taken up by school or training, or health problems.

Another 4.3 million workers told the BLS they were working part-time but wanted full-time work and couldn't find it. We can incorporate these workers into the unemployment count by assuming they work on average half-time and counting half of them as unemployed.

Adding together the discouraged workers, those who are available to work but are unable to search for a job at present, half of the involuntary part-timers, and those the BLS lists as unemployed, the number of unemployed people rises to 11.9 million, a rate of 9.2 percent.

Another 6.2 million people said they wanted a job but had not looked for one within the past twelve months. Even if only a small fraction of them were truly available for work, this would add more than one million people to the unemployment rolls, increasing the true "underemployment" rate to around 12 percent.[6]

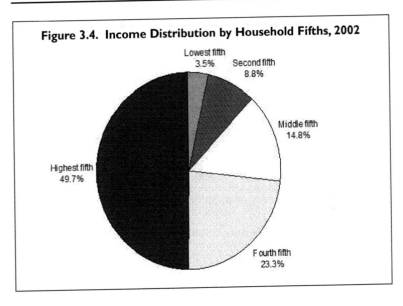

Figure 3.4. Income Distribution by Household Fifths, 2002

Lowest fifth
3.5%

Second fifth
8.8%

Middle fifth
14.8%

Highest fifth
49.7%

Fourth fifth
23.3%

distribution. For instance, the upper half of families or households could be experiencing significant income growth while those in the bottom half are getting poorer and thus the median would remain the same. The median also tells us nothing about how much people have to work for their income. An unfortunate fact about today's economy is that most families and households are working considerably more hours for little or no income growth, compared to past decades. The labor force participation rates help give a better sense of the broader picture, but there are other indicators as well. First, let's look at recent income distribution figures.

INCOME DISTRIBUTION

In 2002, the fifth of American households with the lowest income received just 3.5 percent of all the nation's income (see Fig. 3.4). The fifth with the highest income, in contrast, received 49.7 percent. In other words, the richest fifth receives over fourteen times more income than the poorest fifth. In the mid-1970s the ratio was just ten to one. Almost yearly the United States has been reaching a new extreme in the degree of income inequality. The differences are highlighted even more if we look at the highest 5 percent. In 2002, the highest 5 percent of households received 21.9 percent of the nation's

Table 3.2. Productivity versus Compensation[7]

Year	Productivity per hour (1992=100)	Hourly wages (1999 dollars)	Annual hours
1967	64.6	$13.24	1,758
1973	75.2	15.75	1,720
1979	81.3	15.62	1,745
1989	93.5	16.20	1,823
1995	102.4	15.82	1,868
1998	110.2	16.74	1,898

income, compared to 15.9 percent twenty-six years earlier. In other words, in the year 2002, a typical household in the top 5 percent received twenty-five times more income than a typical household in the lowest fifth. In 1975 the ratio was just fourteen to one. As we look at the top end of the income ladder we see families and households that have had rapidly increasing income, but on the middle and lower rungs income has stagnated.

WORKING MORE, EARNING LESS

Another way to look at the relative well-being of Americans besides looking at their income is to look at how much time it takes to make that income. In contrast to the 1950s and 1960s, when income grew steadily, incomes in the past twenty-five years have been relatively stagnant for most Americans. In fact, for many categories of workers, incomes have decreased. Families and households have compensated, in part, by working more or having more members work. The income distribution figures we have looked at so far would be even more unequal if many working-class households didn't increase their time at work. One study showed that new employment resulted in an increase in the number of hours worked per capita of nearly 10 percent from 1970 to 1986.[8]

Table 3.2 shows how the average number of hours worked per year has grown since 1967. The table also shows how much greater productivity per hour has increased compared to hourly wages.

One of the most significant changes has been the influx of more women into the paid labor force. In 1979, married men averaged 2,104 hours per year at work, married women, 969. By 1996, married men were working forty-six more hours in a year (the equivalent of about six additional workdays), and married women increased their work year by 354 hours.[9] Commuting time has most likely increased too. A telling fact is that in the 1950s for every worker there were two nonworkers. Today, however, there is barely more than one nonworker for each worker. In other words, one income nowadays supports fewer dependents.

More people are working extra long workweeks as well. In 1976, 13 percent of nonagricultural wage and salary workers put in forty-nine hours or more at work each week, but by 1996 that number had increased to 18.5 percent of nonagricultural workers.[10] American workers now spend more time at work than do workers in any other economically advanced nation, having recently surpassed Japan in this category. We put in more hours in a typical workweek, have fewer holidays than many countries, and less vacation time (see chapter 6). In addition, the percent of people over age sixty-five who still work rose throughout the last half of the 1990s.[11] This follows a decrease that had been very steady for three decades. In short, more people are in the paid labor force and they are working longer hours—a trend that has been underway since the 1970s.

In spite of this additional work, many Americans have gone deeper in debt. Some of this, no doubt, has to do with the pressures of commercialism and the prevailing ethic that one is successful if one consumes grandly, and that one achieves personal fulfillment through consumption. These are beliefs that are destructive on the personal level as well as from an ecological point of view. However, a big part of the debt problem is simply that wages, for many people, have not kept up with prices. In addition, more household members working brings expenses that consume much of the added income. As individuals take on jobs, the associated expenses such as childcare, transportation, clothes, dining out, and so forth, grow. Accompanying more recent growth trends are some ominous warning signs of future stress. One of these is the growth of personal debt and the decrease in personal savings.

The stagnation that gripped the U.S. economy starting in the mid-1970s was often used to explain stagnating or falling wages, but it did not mean a lack of prosperity for all. For the most part the middle and lower classes suffered more, while the upper 20 percent or so did quite well. In fact, throughout the lean years from 1974 to the mid-1990s, as well as in the growth years of the late 1990s, inequality rose. Inequality has been a major characteristic of American society from its inception. As the nation industrialized in the 1800s it also became more polarized. The great industrial empires of the Rockefellers, the Morgans, the Carnegies, the Vander-

Table 3.3. Internal Revenue Gross Collections, by Source (in percent)[12]

Source	1960	1970	1980	1993	2001
Individual income taxes	49.0%	53.0%	54.9%	49.8%	50.2%
Employment taxes*	12.2	19.1	24.7	35.0	32.3
Corporate income taxes	24.2	17.9	13.9	11.2	10.0
Estate and gift taxes	1.8	1.9	1.3	1.1	NA
Excise taxes	12.9	8.1	4.7	3.0	3.3

*Includes old age, disability, and unemployment insurance.

bilts, and others were made as the United States became more clearly divided between a small class of wealthy capitalists on the one hand, and a large class of wage laborers living in or near poverty on the other hand. The growth of the labor movement and the extension of democratic rights to more and more of the population gradually strengthened the working class, and gains were made in income, hours, benefits, Social Security, etc. However, in the last quarter of the twentieth century the trend toward polarization recurred.

The official income statistics we have been relying on may be reasonably accurate in examining historical trends, but the reader should be aware that they underestimate inequality to a considerable extent. For one thing, certain types of income are not included in the Census Bureau surveys that produce these statistics. Not included are such income sources as food stamps, health benefits, subsidized housing, full or partial payment by business for educational and medical expenses, transportation or vehicle use provided by a business, and other similar noncash benefits. Nor are capital gains included. Another inadequacy in the data results from the underreporting of certain types of income. Interest and dividend income have traditionally been underreported in the income surveys. Various attempts to calculate these other forms of income have been somewhat controversial and haven't always clarified the picture; nevertheless it is quite clear that interest and dividend income, along with capital gains, are types of income that accrue disproportionately to the rich and if they were counted more accurately the income distribution picture would reveal even more inequality.[13]

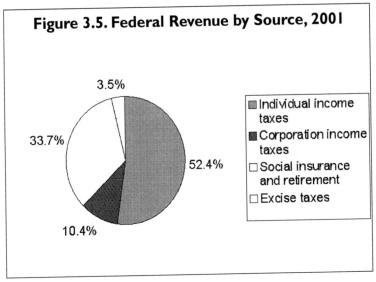

Figure 3.5. Federal Revenue by Source, 2001

- Individual income taxes
- Corporation income taxes
- Social insurance and retirement
- Excise taxes

3.5%
33.7%
52.4%
10.4%

Source: *Statistical Abstract of the United States, 2001.*

TAXES AND INCOME DISTRIBUTION

The income figures cited thus far refer to before-tax income. A number of studies have been done that attempt to measure the effect of taxes on the income distribution picture. Perhaps the most thorough work has been done by Joseph Pechman who found that the income distribution picture doesn't change very much after taxes and, in fact, that in more recent years the burden of taxation has tended to fall somewhat more heavily on the lower end of the income spectrum, while the tax burden has decreased substantially for people near the top. Thus the after-tax picture ought to reveal even greater inequality than we've shown above.[14]

Prevailing analysis shows that overall the tax system has little effect on the distribution of income. Some taxes, particularly the federal income tax and estate taxes are more progressive (taxing higher incomes at a higher rate) and others such as state sales taxes and local property taxes are regressive. Government cash transfers such as Social Security payments and TANF (Temporary Assistance to Needy Families) do help to distribute income a little more equally. But calculations regarding the redistributive effect of government spending often overlook subsidies for certain industries, contributions to health and pension programs, price supports, military contracts, etc., that account for a great deal of government spending and can directly add to the incomes of wealthier Americans while also having a significant indirect effect.

No discussion of federal taxes should overlook the changes that have taken place over recent decades, which have resulted in a greater reliance on payroll taxes and a dramatic drop in corporate income taxes. Table 3.3 and Figure 3.5 show how this shift has occurred since 1960.

The two most notable trends that show themselves in this table are: (1) the greater dependency on employment (payroll) taxes, and (2) the major drop in corporate income taxes as a source of government revenue. Estate and gift taxes have also decreased somewhat, as have federal excise taxes (taxes on alcohol, tobacco, certain manufactured goods, and the windfall profits tax). Tax revenues from corporations have also fallen for municipal governments. In 1957, corporations paid property taxes that accounted for about 45 percent of local property tax revenues; by 1987 they accounted for just 16 percent. This, combined with cutbacks in federal and state contributions to municipalities, has caused personal property tax rates to rise sharply across the nation.[15]

INCOME AT THE TOP

Income inequality has increased because of income stagnation at the low end of the pay scale and rapidly escalating compensation at the high end. Executive pay increased 571 percent from 1990 to 2000 (before adjusting for inflation) compared to 37 percent for workers. Inflation for the period was 32 percent (see Fig. 3.6).[16]

In the United States, CEO pay is 531 times greater than the pay of an average worker. This is phenomenal growth since 1980, when the difference was 42 to 1, and 85 to 1 in 1990. And it is unmatched by any other country (see chapter 6). One way of grasping the significance of this

"There are a lot of Americans who do not recognize that their financial comfort is a consequence of conditions and programs in this country that made it possible for them to be wealthy."

—William Gates Sr.[17]

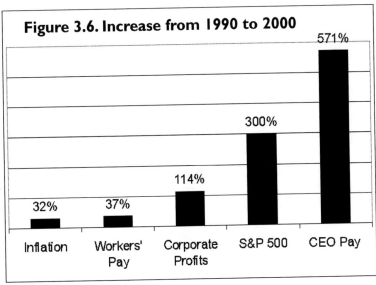

Figure 3.6. Increase from 1990 to 2000

Source: Anderson, et al., p. 3.

increase is to imagine if the pay of other workers had grown at the same rate. In 1990 the minimum wage was $3.80; had it grown at the same rate as CEO pay, it would have been $22.50 in 2000. If the average income for production workers had grown at the same rate as CEO pay, their annual earnings would be $120,491 instead of $23,753.[18]

So how much do the top CEOs in America make? According to *BusinessWeek*'s annual compensation survey, the *average* income for the 362 CEOs surveyed (including salary, bonuses, and the value of exercised stock options) was $13.1 million dollars in 2000.[19]

WEALTH

Wealth is the value of all assets that an individual or family owns. Net wealth is wealth minus debts such as home mortgages, personal loans, credit card debt, etc. There are three useful things to keep in mind about wealth. First, wealth ownership generates income. A significant portion of all income in the United States comes through ownership rather than from wages, salaries, pensions, and other income sources. So wealth and income distribution tend to be correlated. Second, wealth can be considered stored-up purchasing power. Thus, wealth can be tapped to make a large purchase, or to take advantage of a lucrative investment opportunity, or to tide one over during a difficult time that might result from a family member's health problem or similar personal crisis. Third, wealth ownership gives us an idea of who owns and controls America's economic system. We are all a part of the economy, but many of us own no financial assets that give us any control over corporate policy, investment decisions, and other economic considerations that affect how we build our society.

Good data on wealth has been historically much more difficult to come by than that on income. Only recently has a consistent methodology been adopted, so it is difficult to make any certain statements about long-term trends.

Let's look at the most recent figures gathered by the Federal Reserve Board. According to their June 2000 report the wealthiest 1 percent of Americans own 34 percent of all net wealth in the United States.[20] By contrast, the lower 90 percent of Americans own 31.3 percent of all net wealth. In other words, the richest 1 percent (about 2.8 million people) have more wealth than 257 million Americans combined. And while the median net worth of all Americans in the United States is $71,600, the *minimum* net worth of the richest 1 percent is $3.7 million.

Thus there is a tremendous difference in the wealth of the richest Americans and everyone else. In fact, while 1 percent of the population owns a third of all wealth, eight times that number of people (8 percent) actually have negative net worth; that is, they owe more than they own. Another 12 percent of American families have net assets of between zero and $5,000.

Also, consider that for many Americans their home is by far their largest asset. The lower 90 percent also own a large portion of all automobiles. Besides debt, these are the two items that the bulk of Americans own anywhere near their fair share. But homes and automobiles are not true *financial assets*. They do not generate income the way other assets do and their ownership says nothing about control over the means of production. They are valuable utilitarian possessions, but information about the ownership of automobiles and homes doesn't tell us anything about ownership and control of the economy; that is to say, of our productive resources and the power to influence what gets produced and what gets invested in for further development. If we remove autos and homes (principal residences) from the equation, we see that the ownership of financial assets is even more unequally distributed than overall net worth. According to economist Ed Wolff, who analyzed the Federal Reserve Board's 1998 data, the richest 1 percent own 47 percent of all financial assets.

(Reprinted by permission of Andy Singer)

The vast majority of Americans hold only a very small portion of the nation's total financial assets. One can see this especially in the figures on the distribution of investment real estate, stocks, bonds, and businesses ownership (corporations that do not have publicly traded stocks). Ninety percent of all Americans own just 25.5 percent of nonowner-occupied real estate, 17.8 percent of all stocks, 14 percent of all bonds, 10.1 percent of all trusts, and 8.6 percent of all business assets. But they do have nearly 70 percent of all debt and the debt burden for lower and middle America is growing. In 1999 household debt reached a historic high.[21] In 1998 Americans were saving just .5 percent of their disposable income. Compare that to 7.6 percent in the 1960s, 8.2 percent in the 1970s, 6.7 percent in the 1980s, and 4.8 percent in the first half of the 1990s (see Fig. 3.7).

The recent data presented by the Federal Reserve Board fails to look at wealth inequality by race; for that we go back to 1995 and some research done by Edward Wolff. Wolff found that for that year blacks had a median financial net worth of $7,400, compared to $61,000 for whites. For the same year, nearly one out of three black households had zero or negative net worth, twice the rate of whites. It's not surprising then, to find that only two of the four hundred richest Americans (as determined by *Forbes* magazine) are African American.

Hispanics are fairing even worse. Hispanic households had a median net worth of only $5,000.[22]

According to the Federal Reserve Board's recent findings, wealth distribution became a little more unequal during the 1990s, but overall it did

---

Ed Wolff on Wealth:

1. The only segment of the population that experienced large gains in wealth since 1983 is the richest 20 percent of households.
2. Wealth inequality continued to rise from 1989 to 1998, though at a slower pace than during the 1980s.
3. Overall indebtedness continues to rise among American families.
4. The ratio of mean wealth between African-American and white families was very low at 0.19 in 1983, and has barely budged since.
5. The relative wealth holdings of both younger and older families have fallen since 1989.
6. In 1989 middle-income families could sustain their normal consumption for only 3.6 months out of their financial savings. The situation has deteriorated during the 1990s.

Ed Wolff is a professor of economics at New York University and is one of the leading authorities on wealth distribution in the United States. The conclusions listed above are based on his analysis of the 1983, 1989, 1992, 1995, and 1998 Survey of Consumer Finances conducted by the Federal Reserve Board. See Working Paper No. 300, Recent Trends in Wealth Ownership, 1983–1998, available at the Web site of the Jerome Levy Economics Institute, www.levy.org.

Table 3.4. The Richest People in the United States[23]

Rank	Name	Worth	Age	Residence	Source
1	Gates, William H. III	43 Billion	46	Seattle, WA	Microsoft
2	Buffett, Warren Edward	36 Billion	72	Omaha, NE	investments
3	Allen, Paul Gardner	21 Billion	49	Mercer Island, WA	Microsoft
4	Walton, Alice L.	18.8 Billion	53	Fort Worth, TX	Wal-Mart
4	Walton, Helen R.	18.8 Billion	83	Bentonville, AR	Wal-Mart
4	Walton, Jim C.	18.8 Billion	54	Bentonville, AR	Wal-Mart
4	Walton, John T.	18.8 Billion	56	Durango, CO	Wal-Mart
4	Walton, S. Robson	18.8 Billion	58	Bentonville, AR	Wal-Mart
9	Ellison, Lawrence Joseph	15.2 Billion	58	Atherton, CA	Oracle
10	Ballmer, Steven Anthony	11.9 Billion	46	Redmond, WA	Microsoft
11	Dell, Michael	11.2 Billion	37	Austin, TX	Dell Computer
12	Kluge, John Werner	10.5 Billion	88	Charlottesville, VA	Metromedia
13	Mars, Forrest Edward Jr.	10 Billion	71	McLean, VA	candy
13	Mars, Jacqueline Badger	10 Billion	63	Bedminster, NJ	candy
13	Mars, John Franklyn	10 Billion	66	Arlington, VA	candy
16	Anthony, Barbara Cox	9.5 Billion	79	Honolulu, HI	media
16	Chambers, Anne Cox	9.5 Billion	82	Atlanta, GA	media
18	Redstone, Sumner M.	9 Billion	79	Newton Centre, MA	Viacom
19	Johnson, Abigail	8.2 Billion	40	Boston, MA	mutual funds
20	Newhouse, Donald Edward	7.7 Billion	72	Somerset County, NJ	media
20	Newhouse, Samuel Irving Jr.	7.7 Billion	74	New York, NY	media
22	Pritzker, Robert Alan	7.6 Billion	76	Chicago, IL	hotels, investments
22	Pritzker, Thomas J.	7.6 Billion	52	Chicago, IL	hotels, investments
24	Johnson, Samuel Curtis	7 Billion	74	Racine, WI	S.C. Johnson & Son
24	Soros, George	7 Billion	72	Bedford, NY	hedge funds

(Reprinted by permission of *Forbes Magazine* © 2003 Forbes Inc.)

not differ significantly from 1989. However, two studies sponsored by the Joint Economic Committee of Congress, one in 1983 and one in 1989, found that there was a rapid increase in inequality during the 1980s.[24]

The data presented here begins to get at the heart of class structure in the United States. It helps to illustrate the fact that the major dividing line between classes in the United States is located up near the top of the socioeconomic ladder. The fulcrum lies between those who own America's great wealth—its land, factories, corporations, banks, etc.—and those who toil for hourly wages barely affording a decent living (or in many cases not even managing that). It is the elite at the top of the economic pyramid who also exercise disproportionate power in politics. But just as important, if not more so, is the power they exercise through their economic holdings. The economic elite are the major actors when it comes to deciding what our economic system will produce because they control the investment purse strings. Decisions about whether to develop nuclear energy or solar power are made in the corporate board rooms. The economic elite are the ones

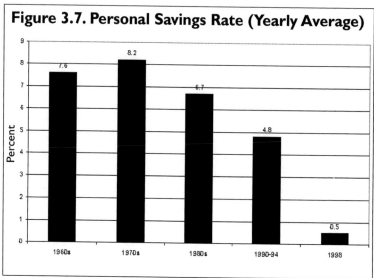

Figure 3.7. Personal Savings Rate (Yearly Average)

who decide whether we will build housing for those who need it or luxury housing for the well-to-do, whether we will provide healthcare for those who need it or build a health system based on the wishes of the pharmaceutical and insurance companies and their top-heavy, well-salaried bureaucracies. It is not uncontrollable market forces that are shaping our society, it is decision making by people with narrow interests but broad power. They make decisions within the constraints of modern-day capitalism that can force out of business those who might choose to consider any goal other than maximizing profits.

A variety of other evidence supports the hypothesis that American society is becoming even more polarized. While the typical occupations held by working-class Americans continue to suffer stagnating earnings, those near the top of the occupational ladder are, for the most part, doing significantly better. Table 3.5 shows how earnings have stagnated for typical American workers. For example, from 1970 to 1993, the real earnings for most typical working-class occupations, be they white collar or blue collar, fell by about 15 percent.

Table 3.5. Average Weekly Earnings in Current and Constant (1982) Dollars for Production and Nonsupervisory Employees[25]

Year	Current Dollars	Constant (1982) Dollars
1970	120	298
1980	235	275
1985	299	271
1990	345	259
1991	354	256
1992	364	255
1993	374	255

In spite of attempts to prove the contrary, these stagnating incomes cannot be explained by a decrease in productivity. For example, from 1973 to 1985 productivity in manufacturing grew by 30 percent while real compensation for manufacturing workers grew just 6 percent. The same trend holds true for the economy as a whole. From 1970 to 1993 output per hour for all nonfarm businesses grew 30.7 percent, but real compensation for workers grew just 15.5 percent (see Table 3.6). In manufacturing industries the discrepancies are even greater. In the period from 1980 to 1993 output per hour in manufacturing grew 46.8 percent, but real compensation grew just 4.3 percent.[26] The reason for the discrepancy between productivity growth and worker compensation is that management has succeeded in commanding for itself a greater share of the surplus value produced by labor.

Corporate executives often claim they need to hold workers' earnings down in order to be more competitive in today's international markets. This attitude was crudely expressed by Stanley Mihelick, one of General Motors' executive vice presidents: "Until we get real wage levels down much closer to those of the Brazils and Koreas . . . we cannot pass along productivity gains to wages and still be competitive."[27] In fact, Mihelick's standards of thriftiness apply only to workers and not to management. Goodyear's chief executive at the time of Mihelick's statement was Robert E. Mercer, who collected salary, bonuses, and stock gains totaling $6.7 million.[28] Such generous compensation for corporate executives and upper management has become the norm for American corporations. Executive compensation is much greater in the United States than it is in other nations. In the mid-1980s the Economic Policy Institute reported that the ratio of CEO pay to workers' pay was nearly twice as great in the U.S. than in West Germany, and nearly 50 percent greater than in Japan. The Institute

Table 3.6. Index of Productivity per Hour and Real Compensation for All Nonfarm Businesses (1982 = 100)[29]

Year	Output per hour	Real hourly compensation
1970	88.5	92.0
1975	96.6	98.4
1980	99.0	99.4
1985	105.4	101.0
1990	108.2	102.8
1992	111.7	105.7
1993	115.7	106.3

also reported that American executives made thirty-one times the salary of the average American worker, a ratio that increased even more in the 1980s and 1990s, reaching over 500 to 1 by the year 2000 (see Fig. 3.8).[30]

Since the mid-1970s, corporate executives have substantially increased their share of the national income. The evidence is overwhelming. Economist Ravi Batra, for instance, noted that average compensation for chief executives of the top 100 corporations rose by 181 percent from 1976 to 1986. In contrast, workers' income rose just 74 percent. Prices, meanwhile, increased 94 percent over the same period.[31]

In 1980 the average chief executive officer had an income of about $624,996; by 1993 the average had skyrocketed to $3,841,273, and exceeded $13 million in 2000.[32] Heading the pack in 2001 was Lawrence Ellison, the CEO of Oracle. His salary, bonuses, and stock options totaled $706 million.[33]

Do corporate executives share the rewards? No, increased productivity and corporate profits have not, for the most part, resulted in higher worker pay. Who suffers most when belts tighten and the ax falls? The CEOs of the twenty companies with the largest layoffs in 1995 had their salaries and bonuses raised by an average of 25 percent compared to the national average of 18 percent (excluding stock options and other long-term compensation). AT&T chairman Robert E. Allen, who directed the company's downsizing that cost 40,000 employees their jobs, benefited from increased stock options that gave him a 143 percent compensation increase—$15.9 million in 1995.[34] Increasingly, executives are being rewarded for downsizing, and it is often profitable companies, not struggling ones, that resort to the ax. During the large wave of layoffs that washed through many U.S. corporations in the first half of 2001 (over three-quarters of a million workers were laid off)

The Ten Highest-Paid Chief Executives[35]
(pay is in *millions* of dollars)

	Salary & Bonus	Long-Term Comp	Total Pay
Alfred Lerner (MBNA)	$9.0	$185.9	$194.9
Jeffrey Barbakow (Tenet Healthcare)	5.5	111.1	116.1
Millard Drexler (GAP)	2.5	88.5	91.0
Dennis Kozlowski (Tyco International)	4.0	67.0	71.0
Irwin Jacobs (Qualcomm)	1.8	61.6	63.3
Charles Cawley (MBNA)	6.3	42.3	48.6
Robert Kotick (Activision)	0.5	42.8	43.3
Ralph Roberts (Comcast)	6.3	33.5	39.8
Charles Fote (First Data)	1.9	37.2	39.1
Orin Smith (Starbucks)	2.5	36.3	38.8
Geoffrey Bible (Altria Group)	3.7	31.1	34.8
Thomas Siebel (Siebel Systems)	0.0	34.6	34.6
David Cote (Honeywell Intl.)	3.9	28.0	31.9
Corbin McNeill Jr. (Exelon)	0.8	29.0	29.8
Richard Fuld (Lehman Brothers)	1.8	26.9	28.7
Scott Mcnealy (Sun Microsystems)	0.6	25.2	25.9
Vance Coffman (Lockheed Martin)	4.4	20.9	25.3
Ray Irani (Occidental Petroleum)	5.4	18.3	23.7
Phillip Purcell (Morgan Stanley)	6.4	17.3	23.7
Ronald McDougal (Brinker International)	2.2	19.7	21.9

And 10 Who Aren't CEOs

	Salary & Bonus	Long-Term Comp	Total Pay
Mark Swartz (Tyco International)	$ 2.2	$72.9	$75.1
Brian Kelly (Activision)	0.5	46.3	46.8
William Schoen (Health Mgmt. Assoc.)	0.4	42.1	42.5
John Cochran III (MBNA)	4.9	31.1	36.0
August Busch III (Anheuser-Busch)	3.6	31.0	34.7
Archie Dunham (Conocophillips)	28.3	4.9	33.1
Jeffrey Vanderbeek (Lehman Brothers)	1.5	27.7	29.2
Joseph Gregory (Lehman Brothers)	1.5	27.1	28.6
Bruce Hammonds (MBNA)	4.9	23.7	28.6
Thomas Fitzpatrick (Sallie Mae)	1.8	25.5	27.2

Source: *BusinessWeek*, April 21, 2003 [online], www.businessweek.com/magazine/content/03_16/b3829003.htm

executives were being rewarded handsomely. The fifty-two U.S. firms that announced layoffs of one thousand or more workers paid their CEOs an average of $23.7 million compared to an average of $13.1 million paid to CEOs of comparable companies. Disney's CEO, Michael Eisner, reported a 33 percent increase in operating profits for the first quarter of 2001 at the same time he announced plans to cut his workforce by 4,000.[36]

Many executive are highly paid in spite of their company's poor performance. The Council on International and Public Affairs claims that "if you invested $10,000 in 1993 in the 10 companies that paid their CEOs the most, by last year [2000] your investment would have been worth $3,585."[37]

One of the more extreme examples of paying dearly for poor performance is the case of the Webvan company, which paid George Shaheen (a former CEO of Andersen Consulting) a $13.5-million signing bonus, plus options on fifteen million shares of the company, in addition to his salary and other bonuses, to head the fledgling company's Internet shopping service. Within two years the company lost nearly $500 million and its stock dropped from $34 a share to twelve cents. Shaheen's punishment? He was forced to resign with a severance package that will pay him $375,000 a year for the rest of his life, and Webvan forgave almost all of a $6.7-million-dollar loan it had made to the CEO to pay his federal income taxes.[38]

POVERTY AND RACIAL INEQUALITY

As more income and wealth is accumulated by the richest Americans, those in the middle-income groups are struggling, and at the lowest end poverty and suffering have increased. We have already seen how unemployment rates have been consistently higher since the early to mid-1970s; the same trend pretty much holds true with poverty rates.

Table 3.7 shows the poverty rate for various years since 1959. The most salient fact revealed by these figures is that as a nation we made significant progress in reducing poverty throughout the 1960s, but that progress stopped in the mid- to late 1970s. Poverty then rose dramatically in the early 1980s and early 1990s, and then dropped in the final years of the millennium.

During the 1960s and part of the 1970s, significant headway was made in reducing poverty in the United States and in closing the economic gap between black and white Americans. The lowest poverty rate ever recorded came in 1973, and after 1973 there was a great deal of backsliding with

Table 3.7. Number and Percent Below the Poverty Line[39]

Year	Number	Percent	% White Non-Hispanic	% Black	% Hispanic
2001	32,907	11.7	7.8	22.7	21.4
2000	31,139	11.3	7.5	22.1	21.2
1999	32,258	11.8	7.7	23.6	22.8
1998	34,476	12.7	8.2	26.1	25.6
1997	35,574	13.3	8.6	26.5	27.1
1996	36,529	13.7	8.6	28.4	29.4
1995	36,425	13.8	8.5	29.3	30.3
1994	38,059	14.5	9.4	30.6	30.7
1993	39,265	15.1	9.9	33.1	30.6
1992	38,014	14.8	9.6	33.4	29.6
1991	35,708	14.2	9.4	32.7	28.7
1990	33,585	13.5	8.8	31.9	28.1
1989	31,528	12.8	8.3	30.7	26.2
1988	31,745	13.0	8.4	31.3	26.7
1987	32,221	13.4	8.7	32.4	28.0
1986	32,370	13.6	9.4	31.1	27.3
1985	33,064	14.0	9.7	31.3	29.0
1984	33,700	14.4	10.0	33.8	28.4
1983	35,303	15.2	10.8	35.7	28.0
1982	34,398	15.0	10.6	35.6	29.9
1981	31,822	14.0	9.9	34.2	26.5
1980	29,272	13.0	9.1	32.5	25.7
1979	26,072	11.7	8.1	31.0	21.8
1978	24,497	11.4	7.9	30.6	21.6
1977	24,720	11.6	8.0	31.3	22.4
1976	24,975	11.8	8.1	31.1	24.7
1975	25,877	12.3	8.6	31.3	26.9
1974	23,370	11.2	7.7	30.3	23.0
1973	22,973	11.1	7.5	31.4	21.9
1972	24,460	11.9		33.3	22.8
1971	25,559	12.5		32.5	
1970	25,420	12.6		33.5	
1969	24,147	12.1		32.2	
1968	25,389	12.8		34.7	
1967	27,769	14.2		39.3	
1966	28,510	14.7		41.8	
1965	33,185	17.3			
1964	36,055	19.0			
1963	36,436	19.5			
1962	38,625	21.0			
1961	39,628	21.9			
1960	39,851	22.2			
1959	39,490	22.4		55.1	

Table 3.8. Persons Below 125% of Poverty Line

Year	Number (in millions)	Percent
2000	43.4	15.7
1999	44.3	16.2
1998	46.0	17.0
1997	47.9	17.8
1996	49.3	18.5
1995	48.8	18.5
1994	50.4	19.3
1993	51.8	20.0
1992	49.2	19.4
1991	47.8	18.9
1990	44.8	18.0
1989	42.7	17.3
1988	42.6	17.5
1987	43.0	17.9
1986	43.5	18.2
1985	44.2	18.7
1984	45.3	19.4
1983	47.2	20.3
1982	46.5	20.3
1981	43.7	19.3
1980	40.7	18.1
1979	36.6	16.4
1978	34.2	15.8
1977	35.7	16.7
1976	35.5	16.7
1975	37.2	17.6
1974	33.7	16.1
1973	32.8	15.8
1972	34.7	16.8
1971	36.5	17.8
1970	35.6	17.6
1966	41.3	21.3
1960	54.6	30.9

Source: U.S. Census Bureau, *Poverty in the United States*, pp. 60–214, and *Statistical Abstract of the United States, 2001*, p. 442.

poverty rates climbing up to 15.2 in 1982, and 15.1 in 1993. Economic growth in the late 1990s brought down both the unemployment rate and the poverty rate.

One might wonder what would be the cost of bringing every American

Figure 3.8. CEO Total Remuneration As a Multiple of Manufacturing Employee total Remuneration

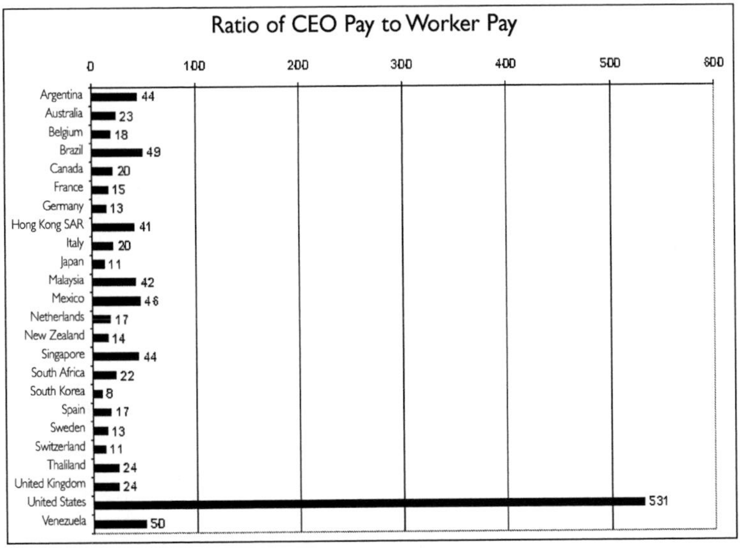

Ratio of CEO Pay to Worker Pay

Country	Ratio
Argentina	44
Australia	23
Belgium	18
Brazil	49
Canada	20
France	15
Germany	13
Hong Kong SAR	41
Italy	20
Japan	11
Malaysia	42
Mexico	46
Netherlands	17
New Zealand	14
Singapore	44
South Africa	22
South Korea	8
Spain	17
Sweden	13
Switzerland	11
Thailand	24
United Kingdom	24
United States	531
Venezuela	50

Ratio of CEO-to-work Pay

Source: Towers Perrin. www.aflcio.org/paywatch/ceopay.htm

up above the poverty level. Is it an insurmountable problem? Is it beyond the capability of our national resources? Available Census Bureau data allows us to calculate the cost. Based on the "income deficit" figures for the year 2000 the total amount of money needed to bring the thirty-one million Americans who are below the poverty line up above the poverty line is approximately $81 billion dollars. The federal budget for that year, by way of contrast, was $1.8 trillion. In other words, it would take less than 5 percent of the yearly federal budget to bring every American above the poverty line. It is not a lack of financial capability that keeps us from making drastic reductions in poverty.

The poverty rate for black Americans in 2000 (22.1 percent) was the lowest rate on record (i.e., since 1959) and the gap between black and white median income also narrowed at the end of the 1990s. While these are good signs, there is a reason to be wary. These advances for blacks occurred during periods of economic growth, but history shows that blacks often suffer disproportionately during recessions.

The discrepancies in the economic plight of black and white Americans is also revealed in the median household income figures for the past few

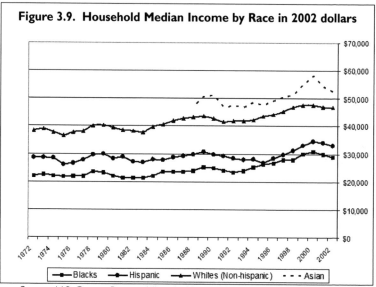

Figure 3.9. Household Median Income by Race in 2002 dollars

Source: U.S. Census Bureau, Historical Income Tables—Housholds

decades. Figure 3.9 shows the median household income for whites, blacks, Hispanics, and Asians. Black median family income has been fluctuating at about 60 percent of the white median. Hispanic median household income has been a little below 70 percent of the white median, lower than it had been a couple of decades ago—most likely a byproduct of higher immigration numbers in the 1990s.

Why are there such significant income differences between blacks and whites? There are several explanations that shed light on these problems, and some that rely on questionable assumptions and data that ultimately tend to justify the status quo.

In explaining income differences between blacks and whites, some have cited low intelligence, poor educational performance, or simply a lower level of educational attainment for blacks compared to whites. However, the available data on education does not support these claims. At times, over the past couple of decades, the economic plight of many blacks worsened in spite of the fact that substantial educational gains were being made. During the 1980s, for example, while the gap in high school and college graduation rates for whites and blacks narrowed, the gap in median family income between the two races was growing. Not until lower unemployment rates arrived in the mid-1990s did the income gap begin to narrow, which, again, makes one wonder about how the black/white income gap will fare in the next long recession.

Furthermore, contrary to popular myth, the average SAT scores for every minority subpopulation in the country have been improving in recent years. Moreover, suburban black students frequently have lower drop-out rates than suburban whites.[40] Another indicator of educational performance is the variety of standardized test scores that are evaluated by the National Assessment of Educational Progress (NAEP). The NAEP points out that modest gains have been made across the board and that "the national data on student performance do not indicate significant declines in any area."[41] In fact, the gap in reading scores for seventeen-year-old whites and blacks fell from fifty to thirty points during the 1980s, and in mathematics the gap fell from thirty-eight points to twenty-one.[42] What all these figures are showing is a narrowing of the educational gap between whites and blacks. If there were a perfect correlation between education and income, then the income gap between whites and blacks ought to be closing as well, but it isn't. Significant income differences exist between blacks and whites at the same educational levels as is shown in Table 3.11. For example, the median income of a white male with a bachelor's degree is more than $17,000 higher than for a black male with the same education. Likewise, the difference between black and white males who have graduated high school is over $5,000.

Researchers who have done extensive analysis of blacks and whites with similar educational levels have found that when black and white workers with similar educational levels are compared, the earnings gap between them, which had decreased in the earlier part of the 1970s, has been increasing in more recent years. Even within the same industry, and with the same education and years of experience, the occupational status and earnings of blacks has fallen compared to whites. A good example of this is cited by economists Richard Freeman of Harvard University and John Bound of the University of Michigan. Freeman and Bound point out that "in the 1970s young black college graduates were as likely to be managers or professionals as were young white college graduates; in 1988–89 black graduates were thirteen percentage points less likely to be in those occupations than whites."[43] In addition, in the 1974 to 1977 period black college graduates were actually earning slightly more than white graduates, but by 1989 they were earning 17 percent less. Clearly something other than educational attainment is causing the currently existing economic disparities.

Some of the factors that are having an impact on median black income

Table 3.9. High School Graduate or More
(in percent, for persons twenty-five years old and over)[44]

Year	White	Black
1960	43.2	20.1
1970	54.5	31.4
1980	68.8	51.2
1990	79.1	66.2
2000	84.9	78.5

Table 3.10. College Graduate or More
(in percent, for persons twenty-five years old and over)

Year	White	Black
1960	8.1	3.1
1970	11.3	4.4
1980	17.1	8.4
1990	22.0	11.3
2000	26.1	16.5

are the economic decline of inner cities, the loss of manufacturing jobs, the decrease in the real minimum wage, racism in hiring and promoting, and the drop in unionization rates. Black unemployment rates were often higher in the 1990s than they were twenty years earlier, but the increase is particularly evident among black teenagers whose unemployment rate was 28 percent in 1973 but 40 percent in 1993.[45] Those who had jobs also suffered. From 1975 to 1992 the real median weekly earnings for black males fell over 15 percent.[46] In part, this is due to the fact that black Americans are more likely to hold occupations that pay the minimum wage. The real minimum wage fell from $7 per hour in 1970 to less than $5 in 1995 (see Fig. 3.10).[47]

Some analysts, sociologist William Julius Wilson for one, have claimed that there is a growing black underclass in the United States.[48] According to Wilson, the concentration of the poor in the inner city has led to sharp increases in joblessness, poverty, and the related problems of single-parent households, welfare dependency, housing deterioration, educational failure, and crime.

In a study of differences in underemployment between blacks and whites, Daniel Lichter also found support for the underclass thesis. Like Wilson, Lichter concluded that a decline in entry-level blue-collar jobs was a major contributor to the problem:

Table 3.11. Earnings by Highest Degree Earned[49]

	HS grad	Some College	Bachelor s	Master s	Professional	Doctorate
White (both sexes)	25,270	27,674	46,894	55,622	103,450	87,746
Male	31,279	34,825	59,606	68,831	123,086	97,076
Female	18,381	20,188	32,507	41,485	57,314	64,080
Black (both sexes)	20,991	24,101	37,422	48,777	75,509	*
Male	25,849	27,538	42,530	54,642	*	*
Female	16,506	21,355	33,184	44,761	*	*
Hispanic (both sexes)	20,704	23,115	36,212	50,576	64,029	*
Male	23,736	27,288	42,733	60,013	*	*
Female	16,653	18,782	29,249	41,118	*	*

*Number in sample is too small to meet standards of statistical reliability.

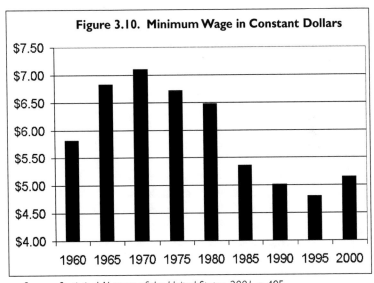

Figure 3.10. Minimum Wage in Constant Dollars

Source: *Statistical Abstract of the United States, 2001*, p. 405

Economic underemployment among blacks increased substantially during the 1970–82 period, especially among young adults and those with little education. . . . The nation's urban centers are now undergoing a process of accelerated racial polarization rather than convergence. These findings reinforce speculation by proponents of the spatial mismatch hypothesis that recent central city declines in entry-level blue-collar jobs and changing racial concentration have disproportionately affected those on the bottom rungs of the social and economic ladder, including many blacks.[50]

The spatial mismatch hypothesis points out that the better jobs are not located in areas where many blacks are likely to live. How much of this is a direct result of intentional racism is hard to say. But it is clear that residential patterns throughout the country show a great deal of segregation between blacks and whites, and the availability of good jobs mirrors this. Nevertheless, conscious racial discrimination may play a substantial part in maintaining, and even increasing, economic differences between blacks and whites.

The ways in which people are likely to obtain employment offer some insights into how segregation occurs in the labor market. Certain skilled trades, such as plumbing, masonry, electrical work, and carpentry, are still based on an apprentice system that may easily exclude blacks. In addition, success at getting many other jobs, or even finding out about their availability, is often dependent on whether one is connected to the informal network of friends and acquaintances who are inside the system. Like an apprentice system, this informal network is more likely to recruit from a somewhat homogeneous pool of talent that reflects the social and cultural characteristics of those already on the inside. These may not be conscious or malevolent forms of discrimination, but they may substantially block the occupational advancement of blacks. In addition, there is a multitude of evidence that documents the existence of racial discrimination in hiring. One especially illuminating study was conducted by the Urban Institute in 1990. The Institute used ten pairs of testers who were carefully matched in age, education, experience, and even physical size and social skills. The Institute conducted 476 "audits" in Chicago and Washington D.C., and found that in each stage of the hiring process (getting an application, getting an interview, and being offered a job) whites were more likely to advance to the next stage. Ultimately, the whites were three times as likely to be offered a job.[51]

The total impact of discrimination in hiring and promoting may be incalculable, but it definitely exists and its impact is significant. Discrimination is illegal, but it is not investigated systematically. The federal government does not seem to take the enforcement of antidiscrimination laws very seriously. For example, at times, the Equal Employment Opportunity Commission has had a backlog of as many as 90,000 cases. Clearly this is a serious problem that is not given a high priority.[52]

Two broad economic trends have also contributed to the growth of poverty among black Americans and the gap in black-white income. The first is the tremendous loss of manufacturing jobs that the nation has experienced since the mid-1970s. This *deindustrialization* closed off an avenue of economic security and advancement for many Americans, but studies have shown that blacks were more likely to lose jobs and, subsequently, were less likely to find new jobs that paid as well.[53] A similar pattern was caused by cutbacks in government hiring and public sector layoffs, particularly during the 1980s. Layoffs of public sector workers had a disproportionate impact on blacks; 29 percent of black women and 21 percent of black men had federal, state, or local government jobs in the mid-1980s. By the early 1990s these percentages had fallen significantly.[54]

One study of the effects of deindustrialization on the wages of black males in the Midwest showed that their wages fell 23 percent when compared to white males over the period from 1973 to 1989. Marc Breslow points out that "blacks began the period with proportionately more workers employed in durable goods manufacturing than whites, but by 1988 had far lower employment than whites."[55] This fact is illustrated by the data presented in Table 3.12.

Trends in unemployment in general, and deindustrialization in particular, make it apparent that blacks disproportionately serve the function of a reserve army of labor. That is to say, they are more likely to be on the fringes of the labor market. They are often the most recently hired workers, therefore they are the first to be let go when a recession hits. They may be rehired during times of economic expansion but without many of the advantages that longer job tenure brings.

Another factor that helps explain black-white economic differences and shows how the advantages of social class are transmitted from generation to generation, to the exclusion of those who have been deprived, has to do with wealth distribution in the United States. Economist Ed Wolff has shown that the wealth gap between blacks and whites is even larger than the income gap. Whereas the median family income of blacks is 54 percent of the white median, the median wealth holdings of non-white families is a mere 5 percent of the median for whites.[56] In addition, 35 percent of non-white families have zero or negative net worth compared to just 12 percent of whites.[57] Wolff sees two main explanations for this. One is that intergenerational transfers play a crucial role in wealth accumulation. White families, on average, receive much larger transfers of wealth, both while their parents are alive and through inheritance, than do nonwhite families. A second explanation is that it may be harder for nonwhites to get mortgages and consumer loans, etc., which can play an important part in accumulating

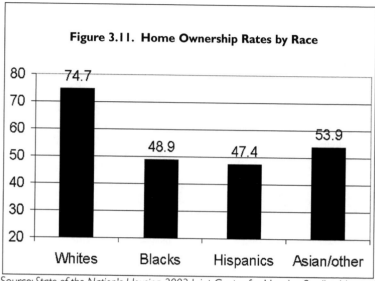

Figure 3.11. Home Ownership Rates by Race

Source: *State of the Nation's Housing, 2003,* Joint Center for Housing Studies, Harvard University

wealth. This assertion is supported by findings made by the Federal Reserve Bank of Boston, which showed that among blacks and whites who were equally credit worthy, blacks were 56 percent more likely to be turned down for mortgages than whites.[58] Likewise, a study of nearly 100,000 mortgage-loan applications, done by the Long Island-based newspaper *Newsday*, found that blacks were almost three times as likely to be rejected than whites, even when they had the same income.[59]

Discrimination and lower financial resources results in fewer blacks being able to share in the dream of home ownership. Home ownership rates for whites, blacks, Hispanics, and Asians/others are shown in Figure 3.11.[60]

It would be a mistake to give the impression that stagnation has affected all blacks in the same way. In point of fact, the percentage of black families with incomes over $75,000 has increased substantially since the mid-1970s, just as it has done for whites. Likewise, it would be a mistake to think of poverty purely as a problem for blacks. The large majority of people below the poverty line in the United States are white (twenty-two million compared to eight million blacks). Nevertheless, the stagnation that the country experienced from the early 1970s to the mid-1990s resulted in falling incomes for many working-class occupations and a reduction in leisure time for many people. Within society as a whole, the working class

Table 3.12. Percentage of Males in the Midwest Employed in Durable Goods Manufacturing[61]

Year	Blacks	Whites
1973–74	42.1%	33.0%
1988–89	12.5%	21.3%

suffered disproportionately, and within the working class black Americans were particularly hard hit.

The divisions that are widening in the country today have to do with the decline of power among African Americans and of the working class in general. For example, the greater share of the nation's income that the upper class has been able to secure for itself and the higher and higher compensation rates for executives has not been challenged by any broad-based working-class movements with demands for higher pay and greater benefits. Nor are strong social movements putting demands on the government to provide programs that would increase healthcare, housing, job training,

---

Racism or Just Good Business?[62]

During the 1990–91 recession, at corporations with federal government contracts, blacks lost 60,000 jobs, while whites, Hispanics, and Asians gained a total of 186,000 jobs, according to a study by the *Wall Street Journal*. The *Journal* analyzed data from 35,000 companies that are required to file reports with the Equal Employment Opportunity Commission.

Companies interviewed by the *Journal* claimed the dramatic racial differences were due to economic restructuring, not racism. At General Electric 13 percent of black workers lost their jobs. GE spokesman Bruce Bunche said, "We closed two plants—one in Columbia, Maryland, which was 39 percent black and one in Cicero, Illinois, which was 80 percent black."

At Sears, African Americans held 16 percent of the jobs in 1990, but lost at least 20 percent of those jobs eliminated. Sears claims the cause was their relocating two distribution centers from inner cities to suburbs, to which blacks without cars could not commute.

USX Corporation (formerly U.S. Steel) laid off nearly 10 percent of its workers in 1991. Although blacks made up only 12.6 percent of the workforce before the recession, they suffered 20 percent of the layoffs. One reason for the disproportionate losses was that African Americans had less seniority than whites. Other problems, said union official Billy Hawkins, included GE's instituting new skills tests that blacks had difficulty passing, and the company's elimination of training programs for crafts jobs, due to the availability of unemployed craftspeople.

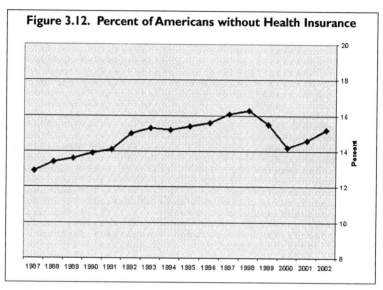

Figure 3.12. Percent of Americans without Health Insurance

Source: *Health Insurance Coverage: 2001*. Current Population Reports P60-220. Issued September 2002.

mass transportation, or similar social programs that would increase the level of social services available to the general public.

HEALTH INSURANCE AND OTHER SOCIAL BENEFITS

Health insurance coverage is a valuable asset that does not show up in the income and wealth distribution figures, but it is a significant factor in inequality and can have a major effect on one's life chances.

In the United States, 14.6 percent of the population was without any type of health insurance for the entire year of 2001. That means 41.2 million people lacked coverage (see Fig. 3.12).[63] More people are without health insurance in the United States than the combined population of the seven countries that comprise Central America. Lack of health insurance is associated with a shorter life expectancy. In fact, people who lack health insurance have a 25 percent higher risk of death.[64] This is an astonishing proportion of people who lack coverage, especially for a country that likes to consider itself a world leader, and it is remarkably behind other advanced nations, many of which provide free and universal healthcare (see Fig. 3.13 for more information on health insurance and race).

The inequality that exists in the United States permits those with the resources to move to more desirable neighborhoods. It also allows wealthier Americans to purchase comprehensive health insurance coverage if it isn't already a benefit of their employment. The income and wealth of the upper class also means that having children is not the major economic burden that it is for people of the lower and middle class.

The ability of different social classes to pay for healthcare, maternity, education, etc., contributes to the lack of agreement on a vision of the future of America. Some people clamor for more services, some for more tax cuts. In Europe, where there are often working-class political parties, stronger unions, and, in some cases, greater representation of women in the national political institutions, many nations have instituted social programs that address the needs of the entire citizenry. In Europe, a national healthcare system is the norm and maternity-leave programs are far superior to the existing U.S. program.

In the United States roughly forty-one million people are without any type of health insurance and most workers are without any paid parental leave benefits. The Family and Medical Leave Act adopted under the Clinton administration only provides for an unpaid leave of twelve weeks, and it only covers about half of the workforce (workers employed by companies with fewer than fifty employees are exempt). In comparison, in Finland, a mother gets a twelve-month paid maternity leave, after which either parent can stay at home until the child is three years old. The parent receives financial compensation for that time and the parent's employment is guaranteed at the end of the leave. Finland also permits parents with children under the age of four the right to shorten their workday by two hours. Sweden, also, has a very extensive paid maternity- and paternity-leave policy, permitting parents to shorten their workweek by two hours per day until the child reaches age ten.

Sweden and Finland may be exceptional in their generous maternity policies, but other European nations also have very good policies. In Italy mothers receive five months off with full pay. In Germany women receive full pay for their fourteen-week leave. In Great Britain women receive eighteen weeks of leave, six weeks are paid at 90 percent of their average earnings, and after that they receive a reduced payment.

The pervasive economic inequality that exists in the United States contributes to individualistic and limited solutions to the loss of community and other social problems. Instead of enacting broad reforms that improve

Going Nowhere?

After urban riots spread throughout the nation in 1967, the Kerner Commission, a presidential commission, concluded that "our nation was moving toward two societies, one black, one white—separate and unequal."[65] In 1988, a follow-up study was released that found "life for inner city blacks has worsened as the races have grown further apart socially and economically: and the poorest blacks have become poorer and more isolated."[66] Over and over, this message has been broadcast, yet the problem, in large part, remains. One reason for the failure is that those who are the victims of racism and poverty generally have very little power in our society, and those who have the power to enact corrective measures have little to gain.

The problem of economic disenfranchisement is clearly connected to a host of other social problems. At the time of the riots in Los Angeles in the spring of 1992, after white police officers were acquitted of brutality against Rodney King, teenage unemployment among blacks was nearly 50 percent, the unemployment rate for black men aged twenty and up, was 43 percent. Well-paying jobs had been disappearing from south central Los Angeles for years as local industrialists moved their facilities to suburban areas of California, or even to Mexico.[67] New employment in south central Los Angeles did not develop in sufficient quantity or quality to replace what had been lost. (This is not to suggest that what existed before had even come close to being adequate.) In the words of one writer, it was the "Reagan revolution [that] sparked L.A.'s rebellion."[68]

The abandonment of many social programs by the Reagan administration, along with massive capital flight in pursuit of profits, has led to a growth of inequality and an increase in social problems including greater racial divisions.[69] Such divisions have been recognized by many community and civic organizations. One especially succinct description was provided by the New Jersey Council of Churches, which noted a growing trend toward a racially and geographically divided state that has resulted in "a transportation system that moves people from places of poverty in the cities to jobs in elegant malls, stores and hotels but returns them to their poverty ghetto at the end of each day."[70] The Council concluded that "New Jersey has two societies—one well off, one poor; and the latter society preponderantly comprised of city-dwellers, minorities and women."[71]

the *social wage* (the benefits of which every member of society can take advantage), we continue a course that is allowing inequality to grow and is leading to a greater alienation of each individual from every other.

Issues such as education, crime, housing affordability, etc., are often discussed from perspectives with very limited vision. Poor academic performance is seen as a result of lousy schools, crime grows due to broken homes and bad parenting, etc., but we need to look more holistically at these problems and recognize that they are, in many ways, outgrowths of the overall inequality that exists in our society. Without addressing the problem of structured economic inequality that causes many people to work long hours for wages that do not provide an adequate standard of living for the area where they live, then we will continue to have people who cannot afford decent housing, and people who have a difficult time finding the time and energy to devote to their children. It's hard to build democratic and caring communities when the economic system has distributed resources so unevenly, allowing great freedom of choice for some and very few options for others.

WOMEN'S PROGRESS AND THE "GLASS CEILING"

Over the past several decades the participation of women in the labor force has grown substantially—from 43.3 percent in 1970 to 60.2 percent in the year 2000.[72] During this time women's pay compared to men's has improved. In 1970 full-time year-round women workers were earning 59 percent of what their male counterparts were paid, and by 1993 women were making 73 percent. But serious differences continue to exist between men and women when it comes to financial compensation for their work. As is the case with black and white earnings these differences cannot be explained by differences in educational attainment. Table 3.13 shows that even at the

Table 3.13. Mean Earnings of Full-Time, Year-Round Workers, Age Twenty-Five and Up (1999)[73]

Educational Attainment	Male	Female	Ratio
Total twenty-five years and over	$ 49,771	$32,222	65%
Less than Ninth grade	23,139	16,636	72
Ninth to Twelfth (no diploma)	27,067	19,620	72
High school graduate	36,805	24,228	66
Some college, no degree	44,558	30,157	68
Associate degree	45,876	31,855	69
Bachelor's degree or more	73,715	45,458	62
Bachelor's degree	63,491	41,106	65
Master's degree	75,527	49,844	66
Professional degree	130,711	72,188	55
Doctorate degree	108,334	69,085	64

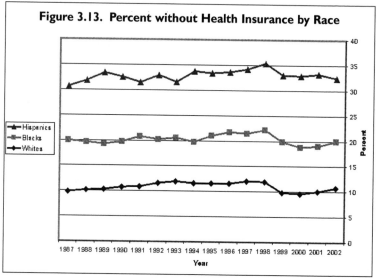

Figure 3.13. Percent without Health Insurance by Race

same educational levels the earnings of full-time year-round male workers are significantly higher than their female counterparts. For example, the typical woman with a high school diploma earns just sixty-six cents for every dollar her male counterpart makes. At the doctoral level the ratio is nearly the same—sixty-four cents for every dollars a male doctorate earns.

In part the differences in pay between men and women can be explained by the notion of *labor market segmentation*, or the *dual labor market*. These terms have been used to point to the fact that women are often funneled into certain types of jobs (secretarial work, retail work, healthcare, teaching, etc.) that tend to be lower paying than the types of jobs men get. While there is a certain amount of truth to this (the increase in women in the labor force that has occurred during the past several decades has coincided with a period of rapid growth in low-paying service sector jobs and nearly 70 percent of full-time women workers are in low-paying occupational categories), significant pay differences exist not just among job categories but within them as well.[74] Table 3.14 shows the ratio of women's pay to men's within a variety of occupations.

Although women in the workforce is commonplace, women still face considerable discrimination that keeps them from advancing farther up the occupational ladder. In recent years the term *glass ceiling* has come into vogue as a metaphor to describe the barrier that confines women to the lower levels of employment. Like glass, this barrier is transparent, which makes it hard to see, especially for men. According to one poll 73 percent of male chief executive officers said they don't think there is a glass ceiling, but 71 percent of female vice presidents think there is.[75]

As one travels up the corporate structure the scarcity of women, blacks, and other minorities becomes apparent. Surveys of the Fortune 1500 companies have found that 95 to 97 percent of senior managers (vice presidents and above) are men. Furthermore, 97 percent of male top executives are white. Of the small fraction of top managers who are women, 95 percent of them are white non-Hispanic. In 1994 there were just two women CEOs in the Fortune 1000. The boards of directors of the large corporations are also dominated by men. Only 10 percent of the Fortune 1500 have women on their board of directors.[76]

One might wonder what the practical differences would be if gender and racial inequality were eliminated but with the continued existence of class inequalities. Is it possible that the inequalities of class are partly built on (and dependent on) other forms of inequality?

THE DECLINE OF UNIONS

The lack of pressure on the government and on private corporations to bridge socioeconomic gaps can be seen in two important indicators of working-class consciousness and activity. The first of these is the dramatic decline in the percentage of workers belonging to unions. In 1975, 28.9 percent of all employed workers were members of unions; by 1986, just 15.5 percent were. The second, and probably more revealing indicator of working-class strength (or weakness, in this case), is the amount of strike activity. Since the 1970s, there has been a tremendous drop-off in the number of work stoppages and the number of workers involved in them. In the 1960s and 1970s, there were an average of over 280 work stoppages per year (of at least 1,000 workers) involving a total of well over one million workers per year. In contrast, the 1980s averaged eighty-three work stoppages per year involving far fewer workers, even though many more people were in the workforce. Thus far the averages for the 1990s have been even lower. See Figure 3.14 for Unionization Rates.[77]

The decline of unions is not simply the result of their possible irrelevance to present-day workers but of active attacks on the working class by corporate America along with its allies in government. Confident that the government will not take up the cause of the unions, corporations have

Table 3.14. Median Weekly Earnings of Full-Time Wage and Salary Workers by Detailed Occupation and Sex[78]

Occupation	Median Weekly Income for Men	Median Weekly Income for Women	Women s % of Men
Managerial and professional specialty	$1,038	$ 732	71%
Engineers	1,142	1,022	89
Teachers, college and university	1,126	844	75
Teachers, except college and university	780	707	91
Technical, sales, and administrative support	667	473	71
Sales occupations	692	429	62
Administrative support, including clerical	576	469	81
Service occupations, except private household and protective	374	332	89
Precision production, craft, and repair	648	479	74
Operators, fabricators, and laborers	501	368	73
Transportation and material moving occupations	587	439	75

become much more willing to harass workers who push for union representation or union assertiveness. The number of workers illegally fired for union activity increased from 2,723 in 1970 to 8,592 in 1980. Likewise, the percentage of union victories in representative elections has dropped, and corporations have become much more likely to push for decertification elections. Such elections increased from about 240 per year in the 1960s to nearly 900 a year in the 1980s.[79] More recently, a study done by the National Labor Relations Board found that from 1992 to 1997 more than 125,000 workers were fired or otherwise punished for supporting a union in spite of the fact that the National Labor Relations Act prohibits employers from taking retaliatory actions against workers who participate in unionization activities.[80]

Table 3.15. The Decline of Strike Activity[81]

Years	Average # of work stoppages per year	Average # of workers involved per year*	Average # of days idle in year*
1950–59	352	1,588,000	26,615,000
1960–69	283	1,234,000	18,882,000
1970–79	289	1,488,000	26,049,000
1980–89	83	507,000	11,754,000
1990–99	36	274,000	4,577,000

*Excludes work stoppages involving fewer than 1,000 workers and lasting less than one day.

Inequality and the Frayed Social Fabric

In a speech at Wake Forest University in March 1995, Felix Rohatyn, a senior partner at Lazard Freres, one of the most prestigious investment firms on Wall Street, displayed a clear awareness of the divisions being created by the policies pursued by corporate America and its allies in the government:

> The big beneficiaries of our economic expansion have been the owners of financial assets and a new class of highly compensated technicians working for companies where profit-sharing and stock ownership was widely spread.
>
> What is occurring is a huge transfer of wealth from lower-skilled middle-class American workers to the owners of capital assets and to the new technological aristocracy.
>
> As a result, the institutional relationship created by the mutual loyalty of employees and employers in most American businesses has been badly frayed. . . . These relationships have been replaced by a combination of fear for the future and a cynicism for the present as a broad proportion of working people see themselves as simply temporary assets to be hired or fired to protect the bottom line and create "shareholder value."[82]

The decline in the power of unions is further illustrated by the fact that in many recent years the wages of union members have actually grown more slowly than nonunion members.[83] For instance, in 1986 and 1987 compensation for union members grew 2.1 percent and 2.8 percent, compared to 3.7 and 3.6 percent for nonunion workers. The proliferation of union-management contracts incorporating "give backs" and two- or even three-tier pay scales, with lower wage scales and benefits for newer

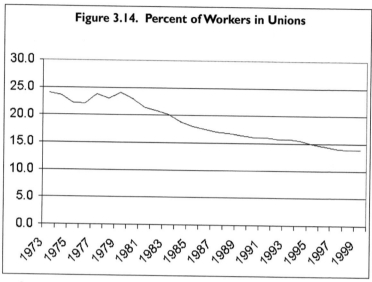

Figure 3.14. Percent of Workers in Unions

Source: EPI's Datazone

workers, has undoubtedly had a strong impact on the earnings of union workers in recent years.

The lack of bargaining leverage for unions today has most likely had a spill-over effect. Historically, without a strong labor movement, minimum-wage laws would have never been enacted, and in the absence of a strong labor movement today the real minimum wage has deteriorated steadily.

Currently, working people lack organized power capable of checking corporate excesses and winning progressive reforms from the government. Workers' unions were responsible for the advent of the eight-hour day and were able to pressure the government for Social Security, unemployment insurance, and publicly funded colleges available at low tuition. From corporations, unions were able to secure pensions, paid vacations, paid sick leave, health plans, better working conditions, and the regulation of on-the-job safety and health concerns. Without a strong working class movement these gains have been gradually eroding. Fewer workers today are covered by pension or health plans, more and more of the unemployed are not eligible for unemployment insurance, and much of the working class works longer and harder for economic security, a security that is becoming more elusive.

NOTES

1. U.S. Bureau of the Census, *The Changing Shape of the Nation's Income Distribution, 1947–1998; Current Population Reports*, P60–204.

2. Ibid., p. 1.

3. Michael Yates, *Longer Hours, Fewer Jobs* (New York: Monthly Review Press, 1994), pp. 55–56. Unemployment rates come from the *Statistical Abstract of the United States*, various years.

4. *Statistical Abstract of the United States, 1995*, p. 399.

5. Labor Force Participation Rates are from the U.S. Bureau of Labor Statistics.

6. Excerpted from Marc Breslow and Mathew Howard, "The Real Un(der)employment Rate," *Dollars and Sense*, May/June 1995, p. 23. See also *Statistical Abstract of the United States, 1995*, p. 396.

7. Lawrence Mishel, Jared Bernstein, and John Schmitt, *The State of Working America, 2000–2001* (Ithaca, N.Y.: Cornell University Press, 2001), p. 115.

8. William Cox, *Measures of Real Earnings Since 1970*, The Congressional Research Service, November 13, 1987, p. 21.

9. Philip L. Rones, Randy E. Ilg, and Jennifer M. Gardner, "Trends in Hours of Work since the Mid-1970s," *Monthly Labor Review* (April 1997): 3–18.

10. Similar increases took place for men and women as a whole. Average annual work hours for men increased by 100 from 1976 to 1993, and 233 hours for women (Rones et al., "Trends in Hours of Work").

11. Mary Williams Walsh, "Reversing Decades-Long Trend, Americans Retiring Later in Life," *New York Times*, February 26, 2001.

12. Harold Kerbo, *Social Stratification* (New York: McGraw-Hill, 1991), p. 51, and *The Statistical Abstract of the United States, 1995*, p. 344; *2001*, p. 305.

13. For more on taxation and income distribution see Edward S. Herman, "The Income 'Counter-Revolution,'" in *Crisis in American Institutions*, edited by Jerome Skolnick and Edward Currie, 3d ed. (Boston: Little, Brown and Co, 1976); Joseph A. Pechman, *Who Paid the Taxes, 1966–85* (Washington, D.C.: Brookings Institute, 1985); Donald L. Barlett and James B. Steele, *America: Who Really Pays the Taxes* (New York: Touchstone, 1994); and Lawrence Mishel and Jared Bernstein, *The State of Working America, 1992–93* (Washington, D.C.: Economic Policy Institute, 1993), chap. 2.

14. Joseph Pechman, *Who Paid the Taxes*.

15. Sidney Plotkin and William E. Scheuerman, *Private Interests, Public Spending* (Boston: South End Press, 1994), p. 22.

16. Sarah Anderson, John Cavanagh, Chris Hartman and Betsy Leondar-Wright, *Executive Excess, 2001* (Boston: United for a Fair Economy, 2001), p. 1.

17. *Too Much* (summer 2001): 9.

18. Anderson et al., *Executive Excess*, p. 1.

19. Ibid.

20. Arthur B. Kennickell, *An Examination of Changes in the Distribution of Wealth from 1989 to 1998: Evidence from the Survey of Consumer Finances* (Washington, D.C.: Federal Reserve Board, June 2000).

21. Economic Policy Institute, *Datazone* [online], www.epinet.org.

22. Chuck Collins, Chris Hartman, and Holly Sklar, *Divided Decade: Economic Disparity at the Century's Turn* (Boston: United for a Fair Economy, 1999).

23. [Online], www.forbes.com. List is for 2002.

24. The large standard error on the highest income group in 1989 makes it impossible to conclude that there was a significant change from 1989 to 1998. On the 1983 and 1989 studies, see the first ed. of *Inequality, Power, and Development*, chap. 3.

25. *Statistical Abstract of the United States, 1993*, p. 424; 1994, p. 427.

26. *Statistical Abstract of the United States, 1994*, p. 426.

27. Louis Uchitelle, "As Output Gains, Wages Lag," *New York Times*, June 4, 1987, p. D7.

28. "What the Boss Makes," *Forbes*, June 15, 1987.

29. *Statistical Abstract of the United States, 1994*, p. 426.

30. Lawrence Mishel and Jacqueline Simon, *The State of Working America* (Washington, D.C.: Economic Policy Institute, 1988), p. 18.

31. Ravi Batra, "An Ominous Trend Toward Greater Inequality," *New York Times*, May 3, 1987.

32. John A. Byrne et al., "That Eye Popping Executive Pay," *BusinessWeek*, April 25, 1994. See also Anderson et al., *Executive Excess*.

33. *BusinessWeek*, April 15, 2002.

34. Byrne, "That Eye Popping Executive Pay," p. 23.

35. *BusinessWeek*, April 21, 2003.

36. Anderson et al., *Executive Excess*, p. 6.

37. "Sometimes Failure Is an Option," *Too Much* (summer 2001): 9.

38. Ibid.

39. U.S. Census Bureau, *Poverty in the United States*, Current Population Reports, P60–214, issued September 2001.

40. Kendrick Frazier, "The State of American Education," *Rethinking Schools* (winter 1993): 16–17.

41. Ibid.

42. Marc Breslow, "The Racial Divide Widens," *Dollars and Sense*, January/February 1995, p. 9.

43. *Statistical Abstract of the United States, 2001*, p. 11.

44. Ibid., p. 139.

45. Breslow, "The Racial Divide Widens," p. 8.

46. Ibid., p. 9.

47. *Statistical Abstract of the United States, 2001*, p. 405.

48. William Julius Wilson, *The Truly Disadvantaged* (Chicago: University of Chicago Press, 1987).

49. *Statistical Abstract of the United States, 2001*, p. 140. Figures are for 1999, for persons eighteen years old and over with earnings.

50. Daniel T. Lichter, "Racial Differences in Underemployment in American Cities," *American Journal of Sociology* (January 1988): 788–89.

51. Breslow, "The Racial Divide Widens," p. 38.

52. Steven A. Holmes, "Programs Based on Sex and Race Are Challenged," *New York Times*, March 16, 1995.

53. See the U.S. Department of Labor, Bureau of Labor Statistics, July 1985, bull. 2240. A good summary is available in the October 1985 issue of *Dollars and Sense*. See also Barry Bluestone and Bennet Harrison, *The Deindustrialization of America* (New York: Basic Books, 1982).

54. For more information on the impact of public sector layoffs, see Don Terry, "Cuts in Public Jobs May Hurt Blacks Most," *New York Times*, December 10, 1991; and Gary Orfield and Carole Ashkinaze, *The Closing Door: Conservative Policy and Black Opportunity* (Chicago: University of Chicago Press, 1991).

55. Breslow, "The Racial Divide Widens," p. 11.

56. Edward Wolff, *Income and Wealth*, series 40, no. 2 (June 1994): 165.

57. Ibid.

58. Breslow, "The Racial Divide Widens," p. 39. For more on discrimination in home mortgage lending and a detailed discussion of the Federal Reserve Bank of Boston's study, see Jim Campen, "Lending Insight: Hard Proof That Banks Discriminate," *Dollars and Sense*, January/February 1994.

59. Peter Passell, "Race, Mortgage and Statistics: The Unending Debate Over a Study of Lending Bias," *New York Times*, May 10, 1996.

60. Joint Center for Housing Studies, Harvard University, *State of the Nation's Housing, 2001*.

61. Breslow, "The Racial Divide Widens," p. 10.

62. Reprinted from *Dollars and Sense*, January/February 1995.

63. Robert J. Mills, *Health Insurance Coverage*, U.S. Census Bureau, Current Population Reports P60–211, September 2000.

64. Chuck Collins, Chris Hartman, and Holly Sklar, *Divided Decade: Economic Disparity at the Century's Turn* (Boston: United for a Fair Economy, December 15, 1999).

65. The National Advisory Commission on Civil Disorders, *Report of the National Advisory Commission of Civil Disorders* (New York: Bantam, 1968). Commonly referred to as *The Kerner Report*.

66. Isabel Wilkerson, "Two Decades of Decline Chronicled by Kerner Follow-up Report," *New York Times*, March 1, 1988. See also *The Kerner Report Updated: Report of the 1988 Commission on the Cities, Race and Poverty in the United States Today*.

67. Bernard D. Headley, "Race, Poverty, Crime and Powerlessness in America's Inner Cities," in *Critical Perspectives in Sociology*, ed. Berch Berberoglu (Dubuque, Iowa: Kendall/Hunt Publishing, 1993), p. 225.

68. Ronald Walters, "The Reagan Revolution Sparked L.A.'s Rebellion," *Wall Street Journal*, May 7, 1992.

69. For a good examination of the attempts by the Reagan administration to cut back social programs, see Frances Fox Piven and Richard A. Cloward, *The New Class War* (New York: Pantheon, 1985).

70. New Jersey Council of Churches, *The Reshaping of New Jersey: The Growing Separation*, February 3, 1988, pp. 3–4.

71. Ibid., p. 35.

72. *Statistical Abstract of the United States, 2002*, p. 367.

73. *Money Income in the United States, 1999*, Current Population Reports, P60–209; U.S. Census Bureau, pp. 37–39.

74. The Federal Glass Ceiling Commission, 1995, *Good for Business: Making Full Use of the Nation's Human Capital*, March, p. 232.

75. Ibid., p. 144; the poll was taken in 1990.

76. The Federal Glass Ceiling Commission, 1995, p. 12.

77. Economic Policy Institute, Datazone.

78. Bureau of Labor Statistics [online], ftp://ftp.bls.gov/pub/special.requests/lf/aat39.txt.

79. Plotkin and Scheuerman, *Private Interests, Public Spending*, p. 49.

80. Steven Greenhouse, "A Potent, Illegal Weapon Against Unions," *San Francisco Chronicle*, October 24, 2000.

81. *Statistical Abstract of the United States, 1993* and *1995*; *Handbook of Labor Statistics*, 1985; and *Monthly Labor Review*, July 1986 and April 1988. Bureau of Labor Statistics [online], www.bls.gov/data/home.htm.

82. Quoted in A. M. Rosenthal, "American Class Struggle," *New York Times*, March 21, 1995.

83. John Lacombe and Joan Borum, "Major Labor Contracts in 1986 Provided Record Low Wage Adjustments," *Monthly Labor Review* (May 1987); Linda LeGrande, *Who's Keeping Up in the 1980s? Compensation as an Indicator* (Congressional Research Service, November 4, 1987).

4 CORPORATE POWER

The decline of the power of unions and of labor's influence in the Democratic Party stands in sharp contrast to the growth in the size and influence of the modern transnational corporation and of various global institutions designed to extend the influence of private capital. In recent years, the term *globalization* has been commonly used when referring to trends in the world economy. Economist Michael Tanzer explains the concept well: "Globalization . . . refers to the explosive growth in the past twenty to twenty-five years of huge multinational corporations and vast pools of capital that have crossed national borders and penetrated everywhere. This globalization, in turn, is seen as largely the result of a parallel technological explosion in computerization, telecommunications, and rapid transportation."[1]

Globalization, of course, is not entirely new. It has been an ongoing process since the time of Columbus, and it is not only something in which corporations are involved but also national governments and, today more than ever, powerful extragovernmental organizations such as the International Monetary Fund (IMF), the World Bank, and the World Trade Organization (WTO). But to begin our examination of globalization, let us start by looking at its driving force, the transnational corporation.

In 1996, the Coca-Cola company announced that it was eliminating the very concepts of "domestic" and "international" from the administrative structure of its worldwide operations. Coca-Cola chairman Roberto C. Goizueta explained that "the labels 'international' and 'domestic,' which adequately described our business structure in the past, no longer apply."[2] General Motors (GM) had already announced that it was a global company over a decade before. Likewise, in 1989, a top executive of Colgate Palmolive expressed his company's global orientation by stating, "The United States doesn't have an automatic call on our . . . resources. There is no mindset that puts this country first." The Dow Chemical Company had even gone so far as to consider buying a Caribbean island and chartering itself as an independent nation.[3] These examples show that many of the world's largest corporations feel no special need for a national identity and no allegiance to one nation over another. But more importantly, they reflect a growing tendency of large companies to transfer capital across borders to develop their interests wherever the economic opportunity is greatest and labor is the most compliant.

The return on investment for U.S.-based multinationals is 50 percent greater in the underdeveloped nations of the world. From 1985 to 1990 alone, U.S. corporate foreign investment grew 84 percent. There are now over 37,000 transnational corporations, but the majority of international business is concentrated in the largest companies. Just 400 companies control about 80 percent of the capital assets of the global market. The top 100 transnationals make nearly half their income from sales outside their home nation.[4]

Globalization has been spurred on by the overaccumulation of capital in the advanced capitalist nations, that is, by the failure of investors to find sufficiently profitable avenues of investment within their own borders. The development in recent years of sophisticated communications systems facilitated by computer and satellite technology, along with the continual development of air and sea transportation, has made it easier for corporations to do business on a global scale. This, in turn, allows corporations to increase their *capital mobility*, often to the detriment of the working classes in the developed nations. The threat of capital withdrawal can be used to gain concessions from workers or even from governments. One study on the impact of capital mobility on union organizing drives found that

> The recent acceleration in capital mobility has had a devastating impact on the extent and nature of union organizing campaigns. Where employers can credibly threaten to shut down and/or move their operations in response to union activity, they do so in large numbers. Overall,

The world's top 200 corporations account for over a quarter of economic activity on the globe while employing less than 1 percent of its workforce.[5]

more than half of all employers [in the study] made threats to close all or part of the plant during the organizing drive. The threat rate is significantly higher, 68 percent, in mobile industries such as manufacturing, communication, and wholesale/distribution, compared to 36 percent threat rate in relatively immobile industries such as construction, healthcare, education, retail, and other services.[6]

To help grasp the size and influence of modern transnational corporations, let's take a look at one of them in detail while highlighting some general trends in the modern corporation.

A CASE STUDY: GENERAL MOTORS

General Motors is the third largest corporation in the world. In 2001, the company had a total revenue of $177 billion and the estimated value of GM's assets was $324 billion. GM, however, like so many large corporations, is not purely an American company. GM has manufacturing operations in more than thirty countries, and its vehicles are sold in about 200 countries. Principal assembly or manufacturing operations outside the United States and Canada include facilities in Germany, the United Kingdom, Australia, Brazil, Mexico, Austria, Belgium, and Spain. Lesser operations are owned in such distant nations as Kenya, Ecuador, and Venezuela. GM has a 49 percent stake in Isuzu Motors and 20 percent stakes in Fuji Heavy Industries (Subaru), Suzuki Motor, and Fiat Auto (Alfa Romeo, Lancia). Recently, GM agreed to take a 42 percent stake in South Korea's Daewoo Motor.[7]

For decades, GM has been investing in automobile companies based in other countries. The phrase "buy American" has become a meaningless slogan, particularly as it is used in automobile advertising. One could buy a GM car only to discover that it was assembled in Mexico or Brazil or that, more likely, different parts of it were made in different countries. The same holds true for Ford and Chrysler. Conversely, one could buy a "Japanese" car, like an Isuzu, that was made by a company partly owned by GM and developed by GM capital. Like GM, the other "American" automobile companies have been investing in foreign companies. Mitsubishi, for example, is partly owned by Chrysler. These internationalist trends exist not just in the auto industry but in other industries as well. The electronics industry may be the best example. General Electric started investing in the Japanese electronics company Toshiba in 1953, and Westinghouse is a principal shareholder in Mitsubishi electronics.[8] The electronics industry has been labeled the quintessential runaway industry. From 1980 to 1985, over 500,000 jobs were created in Asia alone by U.S. electronics companies.[9] These figures illustrate the problem of *capital flight*: the exporting of capital that could be used to develop domestic industries or to put people to work at productive occupations with decent wages in the United States.

The size and resources of a company like GM enable it to influence aspects of daily life that we might normally take for granted. The major auto companies in the United States, for example, have been very influential in determining the nation's transportation policy. Each year they spend millions of dollars to finance lobbying and other political activities. They were among the prime forces behind the Interstate Highway Act of 1956, which was responsible for the construction of 41,000 miles of highways throughout the United States, which, coupled with extensive advertising campaigns, helped stimulate auto use.[10] In fact, GM went well beyond what the typical American citizen might consider the boundaries of fair play, when decades ago it acted to destroy various mass transit systems in numerous American cities. The rise of the automobile directly corresponded to the demise of city trolley systems and intercity rail transportation.

It is generally acknowledged that by the 1920s most of the people who wanted, or were able to afford, an automobile already owned one. The automobile market was saturated.[11] About that time GM acquired the nation's largest bus manufacturer. Shortly afterward it began buying up interurban electric railways and electric streetcar systems and converting them to diesel bus systems. According to Bradford Snell: "By the mid-1950s, it [GM] could lay claim to having played a prominent role in the complete replacement of electric street transportation with diesel buses. Due to their high cost of operation and slow speed on congested streets, however, these buses ultimately contributed to the collapse of several hundred public transit systems and to the diversion of hundreds of thousands of patrons to automobiles."[12]

By 1949, GM had taken over and converted more than 100 electric transit systems in 45 cities across the country. At one point a federal jury convicted GM, along with Standard Oil of California, Firestone Tire, and others of criminal conspiracy. However, in keeping with the legal system's probusiness bias and the corporate structure that shields individuals from accountability, the court fined GM $5,000 and its treasurer $1.[13] Over the years the courts have done little to curtail the destruction of mass transportation by the auto industry, and the federal government has consistently favored tremendous subsidies for the auto over the development of any modern mass transportation system or funding for alternative transportation.

The chaotic, energy-inefficient, heavily polluting system of transportation that currently exists in the United States was planned and developed in the boardrooms of companies like GM with little input from the general public, and with little thought given to considerations other than the accumulation of tremendous profits that have made GM one of the world's largest corporations.

GM's lack of regard for the well-being of the American citizenry has also been displayed in the arena of world politics. The "big three" auto companies clearly put their own interests above those of the American public when they supplied both the Allied forces and the Axis powers with military equipment before and during World War II. In 1935, GM built its Opel subsidiary in Brandenburg, Germany, where military officials advised that it would be less vulnerable to attack, and in the following years supplied Hitler's army with trucks. In 1938, GM's chief executive for overseas operations was awarded the Order of the German Eagle, first class, by Adolf Hitler. Ford also built troop-transport vehicles for the Nazis, and its chief executive also received the German Eagle award.[14] (Overall, U.S. corporate investment in Hitler-run Germany expanded rapidly while falling in every other European nation at that time.)[15]

GM and Ford remained in control of their facilities and continued to build trucks and warplanes after the United States declared war on Germany. According to Snell, "Communications and material continually flowed between GM plants in Allied countries and GM plants in Axis-controlled areas."[16] After the war ended, Snell noted, "GM and Ford demanded reparations from the U.S. Government for wartime damages sustained by their Axis facilities as a result of Allied bombing. By 1967 GM had collected more than $33 million in reparations and Federal tax benefits for damages to its warplane and motor vehicles properties in Germany, Austria, Poland, Latvia, and China. Likewise, Ford received a little less than $1 million."[17]

Of no small significance is the fact that in the 1950s, the U.S. Department of Defense was headed by Charles Wilson, who had been president of GM. Wilson was succeeded by Robert S. McNamara, who had been president of Ford Motor Company and later went on to become the president of the World Bank.[18] These are two examples of the interchange of personnel between the upper echelons of government and the corporate world, an issue that will be examined further in the next chapter.

The rise of the automobile to prominence over the course of the twentieth century created a state of autodependency that fueled auto industry profits but burdened American society with a number of serious problems, including unhealthy air and a dependence on petroleum that often resulted in support for undemocratic regimes in oil-producing nations. The problem of dirty air was exacerbated by a concerted effort made by the petrochemical industry to make sure that the gas used by American automobiles contained tetraethyl lead (TEL). Lead was prohibited as an additive to automotive gasoline in the United States in 1986, but not until after it had been wreaking havoc on the health of Americans for six decades. Lead is not naturally a component of gasoline, but it became a ubiquitous additive due to the efforts of Du Pont, General Motors, and Standard Oil of New Jersey (the predecessor of Exxon/Mobil). By the time lead was discontinued as a fuel additive in the United States, it was estimated that lead-related heart disease was killing about 5,000 Americans per year.[19]

Originally, lead was added to gasoline in order to prevent engine knock; however, according to an in-depth exposé by Jamie Lincoln Kitman, it is quite clear now that the benefits of antiknock additives were grossly overstated, that lead is poisonous to humans, that lead is actually bad for cars, and that other much less harmful additives for reducing engine knock were available. The Du Pont Corporation, the major proponent of lead as an additive, concealed much of the above information in order to protect its investment in TEL and to monopolize the market for antiknock additives. In 1922, when General Motors contracted to buy TEL from Du Pont, the chemical giant owned more than 35 percent of GM.

Standard Oil also played a role in the great lead scam. Neither Du Pont nor Standard Oil wanted to see ethanol, an alcohol-based fuel produced from plant matter, emerge as a popular alternative to petroleum. Ethanol is made from a renewable fuel source, burns cleaner than gasoline, has a higher octane rating, and can provide better engine performance. In addi-

Pierre-Samuel (1870–1954) and Irenee (1877–1963) du Pont were the scions of a 200-year-old family-run explosives business. They used windfall profits made from selling gunpowder during World War I to purchase a controlling interest in GM. Their firms produced TEL and earned royalties on gas sold around the world between 1924 and 1992. They ignored the dangers of TEL production while hundreds died or suffered poisoning at their factories, and they misled the press and public as to the hazards posed by leaded gasoline. Their company also aided the Nazi war effort through deals made with the German chemical giant I. G. Farben.[20]

tion, it was cheaper and more readily available. The fact that it was cheaper and readily available were reasons enough for Du Pont and Standard Oil to conspire against ethanol's market success. Du Pont could patent TEL but not ethanol, and the profits of a few corporations were a higher priority than the health of the nation.

ENRON AND THE CORPORATE SCANDALS OF 2001-2002

The late twentieth century witnessed the rise of a few global corporations that produce little but make most of their profits by buying from and selling to others. In 2002, Wal-Mart, the retail giant, was ranked by *Fortune* magazine as the largest American corporation, number two globally (after Exxon/Mobil). For the year 2001, Enron, an energy trading company, was ranked as the sixth-largest corporation in the world, but before the year was out Enron was rocked by scandal and the company filed for bankruptcy in February of 2002.

Enron initially made its mark in the 1980s by buying and selling natural gas futures. Kenneth Lay, the company's CEO, had convinced the Federal Energy Regulatory Commission to deregulate the wholesale natural gas market. Enron was able to make millions speculating on the price of natural gas. The company then set its sights on the electricity market and funded a $25 million campaign to have electricity deregulated. This successful campaign allowed companies to buy and sell kilowatts many times over before the electricity reached consumers. Needless to say, the practice added significantly to the price ultimately paid by the end-use consumer. It cost Californians, for example, nearly $50 billion.[21] Where Enron couldn't change the law, it broke it. In October 2002, Timothy Belden, a former senior executive, pleaded guilty to illegally manipulating the California power market, increasing Enron's profits by defrauding consumers and driving up prices.[22]

In 2001, Enron's accounting practices drew negative attention to the Texas-based corporation. Enron had set up dummy corporations to hide its expenses so that its profits would appear much larger than they actually were (Enron had 874 offshore partnerships). The revelations about Enron's illegal accounting practices caused the company's stock to plummet, and although company executives got out while the getting was still good, employees were prevented from cashing pension funds that were held in the form of company stocks. By the time employees were allowed to cash out, the stocks were nearly worthless, and employees lost $1.2 billion in retirement savings. Many middle-class Americans were also hurt by the company's crash. Approximately 64 percent of Enron's stock was owned by institutional investors, many of these are mutual funds or pension funds that are important sources of retirement income for middle-class Americans. It is estimated that ordinary Americans lost some $25–50 billion as a result of Enron's fraudulent practices.[23] The day after filing for bankruptcy, Enron laid off 4,000 employees, and this came just three days after Enron arranged for $55 million in bonuses for its top 500 executives.[24]

Meanwhile, speculation grew that Enron had used its close ties with the Bush administration to advance its investment interests, and that Vice President Dick Cheney had been unduly influenced by Enron as he developed national energy policy. Enron officials had at least six meetings with Cheney in 2001, and the administration's energy recommendations, which emphasized increasing supplies of nonrenewable energy sources at the expense of environmental considerations, were very favorable to Enron's interests. Enron's government influence was extensive; the company had made $6 million in political contributions over the course of a decade, with donations to 186 members of the House of Representatives and 71 senators.[25] President George W. Bush had been an Enron favorite. According to the Center for Responsive Politics, Enron and its employees contributed $312,500 to Bush's 1994 and 1998 Texas gubernatorial campaigns, and later gave $113,800 to the Bush 2000 presidential campaign. Enron also gave $10,500 to the Bush-Cheney Recount Fund and $300,000 to the Bush-Cheney 2001 Inaugural Fund.[26] The Council on International and Public Affairs claims that overall Enron invested $2 million in George W. Bush.[27]

In June 2002, a similar "accounting" scandal rocked WorldCom, the world's ninetieth largest corporation (the scandals were often referred to as "accounting scandals," but the problem, at least in Enron's case, consisted of much more than deceptive accounting practices). WorldCom had used illegal accounting practices to disguise $3.8 billion in expenses (WorldCom counted operating expenses as capital expenditures so they could be amortized over many years), thereby artificially inflating declared profits.[28] Higher profits inflated the price of WorldCom stock, enhanced the reputation of the company's management, and justified high executive salaries. WorldCom's bookkeeping practices set a standard of profitability with which its competitors could not keep pace and cost many employees in other companies their jobs. Shortly after the WorldCom scandal broke, the company announced that it would lay off 17,000 employees, and in July 2002, WorldCom filed for bankruptcy.

Scandalous corporate fraud by Enron, WorldCom, and other companies such as Global Crossing and Adelphia, combined with the September 11, 2001, terrorist attack on the World Trade Center, sent the stock market into a tailspin, and by October of 2002, the Dow Jones stock index had fallen over 25 percent, and had the *New York Times* wondering "Could Capitalists Actually Bring Down Capitalism?"[29] But these scandals made the headlines in the United States well after many people in less-developed nations had been exposed to corporate practices that were much more harmful than fraudulent bookkeeping.

Globally, Enron had been advocating, and taking advantage of, neoliberal economic reforms such as increased trade liberalization, privatization, and reductions in government regulations (issues that will be discussed in more detail in chapters 7, 8, and 9) to make deep inroads into the economies of many nations, and billions of dollars of profits as well. In 1992, when the government of India announced that it was privatizing its energy sector, Enron began planning to build the largest electricity generating plant in the world, in the state of Maharashtra. As details of the $2.9 billion plant became known, many of India's economists, academics, trade unionists, and nongovernmental organizations began to express reservations about the project. Eventually, these reservations grew into outright opposition by local residents concerned about their livelihood and by many others throughout India who had environmental and economic concerns. The protest movement, however, was callously dismissed by Enron and state officials, and was, at times, forcibly repressed. According to Human Rights Watch, opponents of the Dabhol power plant

> have been subjected to beatings and repeated short-term detention. In many cases, they have been detained for periods ranging from several days to two weeks without being produced before a magistrate as required under Indian law. During mass arrests at demonstrations in villages surrounding the project site, protesters have been beaten with canes (lathis) or otherwise assaulted by the police, in some cases sustaining severe injuries. Police have also tear-gassed peaceful demonstrations.[30]

Human Rights Watch goes on to point out that the Dabhol Power Corporation, of which Enron is the principal partner, "paid the abusive state forces for the security they provided to the company."

Enron has also used its political connections to get its way in the African nation of Mozambique. Mozambique, under pressure from the IMF and President Bill Clinton (who threatened to cancel development aid to the country), accepted a plan to have Enron construct a pipeline to South Africa. Enron brought similar pressure to bear on Argentina so that it would be able to construct a natural gas pipeline to Chile.[31]

One of the entities that bankrolled Enron's "development" projects is the U.S. Overseas Private Investment Corporation (OPIC). OPIC loaned Enron at least $2.4 billion dollars for its overseas projects. But OPIC is taxpayer-backed, and if Enron's bankruptcy means that it is unable to pay back OPIC, then taxpayers will have to foot the bill.

OPIC also played a role in Enron's ventures in Bolivia. One of these, the Cuiaba natural gas pipeline, became the focal point of dispute for many environmentalists and for many of Bolivia's indigenous villages. The pipeline runs for nearly 400 miles from eastern Bolivia to Cuiaba, Matto Grosso, Brazil, where it fuels Enron's 480-megawatt thermal power plant. Along the way the pipeline passes through the fifteen-million-acre Chiquitano forest, a rare, rich, and "biologically outstanding" forest. The Chiquitano is a habitat for approximately ninety species of mammals, birds, and reptiles that are listed as endangered, and it is a very sensitive ecoregion. OPIC decided to help fund Enron's pipeline through the Chiquitano over the objections of numerous environmental organizations whose firsthand studies led them to declare the forest "a primary tropical ecosystem of global importance."[32]

OPIC's backing of Enron, as well as Enron's close relationship with top Bolivian officials (including President Gonzalo Sanchez de Lozada), helped the company take advantage of Bolivia's new privatization schemes. However, Enron became the object of heavy criticism in January 2000, when the company's Sica Sica Arica oil pipeline burst, spilling nearly 30,000 barrels of oil along 160 miles of the Desaguadero River, ruining the livelihood of many communities. Enron had been warned that the pipeline was old and in need of repair but it failed to heed the warnings. It also failed to shut off valves in the pipeline for more than twenty-three hours after the pipe burst. Enron's disregard for the environment along with its failure to include the participation of indigenous people in development decisions were two of the factors that eventually caused OPIC to cancel its loan in February of 2002. In the meantime, the ecosystem of the Chiquitano forest and the livelihood of many of its inhabitants has been badly damaged. Roads built or "improved" by Enron have facilitated illegal logging in the forest, and hunting and cattle ranching have increased, adding to the ecological damage.

During Enron's peak years it was the beneficiary of the powerful influence of government leaders in Washington, made millions of dollars for stockholders and upper management, and tapped into capital reserves created out of public funds (OPIC). But in four of the five years before the scandal broke, Enron paid not one penny in corporate taxes to the U.S. government. In fact, over the five-year period from 1996 to 2000, Enron received a net tax rebate of $381 million from the federal government. The company's profits over that same period totaled $1.785 billion.[33]

The Overseas Private Investment Corporation's loans and political risk insurance help U.S. businesses of all sizes invest and compete in more than 140 emerging markets and developing nations worldwide. OPIC, a U.S. government agency, assists U.S. private investment overseas because, according to the organization's Web site, "it is in America's economic and strategic interest." The site also points out that "All of OPIC's guaranty and insurance obligations are backed by the full faith and credit of the United States of America."[34]

FOREIGN INVESTMENT

In addition to the increased concentration of corporate assets, a rapid increase in the overseas investments of American corporations has taken place over the past two or three decades. For the year 2000, direct corporate investment abroad was nearly $2.5 trillion, a 196 percent increase since 1989.[35] According to Howard Sherman, "The top 298 U.S.-based transnational corporations earn 40 percent of their entire net profit overseas, and their rate of profit from abroad is much higher than their domestic profit rate." In particular, the rate of profit made by U.S.-based corporations is several times higher in the Third World than it is in developed nations.[36]

Foreign investment accounts for over 30 percent of all corporate after-tax profits compared to 13 percent in 1960.[37] But although corporations have become more and more global, there are few mechanisms for holding them accountable on an international level. Many of the Fortune 500 corporations have yearly sales far greater than the GDP of many less-developed countries. (For example, GM's yearly sales exceed the combined Gross Domestic Product of the seven nations of Central America, and Exxon's sales are four times the GDP of Kuwait.)[38] And although workers may organize themselves into nationwide unions and countries may pass laws regulating business practices or establishing rules for workplace safety, there is little any single nation can do to prevent a corporation from closing down its operations and moving elsewhere. The mobility of capital in the contemporary

The Top 100 Economies, Countries, and Corporations Combined[39]

	Country/ Corporation	GDP/ sales ($mil)		Country/ Corporation	GDP/ sales ($mil)
1	United States	8,708,870.0	51	Colombia	88,596.0
2	Japan	4,395,083.0	52	AXA	87,645.7
3	Germany	2,081,202.0	53	IBM	87,548.0
4	France	1,410,262.0	54	Singapore	84,945.0
5	United Kingdom	1,373,612.0	55	Ireland	84,861.0
6	Italy	1,149,958.0	56	BP Amoco	83,556.0
7	China	1,149,814.0	57	Citigroup	82,005.0
8	Brazil	760,345.0	58	Volkswagen	80,072.7
9	Canada	612,049.0	59	Nippon Life Insurance	78,515.1
10	Spain	562,245.0	60	Philippines	75,350.0
11	Mexico	474,951.0	61	Siemens	75,337.0
12	India	459,765.0	62	Malaysia	74,634.0
13	Korea, Rep.	406,940.0	63	Allianz	74,178.2
14	Australia	389,691.0	64	Hitachi	71,858.5
15	Netherlands	384,345.0	65	Chile	71,092.2
16	Russian Federation	375,345.0	66	Matsushita Elec. Ind.	65,555.6
17	Argentina	281,942.0	67	Nissho Iwai	65,393.2
18	Switzerland	260,299.0	68	ING Group	62,492.4
19	Belgium	245,706.0	69	AT&T	62,391.0
20	Sweden	226,388.0	70	Philip Morris	61,751.0
21	Austria	208,949.0	71	Sony	60,052.7
22	Turkey	188,374.0	72	Pakistan	59,880.0
23	General Motors	176,558.0	73	Deutsche Bank	58,585.1
24	Denmark	174,363.0	74	Boeing	57,993.0
25	Wal-Mart	166,809.0	75	Peru	57,318.0
26	Exxon/Mobil	163,881.0	76	Czech Republic	56,379.0
27	Ford Motor	162,558.0	77	Dai-Ichi Mutual Life Ins.	55,104.7
28	Daimler Chrysler	159,985.7	78	Honda Motor	54,773.5
29	Poland	154,146.0	79	Assicurazioni General	53,723.2
30	Norway	145,449.0	80	Nissan Motor	53,679.9
31	Indonesia	140,964.0	81	New Zealand	53,622.0
32	South Africa	131,127.0	82	E.On	52,227.7
33	Saudi Arabia	128,892.0	83	Toshiba	51,634.9
34	Finland	126,130.0	84	Bank of America	51,392.0
35	Greece	123,934.0	85	Fiat	51,331.7
36	Thailand	123,887.0	86	Nestlé	49,694.1
37	Mitsui	118,555.2	87	SBC Communications	49,489.0
38	Mitsubishi	117,765.6	88	Credit Suisse	49,362.0
39	Toyota Motor	115,670.9	89	Hungary	48,355.0
40	General Electric	111,630.0	90	Hewlett-Packard	48,253.0
41	Itochu	109,068.9	91	Fujitsu	47,195.9
42	Portugal	107,716.0	92	Algeria	47,015.0
43	Royal Dutch/Shell	105,366.0	93	Metro	46,663.6
44	Venezuela	103,918.0	94	Sumitomo Life Insurance	46,445.1
45	Iran, Islamic Rep.	101,073.0	95	Bangladesh	45,779.0
46	Israel	99,068.0	96	Tokyo Electric Power	45,727.7
47	Sumitomo	95,701.6	97	Kroger	45,351.6
48	Nippon Tel & Tel	93,591.7	98	Total Fina Elf	44,990.3
49	Egypt, Arab Rep.	92,413.0	99	NEC	44,828.0
50	Marubeni	91,807.4	100	State Farm Insurance	44,637.2

City Held for Ransom!

General Motors announced in 1980 that it was preparing to close down its last two production facilities in Detroit, but that it would be willing to build a brand-new Cadillac assembly plant locally if the city would make some concessions to the corporation.

The nation's largest automaker asked for two-thirds of a square mile of land in the middle of the city. The area it wanted cleared was one of the most integrated in the city (51 percent of residents were white, predominantly Polish, and 49 percent were black), where more than 3,000 people lived. Second, it wanted the city (at the taxpayers' expense) to relocate these 3,000 people, tear down and compensate 160 small businesses in the area, knock down a 170-bed hospital, remove three nursing homes, redirect two expressway ramps, move a railroad right-of-way, and do something about the two-acre Jewish cemetery in the middle of the plot. The corporation wanted the city to then clear the land to a depth of ten feet below grade so GM would not have to worry about underground water, sewer, telephone, and gas lines. Finally, if the city agreed to all of this and then gave GM a twelve-year, 50 percent local tax abatement, the corporation would agree to build in Detroit. A conservative estimate of the cost to the city (including state and federal contributions) was $450 million.

WHAT WOULD YOU DO?

Eventually, the Detroit City Council voted unanimously to give in to GM's demands. The people were removed by eminent domain; the houses, churches, businesses, nursing homes, and hospital were bulldozed. Ultimately, a Cadillac factory was built that created far fewer jobs than GM said it would.[40]

GM's capital flight has also had a severe impact on the city of Flint, Michigan, so much so that in 2002, Flint became the largest municipality (pop. 125,000) ever to have its city government stripped of power and put under control of the state. In the 1970s, GM had fifteen factories in Flint and employed eighty thousand people. Three decades later there were just three plants operating with twenty thousand workers. Many of the factories were relocated to the south, where labor costs are lower and unions not as common, but expanded overseas production was probably a much bigger factor contributing to the loss of jobs in Flint, as well as in other northern industrial centers.[41]

world economic system has given it a significant upper hand in dealing with workers and in forcing concessions from host governments.

The tremendous resources that corporations have are controlled, on the immediate level, by a board of directors typically consisting of fifteen to twenty people (the overwhelming majority of whom are white males). On the broader level, the vast power of corporate America is in the hands of a relatively small percentage of the American population. In addition, the corporate entity is, in many respects, immune to many of the democratic practices that exist in other organizations and institutions. The general public, or even the employees of the corporation, do not elect the board of directors. Nor do citizens and workers get to vote on any corporate decisions that may have far-reaching consequences. In fact, external input of any kind into the corporate decision-making process is nil. Yet the resources at the disposal of large corporations are often used to shape public policy on the most basic issues of American life. A good example of this is the way that public pressure for healthcare reform in the United States was perverted and fractionalized by major corporate interests.

CORPORATE CONTROL OF HEALTHCARE

With medical costs rising and over thirty-eight million Americans having no health insurance and another sixty million underinsured, healthcare reform became a major plank in Bill Clinton's 1992 presidential campaign. Essentially, this was a position that Clinton was forced into by one of his opponents in the Democratic primary election. Bob Kerrey was making a major issue of healthcare and this was having an impact on the race for the presidential nomination. Shortly before the presidential primary, Harris Wofford won a seat as a U.S. senator from Pennsylvania by making healthcare virtually his sole campaign issue.[42] Clinton, seeing the popularity of healthcare reform among the electorate, made healthcare reform part of his campaign platform and went on to win his party's nomination and, later, the presidential election. But no sooner did Clinton take office than he embraced the industry that he had claimed needed fundamental reform.

Clinton's eventual healthcare reform plan became known as *managed competition*. It rejected the *single-payer plan* used in Canada and more widespread healthcare reform that exists in many other countries. The plan was drawn up by insurance company analysts brought together by Alain Enthoven at a Jackson Hole, Wyoming, ski resort. Enthoven had worked as a military analyst under Secretary of Defense Robert McNamara during the 1960s, and later became president of Litton Medical Products. At the time of the Jackson Hole meetings Enthoven was a highly paid consultant for one of the nation's largest health maintenance organizations (HMO). In prior years he had been a director of PCS, Inc., a pharmaceutical managed-care company.[43]

Enthoven invited executives of the largest managed-care corporations

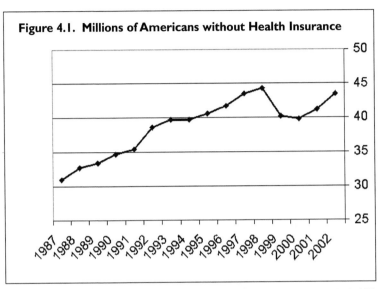

Figure 4.1. Millions of Americans without Health Insurance

Source: *Health Insurance Coverage: 2001.* Current Population Reports P60–220. Issued September 2002.

and commercial health insurers to meet in Jackson Hole and together they developed a complex plan to save the insurance companies from any real heath care reform while maintaining the appearance of reform. The insurance companies comprised the group most clearly threatened by healthcare reform, since the most popular choice for change was the single-payer system, which is in place in Canada. The advantages of a single-payer system for many Americans could be enormous. The U.S. General Accounting Office estimated that a Canadian-style public health insurance program would save nearly $70 billion dollars per year—enough to provide health insurance for the thirty-eight million Americans who are uninsured and eliminate copayments and deductibles for everyone else.[44]

In 1971, both the United States and Canada spent about 7 percent of their GDP on healthcare. However, in 1971 Canada began a federally financed healthcare system that provided guaranteed universal coverage. The impact on healthcare costs was significant; by the 1990s Canada was spending 10 percent of its GDP on healthcare while the U.S. share shot up to 14 percent.[45] The average American spends $3,160 more per year than the average Canadian—about 45 percent more. But paying more money hasn't gotten Americans better care. For instance, Canada ranks tenth in infant mortality while the United States ranks twenty-first. On the average,

Canadians live two years longer, are less likely to die from heart disease, and get faster access to medical services. A ten-nation survey done by Louis Harris and the Harvard School of Public Health found that Canadians were the most satisfied with their system and Americans the least.[46]

In the overall healthcare picture, insurance companies are nonproductive and expensive. They provide no health service, yet they account for a large proportion of total healthcare expenses. The 1991 salaries of the top executives of ten insurance companies ranged from $648,000 to $2,396,000. A total of about 20 percent of our healthcare dollars goes to pay insurance company salaries, profits, and overhead.[47]

How would a national single-payer health insurance program stack up against a private one? For the sake of comparison, Massachusetts' Blue Cross/Blue Shield insures 2.7 million people and employs 6,682 workers. This is more workers than are employed by all of Canada's single-payer system, which insures ten times as many people. Overhead costs among U.S. private insurance firms are six times greater than they are in Canada.[48] Cutting away insurance company profits and the unnecessary layers of bureaucracy permits Canada to provide more real healthcare per dollar spent.

A single-payer system would also have a greater ability to keep other medical costs down. In Canada a hospital stay costs about 40 percent less than in the United States, and prescription drug prices are considerably lower. A patient is also much less likely to undergo unnecessary surgery. In the United States, hospital expenses and drug prices have been rising rapidly, as have the profits for privately owned hospitals and the major pharmaceutical companies. In 1992, the major U.S. pharmaceutical companies had an estimated $10 billion profit on sales of $76 billion. Top executives in six leading companies in 1991 had salaries ranging from $1,979,000 to $12,788,000.[49] According to *Fortune* magazine, the pharmaceuticals industry had the highest rate of return on sales of all industries.[50] In 1992, the highest-paid CEO in the country was Thomas Frist, the head of the Hospital Corporation of America. Frist's total compensation, including stock options, was estimated at a staggering $127 million. The fourth- and seventh-highest paid CEOs also headed healthcare companies and received $62 million and $30 million respectively.[51]

It is clear who benefits from the current healthcare system in the United States. It is also clear who the losers are. Over a third of all Americans avoid using healthcare because of its expense and, according to one estimate, 300,000 Americans yearly are denied care at hospital emergency rooms because they are uninsured or underinsured. Poor Americans are much more likely to suffer illness than wealthy Americans, and black Americans suffer more illness and higher mortality rates than whites.[52] In the United States the healthcare status quo is being upheld not because it provides healthcare but because it provides profits. Proven alternatives such as the single-payer plan have been endorsed in the *New England Journal of Medicine*, *Consumer Reports*, and by the Physicians for a National Health Program, and the single-payer system has been the most widely favored plan among American citizens according to several public opinion polls. Why has such a proven and potentially popular plan received such little attention in the press? One reason is the overlapping of personnel in the upper echelons of the media and the insurance industry. At the time that the Clinton Administration was considering serious healthcare reform, four of the fourteen directors of the *New York Times* were directors of insurance companies, and two were on the board of Bristol-Meyers, a healthcare and pharmaceutical company. Not surprisingly, the *Times* tended to favor healthcare reform that did not threaten the interests of the insurance companies, and usually ignored or dismissed with little discussion single-payer proposals.[53]

On a more general level, both the corporate media and the healthcare industry are owned and managed by the financial elite of American society who rally together whenever profit making is threatened. They also pump a lot of money into the campaign coffers of many politicians. Former speaker of the House, Newt Gingrich of Georgia, for example, received nearly a half million dollars from health and insurance interests.[54] Insurance companies also donated $850,000 to the Democratic Party to help Clinton get elected in 1992.[55] In the 2000 election cycle, the pharmaceutical/health industry contributed over $26 million to candidates and their parties (69 percent to Republicans).[56] These interests also spend millions of dollars lobbying Congress and trying to influence public opinion through advertising and by persuading various *opinion makers* to take up their cause.

Corporate donations to candidates and political parties have contributed to the public's disillusionment with the political process. Polls frequently find that the American public feels that big business's influence on government is too great. For example, a 2002 *New York Times/CBS News Poll* found that when asked if George W. Bush was more interested in protecting the interests of ordinary Americans or in protecting the interests of large corporations, the public was split with 42 percent responding "ordinary Americans" and 42 percent responding "large corporations." When asked the same question with a slightly different twist ("Do you think *members of the Bush administration* are more interested in protecting the interests of ordinary Americans or in protecting the interests of large corporations?"), 61 percent responded, "large corporations" and just 27 percent said, "ordinary Americans."[57]

Corporate Free Speech

The right of corporations to fund electoral campaigns, although often severely criticized, has been upheld by the Supreme Court. In 1976, on the bicentennial of the nation's independence, the Supreme Court ruled (*Buckley* v. *Valeo*) that corporations had freedom of speech and that restrictions on corporate contributions to political campaigns could be considered a violation of their First Amendment rights.[58] Two years later, in the *First National Bank* v. *Bellotti*, the right to pay for electoral campaigns was reaffirmed. Expressing the majority ruling in the case, Justice Lewis Powell explained that giving cash to influence an election "is the type of speech indispensable to decision making in a democracy, and this is no less true because the speech comes from a corporation than an individual."[59]

The roots of these recent Supreme Court rulings are in an 1886 decision that defined corporations as "persons" who could not be taxed differently than real people, and that as "persons" corporations also had First Amendment rights. In making the 1886 ruling (*Santa Clara County* v. *Southern Pacific Railroad*), the Court invoked the Fourteenth Amendment to the Constitution. The Fourteenth Amendment was adopted after the Civil War to protect emancipated slaves and stated that "no state shall deprive any person of life, liberty or property, without due process of law." Although to many people the idea that corporations are people is ludicrous, the courts have protected corporate rights to "free speech" as expressed through political contributions. Corporations don't breath the air or drink the water, and can theoretically live forever; moreover, the idea of money representing free speech contradicts the democratic principle of *one person, one vote*, since corporations are able to express themselves by contributing much more money than an ordinary real American person.

The ruling that corporations cannot be taxed differently than persons has since been changed and in criticizing the use of the Fourteenth Amendment to justify the procorporate stance of the Supreme Court, Justice Hugo Black (in 1938) pointed out that in the five decades since the landmark Santa Clara decision, "less than one-half of 1 percent [of Supreme Court rulings that invoked the Fourteenth Amendment] invoked it in protection of the Negro race, and more than 50 percent asked that its benefits be extended to corporations."[60]

The subject of corporate influence in electoral campaigns will be taken up in the next chapter in further detail.

CONCLUSION:
WHY DOES INEQUALITY MATTER?

The last three chapters have all dealt mainly with economic inequality and, to a lesser extent, the inequality of power. Why does inequality matter? Although many people are willing to accept a good deal of inequality, and although social theorists often see a practical purpose to it, there are a variety of reasons to be concerned about the extremes in inequality that have become commonplace today.

The Moral Critique of Inequality

The first of the reasons one should be concerned about inequality is the moral question of whether or not it is fair for some people to have so much more wealth than others or to be paid so highly while others live in poverty or are paid much less even though they may work harder. As shown in chapters 2 and 3, great wealth does not come from hard work—certainly not harder than those who labored as slaves on plantations, or those who spent twelve-hour days working in the coal and iron mines in the 1800s, or those who suffered in sweatshops in the nineteenth century or even today; great wealth comes primarily from the exploitation of the labor of others. Furthermore, even if we agree that some people are smarter or more talented than others, there are no moral grounds for rewarding those people with better housing, better healthcare, a better education for their children, more leisure, and other advantages.

Critics of the moral perspective on inequality sometimes dismiss these arguments because there is no scientific way to measure and quantify the morality of inequality—too many value judgments are necessary. Nevertheless, if social scientists are reluctant to make value judgments, the public at large is not. Moral considerations have often been a factor in attacking social institutions and bringing about social change. Slavery in the United States, for instance, was not abolished simply because northern industrialists wanted to expand the pool of available wage laborers but because many people found slavery to be morally reprehensible. Likewise, human rights activists often take up the cause of oppressed Third World people, not because they believe it would somehow aid the self-interests of whatever social group the activist sees himself or herself as a part of but because of genuine altruism. Moral issues, in sum, are often major motivating factors in social action.

The Social Critique of Inequality

A second major criticism of inequality is that it erodes social solidarity. There is a great deal of sociological evidence that shows that the greater the inequality, the higher the incidence of social disorder. Differences in wealth, income, lifestyle, residences, power, and so forth, are all forms of inequality that create social distance among people. When these distances are substantial people no longer view one another as being in the same boat. They do not share a sense of belonging to the same social group; they become alienated from one another with no sense of camaraderie. When this happens, resentment, jealousy, racism, sexism, and other forms of hatred or rage are likely to flourish. When people don't see one another as brothers or sisters, it becomes easier for them to commit acts of theft or violence against one another, and this is precisely what we see more and more of in the United States today. Corporations too often regard consumers simply as sources of profit, and regulations protecting the health and safety of workers and the general public are regarded as nuisances that impose expenses that should be kept to a minimum, not as part of the corporation's responsibility to act in the public good.

In recent years, groundbreaking research has been published that shows that nations (and states within the United States) with great inequality have reduced levels of trust and social involvement. These, in turn, are correlated with higher rates of illness and death.[61] Some examples of the connections between inequality, poverty, unemployment, and such social disorders as mortality and crime are shown in Table 4.1.

Inequality also contributes to a decline in important public social institutions and services because it permits the well-off to seek individual solu-

> "[People] . . . proceed as though a house can substitute for a community if only it is spacious enough, entertaining enough, comfortable enough, splendid enough—and suitably isolated from that common horde that politicians still refer to as our 'fellow Americans.'"
>
> —Ray Oldenburg in *The Great Good Place*[62]

NO EXIT © Andy Singer

"YOU GET WHAT YOU PAY FOR"

(Reprinted by permission of Andy Singer)

Table 4.1. Estimated Effects of Unemployment, Poverty, and Wage Inequality on Social Stressors, 1975–1990[63]

	Effect of a 1 Percent Point Change In:		
	Unemployment	Poverty*	Wage Inequality
Mortality			
Heart attack	2.2	—	—
Stroke	1.9	—	—
Suicide	—	—	—
Crime			
Homicide	5.6	2.8	.59
Aggravated assault	1.8	2.9	.57
Forcible rape	1.9	1.5	—
Larceny/theft	2.7	1.3	.28
Motor vehicle theft	—	0.9	.40
Robbery	1.7	2.8	—
Burglary	3.7	2.0	—

*Since poverty rarely rises a full point in a year, these are the effects of a half-point change.
†As measured by the Gini coefficient.

tions to problems. If there is crime in their neighborhoods, they can move to a safer place. If their schools are inadequate, they can send their children to private schools or move to a place with better public schools. If there is pollution, move somewhere else, and so on.

The Economic Critique of Inequality

The third major criticism of inequality has to do with its effect on the economic system as a whole. Numerous authors have pointed out that in the United States an extreme in wealth and income distribution was reached just before the stock market collapsed in 1929, triggering the Great Depression that lasted more than ten years. Economists are continually pointing out that increased inequality invariably means less money in the hands of many consumers, resulting in slack consumer demand and periodic recession. Ravi Batra has noted that when wealth ownership becomes concentrated the number of people with few or no assets rises, thereby forcing more people to go into debt. When this happens it is likely that banks are making loans that are more and more risky. Thus, the higher the concentration of wealth, the greater the number of potential bank failures.[64] Empirically, this is borne out by what happened in the Great Depression and also in the recession of 1981. Furthermore, increased debt among the working classes usually guarantees that inequality will grow more rapidly in the future as the borrowers have to pay back their wealthy creditors.

There is also the more general problem that in an economic system fueled by consumer demand (and demand really means *ability to pay*) production becomes more and more oriented to fill the wants and needs of the wealthy. That is to say, since it's generally not profitable to sell to the poor and near-poor, industries gear their production to higher-income markets. Ultimately what happens, and *is* happening throughout the world, is that the entire system of production becomes oriented to the wants of the wealthy, and the needs of all others become neglected. The planet becomes economically and socially out of balance. So-called dessert crops are grown and exported to wealthy nations while the local people run short of food staples.

In addition, a higher concentration of wealth in tandem with economic stagnation means there is a problem of surplus absorption. This is a situation where there is plenty of capital available for investment purposes but not enough places to make a profit. Imagine having a million dollars but only $500,000 worth of profitable stock to buy. There's little one can do with the extra $500,000. If there are other investors in the same situation, competition for that $500,000 worth of stock ensues, driving its price up without any increase in its real value. This is exactly the situation as it has been played out in the United States over the past few decades. And typically the cycle includes a serious stock market collapse that leads to investor panic, large-scale layoffs, declining revenues for state and federal governments, and other forms of economic contraction; precisely what happened to the United States in 2001–2002. Quite often, the inflation of stock prices is an indication not of increased productivity or total real wealth, but of an increased expropriation of wealth and income from the working classes.

NOTES

1. Michael Tanzer, "Globalizing the Economy," *Monthly Review* (September 1995): 1.

2. Glenn Collins, "Coke Drops 'Domestic' and Goes One World," *New York Times*, January 13, 1996.

3. Michael Parenti, *Against Empire* (San Francisco: City Lights Books, 1995), p. 31.

4. Ibid., pp. 4–5; Michael Kidron and Ronald Segal, *The State of the World Atlas* (London: Penguin Books, 1995), p. 69.

5. The Corporate Accountability Project [online], www.corporations.org/system [October 2002].

6. Kate Bronfenbrenner, *Uneasy Terrain: The Impact of Capital Mobility on Workers, Wages, and Union Organizing*, September 2000, p. v. Paper submitted to the U.S. Trade Deficit Review Commission.

7. [Online] www.fortune.com and www.gm.com.

8. Barry Bluestone and Bennet Harrison, *The Deindustrialization of America* (New York: Basic Books, 1982), p. 143.

9. Carl Proper, "Fighting for Fair Trade," *Dollars and Sense*, April 1986, p. 12.

10. Peter Freund and George T. Martin, *The Ecology of the Automobile* (Montreal: Black Rose Press, 1994), p. 132.

11. Bradford Snell, "American Ground Transport," in Jerome H. Skolnick and Elliot Currie, *Crisis in American Institutions*, 6th ed. (Boston: Little, Brown and Company, 1985), p. 322; and Freund and Martin, *The Ecology of the Automobile*, p. 62.

12. Snell, "American Ground Transport," p. 322.

13. Ibid., p. 326.

14. Bradford Snell, "GM and the Nazis," *Ramparts* (June 1974). For more on corporate support of the Nazis and on American corporations that continued to do business with the Nazis during the war, see Charles Higham, *Trading with the Enemy* (New York: Delacorte Press, 1983).

15. Christopher Simpson, *The Splendid Blonde Beast: Money, Law, and Genocide in the Twentieth Century* (Monroe, Maine: Common Courage Press, 1995), pp. 11, 64.

16. Snell, "GM and the Nazis," p. 16.

17. Ibid.

18. G. William Domhoff, *Who Rules America?* (Englewood Cliffs, N.J.: Prentice Hall, 1967), p. 102; and Cheryl Payer, *The World Bank: A Critical Analysis* (New York: Monthly Review, 1982).

19. Jamie Lincoln Kitman, "The Secret History of Lead," *Nation*, March 20, 2000.

20. Ibid., p. 17.

21. "Here's What Enron Actually Did," *Too Much* (winter 2002): 7.

22. Kurt Eichenwald with Matt Richtel, "Enron Trader Pleads Guilty to Conspiracy," *New York Times*, October 18, 2002.

23. William Greider, "There Are More Enrons Out There: The Rot Is Systemic," *Nation*, February 4, 2002.

24. *Too Much* (winter 2002).

25. John Nichols, "Enron's Global Crusade," *Nation*, March 4, 2002.

26. "Enron and Campaign Finance Reform," *Public Citizen* (January 24, 2002) [online], www.citizen.org/congress/campaign/legislation/shays-meehan/articles.cfm?ID=6693.

27. *Too Much* (winter 2002).

28. Jeff Sommer, "Shares Absorb a New Shock to the System," *New York Times*, June 30, 2002.

29. Kurt Eichenwald, "Could Capitalists Actually Bring Down Capitalism?" *New York Times*, June 30, 2002.

30. Human Rights Watch, *The Enron Corporation, Corporate Complicity in Human Rights Violations*, 1999 [online], www.hrw.org/reports/1999/enron/index.htm.

31. Nichols, "Enron's Global Crusade," pp. 12, 14.

32. Jimmy Langman, "Enron's Pipe Scheme" [online], www.corporatewatch.org [May 9, 2002].

33. "Less Than Zero: Enron's Income Tax Payments, 1996–2000," Citizens for Tax Justice [online], www.ctj.org/html/enron.htm [January 17, 2002].

34. [Online], www.opic.gov/.

35. Kenneth Peres, *The Corporate Political and Economic Offensive and Its Impact on Labor*, Communications Workers of America, District One, p. 48. The information cited is from *The Economic Report of the President, 2002*, p. 443.

36. Howard J. Sherman, "The Concentration of Economic Power in the United States," in *Critical Perspectives in Sociology*, ed. Berch Berberoglu (Dubuque, Iowa: Kendall/Hunt Publishing, 1993), p. 76.

37. Arthur MacEwan, "Markets Unbound: The Heavy Price of Globalization," *Dollars and Sense*, September/October 1994, p. 9.

38. Sales figures are from *Fortune* magazine, May 15, 1995; GNP and GDP figures are from the Rand McNally, *World Facts and Maps*, 1996 ed.

39. Sarah Anderson and John Cavanagh, *Top 200, The Rise of Corporate Global Power*, Institute for Policy Studies, December 2000.

40. Harry Browne and Beth Sims, *Runaway America* (Albuquerque, N.M.: Resource Center Press, 1993), p. 69. "Testimony of Ralph Nader Before the Committee on the Budget," U.S. House of Representatives, June 30, 1999, www.nader.org/releases/63099.html.

41. Danny Hakim, "For Flint, Mich., Takeover Adds to the List of Woes," *New York Times*, July 10, 2002.

42. Melvin Konner, M.D., *Dear America* (New York: Addison-Wesley Publishing Company, 1993), p. 68.

43. Ibid., pp. 69–71.

44. Lawrence D. Weiss, "Excellent Benefits: Clinton Embraces the Private Health Insurance Industry," *Socialist Review* 23, no. 1 (1993).

45. *Statistical Abstract of the United States, 1995*, p. 853.

46. Weiss, "Excellent Benefits," p. 55; and Cathy Hurwit, "A Canadian-style Cure," *Dollars and Sense*, May 1993, p. 10.

47. Konner, *Dear America*, pp. 53, 17.

48. David Himmelstein, M.D., and Steffie Woolhandler, M.D., *The National Health Program Book* (Monroe, Maine: Common Courage Press, 1994), pp. 122–23; Hurwit, "A Canadian-style Cure," p. 10.

49. Konner, *Dear America*, p. 54.

50. *Fortune*, April 18, 1994, p. 280.

51. *BusinessWeek*, April 26, 1993.

52. Himmelstein and Woolhandler, *The National Health Program Book*, pp. 36, 53, 63–75.

53. Konner, *Dear America*, pp. 53, 59.

54. Ibid., p. 60.

55. Norman Solomon, *False Hope* (Monroe Maine: Common Courage Press, 1994), p. 188.

56. Center for Responsive Politics [online], www.opensecrets.org/industries/indus.asp?Ind=H04 [July 8, 2002].

57. Richard W. Stevenson and Janet Elder, "Poll Finds Concerns That Bush Is Overly Influenced by Business," *New York Times*, July 18, 2002.

58. "Corporate Crime, Welfare, and Influence" [online], www.spiritone.com/~gdy52150/corplaw.html.

59. Joel Bleifuss, "Know Thine Enemy: A Brief History of Corporations," *In These Times*, February 1998.

60. Ibid.

61. See, for example, Ichiro Kawachi, Bruce P. Kennedy, and Richard G. Wilkinson, eds., *The Society and Population Health Reader: Income Inequality and Health* (New York: New Press, 1999).

62. Ray Oldenburg, *The Great Good Place* (New York: Marlowe and Company, 1999), p. 7.

63. Lawrence Mishel and Jared Bernstein, *The State of Working America, 1994–1995* (Washington, D.C.: Economic Policy Institute, 1994), p. 83.

64. Ravi Batra, *The Great Depression of 1990* (New York: Simon and Schuster, 1987), p. 120.

STATE POWER

ELITES, CLASSES, AND INTEREST GROUPS

In modern societies the state has become increasingly involved in more and more aspects of life. Major sociological issues regarding the state involve disputes over the true functions of the state, and the extent to which a given state is democratic. The word *democratic* is used here not as a measure of voter activity but as an indicator of actual involvement in decision making and the sharing of power. We have already seen that a great deal of power and decision making in our society lies with private economic institutions, so it is worth remembering that the state is just one part of the total picture of power.

Theories of the modern state can be classified in many different ways, but for our purposes we will start by looking at four general types commonly referred to as pluralist theory, functional elite theory, critical elite theory, and structuralist theory.

PLURALIST THEORY

Pluralist theory generally sees American society as composed of various special-interest groups, none of which have any major advantage in terms of their ability to influence government decision making. The state in the pluralist model is regarded as reasonable and unbiased, not favoring one group over another. When an issue confronts the state, or the society as a whole, the various interest groups that have a stake in the issue lobby their representatives in an attempt to influence the decision or shape the state's policy in some way.

The fundamental principle of the pluralist model is the notion that the state is autonomous and unbiased. The state is like a balance scale, and the input from various interest groups is weighed on the scale. The state then makes a decision, or a policy, based on the weight of the arguments put forth by the interest groups, or based on the sheer number of people lined up on each side of the issue.

The pluralist model is the type of political science typically taught in high school civics classes, and is the dominant strain in college political science departments. In the United States, it could be argued, the pluralist model of government is how things are supposed to work. However, the way things really work is much different. Political scientist Michael Parenti has suggested that our understanding of politics would be greatly improved if we thought of our system of government as a "dual political system":

> First, there is the *public* system centering around electoral and representative activities, including campaign conflicts, voter turnout, political personalities, public pronouncements, official role-playing, and certain ambiguous presentations of issues that bestir presidents, governors, mayors, and their respective legislatures. Then there is the *covert* system, involving multibillion-dollar contracts, tax write-offs, protections, rebates, grants, loss compensation, subsidies, leases, giveaways, and the whole vast process of budgeting, advising, regulating, protecting, and servicing major companies, now ignoring or rewriting the law on behalf of the powerful, now applying it with full punitive vigor against heretics and "troublemakers." The public system is highly visible, taught in the schools, dissected by academicians, gossiped about by news commentators. The covert system is seldom acknowledged.[1]

There are three major criticisms of pluralism as a theory of how government works. The first has to do with the interest groups that attempt to influence government policy. Many people have no connection whatsoever with these interest groups; in fact, only about half of the American population belongs to voluntary associations and most of these associations have very little to do with politics. Many of these are church groups or social clubs, etc., most of which are not usually involved in politics.[2] In addition, the organizations to which people belong rarely consult their membership when they do attempt to influence policy. For example, for most union members their only union participation consists of paying their dues. Furthermore, it is not unusual for unions, or other mass-based organizations, to have official policies that contradict the opinions of their members.

A related point concerning interest groups is that their power in the real world is not proportionate to the size of their membership. The American Federation of Labor and Congress of Industrial Organizations (AFL-CIO), for example, has over fifteen million members but not nearly as much influence as the Council on Foreign Relations, which has just three thousand members.[3]

The second area of criticism has to do with the common class background of many of the people who occupy positions of power in the United States. Research has shown that people who hold power often come from families of considerable wealth, they attend elite private schools, and belong to exclusive social clubs. In contemporary society people from working- or middle-class backgrounds have very little chance of ever holding a position of significant power in American society.

The third criticism has to do with the ability of the state to set policy. Pluralist theory tends to overlook the constraints set on the state, particularly by economic conditions. For example, if a municipal government such as New York City doesn't provide adequate tax subsidies to corporations, they may move across state lines to Connecticut or New Jersey. If these states don't provide the kind of tax breaks and support services that the corporations want, then perhaps they move to South Carolina. If South Carolina doesn't provide the support corporations want, then perhaps they move to Thailand or Indonesia. The point is that governments often face economic coercion that forces them to make decisions they would rather not. GM's "blackmail" of the city of Detroit, discussed in chapter 4, is an example of this.

In sum, pluralist theory neglects to account for the tremendous influence of the upper class—specifically, the interests of large corporations—in determining state policy, a point that is greatly emphasized by many elite theorists.

FUNCTIONAL ELITE THEORY

It has become difficult to deny that the top power holders in American society, or nearly any other society for that matter, do not represent the population at large in terms of their class or educational background. In some cases single individuals may occupy a variety of high-level government positions over the period of several decades, or we may see the same family name cropping up from time to time when we examine power. This has caused many theorists to claim that there is an elite that governs society. Some of those who acknowledge the existence of an elite, however, claim that it is useful and functional: If some people are more qualified, then they ought to hold society's most powerful positions; and if we are developing an intelligentsia that tends to supply people for positions of power, then so be it. If these people are more qualified, then we are better off with an elite running things than with a more equal distribution of power.

In essence, the functional elite perspective claims that as societies become more complex we need individuals with specialized skills to fill the important leadership posts. We are not going to get these people from the public at large, so it is natural for an elite to develop. Strong elites with broad authority are necessary for running society in a way that unifies people and institutions so their duties can be performed without serious breakdowns in order. Functional elite theorists, in sum, do not deny the existence of elites, but similar to pluralists, they feel that the elite will make their decisions with the best interests of the nation as a whole in mind, and not in pursuit of their own enrichment. E. Digby Baltzell, for example, felt that the U.S. upper class operated as such an elite and was successfully guided by a strong sense of moral responsibility to the population as a whole.[4] This sense of responsibility is one of the values emphasized in the elite private schools that many of the elite have attended. The functional elite view is capsulized by the words of the late sociologist Talcott Parsons (1902–79): "We must have a stronger government than we have tradition-ally been accustomed to, and we must come to trust it more fully."[5] Par-sons, in fact, went so far as to declare the need for a "functional equivalent of aristocracy."

CRITICAL ELITE THEORY AND INSTRUMENTALISM

Critical elite theory claims that power lies in the hands of a relatively small group of people who use it mostly for their own benefit. Among the social theorists usually placed in this category are Thorstein Veblen, C. Wright Mills, Ralph Miliband, and G. William Domhoff.[6] Mills, in particular, can be considered the seminal theorist for contemporary critical elite theory. In Mills's landmark work, *The Power Elite*, he made the claim that power had become concentrated within three major social institutions: (1) the economy, which is dominated by 200 or 300 large corporations that hold the keys to many economic decisions that affect large numbers of people; (2) the political order, which Mills described as a centralized executive establishment with many powers that "enters into each and every cranny of the social structure"; and (3) the military, "the largest and most expensive feature of government."[7]

Mills was quick to emphasize that these three areas of power were interlocking, that decisions in one area affected the other areas, and that the personnel of the three areas were increasingly interchangeable. The power elite are those people in the upper echelons of these three social institutions:

> At the pinnacle of each of the three enlarged and centralized domains, there have arisen those higher circles which make up the economic, the political, and the military elites. At the top of the economy, among the corporate rich, there are the chief executives; at the top of the political order, the members of the political directorate; at the top of the military establishment, the elite of soldier-statesmen clustered in and around the Joint Chiefs of Staff and the upper echelon. As each of these domains has coincided with the others, as decisions tend to become total in their consequence, the leading men in each of the three domains of power—the warlords, the corporation chieftains, the political directorate—tend to come together, to form the power elite of America.[8]

There are two important aspects of Mills's analysis that need to be mentioned. The first is that Mills does recognize gradations of power within the elite and within American society as a whole. That is to say, some of the elite are more powerful than others, the elite do not always agree with one another, and there are groups outside the power elite capable of challenging their power to some extent. Although Mills never elaborated much on how power in America is challenged, he did note that the power elite were not omnipotent.

The second aspect of Mills's work that should be highlighted is his claim that the elite tend to come from similar class and educational backgrounds. The significance of this is that the elite tend to know one another, they see each other socially, and they feel themselves to be in the inner circle of the upper social class. The power elite accept one another, more or less, as equals and tend to view the world in similar ways.

This aspect of critical elite theory, that the people who hold positions of power in American society tend to come from a socially aware upper class, became an important part of the work of G. William Domhoff, who was heavily influenced by Mills. Domhoff spoke of the elite as a *governing class* and defined it as: "a social upper class which owns a disproportionate amount of a country's wealth, receives a disproportionate amount of a country's yearly income, and contributes a disproportionate number of its members to the controlling institutions and key decision-making groups of the country."[9]

Domhoff's concept of the upper class put an emphasis on its social nature. That is, Domhoff saw the upper class as a group of families who interact socially, freely intermarry, and perceive one another as equals. According to Domhoff, the upper class has a definite boundary that excludes others. Its members have similar aspirations and values, attend exclusive schools, and belong to exclusive clubs. In order to prove his theory, Domhoff offers ample evidence of the upper class's self-awareness, and of the network of schools, clubs, and organizations to which upper-class individuals belong. He also goes to great lengths to show the interchange of personnel between the upper class and "controlling institutions and key decision-making groups."

It is Domhoff's work, in particular, that has become known as *instrumentalist theory*. The instrumentalist label was tagged on to Domhoff (Ralph Miliband was also cited as an example of this perspective) in a frequently cited essay by David A. Gold, Clarence V. H. Lo, and Erik Olin Wright, in which the authors defined instrumentalism as "a theory in which the ties between the ruling class and state are systematically examined, while the structural context within which those ties occur remains largely theoretically unorganized."[10] The term fits well since Domhoff's work tends to emphasize how state power is used as an *instrument* that furthers the interests of the social upper class. Domhoff himself prefers to call his perspective *class dominance theory*, and others refer to Domhoff's work (and similar perspectives) as the *business dominance theory*.[11]

The interchange of personnel between big business and government is often referred to as *cross-fertilization*, and many examples of it can be found in looking at the people who have filled important government positions over the years: Alexander Haig is a prime example of this. Haig served in the Defense Department during the 1960s and under President Nixon in the 1970s; in the 1980s, he was named secretary of state by President Reagan. Haig was president of United Technologies; a director of the Chase Manhattan Bank, Crown Cork & Seal, Texas Instruments, and Conagra; and a member of the Council on Foreign Relations. Likewise, George Schultz, who also served as Reagan's secretary of state, was president of the Bechtel Corporation and a director of Morgan Guaranty Trust, as well as the Council on Foreign Relations.[12] Schultz had also been secretary of labor and secretary of the treasury under President Nixon. Another example is Caspar Weinberger, Reagan's secretary of defense, who served in three different positions in the federal government from 1970 to 1975. His corporate background included stints as a vice president of the Bechtel Corporation and as a director of Pepsico and Quaker Oats. These examples serve to illustrate the revolving door that exists between the corporate world and the government, which Domhoff and Mills see as being more and more commonplace.[13]

One might wonder what makes these individuals so exceptional that they can move from post to post in the government. How can a man like George Schultz go from being, presumably, one of the nation's leading authorities on labor to the nation's preeminent treasury official? And how can Caspar Weinberger go from being secretary of defense to heading up the Department of Health, Education, and Welfare? How can individuals change their area of expertise just like that? The answer is that they don't. These individuals occupy the positions they do, not because of their expertise, but because they embody the interests of their class. By filling important positions in government and other influential positions with what essentially amounts to spokespeople or emissaries of the upper class, the upper class is able to ensure that its wishes will be expressed and that the system will continue to shower its members with a disproportionate amount of the nation's wealth, along with elevated status and power. These appointments are ideological and class-based much more than they are based on any individual's expertise.

A clear example of how cross-fertilization works to influence government policy for the benefit of the wealthy is the case of American involvement in Guatemala during the 1950s. In 1950, Jacobo Arbenz was elected president of Guatemala with about 72 percent of the vote. Arbenz was a *progressive nationalist* who favored reforms that would help keep Guatemala's wealth for its people. In 1953, Guatemala nationalized 387,000 acres of *unused* land owned by the American-based United Fruit Company. At the time, United Fruit controlled 40,000 jobs in Guatemala, owned almost all the railroad tracks, and owned half the country's arable land. It was known as "the octopus" and made $65 million a year in profits, twice as much as the revenue of the Guatemalan government.[14] United Fruit responded to the nationalization by initiating a campaign to slander the Arbenz government and manipulate U.S. public opinion. These efforts are well documented in a book by Thomas McCann, former director of public relations for United Fruit, as well as other sources.[15] United Fruit's efforts were rewarded as the

State Department and the Central Intelligence Agency undertook a successful effort to overthrow the Arbenz government. The ties between United Fruit and the U.S. government illustrate the concept of cross-fertilization and make a good case for the validity of instrumentalist theory:

> John Foster Dulles, U.S. Secretary of State at the time, had for a long time been the legal counsel to United Fruit Company; his brother Allen Dulles, Director of the CIA at the time, had been president of the United Fruit Company; Henry Cabot Lodge, the U.S. Ambassador to the United Nations at the time, was on the Board of Directors of United Fruit; John Moors Cabot, then Assistant Secretary of State for Inter-American Affairs, was a large shareholder in United Fruit; and Walter Bedell Smith, Director of the CIA before Dulles, became the president of United Fruit after the Arbenz government was overthrown. The day after the invasion an urgent request was made by the Guatemalan Government that the United Nations Security Council be called into session to deal with the events. The request was turned down by the then President of the Security Council, who happened to be the same Mr. Henry Cabot Lodge.[16]

The instrumentalist approach goes a long way in terms of debunking the pluralist belief that the state weighs the input of many interest groups and makes its decisions without consistent favor to any particular group. The instrumentalist model shows that the state is not above class and factional conflict and is not an impartial mediator. The model holds no illusions that we live in a politically egalitarian society.

The Powers That Be

How does the upper class maintain its powerful grip on American political institutions? In his book *The Powers That Be*, Domhoff outlines four major processes of ruling class domination.

1. *The special-interest process:* This refers to the means by which individuals, families, corporations, and business sectors within the ruling class obtain tax breaks, favors, subsidies, and favorable rulings that are beneficial to their short-run or limited interests. A good example of this is the way the stated functions of regulatory agencies are thwarted. Very often regulatory agencies end up regulating various industries not to protect the consumer or the public at large but to ensure fair competition between businesses, or to divide up markets, or to share certain responsibilities so that the companies can operate more efficiently and with less duplication of services.

As part of the special-interest process, Domhoff includes the tremendous amount of lobbying that is done by large corporations and other special interests. In this regard, Parenti states, "Lobbyists make themselves so helpful that members of Congress sometimes rely on them to perform tasks normally done by congressional staffs. Lobbyists will draft legislation, write speeches, and plant stories in the press on behalf of cooperative lawmakers. Lobbyists 'put in millions of hours each year' to make the world a better place for their clients, and 'they succeed on a scale that is undreamed of by most ordinary citizens.'"[17]

Domhoff is emphatic in pointing out that the special-interest process demonstrates only the power of special interests and not the power of a

A bill introduced to the House of Representatives by Republicans in 1995 proposed a series of revisions to the Clean Water Act, which contained many new provisions desired by industry. The bill's sponsors worked side by side with a committee of lobbyists "inserting one provision after another to satisfy industry groups like the Chemical Manufacturers Association" and companies like International Paper. The Chemical Manufacturers Association, for instance, won a provision that would define factories as being in "statistical compliance" with their pollution discharge permits "as long as pollution levels were not exceeded with unusual frequency." The paper industry won a provision that would require the Environmental Protection Agency (EPA) to give greater weight to cost-benefit analysis and risk calculations when determining which technologies should be relied on in meeting water quality goals. One industry coalition won a provision that would significantly weaken an EPA regulation governing discharges of toxic wastes in the Great Lakes region. Senior EPA officials and environmental groups objected to being excluded from the process.

Another bill, introduced by Republican Bob Dole of Kansas and refined by Senators Orrin Hatch and Charles Grassman, gives industry more power to challenge government regulations in court and imposes complex requirements on government regulators. The bill was written in close consultation with industry representatives. According to the *New York Times*, staff workers on the Senate Judiciary Committee, mostly Democrats, were "dumbfounded" when the bill was presented to them by Larry Block, the staff director, by whom were seated three lawyers from the Hunton and Williams law firm, which represented dozens of electric companies in court cases against environmental regulators. The lawyers outlined many of the provisions of the bills, and Block frequently deferred to the lawyers about what exactly the bill meant. The firm had been hired by about fifteen companies to lobby on the bill, but it was apparently able to take on a much bigger role. The director of a Washington-based citizen's group denounced the firm's role in creating the bill: "This is a bill by big business, for big business, and of big business."[18]

class. The class perspective comes about through the second major process of domination.

2. *The policy-formation process:* This is the means by which the power elite formulate policy on larger issues. Within this network, the various special interests join together; and it is within the policy-formation process that the class interests of the elite are given a chance to be more clearly formed and to have some consensus developed. Some of the most important policy-formation organizations are the Council on Foreign Relations, the Committee for Economic Development, the Business Council, the National Association of Manufacturers, and the Trilateral Commission. In the past few decades a variety of policy and opinion organizations with a more right-wing perspective have come into prominence. Among these are the Heritage Foundation (which has sponsored much of the work of archconservative Rush Limbaugh), the Manhattan Institute, and the American Enterprise Institute, both of which have sponsored the work of Charles Murray. In the 1980s, Murray authored *Losing Ground*, which argued that government relief programs actually cause poverty; and in 1994, he coauthored *The Bell Curve* with Richard Hernstein, which argued that the reason black Americans have not been able to succeed in the American class structure is because of their inferior intelligence, which is primarily a result of genetic factors.

Groups such as these serve a variety of important functions, most of them revolving around the need to promote class cohesion and unity. Domhoff points out that they provide a setting where the power elite can familiarize themselves with general issues in an environment that is out of the public eye and relatively free of pressure. They also provide a forum where disagreements within the power elite can be worked out and where the elite can hear the findings of various academic experts on issues of their concern. Policy-formation groups may also commission their own studies to further clarify certain issues. Additionally, they take part in what might be best described as "grassroots lobbying." This consists of doing propaganda work aimed at the general public and designed to help maintain or create a social climate that is more amenable to a social and political agenda set by members of the upper class.

Furthermore, policy-formation groups act as informal training grounds where new leaders can be cultivated and promoted. Both Henry Kissinger and Gerald Ford are good examples of this, as the Council on Foreign Relations helped nurture their talents and champion them as candidates for various positions in government. In a similar vein, these groups provide an informal recruiting ground for determining which "experts" may be suitable for government service. In other words, policy-formation groups are an important part of what Domhoff calls the "co-optation process" whereby individuals, perhaps from other social classes, assimilate the values and interests of the dominant class.

3. *The candidate selection process:* The upper class is able to dominate the government because it has a major advantage in the candidate selection process. Electoral campaigns typically cost tens of millions of dollars, and in some cases hundreds of millions. This effectively excludes lower- and middle-class individuals, and even many from the upper middle class, from running for public office. One must have either a vast personal fortune that he or she is willing to spend or the backing of other wealthy individuals, corporations, and political action committees in order to run a serious campaign.

Numerous studies have shown the preponderance of the upper class in both elected and appointed offices. Domhoff himself estimates that about 90 percent of state and national officeholders come from the top 15 percent of the occupational ladder.[19] Working-class and minority Americans are particularly underrepresented in government, both because they lack the funds necessary to mount a modern successful political campaign and because they have been the victims of partisan *redistricting*—redrawing the boundaries of electoral districts. Redistricting has often been used to break up working-class and minority constituencies, particularly those that favor progressive economic and social reform. Establishing highly contorted district lines is often referred to as *gerrymandering*, a term named after Massachusetts governor Elbridge Gerry, who redrew the boundaries of one particular district in 1812, which ended up looking a bit like a salamander. Parenti provides some examples of how redistricting has been used to exclude minorities from elected office:

> In 1981, in Philadelphia, a Latino community of 63,000 anticipated control of at least one, and possibly two, seats, in the Pennsylvania Assembly. Instead, their cohesive community was divided into a number of districts, none of which had more than a 15 percent Latino population. Chicago's Puerto Rican and Mexican-American community suffered a similar plight that same year. And the New York City Council split 50,000 working-class Black voters in Queens into three predominantly White districts, making them a numerical minority in all three. Although composing nearly 50 percent of New York's population, Blacks and Latinos have been able to elect only eight representatives of a forty-three member council in part because of gerrymandering.[20]

Jamin Raskin, a professor of constitutional law, has pointed out that no black has ever been elected to Congress from the southern United States in a district populated mostly by whites. The carefully drawn lines of voting districts are so important that Raskin charges: "Voters don't really pick public officials on election day because public officials pick voters on redistricting day."[21]

Another factor that contributes to upper-class domination of the electoral process is our winner-take-all system of representation. In this system the candidate with the largest number of votes wins, and the other candidates get nothing even though they may have received a significant share of the vote. One alternative to this is called *proportional representation*, which is used in many democratic nations throughout the world. Proportional representation means that the representative body (the congress, national assembly, or parliament) is constructed to reflect the voting as it actually tallied up throughout the nation. In other words, if party A received 50 percent of the votes then it gets 50 percent of the seats in Congress. And if party B received 20 percent of the votes it would get 20 percent of the seats. Other parties would fill the remaining 30 percent of the seats. But in our current winner-take-all system, the losers receive nothing. The advantage (at least a potential advantage) of the proportional system is that smaller parties can be represented in the Congress, where they can then establish a presence and visibility that could be a stepping-stone toward becoming a major party. In the United States today the two major parties

---

The Price of Democracy?[22] (all figures are for 2000)

Amount spent on campaigns for the U.S. Senate: $457 million
Amount spent on campaigns for the House of Representatives: $559 million
Amount spent for the presidential elections: $355 million
Amount spent by each presidential candidate:

George W. Bush:	$186 million
Al Gore:	$120 million
Pat Buchanan:	$39 million
Ralph Nader:	$7.8 million
Harry Browne:	$2.2 million

Are losers bad candidates, or are they just a little short on money? In the 2000 race for Senate, the average winner spent $7.7 million compared to $3.9 for the average losing candidate. In the House races, the average winner spent $842,000 compared to $306,000 for the average loser.

have become so entrenched and, many would argue, conservative and unresponsive that there seems to be almost no possibility of an alternative party ever making inroads into the mainstream of American politics.

4. *The ideology process:* This refers to the many ways that the dominant class attempts to shape the beliefs and opinions of the population as a whole. Many of the policy-formation groups are very involved in the ideology process. Groups such as the Council on Foreign Relations expend a great deal of effort to reach and influence opinion makers and the mass media. The Advertising Council, for example, runs ad campaigns directed at the public that attempt to "promote the image of corporate business."[23] The Ad Council is able to do much of its work at very little cost, for as Domhoff reports, the council uses at least 80 percent of the public-service advertising time that television networks are required by law to provide.[24]

Although efforts to mold public opinion and create a unified consensus have had limited success, Domhoff feels that they have "been able to ensure that opposing opinions have remained isolated, suspect and only partially developed."[25] "Thus, the most important role of the ideology network may be in its ability to help ensure that an alternative view does not consolidate to replace the resigned acquiescence and disinterest that are found by pollsters and survey researchers to permeate the political and economic consciousness of Americans at the lower levels of the socioeconomic ladder."[26]

However, not everyone falls into complacency and acquiescence. Some people can be quite outspoken in their opposition to the status quo, and occasionally groups are organized that threaten the powers that be. These people may be forced out of their jobs, excluded from social groups, or attacked by the media as a consequence. Domhoff includes repressive acts by the state as part of the ideology process but only briefly acknowledges the crucial role they have played: "The fact remains that leaders within the American ruling class have turned loose strikebreakers, the police, the FBI and the CIA on trade-union organizers, civil-rights activists, anti-war protesters and left-wing political leaders, sometimes murdering them in the process. These actions are part of the ideology process, and they suggest that the power elite will use the most drastic methods to defend its position."[27]

It is important to recognize that government institutions are not the only sources of power in a nation. In Domhoff's definition of the ruling class, he includes certain organizations outside of government as being very important controlling institutions or decision-making groups. One type of group that I have not yet mentioned but that can play a very significant role, particularly in the ideology process, is the large charitable foundation. Domhoff points out that the trustees of the big charity foundations are almost all from the upper class. They provide "seed" money for various intellectual and cultural projects that help, in one way or another, to shape the beliefs and ideals of American society.

When a foundation sponsors a project, one can assume that the project meets with the approval of at least some members of the upper class. By encouraging some projects and not others, the foundations create implicit values and set limits within which cultural and intellectual quests are taken. A good example of this is the numerous population studies funded by the Rockefeller Foundation and the Ford Foundation. Both foundations were influential in portraying the problems of hunger and health in the Third World as the result of overpopulation. A more accurate picture, as we shall see in later chapters, would describe these problems as the result of very unequally distributed resources—a problem that is usually compounded by the development policies of the industrialized nations and large multinational corporations. The same bias is found in the solutions proposed by these foundations, e.g., birth control and the "green revolution." These proposed solutions tend to rely on technology and not on social reforms, which may threaten the great imbalance between the developed and the undeveloped nations.

The major foundations also have close ties with the major policy groups such as the Council on Foreign Relations.[28] According to Robert F. Arnove, organizations like the Carnegie, Ford, and Rockefeller Foundations

> have a corrosive influence on a democratic society; they represent relatively unregulated and unaccountable concentrations of power and wealth which buy talent, promote causes, and, in effect, establish an agenda of what merits society's attention; . . . they help maintain an economic and political order, international in scope which benefits the ruling class interests . . . [and] works against the interests of minorities, the working-class, and Third World peoples.[29]

Concern over the power of foundations has been expressed for decades, but little has been done to curb their power and influence. In 1914, a citizens' Commission on Industrial Relations (CIR, also known as the Walsh Commission) was established by Congress to look into a variety of labor-related issues. Shortly after its establishment the commission decided to conduct a "sweeping investigation of all of the country's great benevolent organizations."[30] Speaking for the commission, Frank Walsh said that charges had been made to the CIR that "the creation of the Rockefeller and other foundations was the beginning of an effort to perpetuate the present position of predatory wealth through the corruption of sources of public information."[31]

Ultimately, the Walsh Commission submitted an eleven-thousand-page report (the Manley Report) to Congress that claimed "the giant, general purpose foundations were so grave a menace to society that if they could be clearly differentiated from other forms of voluntary altruistic effort, it would be desirable to recommend their abolition."[32] But although the Walsh Commission did make some recommendations regarding investigation and regulation of these foundations, very little has been done to restrict their power. A few minor, tax-linked restrictions put into effect in 1969 caused the foundations some concern, but essentially they remain a truly powerful group of latently political institutions.

In spite of instrumentalism's advance over pluralism and functional elite theory, it still has some shortcomings. First, instrumentalism overemphasizes the actions and intentions of various individuals and groups and assumes a high degree of self-consciousness and solidarity among the upper class. This can be quite difficult to prove. Second, class struggle, or political conflict, exists only faintly in the background of instrumentalist analysis. Change appears to come from the top down rather than as a result of the tensions among different social forces. Third, the state's role in the economic process is somewhat neglected or misrepresented. Fourth, the instrumentalist approach fails to adequately account for the state's ability to act against any particular sector or interest of the capitalist class, that is, the state's ability to function independently of particular interests. Last, and perhaps most important, instrumentalism gives the impression that major social change can occur simply by changing the people who are in power; it neglects the external constraints placed on the state by the economic system and by the capitalist class as a whole.

STRUCTURALIST THEORY

Some of the shortcomings of instrumentalism have been addressed by a number of writers whose work has become known collectively as the "structuralist theory of the state." The structuralist theory of the state emphasizes a number of important points. One is that the state is the product of social relations: it does not develop independent of social classes and conflict but, rather, as an outgrowth of these forces. The state is highly conditioned by all spheres of social relations, and in turn acts upon these relations and other social structures. From the structuralist viewpoint, the state is the product of a constellation of social forces that develops independently of anyone's particular will and then acts with a fairly high degree of autonomy. So whereas instrumentalism emphasizes the primacy of capitalist actors who are acutely aware of their interests and completely willful in their actions, the structuralist approach poses a state that is the coalescing of various structural elements, all of which condition or constrain the actor to the point where individual consciousness or will is barely relevant.

One of the key concepts of structuralist analysis is the notion of *relative autonomy*. This means that the state, both as a result of historical struggles and in order to fulfill its functions, has a high degree of independence from any existing social classes or power blocs. In the words of Martin Carnoy, it means "that in order to represent class interests—that is, to be legitimate in the context of class and group conflict—the state bureaucracy must appear to be autonomous from the dominant class."[33] For this reason, structuralist theories of the state are sometimes collectively referred to as *state autonomy theory*, a label that can be confusing because pluralist theory also denotes an autonomous state. Others distinguish between *state-centered theory* and *capitalist-state structuralist theory*. The former includes theories of the state that perceive the state as being able to act independently of outside forces (especially class interests), and the latter includes theories that downplay the ability of sectors of any class to influence the state and instead emphasizes that state officials are "constrained by imperatives of capitalist political economy."[34]

From the structuralist perspective, relative autonomy provides the appearance of state impartiality that helps the government maintain legitimacy in the eyes of the masses, but also gives the state the ability (to a limited extent) to act against the wishes of the capitalist class either in part or in whole. Structuralists often explain the Bonapartist state in France (1852–70) in these terms, along with the Bismarck regime in Germany (late 1800s), the czarist reign in nineteenth-century Russia, and perhaps even the fascist states of mid-twentieth-century Europe (controlled by Hitler, Mussolini, Franco, etc.).

From the structuralist perspective, the state need not be controlled by a willful capitalist class in order to function in its service. For example, German industrialists under Bismarck were willing to tolerate a monarchy so long as the latter understood how to further the interests of German industry and its owners: through the tariff policies it established, by placing diplomacy in the service of commerce, by permitting cartels and monopolies, and by encouraging export trade through subsidized shipping and other privileges. They also trusted the monarchy to protect them from revolt from below by instituting antisocialist laws, along with strike and picketing restrictions. To gain their security, they even submitted willingly to the Bismarckian social insurance program, even though it placed a greater financial burden upon industry.[35]

In the United States, the administration of Franklin Roosevelt has sometimes been explained in the same way. Roosevelt instituted many social reforms and work programs that were not popular with the owning class and that may not ever have come about if the state was not somewhat independent of the capitalist class. And although some were quick to decry Roosevelt's policies as socialistic, Roosevelt took pride in pointing out that it was his administration that "saved the country from socialism."

Another important component of structuralist analysis is the notion that the structure of the various state institutions forces it to perform certain functions regardless of the personnel who hold the positions. Even if proworking-class officials attempt to carry out anticapitalist policies, the state's institutional structure enables the bourgeoisie to transport the role of dominance from one sector to another.[36] Thus when socialist candidate Salvador Allende was elected president in Chile in 1970, the capitalist class and some state officials managed to subvert much of the president's power and to concentrate power in the hands of the military, which eventually overthrew the president.

Parenti has argued that making a conceptual distinction between the state and the government can help us to better understand the relationship between politicoeconomic power and popular governance. Although the government and the state are "empirically overlapping phenomena," one can think of the government as that part of the U.S. political system that mediates public policy, and the state as the set of institutions and processes that "orchestrates coercion and control, both overtly and covertly."[37] Such a distinction can help to explain the complexities in challenging political power in contemporary societies and the roadblocks to change that can be faced by newly elected governments or by revolutionary movements. For instance:

> When Salvador Allende, a Popular Unity candidate dedicated to democratic reforms on behalf of the laboring classes, was elected president of Chile in 1970, he took over the reins of government and was able to initiate certain popular policies. But he could never gain control of the state

apparatus, that is, the military, the police, the security forces, the intelligence services, the courts, and the fundamental organic law that rigged the whole system in favor of the wealthy. When Allende began to advance into redistributive politics and against class privilege, the military seized power and murdered him and thousands of his supporters. The CIA-backed, procapitalist state destroyed not only Allende's government but the democracy that produced it.

In Nicaragua, after the Sandinistas lost the 1990 election to a right-centrist coalition, the army and police remained in their hands. However, in contrast to the Chilean military, which was backed by the immense power of the United States, the Nicaraguan military was the target of that power and was unable to keep the government on its revolutionary course. At the same time, the anomaly of a left military sufficiently diffused state power so as to make it difficult for the newly installed Chamorro government to effect procapitalist changes at a speed pleasing to Washington.[38]

THE STATE'S ROLE IN THE ECONOMY

Perhaps the key area of study for those who wish to understand state power is the role that the economy plays in shaping the state and vice versa. In terms of the relationship between the state and capitalist economy, Carnoy asserts that the state must fulfill certain conditions in order to ensure its own reproduction. These are:

1. Since accumulation takes place on a private basis, the state can control production only to a limited degree.
2. The state is dependent on the private sector for revenue (through taxation), thus the state is not likely to pursue policies that would inhibit accumulation.
3. Likewise, the state has a mandate to advance the accumulation process.
4. The personnel of the state does not have a power base of its own and thus needs to promote itself as representing the "common and general interests of society as a whole."[39]

Thus the state operates with a great deal of independence from any class or class fraction and is continually caught up in the need to promote the accumulation process while at the same time maintaining its legitimacy by *appearing* to act in the general interest of society and in the particular interest of no one.

Two American theorists who analyze the state in this way are Fred Block and James O'Connor. Block and O'Connor see the state as a political power independent of capital and labor's *fractionalized interests*, which tries to promote the contradictory goals of accumulation and legitimation. According to Block, sectors of capital are able to influence the state directly through lobbying and other policy-influencing activities, and by having some of their personnel in government service (Block is acknowledging the partial validity of instrumentalism). Bourgeois cultural hegemony is also a factor since there is "widespread acceptance of certain rules about what is and what is not legitimate state activity."[40] But for Block these are only "subsidiary structural mechanisms," and do not explain the state's ability to carry out policies that may go against the short-term or particular interests of capital.

Block's next step, then, is to outline the "major structural mechanisms" of the modern capitalist state, which ensure that overall it will act in the general interest of capital but that it will also have the ability to act against capital when necessary. Block points out that the capacity of the state to finance itself through taxation or borrowing depends on the general level of economic activity. Thus the state is an active independent agent to the extent to which it pursues policies to promote economic activity favorable to capitalism. It does so not only because it needs to finance itself, but also because public support will drop if there is a serious decline in economic activity and a consequential rise in unemployment and shortages of consumer goods. The state is also constrained because the level of economic activity is largely determined by private investments, which means the private sector has the power to "veto" or sabotage the activities of the state.[41] In short, the state is highly dependent on maintaining a substantial level of business confidence. If private enterprise does not have a relatively high degree of confidence in the state's ability to provide favorable investment conditions, then the state's legitimacy will be called into question.

One of the factors that can force the state to be more independent of the ruling class is the general level of class struggle in the society. We have seen that union activity in the United States has dropped off dramatically in the past couple of decades and that without strong movements for social change, social programs and services have consequently been rolled back. Both Block and O'Connor attempt to incorporate class struggle into their analysis, something that is deficient in instrumentalist theory and early structuralist theory. Block, for instance, points out that when workers successfully strive for higher wages and greater benefits, capitalists are compelled to develop more technology and more efficient ways of organizing work. They must do this in order to restore their previous rate of profit. But by increasing the rate of exploitation or productivity, they displace many workers. This can relieve some of the pressure for higher wages and better working conditions, and it frees up more capital for new investments that can start the cycle all over again. The point is that pressure from the working class has contributed to rationalizing capitalism. Class struggle also contributes to the expansion of the state's role in the regulation of the economy and in the provision of social services. It is in these ways that class struggle is often referred to as the "dynamic" or "motive force" of capitalism.

James O'Connor's groundbreaking book, *The Fiscal Crisis of the State*, analyzes government expenditures (and indirectly, all government activity) and sees them as corresponding to the capitalist state's two basic functions: accumulation and legitimation. O'Connor labels as *social capital* all expenditures that are aimed at increasing the productivity of labor and lowering the reproductive costs of labor. All projects and services that are required to maintain social harmony are called *social expense*.[42] A *fiscal crisis of the state* exists to the extent that the state is unable to collect revenues to match its expenditures.

The growth of the government's involvement in the economy and society has reached tremendous proportions. In 2002, the federal government spent nearly $1.9 trillion; state and local government outlays added an additional $2 trillion.[43] As mentioned earlier, during the last two decades in particular, government expenditures have tended to exceed revenues by substantial amounts. In 2000, the accumulated federal debt was $5.6 trillion, and state and local government indebtedness was nearly $1.5 trillion.[44] For what purposes is this money spent? The essence of O'Connor's analysis, and of others such as Sidney Lens, is that the vast bulk of it goes to shore up capitalism's various support systems. O'Connor claims the primary role of the state is to help ensure the proper conditions for the accumulation of capital. In other words, much of the state's expenditures are allocated to projects and services that help private investors, especially large corporations, make money.

Lens points out a number of ways in which the government props up big business. One is through various types of subsidies—when the government pays for part of the cost of running a particular business, or in many cases, it assumes part of the cost for a whole business sector. The govern-

Facts and Figures on the Budget Deficit[45]

2001 Federal Budget Outlays: $1.856 trillion
Accumulated Federal Debt: $5.625 trillion
Total Personal Income (2000): $8.282 trillion
Federal Debt Per Person: $20,455
2001 Federal Interest Payments: $206 billion
2001 Federal Interest Payments as Percent of Federal Outlays: 11%
2000 State Debt: $548 billion
2000 State Debt Per Person: $1,950
2000 Local Government Debt: $800 billion

ment routinely subsidizes airlines, airports, shipping ports, agribusiness, and other industries. In the case of farm subsidies, farmers are actually paid not to grow food. This was a price support program originally started in the 1930s to help struggling farmers. For decades, though, the bulk of the farm subsidy program has gone to the nation's largest farms and to high-income farming households. For example, it is estimated that the $180 billion farm subsidy bill signed into law by George W. Bush in 2002 will give 47 percent of commodity payments to farms run by owners whose *household* incomes average $135,000.[46]

The federal government also loans out a good deal of money to commercial enterprises, or it may guarantee loans made by private banks. Major loans have been granted to such industrial giants as Lockheed and Chrysler. However, in cases where the company folds in spite of the government's financial support, taxpayers are left footing the unpaid portion of the bill. Such was the case with the savings-and-loan bailout that cost American taxpayers some $500 billion and that, incidentally, was directly the result of the banking deregulation sponsored by the Reagan administration.[47] Overall, the federal government has bailed out over 400 corporations.[48]

Another way in which the federal government uses public tax money to promote private-sector profit is through its expenditures on research and development. The government has spent hundreds of billions of dollars for research now used by private utilities and nuclear power companies and by communications companies such as AT&T. All sorts of advancements in consumer goods, such as wash-and-wear clothes, frozen foods, and aerosol sprays, were made by Department of Agriculture researchers. The benefits of this research were simply handed over to private companies, which then used them to increase their profits.[49]

Occasionally, an industry that is vital for the functioning of other industries, or essential to a large portion of the public, is unable to continue its operations. In many of these cases, the government takes over the operation and continues to run it even though it loses money. A prime example of this is Amtrak, which was created to take the place of the crumbling Penn Central railroad. Lens calls these "quasi-public" corporations.[50] The government runs them at a loss and the taxpayer has to make up the difference. If the government had nationalized the entire railroad industry, the tax burden would have been lightened since the profitable freight sector could have easily paid for the unprofitable passenger services.

The government never takes over a profitable industry, and in the rare cases where it takes over a losing enterprise and turns it into a bit of a profit maker, it does its best to get rid of it quickly. An example of this is the case of Conrail, which was created from the remains of seven northeastern railroads. According to Parenti, Conrail was transformed by the government into "an efficient and profitable giant railroad system with $800 million in cash reserves by 1985."[51] After its transformation into a moneymaker, Conrail was sold by President Reagan to private stockholders at less than half its real value.[52]

Lens calls this arrangement between government and corporate America *corporate socialism.* It is a system whereby the risks, losses, and normal operating expenses of big business are taken on by the population at large, but the benefits accrue disproportionately to the owners of capital—the upper class.

Consumer advocate Ralph Nader has called this set of arrangements the *corporate welfare system.* Nader points out that there are over 120 federal programs that take the form of "handouts" and "giveaways" to big corporations and that "they dwarf the poverty welfare services coming out of Washington."[53] Nader asserts that "if a program involves the government giving more to private companies than it gets back . . . then it should be considered corporate welfare."[54]

Estimates on the amount of corporate welfare range from $85 billion to $448 billion per year, but, in truth, it is difficult to discern the line between corporate welfare and other functions of the state.[55] One could argue that everything from guaranteed loans to Enron, to building prisons and jails, from dredging shipping ports to providing public education serves a role in maintaining and reproducing the entire system. And overall, it is a system dominated by corporate interests, in which the benefits are distributed disproportionately to the upper class.

Davita Glasberg and Dan Skidmore provide a more elaborate answer to the question "what is corporate welfare?" They define corporate welfare as

> Those efforts made by the state to directly or indirectly subsidize, support, or rescue corporations, or otherwise socialize the cost and risk of investment and production of private profits and capital accumulation of corporations. These include corporate tax loopholes, reductions in capital gains taxes, subsidies to industries such as defense contractors and agriculture, tax abatement to encourage corporate development, and bailouts of ailing corporations.[56]

The concepts of corporate welfare and corporate socialism can even be extended to include many progressive reforms. Publicly funded institutions such as schools or subsidized low-income housing, and nonprofit social institutions such as prisons or even water utilities, are typically structured in such a way as to make a profit for private interests. This market function

Annual "wealthfare" expenditures:[57]

Military waste and fraud	$172 billion
Social Security tax inequities	$53 billion
Accelerated depreciation	$37 billion
Lower taxes on capital gains	$37 billion
Savings-and-loan bailout	$32 billion
Homeowners tax break	$26 billion
Agribusiness subsidies	$18 billion
Tax avoidance by transnationals	$12 billion
Tax-free municipal bonds	$9.1 billion
Media handouts	$8 billion
Excessive government pensions	$7.6 billion
Insurance loopholes	$7.2 billion
Nuclear subsidies	$7.1 billion
Aviation subsidies	$5.5 billion
Business meals and entertainment	$5.5 billion
Mining subsidies	$3.5 billion
Oil and gas tax breaks	$2.4 billion
Export subsidies	$2 billion
Synfuel tax credits	$1.2 billion
Timber subsidies	$427 million
Ozone tax exemptions	$320 million
Miscellaneous	$1.6 billion

is often given a higher priority than the institution's officially proclaimed purpose. Many of today's publicly financed projects are funded through the sale of bonds. These bonds are seen as an alternative to funding through taxation, although in the long run, they require higher taxes to pay them off.

A state government may, for instance, authorize the sale of $100 million in bonds to pay for new prison construction. These bonds are bought by investors and normally provide the investors with tax-free interest income. The bonds are often of a twenty-year term, which means that for twenty years the bond holders, who are almost exclusively wealthy to begin with, receive nontaxable interest payments for twenty years, and at the end of that period their initial investment is returned to them. In the meantime, the state has had to come up with the revenue to make the yearly interest

---

Some examples of corporate welfare programs:

- The Department of Agriculture's Foreign Agricultural Service spent $110 million a year advertising American products in other countries. Among the products promoted by this program are Sunkist oranges, Pillsbury muffins, and Chicken McNuggets.
- The government's advanced technology program transferred $400 million in 1994 to such corporate giants as Chevron, General Electric, IBM, and Texaco.
- A "clean car initiative" requested by the government would cost $333 million. The program has the stated aim of producing a more fuel efficient car and ensuring "the global competitiveness of the U.S. automobile industry." The money would go to General Motors, Ford, and Chrysler, whose combined profits are often over $10 billion per year.
- The government hands out approximately $2 billion in subsidies to large and profitable electric utility cooperatives. In doing so the government is underwriting the costs of, among others, some ski resorts in Aspen, Colorado, and luxurious hotels in Hilton Head, South Carolina.
- In 1994, the U.S. Forest Service spent $140 million to build roads in national forests, thus facilitating the removal of timber by private lumber companies. From 1975 to 1995 the Forest Service built 340,000 miles of roads (eight times the length of the interstate highway system), which are mainly used by lumber companies.[58]
- The Mining Act of 1872 allows companies to purchase federal land for $5 an acre or less and to mine valuable minerals from federal land without paying a cent in royalties. The Mineral Policy Center estimates that mining companies extract $2 billion to $3 billion worth of minerals from public lands every year without paying any royalties. According to the Center, from 1872 to 1993, mining companies took more than $230 billion from federal lands.[59]

payments and then the final investment return. If, for instance, the interest on the bonds is calculated at 5 percent per year, then by the end of the twenty-year period the state will have shelled out $100 million in interest, which means it has spent twice as much for the prisons than it would have if it had simply raised taxes. Of course, we have not taken into account the decreased value of the dollar that would occur due to inflation; but the basic point is that projects funded through bonds create income for the wealthy. They do it by transferring money from the general public to the bond holders through the system of taxation. If we think back to some of the points made in our discussion of surplus value, it becomes quite clear that the need for this support system is a result of falling profits and the crisis of overproduction or, as some call it, "the problem of surplus absorption." In sum, the inability of the capitalist economic system to maintain steady growth and provide jobs and income for the general population forces the state to intervene more and more in order to avoid prolonged crisis.

As we have also seen, without addressing the heart of the problem, the crisis can't be completely avoided anyway. In the United States today, incomes for many workers are stagnant, more than 30 million Americans live in poverty, and high unemployment has become a chronic problem. Furthermore, we have created a debt situation that may place a tremendous burden on future generations. The cumulative federal deficit of $5.6 trillion amounts to a debt of over $20,000 for every single American. Add the debt owed by state and local governments, and per capita debt increases by several thousand more.[60] This is a tremendous amount of debt, and no one seems to have any reasonable idea how to pay it off. To put these numbers in perspective, total personal income in the United States amounts to about $8 trillion annually, so it would take every employed American working for nine straight months and giving their entire income for those nine months, to pay off the existing federal and state debt. To say the least, we have reached a situation in which government spending and taxation have become very difficult to control.

Where does the money come from when the government has to borrow to make ends meet? For the most part the government borrows the money from American banks, although there is also a relatively small amount borrowed from foreign banks. At present the banks are perfectly willing not to collect the principal but merely the interest on the loans. In fact, this may be the ideal situation for the banks because they are receiving regular payments but at such a rate that the loans will never be paid off. It is a situation of permanent debt. Presently, about 11 percent of federal expenditures (around

$200 billion) is allocated for interest payments on the debt. This amount is more than twice the amount needed to raise every single American above the poverty line. However, since most of the debt is held by private corporations and upper-income individuals, the interest payments that the government makes amounts to little more than another form of income transfer from the majority of American taxpayers to the wealthiest of all Americans.

The solution to the debt problem is neither more taxes nor greater cutbacks in government spending. These proposals invariably end up placing a greater burden on the American working class and could perhaps cripple the economy even more. Deficit spending itself is not something that should be avoided at all costs either; it depends on what the objectives of the spending are. During the Reagan years, when the deficit experienced its greatest increase, military spending increased dramatically, defense contractors made profits way above the average for all industries, and the rich received numerous tax breaks. Thus, federal government borrowing financed a wealthier life for the rich at the expense of everyone else. But deficit spending can also be done to finance all sorts of social services—mass-transportation systems, housing construction, healthcare, education, parks and recreation areas, and so forth. The key focus should not be exclusively on balancing the budget, but on what the government actually spends its money for, who pays for these expenditures, and who benefits.

The eventual solution for our present debt situation may be abolition of the debt. This would mean that those who loaned money to the government will never be paid back in full but they will have to settle for the interest payments that they have already received. In other words, the principal could be forgiven or abolished. Another possibility, which may meet less powerful opposition, is to erode the debt by allowing inflation to rise. As long as people's income keeps pace with the inflation rate, rising inflation would have the effect of lowering the relative expense of the debt payments.

CONFLICT AND REPRESSION

As pointed out earlier, instrumentalist theory has been criticized for being somewhat one-sided in the sense that it overemphasizes the ability of the upper class to get its way and underestimates the ability of other classes to shape the social and economic landscape. On the other hand, structuralist theory has been criticized for being too theoretical. Its view of society is one in which social institutions play major roles, but people (their actions, intentions, and motivations) get somewhat lost in the picture. It is important to remember that it is people who make history and that throughout the history of our nation conflict among groups has played an important part in shaping our society. Many times people have had to struggle to gain some of the things that we now take for granted. At times the state has come down very hard on opposition groups, and its tendency to do so in favor of capital reveals the true class nature of the government. With all this in mind, a look at the work of Frances Fox Piven and Richard Cloward, Michael Parenti, and others will help to illustrate how important the concepts of class struggle and repression are to the field of political sociology.

Piven and Cloward are the authors of numerous books that depict the struggle by poor and working people for the expansion of democratic rights and for a larger share of America's wealth. In *The New Class War*, which documents "Reagan's attack on the welfare state," the authors posit that capitalism was not established voluntarily and was not regarded as a better system by many or most people. In order to enforce a system of wage labor, people's subsistence rights were eroded. Property rights superseded them. The social programs existing in the contemporary state were essentially forced upon capitalism and the government because of mass pressure from below. Capitalism has never been able to provide for everyone. The policies of the Reagan administration during the 1980s amounted to a *class war*. However, as Piven and Cloward point out, dismantling these programs is very difficult. They represent structured participation in the state for both the clients of various social service programs and the workers employed by these programs. Any attempt at dismantling them is bound to meet serious resistance.

Much of the theoretical framework of *The New Class War* was established by Piven and Cloward in an earlier book titled *Regulating the Poor*. In this work Piven and Cloward state that most of the "relief" programs established by the government were not established because people needed them but because of mass pressure put on the government. In this regard the authors elucidate some of the latent functions of relief programs. Chief among these are quelling social and political unrest and helping maintain the legitimacy of the state. Furthermore, relief programs are not truly independent, state-run programs, they are an adjunct of the private-sector economy. For instance, in times when the private sector is expanding and creating new jobs, government-run relief programs are usually cut back, forcing more people into the labor force.

Relief programs also degrade the recipients, thereby reinforcing the work ethic and encouraging people to be content with the jobs they have.

If people have a fear of the degradation and deprivation of unemployment and welfare, they are less likely to rock the boat at their workplace. This means they are less likely to form unions or to participate in job actions. Likewise, they are less likely to put pressure on their employers for more pay, greater benefits, or cleaner and healthier working conditions.

The explicit assumptions of Piven and Cloward's work are that the government functions primarily in the service of capitalism, not in service to the population as a whole, and that the system responds more to political pressure than it does to needs. In other words, protest and conflict force change.

The notion that social conflict and class struggle are major forces that shape government policy is also present in the work of Parenti. In *Democracy for the Few* Parenti avers that the original formation of the U.S. government and the Constitution was a very elitist process that deliberately excluded the vast majority of Americans. At the time John Jay, the nation's first chief justice of the Supreme Court (1789–95), declared that "the people who own the country ought to govern it"; and Alexander Hamilton, first secretary to the Treasury (1789–95), felt that "the rich and well-born" ought to have superior power.[61]

One way of ensuring the power of the elite was to exclude the vast majority of the population from the electoral process. Parenti points out:

> Property qualifications disenfranchised the poorest white males in various states. Half the adult population was denied suffrage because they were women. American Indians had no access to the ballot. About one-fourth, both men and women, had no vote because they were held in bondage, and even of the blacks who had gained their legal freedom, in both the North and South, none was allowed to vote until the passage of the Fourteenth Amendment, after the Civil War.[62]

Parenti's *Democracy for the Few* includes a chapter on repression in which he highlights some of the ways in which the power of the state has been used against the working class and political dissidents.[63] By far it has been the labor movement that the state has seen as the greatest threat to the status quo. Many lives have been lost because of the government's willingness to use violent force against the working class. The following are just a few classic examples of this.

- In 1877 General Sheridan and his troops were recalled from fighting the Sioux Indians and brought to Chicago to help end a nationwide strike of railroad workers. Scores of workers were killed and hundreds wounded by government troops in Chicago and by related government actions in Pittsburgh and Baltimore.[64]

- In July 1892, the Pinkerton private police force and government troops were brought into Homestead, Pennsylvania, where workers were locked out of factories in a dispute with Carnegie Steel. Seven workers were shot to death.

- On Easter Sunday in 1914, during a workers' strike in Ludlow Colorado, the Rockefeller-owned Colorado Fuel and Iron Company employed gunmen and National Guardsmen, who drenched the strikers' tents with oil and set them on fire as the miners and their families slept. As they ran from the burning tents, the miners, their wives, and their children were fired upon by machine guns. All told, twenty people were killed. John D. Rockefeller Jr. took full responsibility for the massacre and had the audacity to say that he was protecting the workingman against trade unions.[65]

- On Independence Day in 1936, federal troops were once again dispatched to Chicago to help break a railroad strike. This time thirty men and women were killed, and one hundred others, mostly bystanders, were wounded.

When Americans think of political unrest they no doubt think of the 1960s, but the 1960s were not the only time of political turmoil, and certainly not the only period in which the state took repressive action against political dissidents. Parenti summarizes some of the major acts of repression that took place in this century:

Eugene Debs and some 6,000 other socialists, pacifists, and radical IWW [Industrial Workers of the World] organizers were imprisoned during the First World War or deported during the Palmer raids immediately afterward. The anarchists Sacco and Vanzetti were executed for a crime most investigators say they never committed. Numerous war resisters were arrested during World War II and the Korean War. The Smith Act of 1940 prohibited the mere advocacy of revolutionary ideas and was used to jail scores of American Communists and other leftists, including Gus Hall, General Secretary of the Communist Party, USA, who spent nine years in prison for his political beliefs.[66]

During the 1960s, government repression was aimed more at political dissidents than the working class. In particular, black civil rights leaders and revolutionaries were the targets:

All of the one hundred or so murders of civil-rights activists during the 1960s were committed by police and White vigilantes. Yet the state was able to catch but a few of the perpetrators and none were convicted of murder. From 1968 to 1971, police attacked the headquarters of the Black Panthers (a Black Marxist organization) in more than ten cities, smashing typewriters, stealing thousands of dollars in funds, and arresting, beating, and shooting the occupants in well-planned, unprovoked attacks. More than forty Panthers were killed by police in that period, and over three hundred were arrested, with many imprisoned for long periods without bail or trial.[67]

Repression against American citizens sometimes has taken a violent or very forceful tack, but we should also be aware of the more subtle and insidious violation of our rights. American citizens have been spied on and lied to by their government, we've had our phones tapped and our mail opened, we've been slandered by false stories planted in the press, and rivalries between different groups have been exacerbated by opportunistic agents who sow dissension and division. Two excellent sources for detailed information regarding how the U.S. government has repressed individuals and groups who may oppose it are Alan Wolfe's *The Seamy Side of Democracy* and Brian Glick's *The War at Home*. David Wise's earlier work *The Politics of Lying* also contains a wealth of information about government deception and explores many aspects of the secrecy issue.

During the 1970s, a variety of commissions began to uncover some of the actions that U.S. agencies had taken against Americans. One such action was Operation CHAOS, which began under President Lyndon Johnson and continued under Richard Nixon. According to Wolfe, "CHAOS kept close tabs on the antiwar movement, eventually collecting computerized indices on over 300,000 persons and organizations within the United States."[68]

Also, in the 1970s, the President's Commission on CIA Activities within the United States (established by President Gerald Ford and headed by Nelson A. Rockefeller) brought to light some of the ways in which the CIA violated its charter by spying on Americans at home:

The vice-president and his colleagues also learned that the CIA had been reading our mail for over twenty years, opening 215,820 letters in New York City alone before resealing them and sending them on to their destinations. Other revelations indicated that the agency had followed and photographed American citizens, had carried out break-ins at home, had wire-tapped and bugged, and had obtained citizens' tax records from the Internal Revenue Service.[69]

But the CIA was not the only arm of the government actively spying on the American people:

> During the height of the Vietnam war, army intelligence sent out 1,500 spies to watch and infiltrate domestic political organizations. Data on over 100,000 Americans were collected by the army alone. The army infiltrated the 1963 March on Washington, the 1966 freedom march of James Meredith, the civil rights movement's major organizations, the Americans for Democratic Action, the American Civil Liberties Union, the 1968 Poor People's March on Washington, the 1968 Democratic convention (where agents posed as reporters to gather information), the 1969 moratoria against the Vietnam war, and other political organizations and events. In spite of reforms passed in 1971, military intelligence continues to flourish; eight examples of covert surveillance by the military intelligence services between 1971 and 1975 were noted by the Senate Intelligence Committee.[70]

One of the CIA's most outspoken critics in recent years has been Ralph McGehee, who spent twenty-five years in the agency. McGehee revealed that the CIA infiltrated student groups, labor organizations, and even religious groups. The CIA had thousands of college professors and administrators working for it in a variety of capacities, and "it worked to shape public opinion through some 450 individuals and publications."[71] McGehee also notes that philanthropic organizations were tied in to the CIA's network of deception and surveillance and that the Church Committee described the CIA's "intrusion into the foundation field" as "massive."[72]

One of the more bizarre and irresponsible domestic programs that the CIA ran was called Operation MKULTRA. According to McGehee:

> In the MKULTRA program, physicians, toxicologists, other specialists, and CIA personnel without medical training conducted intensive tests *on human subjects* without telling the victims or Congress or the executive branch. In one scenario, Agency employees would visit restaurants, bars, and beaches, slipping LSD into the drinks of unsuspecting individuals. The number of people damaged by these unlawful and immoral activities is incalculable.[73]

Perhaps the most extensive covert operation directed at the American people was the COINTELPRO (counterintelligence program) of the Federal Bureau of Investigation (FBI). COINTELPRO consisted of six major areas of operations, although the program was primarily directed at black political organizations. The first and largest program ran from 1956 to 1971 and targeted the Communist Party USA, especially the party's civil rights activities. A second program—a little-known one—was directed at groups seeking independence for Puerto Rico, and it ran from 1960 to 1971. During the same time period the FBI also ran a COINTELPRO operation known as the Border Coverage Program. It was directed at radical Mexican organizations and, like the operation against Puerto Ricans, much of its activities were concealed from Congress.

A fourth program was directed against the Socialist Workers Party (SWP) and ran from 1961 to 1969. Much has been revealed about this program because of the many lawsuits that the SWP has filed against the FBI and the U.S. government. The FBI's attacks on the SWP were especially preoccupied with SWP activities connected with Malcolm X and also the National Mobilization Committee to End the War in Vietnam.

A fifth program was aimed at black nationalist "hate" groups. This program ran from 1967 to 1971 and was "the vehicle for the Bureau's all-out assault" on Martin Luther King Jr., the Black Panther Party, the Nation of Islam, and many other black organizations.

A sixth program was directed against the New Left and consisted of attempts to destroy such groups as the Students for a Democratic Society, the Peace and Freedom Party, and the Institute for Policy Studies.

A seventh, mostly bogus, program was directed at white hate groups. According to Brian Glick, "under the cover of being even-handed and going after violent right-wing groups, the FBI actually gave covert aid to the Ku Klux Klan, Minuteman, Nazis, and other racist vigilantes."[74]

SOCIAL CAPITAL

Repression of dissent, along with the ability of big money and corporations to dominate the American political process, has contributed to the lack of confidence that many Americans express toward their government. These factors may partially explain the relatively low voter turnout that exists in the United States (see Fig. 5.1). Low voter turnout is one of the factors that has caused many researchers to wonder what has happened to political life in the United States. Has overall civic activism declined along with voter turnout, or are people politically active in other ways? Has something fundamental changed in the social life of Americans in a way that has weakened our political identities and connections to one another? These and similar questions have sparked a debate over America's *social capital*.

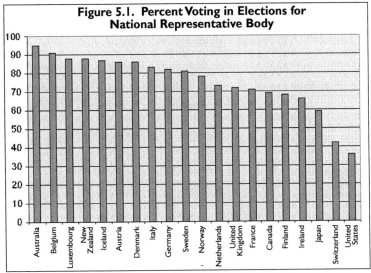

Figure 5.1. Percent Voting in Elections for National Representative Body

Source: UN HDR 1999

What is social capital and is it really declining? The state of social capital in the United States is the object of a flurry of contending claims and counterclaims. One of the leading researchers on the topic is Harvard political scientist Robert Putnam. In 1995, Putnam published an article titled "Bowling Alone" in *The Journal of Democracy*, in which he claimed that political and social involvement in the United States was experiencing a serious decline. The article attracted a great deal of attention and the "bowling alone thesis" sparked widespread reaction. Five years later, Putnam published a much more thorough and persuasive book titled *Bowling Alone: The Collapse and Revival of American Community*.[75]

In its broadest sense, social capital refers to the entire range of connections that individuals make to one another. It consists of all the varied networks that people use (or create) to communicate, set goals, mobilize resources, and coordinate actions. All these connections make up a web of reciprocity and social trust. Questions about social capital fit well with both structural and elite theories of the state. If powerful interest groups, or elites, dominate the political process, wouldn't there have to be a corresponding decline in certain types of political participation on the part of the public?

In Putnam's writing, social capital is clearly viewed as a good thing. What exactly is so good about social capital? Let's take a brief look at some of its benefits:

1. Social capital allows citizens to resolve collective problems more easily.
2. Social capital increases trust and reciprocity and makes business and social transactions less costly.
3. Social capital widens our awareness of the many ways in which our fates are linked. Joiners, with exceptions, become more tolerant, less cynical, and more empathetic to the misfortunes of others.
4. People whose lives are rich in social capital are healthier and happier. They are better able to cope with trauma and they fight illness more successfully. Putnam points out that "over the last twenty years more than a dozen large studies . . . in the United States, Scandinavia, and Japan have shown that *people who are socially disconnected are between two and five times more likely to die from all causes, compared with matched individuals who have close ties with family, friends, and the community.*"[76]
5. Social capital is second only to poverty in its effect on children's lives. Putnam writes, "while poverty is an especially potent force in increasing youth fertility, mortality, and idleness, community engagement has precisely the opposite effect." For example, child abuse rates are higher where neighborhood cohesion is lower.[77]
6. Social capital also has a significant effect on the economic success of individuals. Social ties can influence who gets a job, a bonus, a promotion, and other job benefits.

For social scientists, social capital can be a tricky thing. Not only is it difficult to measure but one must be careful not to fall into the trap of thinking that all of the consequences of high levels of social capital are positive. Putnam points out that "networks and the associated norms of reciprocity are generally good for those inside the network, but the external effects of social capital are by no means always positive."[78] Benjamin Barber makes a similar point in *A Place for Us* when he differentiates between *communitarianism*, which is often ethnocentric, exclusive, and even authoritarian, and *strong democracy*, which is inclusive and more egalitarian and empowering.[79]

Wisely, Putnam distinguishes between *bonding* social capital and *bridging* social capital. Bonding social capital refers to in-group ties. These may have some positive benefits for the members, but bonding social capital is frequently exclusionary and divisive. Bridging social capital refers to networks that create or promote ties among varied individuals and groups.

This type of social capital goes a long way in breaking down the estrangement and conflict that may exist among people, and it helps promote trust and reciprocity. Many forms of bridging social capital are what social scientists refer to as "weak ties," and they are a very good predictor of how much people enjoy their neighborhoods, and of low crime rates and higher academic achievement. When people see each other on a fairly consistent basis and frequently say hello or occasionally make small talk, they are creating weak ties. Lots of weak ties are good.

CIVIC PARTICIPATION IS DECREASING

In large part, what triggered recent research into social capital is the very measurable and well-documented decline in participation of many citizens in the American political process. For example, from 1920 (when women obtained the right to vote) through 1960, voter turnout in presidential elections had risen at the rate of 1.6 percent every four years. But since peaking in 1960, when 62.8 percent of voting-age Americans went to the polls, the voter participation rate has been dropping steadily, and by 1996 it had dropped to 48.9 percent.[80] (See Fig. 5.1 for international comparisons of voter participation).

Research by Putnam and others has turned up a number of variables that correlate with this decline. Two factors clearly connected with the decline in voter participation are the lack of interest in national affairs and the lack of trust in government officials. And while one could argue that the latter is a positive or sensible outcome of the post-Vietnam/Attica/Watergate years, it would be very difficult to make the case that this disillusionment has fueled any significant movement guided by an alternative vision for American society. In other words, even if the disillusionment makes some sense, the possibilities for radically rebuilding American society are slim as long as Americans are so disconnected. An uninformed (or misinformed) and apathetic public is not likely to challenge the policy-making establishment.

One of Putnam's most important findings is that the decline in political and social participation is, for the most part, generational. The participation rates of the younger generations are much lower than those of the older generations. And "the post-baby boom generations—roughly speaking, men and women who were born after 1964 and thus came of age in the 1980s and 1990s—are substantially less knowledgeable about public affairs, despite the proliferation of sources of information."[81]

Participation in civic affairs is facilitated by having an active social life. People who talk to others are more likely to recognize common problems or mutual desires, and they are better able to organize people into groups for political action (in the broadest sense, anything from the PTA to unions, to alternative political parties, or community organizations). Not surprisingly, researchers are finding that social interaction has decreased significantly and may be an underlying reason for the large decline in political participation. For example, the percentage of Americans (as measured by time diary studies) who say they spent any time socializing informally on a given day fell steadily from about 65 percent in 1965 to 39 percent in 1995.[82] Similarly, the average time devoted to visiting with friends, attending parties, hanging out at bars, informal conversations, etc., fell from eighty to eighty-five minutes per day in 1965 to fifty-seven minutes in 1995.

SOCIAL INTERACTION AND TRUST ARE DIMINISHING

Increased social isolation is probably a significant factor leading to the apparent decline in how much people trust each other. Most Americans today believe they live in a less trustworthy society than their parents did. In 1952, Americans were split about 50–50 on the issue of whether our society was then as upright morally as it had been in the past. In 1998, however, after nearly four decades of apparently growing cynicism, we believe, by a margin of three to one, that our society is less honest and moral than it used to be.[83]

Other survey data suggest that social trust rose from the mid-1940s to the mid-1960s, peaking in 1964. But every year since 1964 fewer people agree with the statement that "most people can be trusted" and more Americans agree that "you can't be too careful in dealing with people."[84] The decline in social trust has been sharper among younger Americans. Putnam declares that "by virtually every conceivable measure, social capital has eroded steadily and sometimes dramatically over the past two generations."[85]

Religious institutions are an important mechanism of social engage-ment with a long and influential presence in the United States, but in recent years church attendance is down. Atheists and agnostics may cheer, but consider this offering from Putnam: "Churches . . . are one of the few vital institutions left in which low-income, minority, and disadvantaged citizens of all races can learn politically relevant skills and be recruited into polit-ical action. The implication is vitally important to anyone who values egalitarian democracy: without such institutions, the class bias in American politics would be much greater."[86]

There are some trends that run counter to the overall decline in social capital. For example, there has been a rise in youth volunteering, a vigorous growth of grassroots activity among evangelical conservatives, an increase in self-help groups, and then there is the Internet, a complex issue in itself. Suffice it to say, for now, that the overall impact of the Internet isn't clear, but it's likely that it has a positive impact on social connectivity for some people but facilitates a hermitlike existence for others.

Bowling Alone makes a convincing argument that social capital is declining, but Putnam has his critics, and his argument is not universally accepted. However, in many respects the key question isn't "is social capital declining?" but "how can social capital be built?" And for those who accept the importance of building community and civic participation, *Bowling Alone* provides much insight into the many dimensions of the problem.

SOCIAL CAPITAL SHRINKS AS WE WORK MORE

One notable shortcoming in *Bowling Alone* is Putnam's inadequate and unconvincing discussion of increased work time as a cause of declining social capital. Putnam makes a brief reference to Juliet Schor's important work on the decline of leisure in a footnote, and he otherwise downplays the expansion of work as a factor in the decline of social capital. And he discusses very little of the data. But as we've seen in chapter 3 herein, a greater percentage of the American population is in the labor force than ever before. This expansion of the workforce coincides with Putnam's measured decline in social capital. For example, in 1960 the labor force participation rate (the percentage of Americans over age sixteen who are in the labor force) was 59.4 percent, but currently it is over 67 percent. In addition, the number of hours worked by many Americans has increased as well. From 1989 to 1998 middle-income families added about 135 hours a year to their work time.[87] Survey data from some of the major polling organizations reinforce the data presented in chapter 3, and conclude that leisure time has been diminishing (see Fig. 5.2).

Putnam claims that employed people are more civically and socially active than people outside the labor force and that longer work hours are often linked to more civic engagement. However, he also states that full-time employment appears to reduce home entertaining, club and church attendance, informal visiting with friends, and volunteering. And husbands of full-time working women also have lower participation. These facts lead him to declare that "one practical way to increase community engagement in America would be to make it easier for women (and men too) to work part-time if they wished."[88]

The expansion of work has been accompanied by increased commuting times, thereby further reducing time available for social and civic participation. The impact of commuting on social capital is something that Putnam recognizes, noting that ten minutes of commuting reduces social capital by 10 percent.[89]

Building social capital and building community are complex tasks that require great resources. Knowing the problem is an important first step, but the collapse of community cannot be reversed simply by good will; structural changes need to be made as well—changes that can free up the valuable resources of time and energy that lie within people everywhere. Reducing work and commuting time, creating public spaces, and using architectural planning that facilitates the development of social ties are just some of steps necessary to build social capital.

Building, or reviving, social capital is a complex matter that will require long-term structural change that will challenge many existing forms of power and ways of doing things. But there are also reforms that could be made to the political process to elicit greater citizen involvement. For example, many ideas have been put forth to increase voter participation. These include:

- Same-day voter registration, that is, permit unregistered voters to register on election day and vote right away.
- Have election "day" last more than one day.
- Make election day a half-day holiday, that is, give people time off to vote. (Election day is a two-day holiday in Italy).[90]
- Eliminate state laws that deprive convicted felons the right to vote (felony disenfranchisement deprives approximately 4 million people of the right to vote, see page 159 on felony disenfranchisement).
- Have polling places on college campuses and at work sites where there are more than 200 employees.
- Institute a system of proportional representation whereby parties are awarded seats according to the percentage of votes they receive. In countries with proportional systems, citizens are more likely to vote

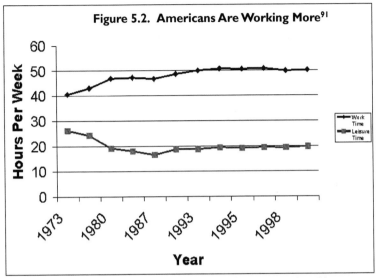

Figure 5.2. Americans Are Working More[91]

The Harris Poll. Latest: June 10–15, 1999. N=1,006 adults nationwide.
Source: www.pollingreport.com/workplay.htm#Prestige

because they know that if their party gets a small share of the vote
(say 10 or 20 percent) they still win a portion of the seats. In a
winner-take-all system, many people who support candidates or parties that have little or no chance of winning simply stay home.

- Institute instant runoff voting that allows voters to rank their choices.
  If no candidate receives a majority of the number 1 votes, the candidate with the least total of number 1 votes is eliminated. The second-
  choice votes from these ballots are then transferred to the other
  candidates and the ballots are recounted.
- Eliminate the Electoral College for presidential elections, and have
  the president selected by a majority of the popular vote.
- Fund campaigns with public money and end contributions to political parties by corporations and large donors.

CONCLUSION

Understanding the functions of the state, and how people interact with it as
citizens, is a very complex task and no short analysis can do it justice.

Based on the material presented in this chapter, there are at least three important state functions that readers should note well:

1. The state is instrumental in preventing serious economic crisis and managing periods of potential crisis. This is done partly through control of the money supply as advocated by the British economist John Maynard Keynes. And today it is done mainly through the lowering of interest rates by the Federal Reserve Board in order to loosen up the money supply when demand shrinks and the economy begins to falter. Or, conversely, the board may raise interest rates in order to tighten up the money supply and cool off the economy guided by the assumption that an "overheated" economy is more likely to crash and burn. The state also manages the general economy through government spending to stimulate demand (or aid the accumulation process). It is in this regard that deficit spending has served a vital role. When the economy goes into a recession, incomes, corporate profits, sales, and the like may all begin to fall, leaving the government with a significant decrease in tax revenue. In order to maintain government activity at prerecession levels, the government must resort to deficit spending; a cutback in government spending would likely cause the economy to take a more severe nosedive. Furthermore, since increased government spending can stimulate the economy and help avoid a major depression, it is important to not just maintain prerecession levels of spending and government activity but to actually increase them. In theory, deficit spending during recessions is balanced out by the increased revenues that accompany economic expansion.

2. The state provides a variety of carrot-and-stick social programs designed to provide a "social safety net" and a system of social control. Welfare, food stamps, Social Security, unemployment insurance, and similar programs, all help to provide a level of comfort for the poor, or the potentially poor, which deters them from making greater demands on the system or participating in various acts of rebellion. If these programs are not effective at pacifying the poor, then there are more coercive measures of social control that exist in the form of the police, the courts, jails, and prisons.

3. The state is important in managing conflicts within the bourgeoisie. The state, through its authority and relative autonomy, is able to find some common ground upon which different segments of the upper class can agree. By minimizing these disagreements the state is able to reduce the possibility of economic crisis and the creation of leadership vacuums in the state itself, of which anticapitalist forces could take advantage.

One other point deserves to be highlighted. The ability of the upper economic class to dominate the state and determine policy is commensu-

---

Felony Disenfranchisement

Most states have laws that restrict the rights of convicted felons to vote. Forty-six states and the District of Columbia prohibit inmates from voting, thirty-two states prohibit felons from voting while they are on parole, twenty-nine states also prohibit probationers, ten states disenfranchise all felons who have completed their sentences. In other words, ten states permanently deprive anyone convicted of a felony the right to vote.

Nearly four million Americans are without the right to vote due to these state laws, including 1.4 million who have completed their sentences. 1.4 million African American men are currently disenfranchised. That's 13 percent of black males, a rate seven times the national average. According to the Sentencing Project, "the scale of felony voting disenfranchisement in the U.S. is far greater than in any other nation." At least a dozen countries even allow offenders to vote while in prison.[92]

Many felony disenfranchisement laws were enacted at the end of the nineteenth century and were intended to exclude black Americans from the electoral process. A Virginia legislator remarked that the disenfranchisement law was passed "with a view to the elimination of every Negro voter." And in Louisiana, the chief justice of the state supreme court urged that such a law be passed "to establish the supremacy of the white race."[93]

---

rate with the extent of the passivity of other classes, particularly the exclusion of other classes from the major decision-making processes.

All in all, the class nature of most states is usually quite evident, and it is abundantly clear in the United States. As we shall see in the next chapter, the governments of other advanced industrial nations generally have provided more services that are beneficial to the working class. Without doubt, it is the political strength of the working class that has been the main reason for the somewhat different character of these governments.

NOTES

1. Michael Parenti, *Democracy for the Few*, 6th ed. (New York: St. Martin's Press, 1995), pp. 315–16.

2. Albert Szymanski, *The Capitalist State and the Politics of Class* (Cambridge, Mass.: Winthrop Publishers, 1978), p. 4.

3. G. William Domhoff, *Who Rules America? Power and Politics in the Year 2000* (Mountain View, Calif.: Mayfield Publishing, 1998), p. 145.

4. Harold Kerbo, *Social Stratification and Inequality* (New York: McGraw-Hill, 1991), p. 257.

5. Ibid., p. 256.

6. In Harold Kerbo's comprehensive textbook on stratification, G. William Domhoff, C. Wright Mills, Ralph Miliband, and others, are grouped together as "critical elite theorists." Kerbo, *Social Stratification and Inequality*, pp. 257–61. Randall Stokes groups Mills and Domhoff together under the heading of "elite theory" and Ian Robertson discusses these under the separate headings of "the power-elite model" and "the governing class." Randall Stokes, *Introduction to Sociology* (Dubuque, Iowa: Wm. C. Brown, 1984), pp. 381–82; Ian Robertson, *Sociology*, 3d ed. (New York: Worth, 1987), pp. 495–96.

7. C. Wright Mills, *The Power Elite* (New York: Oxford University Press, 1956), p. 7.

8. Ibid., pp. 8–9.

9. G. William Domhoff, *Who Rules America?* (Englewood Cliffs, N.J.: Prentice Hall, 1967), p. 5.

10. David A. Gold, Clarence Y. H. Lo, and Erik Olin Wright, "Recent Developments in Marxist Theories of the Capitalist State," *Monthly Review* (October 1975): 31. The classification of pluralist, instrumentalist, and structuralist perspectives was repeated in an article in *Kapitalistate* in 1976 by Gosta Esping-Anderson, Roger Friedland, and Erik Olin Wright. See "Class Struggle and the Capitalist State," in *Capitalist Society: Readings for a Critical Sociology*, ed. Richard Quinney (Homewood, Ill.: Dorsey Press, 1979).

11. See especially, G. William Domhoff, *State Autonomy or Class Dominance* (New York: Aldine De Gruyter, 1996). Regarding "business dominance theory," see Davita Silfen Glasberg and Dan Skidmore, *Corporate Welfare Policy and the Welfare State* (New York: Aldine De Gruyter, 1997), pp. 6–16.

12. G. William Domhoff, *Who Rules America Now?* (Englewood Cliffs, N.J.: Prentice Hall, 1983), pp. 139–40.

13. Ibid.

14. *David Halberstam's The Fifties*, pt. 2, The History Channel.

15. Thomas McCann, *An American Company: The Tragedy of United Fruit* (New York: Crown Publishers, 1976). See also Stephen Schlesinger and Stephen Kinzer, *Bitter Fruit* (Garden City, N.Y.: Anchor/Doubleday, 1983).

16. Felix Greene, *The Enemy* (New York: Random House, 1970), p. 189.

17. Michael Parenti, *Democracy for the Few*, 5th ed. (New York: St. Martin's Press, 1988), p. 204.

18. John Cushman, "Industry Helped Draft Clean Water Law," *New York Times,* March 22, 1995; and Stephen Engelberg, "Business Leaves the Lobby and Sits at Congress's Table," *New York Times,* March 31, 1995.

19. G. William Domhoff, *The Powers That Be* (New York: Vintage, 1978), p. 157.

20. Parenti, *Democracy for the Few*, 5th ed., p. 181.

21. Jamin B. Raskin, "Supreme Court's Double Standard," *Nation,* February 6, 1995, p. 168.

22. Center for Responsive Politics [online], www.opensecrets.org/.

23. Domhoff, *The Powers That Be*, p. 183.

24. Ibid., p. 188.

25. Ibid., p. 192.

26. Ibid.

27. Ibid., p. 196.

28. See Domhoff, *Who Rules America Now?* pp. 92–95 for a discussion of these relationships.

29. *Philanthropy and Cultural Imperialism*, ed. Robert F. Arnove (Bloomington: Indiana University Press, 1980), p. 1.

30. Barbara Howe, "The Emergence of Scientific Philanthropy, 1900–1920: Origins, Issues, and Outcomes," in Arnove, *Philanthropy and Cultural Imperialism*, p. 34.

31. Ibid., pp. 34–35.

32. Ibid., p. 47.

33. Martin Carnoy, *The State and Political Theory* (Princeton, N.J.: Princeton University Press, 1984), pp. 97–98.

34. Glasberg and Skidmore, *Corporate Welfare Policy*, p. 8.

35. Selig Perlman, *A Theory of the Labor Movement* (Philadelphia: Porcupine Press, 1928), p. 67; *Social Welfare in Society*, ed. George T. Martin and Mayer N. Zald (New York: Columbia University Press, 1981), p. 13; and George T. Martin, *Social Policy in the Welfare State* (Englewood Cliffs, N.J.: Prentice Hall, 1990), p. 23.

36. Nicos Poulantzas, *State, Power, Socialism* (London: Verso, 1978), pp. 136–37.

37. Michael Parenti, "Popular Sovereignty vs. the State," *Monthly Review* (March 1995).

38. Ibid., pp. 3–4.

39. Carnoy, *The State and Political Theory*, pp. 133–34.

40. Fred Block, *Revising State Theory* (Philadelphia: Temple University Press, 1977), p. 132.

41. Ibid., pp. 133–36.

42. James O'Connor, *The Fiscal Crisis of the State* (New York: St. Martin's Press, 1973), pp. 6–7.

43. *Statistical Abstract of the United States, 2001*, pp. 282, 286, 303.

44. Ibid., pp. 287, 303.

45. U.S. Census, *Statistical Abstract of the United States, 2001* and [online] www.census.gov/govs/state/00st00us.html.

46. Nicholas D. Kristof, "Farm Subsidies That Kill," *New York Times*, July 5, 2002.

47. Michael Yates, *Longer Hours, Fewer Jobs* (New York: Monthly Review Press, 1994), pp. 110–11.

48. Glasberg and Skidmore, *Corporate Welfare Policy*, p. 3.

49. Sidney Lens, "Socialism for the Rich," in Glen Gaviglio and David E. Raye, *Society As It Is,* 3d ed. (New York: Macmillan, 1980), p. 223.

50. Ibid., p. 225.

51. Parenti, *Democracy for the Few*, 5th ed., p. 111.

52. Ibid.

53. David Barsamian, "Corporate Power: Profits Before People, An Interview with Ralph Nader," *Z Magazine*, February 1995, p. 59. For a detailed statement by Nader, see *Testimony of Ralph Nader Before the Committee on the Budget,* U.S. House of Representatives, June 30, 1999.

54. Testimony of Ralph Nader Before the Committee on the Budget, U.S. House of Representatives, June 30, 1999 [online], www.nader.org/releases/63099.html.

55. See, for example, "The $150 Billion 'Welfare' Recipients: U.S. Corporations," by Charles M. Sennott in the *Boston Globe*, July 7, 1996.

56. Glasberg and Skidmore, *Corporate Welfare Policy*, p. 2.

57. Mark Zepezauer and Arthur Naiman, *Take the Rich off Welfare* (Tucson, Ariz.: Odonian Press, 1996), pp. 4–5.

58. Stephen Moore, "How to Slash Corporate Welfare," *New York Times,* April 5, 1995.

59. Testimony of Ralph Nader Before the Committee on the Budget, U.S. House of Representatives, June 30, 1999 [online], www.nader.org/releases/63099.html.

60. *Statistical Abstract of the United States, 2001.*

61. Michael Parenti *Democracy for the Few,* 6th ed. (New York: St. Martin's Press, 1995). See chap. 9, "A Constitution for the Few."

62. Parenti, *Democracy for the Few*, 5th ed., p. 62.

63. Parenti, *Democracy for the Few*, 6th ed., chap. 9.

64. Richard O. Boyer and Herbert M. Morais, *Labor's Untold Story* (New York: United Electrical, Radio and Machine Workers of America, 1955), p. 59.

65. Ibid., pp. 190–91.

66. Parenti, *Democracy for the Few*, 5th ed., p. 141.

67. Ibid., p. 138.

68. Alan Wolfe, *The Seamy Side of Democracy*, 2d ed. (New York: Longman, 1978), p. x.

69. Ibid., pp. x–xi.

70. Ibid.

71. Ralph McGehee, "Back in the Saddle Again," *Progressive*, August 1985, pp. 32–33.

72. Ibid.

73. Ibid.

74. Brian Glick, *War At Home* (Boston: South End Press, 1989), pp. 12–13.

75. Robert D. Putnam, *Bowling Alone: The Collapse and Revival of American Community* (New York: Simon and Schuster, 2000).

76. Ibid., p. 327.

77. Ibid., pp. 297–98.

78. Ibid., p. 21.

79. Benjamin Barber, *A Place for Us: How to Make Society Civil and Democracy Strong* (New York: Hill and Wang, 1998).

80. Putnam, *Bowling Alone,* pp. 17, 32.

81. Ibid., p. 36.

82. Ibid., p. 107.

83. Ibid., p. 139.

84. Ibid., pp. 139–40.

85. Ibid., p. 287.

86. Ibid., p. 339.

87. Louis Uchitelle, "Working Families Strain to Live Middle-Class Life," *New York Times*, September 10, 2000, p. 32.

88. Putnam, *Bowling Alone,* p. 201.

89. Ibid., p. 213.

90. Fran Shor, "One Person, One Vote—Seize the Time!" *Common Dreams News Center* [online], www.commondreams.org/views/110900-102.htm [November 9, 2000].

91. [Online], www.pollingreport.com/workplay.htm#Prestige.

92. The Sentencing Project and Human Rights Watch, *Losing the Vote: The Impact of Felony Disenfranchisement Laws in the United States,* 1998. Patricia Allard and Marc Mauer, *Regaining the Vote: An Assessment of Activity Relating to Felon Disenfranchisement Laws* (January 2000); Jon Shure and Rashida Mac-Murray, "Restoring the Right to Vote: Isn't It Time?" *New Jersey Policy Perspective* (October 2000).

93. *The Real War on Crime,* ed. Steven R. Donziger (New York: Harper-Collins, 1996), p. 127.

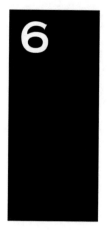

6

A COMPARATIVE VIEW OF DEVELOPED NATIONS

Thus far I have presented a great deal of information on the United States, much of which shows it in a critical light. But how does the United States compare with other nations? After all, no country is perfect, and if the United States outperforms the rest of the world on crucial social indicators, then its failings could be regarded as less serious than this book has suggested. In short, when all is said and done, isn't the United States "number one"?

In an effort to answer this question, this chapter gives the reader a sampling of comparisons primarily between the United States and other developed nations, but some data on the less-developed nations will also be included. There is much to learn by examining how other nations cope with issues such as poverty, healthcare, and crime and by being aware of how different institutional forms can play a major role in addressing various "issues" before they reach the level of "problems." In this chapter, we will see that the notion of the United States as the number one nation in the world is, on many levels, a myth; hopefully, the reader will come to recognize the nation's shortcomings and the ways in which the elite have managed to shape the society mostly according to their own interests. The success of the elite in shaping the social system is partly dependent on the acceptance by the general public that much of the social order, especially the economic system, has a life of its own and operates to the benefit of no one in particular. The belief that success is the result of individual ability and not the result of structural inequities in power and resources plays a very important role in maintaining a highly stratified social order.

International comparisons are, of course, fraught with problems. Countries with vastly different circumstances can't be readily compared. But if we focus on comparisons of the rich nations that do have a great deal of common history, culture, and/or social structure, we can learn something of value about our own society.

ATTITUDES TOWARD GOVERNMENT

Public opinion polls tend to show that American attitudes concerning government are significantly different from those in the democracies of Western Europe (see Table 6.1). Nevertheless, in the United States attitudes still tend to be fairly progressive, though one should note that a lot of the findings of polls are highly dependent on how pollsters phrase the questions. Many Americans express dissatisfaction and skepticism regarding big business and the wealthy; however, this isn't well reflected in the electoral process because many people don't vote and they don't see the candidates as really representing their interests. Figure 5.1 in the previous chapter shows voter turnout in a number of different nations; in most years the United States typically ranks at or near the bottom in voter participation.

One of the major reasons for low voter turnout in the United States is the simple fact that many potential voters are not registered. However, more complex reasons include: (1) the lack of voter identification with the candidates; (2) the inability of the major parties to put forth a sincere political platform that addresses the real concerns and needs of the majority of the population; (3) the relative conservatism on the part of the leadership of organized labor, which has not provided a strong impetus for a labor party; and (4) the role the media has played in encouraging an attitude of resigned acquiescence on the part of the general public and in maintaining a narrow dialogue that excludes many political and economic alternatives.

After the 1994 congressional elections, the conservative "Contract with America" died quickly because, although its rhetoric was popular with many people, the particulars of its programs were not. Americans may favor welfare reform, but they do not advocate abandoning the poor. They may favor tax reform, but they do not favor lowering federal income taxes (perhaps the only significant progressive tax) for the rich via a flat tax plan. And although they agree in principle with the idea of a balanced budget, they are not willing to cut Medicare, Social Security, and other social-service spending for the sake of balancing the budget.

Conversely, in most years, the majority of Americans favor reducing the military budget, but this has consistently been regarded by the conservative, and even moderate, political establishment as out of the question and beyond the limits of reasonable debate. Likewise, in spite of the ever-present barrage of propaganda telling the public that crime and big government should be their major concerns, many people still hold big business responsible for many of the nation's problems. Over 70 percent feel that business has gained too much power over too many aspects of American life, and 95 percent of the population feel that U.S. corporations owe something to the communities in which they operate and should therefore sacrifice some profit for the sake of their workers and communities.[1] Likewise, 81 percent of all respondents in a 1995 poll felt that taxes help corporations more than people.[2] And a joint *New York Times/CBS News* poll found that 79 percent of all adults agree with the statement "government is run by a few big interests looking out for themselves," while 58 percent feel they don't have much say in what the government does. A majority of those polled (55 percent) agreed that the nation needed a new political party to compete with the Republicans and Democrats.[3]

Attitudes about government, as well as the ease of registering and voting, probably have an effect on voter participation rates (see chapter 5), but another factor could be the perception that voters have regarding the possibility for success that their party of choice has. Table 6.2 shows voter turnout in twenty developed nations. The United States, which has a two-party "duopoly," has the lowest voter turnout. Every other nation has a higher voter turnout *and* more than two parties represented in the national legislature.

CROSS-NATIONAL COMPARISONS OF INCOME

One of the most notable differences between the United States and other advanced capitalist nations is the higher degree of income inequality that exists in the United States. One of the more effective ways of summarizing income inequality is by comparing the income of the lowest 10 percent of the population to the income of the highest 10 percent of the population. Table 6.3 shows the share of income received by the lowest and highest 10 percent, and the ratio between them. The United States has a highest to lowest decile ratio of 16.6 to 1. Australia has the next highest ratio (12.5).

Another way of measuring inequality is by use of the Gini index (or

Table 6.1. Attitudes Toward Government Responsibility[4]

Government should provide everyone with guaranteed basic income:

United States	21*
Austria	38
Switzerland	43
United Kingdom	61
Netherlands	50
West Germany	56
Australia	38
Italy	67

Government should provide healthcare for the sick:

United States	89
Austria	93
Switzerland	N.A.
United Kingdom	99
Netherlands	N.A.
West Germany	98
Australia	98
Italy	100

Government should reduce income differences between high- and low-income people:

United States	29
Austria	44
Switzerland	43
United Kingdom	64
Netherlands	65
West Germany	61
Australia	81
Italy	82

Government should give industry the help it needs to grow:

United States	63
Austria	87
Switzerland	N.A.
United Kingdom	95
Netherlands	N.A.
West Germany	54
Australia	75
Italy	84

Government should provide jobs for all who want one:

United States	44
Austria	40
Switzerland	52
United Kingdom	59
Netherlands	75
West Germany	77
Australia	80
Italy	82

People with high incomes should pay taxes at high rates:

United States	58
Austria	65
Switzerland	N.A.
United Kingdom	76
Netherlands	N.A.
West Germany	90
Australia	N.A.
Italy	86

*Figures given per country refer to the percentage of the pollees that agreed with the statement.

Table 6.2. Number of Political Parties and Voter Turnout[5]

Nation	Voter turnout (%)	Parties represented: In lower house	In upper house
Australia	95	3	5
Belgium	91	11	10
Luxembourg	88	5	na (not applicable)
New Zealand	88	6	
Iceland	87	6	
Austria	86	5	3
Denmark	86	10	
Italy	83	4	6
Germany	82	5	1
Sweden	81	7	
Norway	78	7	
Netherlands	73	9	7
United Kingdom	72	10	3
France	71	9	8
Canada	69	5	2
Finland	68	7	
Ireland	66	7	5
Japan	52	7	9
Switzerland	42	11	6
United States	36	2	2

coefficient). The Gini index is a number between 0 and 100 that measures the extent to which the distribution of income deviates from a perfectly equal distribution. A Gini index of 0 would represent complete equality, where everyone in a nation has the same income; conversely, a Gini index of 100 would represent complete inequality. It is a more complete indicator of income distribution than are simple comparisons of the top tenth or fifth with the lowest tenth or fifth. Figure 6.1 shows the Gini index for fourteen countries. Of the world's wealthiest nations, the United States has highest Gini index, with the United Kingdom a relatively distant second.

The Luxembourg Income Study, a sixteen-nation study conducted in the mid-1990s by the Organization for Economic Cooperation and Development (OECD), also found that income is most unequally distributed in the United States and that, in general, income inequality has been on the rise. Among some of the other interesting findings of the study was the fact

Table 6.3. Income Distribution in Fourteen Countries[6]

Country	Share of income Poorest 10%	Share of income Richest 10%	Ratio
Norway	4.1	21.8	5.3
Australia	2.0	25.4	12.5
Canada	2.8	23.8	8.5
Sweden	3.7	20.1	5.4
Belgium	3.7	20.2	5.5
United States	1.8	30.5	16.6
Netherlands	2.8	25.1	9.0
Japan	4.8	21.7	4.5
Finland	4.2	21.6	5.1
Switzerland	2.6	25.2	9.9
Luxembourg	4.0	22.0	5.4
France	2.8	25.1	9.1
United Kingdom	2.6	27.3	10.4
Denmark	3.6	20.5	5.7

Figure 6.1. The Gini Index for Income Distribution

Country	Gini Index
United States	40.8
United Kingdom	36.1
Australia	35.2
Switzerland	33.1
France	32.7
Netherlands	32.6
Canada	31.5
Luxembourg	26.9
Norway	25.8
Finland	25.6
Sweden	25.0
Belgium	25.0
Japan	24.9
Denmark	24.7

Source: UN Human Development Report

Table 6.4. Public Expenditures for Health, Education, and Social Welfare[7] (among the Non-Aged, as a Percentage of GDP)

Country	% of GDP
Sweden	28.6
Netherlands	25.1
Norway	24.8
Finland	24.7
Ireland	21.3
Belgium	21.2
France	20.6
Canada	20.1
Germany	18.5
United Kingdom	17.8
New Zealand	15.1
Spain	14.0
Australia	13.7
Italy	13.6
United States	13.0
Portugal	12.5

that the average income in the lowest 10 percent of American households was just 34.7 percent of the overall median. No other country's poorest population is that far from the median; the second farthest is Canada's at 45.8 percent, and the closest is the Netherlands' at 61.5.[8] The figures may actually understate how far removed from the average lifestyle the poor are in the United States since in many of the other nations there is a higher *social wage*. Healthcare, for example, is often provided at little or no charge in many of the other nations; furthermore, in the United States, other fringe benefits for low-wage workers are virtually nonexistent and mass transit is less available. An indication of the low social wage in the United States is given in Table 6.4.

The Luxembourg Income Study also found that poverty in the United States was greatest among the developed nations it studied, at least in a relative sense. Crossnational comparisons were standardized by examining the percentage of each nation's population that fell below 50 percent of the corresponding nation's median income. Results for some of the OECD nations are shown in Table 6.5.

In addition, the study found that inequality was increasing fastest in the United Kingdom, followed by the United States. Of the sixteen nations

Table 6.5. Poverty Rate in OECD Nations

Country	% of Population Below 50% of Median Income
United States	18.4
Australia	12.3
Canada	12.2
United Kingdom	9.1
Sweden	7.6
France	7.5
Norway	7.3

studied, income polarization increased in eight of them; only two nations (Italy and Portugal) showed any movement toward equality.[9]

CROSS-NATIONAL COMPARISONS OF "THE TAX BURDEN"

Some analysts claim that government spending can perpetuate poverty and that high rates of taxation have a crippling effect on the economy. The tax burden is often a major issue in U.S. electoral campaigns, but as Table 6.6 shows, taxes in the United States (as a percentage of GDP) are considerably lower than those in the developed nations of Western Europe. Furthermore, people in Europe are less hostile to high taxes because they see themselves as directly benefiting from government programs. In many of these nations medical care is inexpensive or free, care of the aged is a minimal expense, college education is inexpensive, and generous pension and unemployment benefits are well established. Europeans also benefit from much lower homicide rates, more advanced mass transportation, and cleaner cities. Does the tax burden act as a brake on the economy? Is it a disincentive to work and save and invest? Probably not. Table 6.6 shows the approximate tax rate and the productivity growth rate for thirteen nations, of the thirteen the United States has the lowest overall tax rate and it also had the lowest productivity growth rate during the period from 1979 to 1997.

POVERTY AND UNEMPLOYMENT

In the United States, where tax rates are considerably lower than they are in nearly all other developed nations, the impact of government transfer

Table 6.6. Government Tax Revenues (as a Percentage of GDP)

	Taxes as % of GDP[10]	Productivity Growth Rate, 1979—97[11]
Denmark	58.6	2.1
Sweden	56.2	2.0
Norway	55.2	1.8
Finland	54.0	3.5
Netherlands	51.2	1.5
Belgium	50.0	1.9
France	49.6	2.2
Austria	48.0	2.3
Italy	46.3	2.0
Germany	46.1	2.2
Spain	39.5	2.7
United Kingdom	36.4	2.0
United States	31.6	0.9

programs on poverty is much less than it is elsewhere. Government figures show that the poverty rate is lowered by 6.6 percentage points, compared to 22.5 percentage points in the United Kingdom, 21.6 points in Sweden, and 21.9 in France (see Table 6.7).

These figures rely on official government statistics, and nations measure poverty in slightly different ways. If measurements are standardized by a methodology similar to that used by the Luxembourg Income Study, the impact of taxes and transfer payments in the United States is found to have a negligible effect on poverty, while that of other nations is found to have very large effects. Table 6.8 shows the results of a study done by the Joint Center for Political and Economic Studies in Washington, D.C. The Center standardized poverty figures from eight different nations by drawing the poverty line at half of the nation's median income and looked at families headed by individuals between twenty and fifty-five years of age. The results show that the combination of taxes and income transfer programs in the United States actually increased poverty by 0.5 percent. This means that collectively, families in the United States that are below one-half of the median income are paying more in taxes than they are receiving in income benefits. In no other country was this the case.

Many nations with lower poverty rates actually have higher unemployment rates (see Table 6.9), but their lower poverty rates suggest that unem-

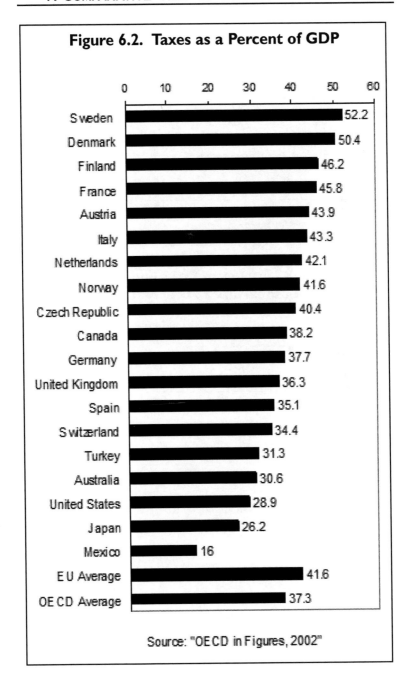

Figure 6.2. Taxes as a Percent of GDP

Source: "OECD in Figures, 2002"

Table 6.7. Impact of Taxes and Transfers on Poverty Rates[12]

Country	% Poor before Taxes and Transfers	% Poor after Taxes and Transfers	Percentage Point Change
United Kingdom	27.7	5.2	−22.5
France	26.4	4.5	−21.9
Sweden	25.9	4.3	−21.6
West Germany	21.6	2.8	−18.8
Netherlands	21.5	3.4	−18.1
Australia	19.1	6.7	−12.4
Canada	17.1	7.0	−10.1
United States	19.9	13.3	− 6.6

Table 6.8. Impact of Taxes and Transfers on Standardized Poverty Rates[13]

Country	Approx. % of Originally Poor Families Lifted Above Poverty
United States	-0.5
Canada	20.0
United Kingdom	46.0
West Germany	36.0
Sweden	44.0
France	51.0
Netherlands	61.0

ployment insurance in these nations offers better compensation and covers a greater number of the unemployed. In the United States in any given year, little more than a third of all unemployed workers actually receive unemployment benefits.[14]

CRIME AND INCARCERATION

Poverty, inequality, unemployment, and other factors combine to create social circumstances that breed crime. Like the laws that punished the poor, the vagabonds, and the thieves in the early stages of capitalism in Europe, the laws today are also designed to punish the poor and to perpetuate an

Table 6.9. Unemployment Rates in Developed Nations[15]

Country	Average annual unemployment rate, 1990—98
Japan	2.9
Switzerland	3.5
Norway	5.0
Austria	5.1
United States	5.9
Netherlands	6.0
Sweden	6.3
Germany	7.6
United Kingdom	8.1
Belgium	8.7
Australia	9.0
Canada	9.8
Italy	10.6
France	11.2
Finland	12.1
Ireland	12.7
Poland	12.7
Spain	20.0

ideology that keeps the focus of public attention on the poor rather than on the economic system that fails to create jobs, provide a living wage, and train people for better employment. Lack of dignified work and the accompanying social stigma can be a devastating blow to the human psyche and one's sense of self-esteem. The connection among employment, self-worth, and social problems is capsulized well by economist Michael Yates:

> We normally think of our economy as producing goods and services, but things are more complicated than that. As we work, we not only make useful things, we also make ourselves. Through our work, we become what we are: our work is part of what defines us as human beings. Seen in this light, unemployment takes on added significance. Work is a social experience, one of the main ways in which we connect to our fellow human beings. An unemployed person cannot make these connections and is therefore made to be less than fully human. It should not be surprising, then, that unemployment is a blow to a person's ego, to his or her sense of self-worth. Not only is the output that the unemployed person could have produced being wasted; the unemployed person is being wasted as well.[16]

Poverty, then, can be seen not only as "encouraging" crime as a means of gaining the material goods needed to survive but as a social situation that may instill the victim with despair, rage, and other powerful emotions that, in turn, may trigger violence and crime. This fact—along with the selective prosecution of many laws, the weeding out of the wealthy at various stages of prosecution and sentencing, and an ideology that sees crime as something committed by individuals from poor inner-city minority subcultures —has led to an extremely disproportionate representation of the poor and of blacks in America's jails and prisons. Perhaps more than any developed nation in the world the United States has attempted to deal with the myriad of problems associated with unemployment and poverty through strictly punitive measures. But these measures have clearly been unsuccessful. Table 6.10 shows the imprisonment rate for a variety of nations, and Table 6.11 shows selected homicide statistics. Among the most notable findings are that Russia has surpassed the United States as the nation with the highest incarceration rate; 558 per 100,000 compared to 519 per 100,000. Economic problems and social disorder have led to more crime and more imprisonment in Russia than in the Soviet Union prior to its dissolution. Before the collapse of the Soviet Union, incarceration rates were estimated to be in the range of 268–353 per 100,000.[17]

From 1989 to 1993, the U.S. incarceration rate increased 22 percent and is now five to eight times greater than the rate of most industrialized nations. Incarceration rates have increased dramatically over the past few decades, much faster than any real growth in crime.[18] Like the royal edicts in the early years of capitalist transition, the power elite in the United States have responded by punishing marginalized portions of the population rather than by making structural changes that would bring about constructive improvements. For the most part, blacks have borne the brunt of these policies. African Americans have an incarceration rate more than six times higher than that of white Americans, 1,947 per 100,000 compared to 306 per 100,000. The rate for black males is especially high; 3,822 per 100,000, more than four times the rate for black males in South Africa (851 per 100,000).[19]

During the 1990s, the homicide rate in the United States dropped significantly. Analysts disagree over the reasons for this, with some crediting stricter law enforcement and higher imprisonment rates, and others citing the improved economy. Regardless of the reason, as seen in Table 6.11, the United States still has a considerably higher homicide rate than all other highly developed nations. Two "transitional" states included in Table 6.11, Russia and

Mexico (both with serious economic displacement and rapidly changing social orders), have higher homicide rates than the United States rate.

Although all of the advanced capitalist nations have significant unemployment problems, many of the extreme social problems are minimized due to extensive social services, income transfers, job training programs, and other pro-working-class measures that exist in these nations. These services are the result of the continual struggle among social classes, which tends to be more widespread elsewhere than it is in the United States. Unionization rates are much higher in most comparable nations (see Table 6.12), and many advanced industrialized nations have strong labor or socialist parties. The political strength of the working class is directly related to its economic status.

Past studies also show that many of the world's most developed nations play a much more active role in redistributing national income and in providing a broader range of government funded services, including such social benefits as pensions, health insurance, public assistance, family allowances, and unemployment benefits.[20] One study ranked the United States seventeenth out of nineteen countries in terms of government spending for social benefits.

On some aspects of social spending, the United States appears to be generous, but often a closer look is needed. For example, according to United Nations figures, the United States spends about 13 percent of its GDP on healthcare, a greater percentage than any other highly developed country.[21] This figure may sound like a positive until one considers that healthcare in the United States tends to be much more expensive than in other countries. Overall, the typical U.S. citizen is likely to pay more for comparable medical procedures or prescription drugs. Complicating the comparison is the great inequality in healthcare delivery that exists in the United States. Access to health services is often dependent on whether or not one has a decent health insurance policy. In the United States, over 40 million people are uninsured. In contrast to many other countries, the United States relies much more heavily on private expenditures for healthcare than on public expenditures; private expenditures run four times higher than do public expenditures. In Norway, by comparison, the ratio is reversed. The U.S. political elite want to keep healthcare in the realm of the private-sector economy.[22]

The private sector does not often take on activity that is not profitable, and in the United States the government has not shown the same commitment to spending money for the social good that the social democracies of Europe have. Another example of this can be seen in the comparative statistics on educational spending (see Table 6.14). United Nations Educa-

Table 6.10. Incarceration Rates, 1992–1993[23]

Country	No. of Prisoners per 100,000 People
Russia	558
United States	519
South Africa	368
Singapore	229
Hong Kong	179
Venezuela[a]	177
Poland	160
Hungary	117
Canada	116
China	111
New Zealand	135
United Kingdom[a]	97
Mexico	97
France	84
Australia	91
Austria	88
Portugal	93
Spain	90
Switzerland	85
Germany	80
Czechoslovakia[a]	72
Denmark	66
Italy	80
Albania[a]	55
Netherlands	49
Ireland[a]	44
Sweden	69
Japan	36
India	23

[a]Figures are for a prior but recent year.

tional, Scientific, and Cultural Organization (UNESCO) figures show that the United States ranks fourteenth out of sixteen industrialized nations in spending for kindergarten through the twelfth grade. When higher education is included, the U.S. ranking goes up substantially. The United States tends to spend proportionally more on tertiary education, but since a smaller section of the population benefits from this, this pattern of spending may contribute to increased inequality.

Table 6.11. Homicide and Suicide Rates, Selected Countries (per 100,000)[24]

	Homicide Rate	Suicide Rate*	Combined Rate
Australia	1.7	14.3	16.0
Austria	0.8	19.0	19.8
Belgium	1.7	21.3	23.0
Canada	1.4	12.3	13.7
Denmark	1.1	17.0	18.1
Finland	2.4	23.8	26.2
France	0.9	19.0	19.9
Germany	0.9	14.2	15.1
Greece	1.4	3.8	5.2
Hungary	2.9	33.1	36.0
Ireland	0.9	11.3	12.2
Italy	1.3	8.2	9.5
Japan	0.6	18.6	19.2
Mexico	17.2	3.2	20.4
Netherlands	1.3	10.1	11.4
New Zealand	1.5	15.1	16.6
Norway	0.9	12.1	13.0
Poland	2.8	14.3	17.1
Russia	22.9	35.3	58.2
Spain	0.9	8.6	9.5
Sweden	1.2	14.2	15.4
United Kingdom	0.7	7.4	8.1
United States	6.6	11.3	17.9

*Cause of death is listed as "self-inflicted injuries."

WORK AND LEISURE

The relative weakness of the American working class is also reflected in a decrease in leisure time. Economist Juliet Schor has documented the loss of leisure in her book *The Overworked American*. Challenging the belief that capitalism has "delivered us from excessive toil," Schor argues that eighteenth- and nineteenth-century Europe and America probably had the "longest and most arduous work schedules in the history of humankind."[25] Twelve-hour, even sixteen-hour workdays were common, and working conditions were deplorable. Medieval societies, in contrast, tended to have many holidays and opportunities for leisure; and leisure time in ancient Greece and Rome appears to have been plentiful. Anthropologists have found that people who lived in primitive hunting and gathering societies

Table 6.12. Labor Force Unionization Rates[26]

Country	% of Total Labor Force in Unions
Sweden	85
Finland	71
Norway	55
Belgium	53
United Kingdom	42
Australia	42
Italy	40
Canada	35
Japan	27
Netherlands	25
United States	17
France	12

might have worked a surprisingly small amount. For example, !Kung Bushmen in Africa worked about fifteen hours per week, and in the Sandwich Islands men worked just four hours a day.[27]

In chapter 3 we saw how the percentage of the American population in the labor force has been growing in the past few decades. In addition, Schor points out that not only are more people working but they are working more.[28] According to Schor's calculations, from 1969 to 1987, the average worker added 163 hours to his or her work year. In particular, the amount that women have been working has increased most substantially, but men's work time has grown as well (see Table 6.15).

How does the number of hours worked in the United States compare to that of similar countries? In the mid-1990s, the typical work year for an American worker was 1,950 hours. The nation with the highest number of yearly work hours was Japan with about 2,150. In Japan overwork was viewed by many as a serious national problem, and it was estimated that in Japan 10,000 workers a year were dying from *Karoshi*—overwork.[29] Due to a concerted effort on the part of many, including Japan's largest labor union, the average number of hours worked per year by Japanese workers has been declining, meanwhile work hours have risen in the United States. Workers in the United States now average more hours on the job than any other high-income nation. U.S. manufacturing employees work about 320 more hours per year than their German and French counterparts (Fig. 6.3).[30]

Compensation for manufacturing workers is often higher in the world's most economically advanced nations than in the United States, and vacation time is usually substantially longer (see Table 6.16 and Fig. 6.4).

Table 6.13. Unemployment Compensation Rates (as a Percentage of GDP)[31]

Country	% of GDP
Netherlands	2.17
Canada	1.92
Australia	1.75
France	1.46
Germany	1.32
United Kingdom	0.95
Sweden	0.80
Italy	0.60
United States	0.58
Japan	0.32

One reason that Americans work more is because their vacations are typically shorter (see Fig. 6.4). Most European workers, for example, receive four to six weeks of paid vacation, which is required by law. But American workers average about three weeks of paid vacation, and since these are not mandated by law, many workers, especially those in the lowest-paying occupations, receive little or no paid vacation. These workers are also less likely to receive job training to improve their status. No comparable nation spends as little as the United States on job training, job creation, or on subsidizing wages.[32]

WHERE WOMEN STAND

The nineteenth-century French social critic and socialist Charles Fourier (1772–1837) declared that "in any given society the degree of women's emancipation is the natural measure of the general emancipation."[33] As we look at the situation of women in today's world, we can see they are far from emancipated; and if Fourier's dictum is accurate, the same holds true for the whole of humanity.

In spite of positive gains, such as increased literacy and increased enrollment in secondary and tertiary schools, there are still many areas of great inequality between men and women. According to the best available data, women make up 70 percent of the world's poor and two-thirds of the world's illiterate. Many legal systems treat them as less than equal. Worldwide they hold just 10 percent of parliamentary seats, 6 percent of cabinet-

Table 6.14. Comparison of
Educational Expenditures (Grades K–12)[34]

Rank	Nation	% of GDP*
1	Sweden	7.0
2	Austria	5.9
3	Switzerland	5.8
4	Norway	5.3
5	Belgium	4.9
6	Japan (tie)	4.8
7	Denmark (tie)	4.8
8	Canada	4.7
9	France (tie)	4.6
10	West Germany (tie)	4.6
11	Netherlands (tie)	4.5
12	United Kingdom (tie)	4.5
13	Italy	4.2
14	United States	4.1
15	Australia	3.9
16	Ireland	3.8

*Percentages have been adjusted for size of school-aged population.

level positions, and 14 percent of managerial and administrative jobs. Women work longer hours than men in almost every one of the world's nations. In developing countries women do an estimated 53 percent of the work, and in industrial nations they do about 51 percent; yet in spite of this greater work burden, women receive far less income than do men. Just 26 percent of all earned income goes to women. In both the developed and the underdeveloped nations of the world, women spend a greater proportion of their time doing unpaid labor.[35]

In general, the relative position of women is better in the developed world, but in some less-developed nations very significant progress has been made. However, the status of women does vary substantially from nation to nation—and in some surprising ways. Table 6.17 shows women's pay in comparison to men's.

An accurate assessment of the status of women can be obtained only by examining gender differences in economics, politics, and culture, but comprehensive measures in each of these realms really don't exist. However, there are some good general indicators. In politics, for example, data is available regarding the percent of government officials of each sex, and, as we shall soon see, this is often a good indication of the general level of

Table 6.15. U.S. Annual Hours of Paid Employment[36]

	1969	1987	Change
All workers	1,786[a]	1,949	+163
Men	2,054	2,152	+98
Women	1,406	1,711	+305

[a] Figures given apply to labor force participants only.

emancipation and power of women in a nation. Table 6.18 shows countries ranked in order of their Human Development Index (to which we shall return shortly) score and includes each nation's Gender Empowerment Measure (GEM) ranking. The GEM is a composite index developed by the United Nations that measures gender inequality in three dimensions—economic participation and decision making, political participation and decision making, and power over economic resources. The United States, while scoring relatively well on some of the economic indicators of gender equality, actually fares quite poorly on some of the political indicators. For example, only 13.8 percent of the seats in Congress are held by women. On the ministerial level, the United States does much better, with 31.8 percent of those positions held by women—no doubt a product of high-level elected officials trying to appease women voters by appointing women to highly visible national positions.

ALTERNATIVE DEVELOPMENT INDEXES

Traditionally, the relative development of nations has been measured in strictly economic terms using the GDP. The shortcomings of this method will be discussed in chapter 7. In recent years some alternate measures of development have been devised, and some of these make a special effort to ascertain the relative well-being of women. One of the most frequently cited is the Human Development Index (HDI) used by the United Nations. Table 6.19 shows the twenty-five countries with the highest scores on the HDI, as well as their GDP per capita. Several less-developed countries are included for the sake of comparison. The HDI combines income with life expectancy and education to give a general indication of the nation's level of development. Note that several of the oil-rich nations have high GDPs but score low on the HDI. The implication is that wealth is highly concentrated and that the population at large does not benefit very much from the

Table 6.16. Hourly Compensation, 2000[37]

United States	$19.86
Canada	16.16
Japan	22.00
Austria	19.46
Belgium	21.11
Denmark	20.44
Finland	19.50
France	16.38
Germany	22.99
Italy	14.66
Netherlands	19.08
Norway	22.05
Spain	10.85
Sweden	20.14
Switzerland	21.24
United Kingdom	15.88

Work and Leisure in Germany

Germany is one of the world's leaders in vacation time, with six weeks of paid time off a year. Public holidays add another ten days. Brigitte Dunst is a typical worker in a BMW factory in Regensburg. She works just four days a week, and since her work schedule varies from week to week she sometimes ends up with five days off in a row. "It's better than a long weekend, more like a mini-vacation. We might go skiing, or it's only a short drive to where we can hike in the mountains. In five days off, I might go for a motorcycle ride, or play tennis with a friend or take the dog for a walk along the Danube."[38]

Diana Orlet is a file clerk for Schering Chemical Company in Berlin. Diana is a single mother, but her situation contrasts sharply with that of many single mothers in the United States: she works just six hours a day, is paid a decent wage, receives full benefits—healthcare, Social Security, and unemployment insurance (all paid for by the government)—and has thirty-one vacation days per year. Her free time enables her to spend time with her child and pursue her hobbies: aerobics, bike riding, and learning other languages.[39]

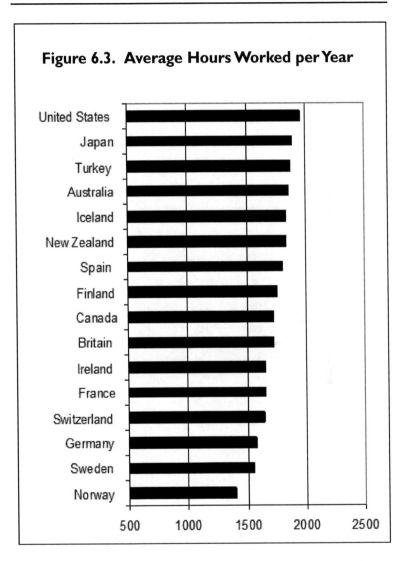

Figure 6.3. Average Hours Worked per Year

Source: The Time Sizing Wire www.timesizing.com/gts0107a.htm
based on figures from the International Labor Organization

Figure 6.4. Number of Vacation Days per Year Required by Law

Note: Figures for Germany and USA are averages, not required by law.
Source: The Timesizing Wire www.timesizing.com/1vacatns.htm

Table 6.17. Ratio of Female Income to Male Income[40]

HDI Rank		
1	Norway	0.63
2	Australia	0.67
3	Canada	0.61
4	Sweden	0.68
5	Belgium	0.43
6	United States	0.61
7	Iceland	0.62
8	Netherlands	0.51
9	Japan	0.43
10	Finland	0.66
11	Switzerland	0.49
12	Luxembourg	na
13	France	na
14	United Kingdom	0.61
15	Denmark	0.70
16	Austria	0.48
17	Germany	0.50
18	Ireland	0.38
19	New Zealand	0.65
20	Italy	0.44
21	Spain	0.42
22	Israel	0.50
23	Greece	0.44
24	Hong Kong	na
25	Cyprus	na
26	Singapore	0.49
38	Poland	0.61
43	Kuwait	na
51	Mexico	0.37
55	Russia	0.63

nation's wealth. Qatar, for example, has a relatively high GDP ($18,789), high enough to place it in the top twenty-five, but when the educational and life expectancy indexes are factored in, it drops twenty-five places. The United States drops four places when the HDI and GDP per capita are compared. Sweden, in contrast, rises fifteen places.[41]

The United Nations has another index designed to give some indication of the relative standing of women compared to men, the Gender-related Development Index (GDI). The GDI ranks nations according to the share of total income that women earn, women's life expectancy and literacy compared to men's, as well as women's enrollment in primary, secondary, and tertiary schools. The GDI rankings for the top twenty-five nations are shown in Table 6.20, as are life expectancy, and adult literacy statistics.

Table 6.18. HDI and GEM

HDI Rank	Country	Gender Empowerment Measure Rank	Seats in parliament held by women (%)	Female legislators, senior officials and managers (%)	Female professional and technical workers (%)	Ratio of estimated female to male earned income
1	Norway	1	36.4	25	49	0.64
2	Sweden	3	42.7	29	49	0.68
3	Canada	7	23.6	35	53	0.62
4	Belgium	14	24.9	19	50	0.44
5	Australia	10	26.5	26	48	0.69
6	United States	11	13.8	45	54	0.62
7	Iceland	2	34.9	27	53	0.61
8	Netherlands	6	32.9	27	46	0.52
9	Japan	32	10.0	9	45	0.44
10	Finland	5	36.5	27	56	0.70
11	Switzerland	13	22.4	22	42	0.50
12	France	na	10.9	na	na	na
13	United Kingdom	16	17.1	33	45	0.61
14	Denmark	4	38.0	23	50	0.70
15	Austria	12	25.1	28	49	0.50
16	Luxembourg	na	16.7	na	na	na
17	Germany	8	31.0	27	50	0.50
18	Ireland	17	13.7	34	50	0.40
19	New Zealand	9	30.8	38	54	0.67
20	Italy	31	9.1	19	44	0.44
21	Spain	15	26.6	32	45	0.43
22	Israel	22	13.3	26	55	0.52
23	Hong Kong	na	na	25	38	na
24	Greece	41	8.7	25	47	0.44
25	Singapore	23	11.8	23	42	0.50
37	Poland	24	20.7	33	61	0.61
45	Kuwait	na	0.0	na	na	na
51	Qatar	na	na*	na	na	na
54	Mexico	38	15.9	24	41	0.38
60	Russia	53	6.4	37	64	0.64
71	Saudi Arabia	na	na*	na	na	na
73	Brazil	na	6.7	na	62	na
96	China	na	21.8	na	na	na
109	Vietnam	na	26.0	na	na	na
110	Indonesia	na	8.0	na	na	na
148	Nigeria	na	3.3	na	na	na
173	Sierra Leone	na	8.8	na	na	na

Source: Human Development Report 2002
*Has never had a parliament.

Some additional nations beyond the top twenty-five are included for the sake of comparison. The United States ranks sixth, although it should be noted that the United States ranked first on the GDI in 1970. In other recent years, Afghanistan had the lowest GDI of all countries rated, but in the 2002 *Human Development Report* Afghanistan was unranked.

The HDI, the GDI, and the GEM all add to our understanding of the level of development existing in various nations, certainly more than do simple GDP per capita figures. However, they still fall short in many ways. For example, these existing rating systems tell us nothing about the degree of racial discrimination or religious persecution that may exist in a society, nor do they give us an indication of the state of the environment or access to various social services such as medical care and public transportation. This may be asking too much from any one (or even several) development indexes, but it nevertheless underscores the fact that a true understanding of any particular society involves an examination of many aspects of life.

An example of an important indicator of well-being (and a society's commitment to its children) not measured by any of the above indexes is a country's maternity leave policy. The United States has a very basic policy that ensures a mother's right to retain her job only within twelve weeks of the date she leaves it to have the baby. No pay is mandated for that twelve-week period, and the law applies only to people who work for companies with at least fifty employees (61 percent of all American workers are employed by companies with fewer than fifty employees). Although some employers have much more generous maternity leave policies, many do not go beyond the minimum. Some of the most progressive maternity leave policies are those that have been instituted in Finland and Sweden. In Finland the mother gets a twelve-month paid maternity leave, after which either parent can stay at home until the child is three years old. The parent receives monetary compensation for that time, and the parent's employment is guaranteed at the end of the leave. Alternatively, the community will arrange child care for parents while they return to their jobs. In addition, Finland permits parents with children under the age of four the right to shorten their workday by two hours. Sweden, also, has a very extensive paid maternity and paternity leave policy, permitting parents to shorten their workweek by two hours per day until the child reaches age ten.[42]

In Italy mothers are required to take five months' leave, and they receive full pay. In Great Britain women receive eighteen weeks of leave: six weeks are paid at 90 percent of their average earnings, and for the remaining twelve weeks they receive about $85 per week. In France

Table 6.19. Human Development Index (Compared to GDP Per Capita)

HDI Rank	Country	GDP per capita (PPP US$)	GDP per capita rank minus HDI rank	Life expectancy at birth
1	Norway	29,918	2	78.5
2	Sweden	24,277	15	79.7
3	Canada	27,840	4	78.8
4	Belgium	27,178	5	78.4
5	Australia	25,693	7	78.9
6	United States	34,142	− 4	77.0
7	Iceland	29,581	− 2	79.2
8	Netherlands	25,657	5	78.1
9	Japan	26,755	2	81.0
10	Finland	24,996	6	77.6
11	Switzerland	28,769	− 5	78.9
12	France	24,223	6	78.6
13	United Kingdom	23,509	7	77.7
14	Denmark	27,627	− 6	76.2
15	Austria	26,765	− 5	78.1
16	Luxembourg	50,061	−15	77.4
17	Germany	25,103	− 2	77.7
18	Ireland	29,866	−11	76.6
19	New Zealand	20,070	5	77.6
20	Italy	23,626	− 1	78.5
21	Spain	19,472	4	78.5
22	Israel	20,131	1	78.7
23	Hong Kong	25,153	− 9	79.5
24	Greece	16,501	10	78.2
25	Singapore	23,356	− 4	77.6
37	Poland	9,051	16	73.3
45	Kuwait	15,799	−10	76.2
51	Qatar	18,789	−25	69.6
54	Mexico	9,023	1	72.6
60	Russia	8,377	− 2	66.1
71	Saudi Arabia	11,367	−26	71.6
73	Brazil	7,625	−13	67.7
96	China	3,976	0	70.5
109	Vietnam	1,996	19	68.2
110	Indonesia	3,043	1	66.2
148	Nigeria	896	9	51.7
173	Sierra Leone	490	0	38.9

Source: Human Development Report, 2002.

Table 6.20. Gender-related Development Index

HDI Rank	Country	GDI rank	Life expectancy at birth Female	Male	Adult literacy rate Female	Male	HDI rank minus GDI rank
1	Norway	3	81.5	75.6	99.9	99.9	− 2
2	Sweden	4	82.2	77.2	99.9	99.9	− 2
3	Canada	5	81.5	76.0	99.9	99.9	− 2
4	Belgium	2	81.5	75.2	99.9	99.9	2
5	Australia	1	81.8	76.1	99.9	99.9	4
6	United States	6	79.9	74.1	99.9	99.9	0
7	Iceland	7	81.5	76.8	99.9	99.9	0
8	Netherlands	9	80.8	75.4	99.9	99.9	− 1
9	Japan	11	84.4	77.4	99.9	99.9	− 2
10	Finland	8	81.1	73.9	99.9	99.9	2
11	Switzerland	14	82.0	75.6	99.9	99.9	− 3
12	France	12	82.4	74.7	99.9	99.9	0
13	United Kingdom	10	80.2	75.2	99.9	99.9	3
14	Denmark	13	78.7	73.8	99.9	99.9	1
15	Austria	15	81.1	74.9	99.9	99.9	0
16	Luxembourg	19	80.5	74.1	99.9	99.9	− 3
17	Germany	16	80.7	74.5	99.9	99.9	1
18	Ireland	17	79.2	74.0	99.9	99.9	1
19	New Zealand	18	80.2	74.9	99.9	99.9	1
20	Italy	20	81.6	75.2	98.0	98.9	0
21	Spain	21	82.0	75.0	96.8	98.6	0
22	Israel	22	80.6	76.7	92.4	96.8	0
23	Hong Kong	23	82.4	76.9	90.2	96.5	0
24	Greece	25	80.9	75.6	96.0	98.5	− 1
25	Singapore	24	79.8	75.4	88.4	96.3	1
37	Poland	36	77.5	69.2	99.7	99.7	0
45	Kuwait	44	78.6	74.5	79.7	84.0	− 2
51	Qatar	48	71.3	68.7	83.1	80.4	− 1
54	Mexico	49	76.0	70.0	89.5	93.4	0
60	Russia	52	72.5	60.1	99.4	99.7	2
71	Saudi Arabia	72	73.0	70.5	66.9	83.1	−10
73	Brazil	64	72.0	64.1	85.4	85.1	0
96	China	77	72.8	68.5	76.3	91.7	3
109	Vietnam	89	70.6	65.9	91.4	95.5	2
110	Indonesia	91	68.2	64.3	82.0	91.8	1
148	Nigeria	124	51.9	51.5	55.7	72.4	1
173	Sierra Leone	na	40.2	37.6	na	na	na

Note: 173 countries have an HDI rank, but only 146 have a GDI rank.
Source: Human Development Report, 2002.

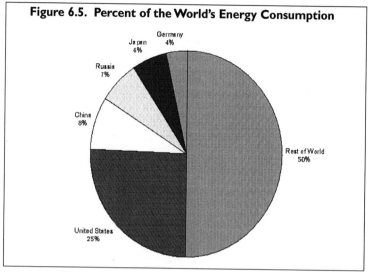

Figure 6.5. Percent of the World's Energy Consumption

women get sixteen to twenty-six weeks of maternity leave, during which time they receive full pay. German women also receive full pay for their fourteen-week leave.[43]

It's important to note that nations with a greater representation of women in the national law-making body have some of the most generous maternity leave policies and best national healthcare programs. Forty-three percent of Sweden's parliamentary members are women, for example, and women hold 55 percent of upper-level ministerial positions. In the United States, where Congress is severely male-dominated, these issues are rarely ever raised for consideration.

ENERGY CONSUMPTION AND POLLUTION

Another area to consider when comparing the state of advanced nations is energy consumption and pollution, especially in view of rapid population growth and depletion of the earth's resources. Figure 6.5 shows that just five nations (United States, China, Russia, Japan, and Germany) consume 50 percent of the world's energy production. Thus when it comes to under-standing resource use and pollution, it may be the wealthy nations of the world that pose the biggest ecological threat, not population growth in the Third World.

Table 6.21. Air Pollution Emissions and Municipal Waste per Capita[44]

Country	Sulfur Oxides (kilograms)	Nitrogen Oxides (kilograms)	Carbon Dioxide (tons)	Municipal Waste Generated (kilograms per capita)
United States	69	80	20	720
Australia	101	118	17	690
Belgium	24	33	12	480
Canada	90	68	16	500
Denmark	21	47	11	560
Finland	20	51	12	410
France	16	29	6	590
Germany	16	22	10	460
Greece	48	35	8	370
Ireland	49	34	10	560
Italy	23	31	7	460
Japan	7	11	9	400
Mexico	24	17	4	310
Netherlands	8	28	11	560
New Zealand	12	46	8	350
Norway	7	51	8	600
Spain	49	32	6	390
Sweden	10	38	6	360
United Kingdom	34	35	9	480

Table 6.22. Nuclear Waste Generated per Year[45]

Country	Tons
United States	2,100
Canada	1,340
France	1,130
Japan	964
United Kingdom	820

The United States ranks in first or second place as the largest per capita producer of major air pollutants, we create more municipal waste per person than any other country, and we are the largest per capita producer of nuclear waste, a dangerous by-product of energy production that remains radioactive for hundreds of years and is extremely difficult, if not impossible, to dispose of safely (see Tables 6.21 and 6.22).

It is estimated that in 2005, over seven billion metric tons of carbon

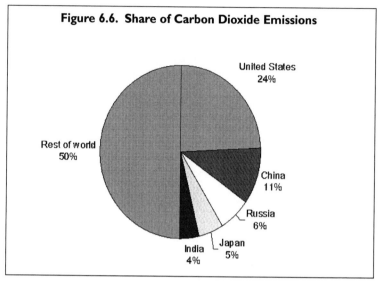

Figure 6.6. Share of Carbon Dioxide Emissions

United States 24%

Rest of world 50%

China 11%

Russia 6%

Japan 5%

India 4%

dioxide will be emitted into the earth's atmosphere as a result of the world's use of fossil fuels (petroleum, natural gas, and coal). The United States will be responsible for roughly a quarter of this amount and the continued mass production and use of auto-centered transportation, along with recently loosened emissions standards for automobiles, will jeopardize the health of the planet. Scientists estimate that for each gallon of gasoline burned by an automobile, five *pounds* of carbon are released into the atmosphere.[46]

One other international comparison is worth a brief mention. It is common for Americans to believe that the United States doles out a great deal of foreign aid, and while spending on international affairs may be fairly high, the bulk of that spending is for military assistance. The U.S. government spends billions of dollars for direct military assistance and U.S. arms manufacturers are the world's largest arms merchants. A report issued by the Congressional Research Service in August of 2002 noted that the United States has had the largest share of both new contracts and deliveries to the world for at least eight years in a row. For the year 2001, U.S. arms manufacturers made new agreements worth $12.1 billion and delivered $9.7 billion worth of arms, making up 45 percent of the world market.[47]* When it comes to real development assistance the United States ranks very low. Figure 6.7 shows that U.S.

---

*The data on new U.S. sales agreements only include government-to-government sales, leaving out potentially large commercial sales numbers. Thus, the amount reported by the CRS is an understatement of the total.

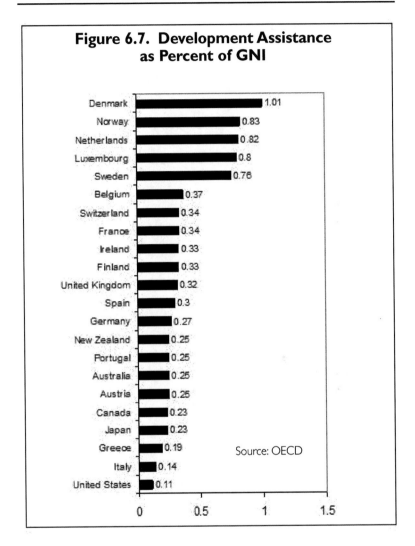

Figure 6.7. Development Assistance as Percent of GNI

Face-off: U.S. vs. Canada

Realizing that the various indexes discussed previously can give only a superficial indication of the relative standings of nations, let us briefly take a look at some more detailed comparisons between two countries, the United States and Canada, which are similar in size (though not total population), history, culture, and per capita GNP.

On most indicators of national well-being, the social democracies of Western Europe outperform both the United States and Canada. But in many categories Canada outperforms the United States, sometimes by a wide margin.[48]

- The poverty rate in the United States hovers around 12 to 14 percent. Canada's poverty rate is just 7 percent.
- The United States spends more on healthcare—13.1 percent of its GDP—than any country in the world, but still does not provide coverage for all of its citizens; over forty million American citizens are without any kind of health insurance. Canada spends 9.1 percent of its GDP and provides coverage for all citizens.
- The United States has a mortality rate of 8 deaths per 1,000 children under age five. Canada's rate is 6 deaths per 1,000.
- Life expectancy in Canada is 78.8 years, in the United States it is 77.
- In Canada, the typical citizen spends $2,391 per year for healthcare (public and private). In the United States per capita expenditures are $4,180 per year.
- Canadians smoke an average of 1,989 cigarettes per year. Americans smoke 2,372.
- The United States has a very minimal maternity leave policy; Canadian women receive seventeen to eighteen weeks of paid maternity leave.
- The U.S. homicide rate is nearly five times higher than Canada's; 6.6 per 100,000 compared to 1.4 per 100,000.
- During the late 1980s, the United States was the world's most prolific producer of hazardous waste—110,000 tons of hazardous waste per 100,000 people; Canada ranked second with less than one-eighth that rate—12,500 tons per 100,000.
- The United States spends 5.4 percent of its GDP in public dollars on education, compared with 6.9 percent in Canada.
- When fourteen-year-olds in seventeen countries were given a science test, the United States ranked fifteenth, above only the Philippines and Hong Kong; Canada ranked fourth.
- The United States has won the most Nobel Prizes in science, but twenty-eight nations have more scientists and technicians per capita than does the United States.
- CEOs in the United States make 531 times more than the average manufacturing worker; in Canada the ratio is 20 to 1.
- The United States has one of the lowest voter turnout rates of any industrialized democracy; 49 percent in the 2000 presidential election. In Canada the rate of turnout among the voting-age population is generally some twenty points higher.

development assistance as a percent of Gross National Income (GNI) is far below the UN target of .7 percent. In fact, in proportion to the size of its economy the United States gives the lowest amount of aid of all the member nations of the OECD's Development Assistance Committee (DAC).

From the information presented in this chapter it is clear that although the United States has a great productive capacity, it is not geared toward meeting the needs of many of its people. Many nations provide their citizens with better social benefits. The willingness of the U.S. government to provide such benefits receded when prolonged economic stagnation set in starting in the 1970s, and was compounded by domestic neoliberal policies enacted by the Reagan administration in the 1980s. More so than in other developed nations, the U.S. corporate class, which holds most of the nation's wealth and makes its key decisions, has elected to pursue profits at the expense of the needs of whole segments of the population. Neither the private sector nor the government has felt compelled to vigorously address such problems as poverty, hunger, health, and housing that are affecting tens of millions of people. Some analysts have even gone so far as to suggest that a process of underdevelopment may be taking place within the United States.[49]

NOTES

1. Louis Harris poll in *BusinessWeek,* March 11, 1996, pp. 64–65.

2. "Deepening Cynicism Leaves Niche for Third Party," *Star Ledger* (Newark, N.J.), August 1, 1995.

3. R. W. Apple Jr., "Poll Shows Disenchantment with Politicians and Politics," *New York Times*, August 12, 1995.

4. Austin Ranney, *Governing: An Introduction to Political Science* (Upper Saddle River, N.J.: Prentice Hall, 1996), p. 163.

5. United Nations, *Human Development Report, 1999*, p. 217.

6. United Nations, *Human Development Report, 2001*, p. 182.

7. OECD, *Income Distribution in OECD Countries* (Paris: OECD, 1995), p. 32.

8. Organization for Economic Cooperation and Development (OECD), *Income Distribution in OECD Countries* (Paris: OECD, 1995).

9. OECD, *Income Distribution in OECD Countries* (Paris: OECD, 1995), p. 80.

10. OECD data, as published in Nathaniel C. Nash, "Europeans Shrug as Taxes Go Up," *New York Times*, February 16, 1995.

11. Lawrence Mishel, Jared Bernstein, and John Schmidt, *The State of Work-*

ing America, 2000/2001 (Washington, D.C.: Economic Policy Institute, 2001), p. 376.

12. Lawrence Mishel and Jared Bernstein, *The State of Working America, 1994–95* (Washington, D.C.: Economic Policy Institute, 1994), p. 349.

13. Reprinted in Randy Albeda, "Left in the Dust: U.S. Trails Other Nations in Support for the Poor," in Randy Albeda et al., eds., *Real World Micro*, 5th ed. (Somerville, Mass.: Economic Affairs Bureau, 1995), pp. 81–82.

14. Economic Policy Institute [online], epinet.org/.

15. Annual averages for 1990–98. *Human Development Report, 2001* (United Nations), p. 199.

16. Michael Yates, *Longer Hours, Fewer Jobs: Employment and Unemployment in the United States* (New York: Monthly Review Press, 1994), pp. 66–67.

17. Marc Mauer, *Americans Behind Bars: The International Use of Incarceration, 1992–1993* (Washington, D.C.: Sentencing Project, 1994), p. 5.

18. See Steven R. Donziger, ed., *The Real War on Crime* (New York: Harper-Collins, 1996), for a wealth of information regarding trends in crime rates and incarceration rates, as well as a provocative analysis of the faulty reasoning underlying U.S. criminal justice policies.

19. Mauer, *Americans Behind Bars*, pp. 6–7.

20. Vincent A. Mahler and Claudio J. Katz, "Social Benefits in Advanced Capitalist Countries: A Cross-National Assessment," in *Comparing Nations and Cultures*, ed. Alex Inkeles and Masamichi Sasaki (Englewood Cliffs, N.J.: Prentice Hall, 1996), p. 358.

21. United Nations, *Human Development Report, 2002*, p. 166.

22. United Nations Development Program, *Human Development Report, 1995*, p. 203.

23. Marc Mauer, *Americans Behind Bars: One Year Later* (Washington, D.C.: Sentencing Project, 1992), p. 5; and Marc Mauer, *Americans Behind Bars: The International Use of Incarceration, 1992–1993* (Washington, D.C.: Sentencing Project, 1994), pp. 3–4.

24. United Nations, *Demographic Yearbook, 1999*.

25. Juliet B. Schor, *The Overworked American: The Unexpected Decline of Leisure* (New York: Basic Books, 1993), p. 6.

26. United Nations, *Human Development Report, 1995*, p. 201.

27. Schor, *The Overworked American*, p. 10.

28. Ibid., p. 29.

29. Oregon Public Broadcasting, *Running Out of Time*, 1994, videotape.

30. Schor, *The Overworked American*, p. 2.

31. Mishel and Bernstein, *The State of Working America, 1994–95*, p. 360.

32. Mishel and Bernstein, *The State of Working America, 1994–95*, pp. 357–59.

33. Friedrich Engels, "Socialism Utopian and Scientific," in *The Essential Works of Marxism*, ed. Arthur P. Mandel (New York: Bantam Books, 1961), p. 52.

34. Economic Policy Institute, *Shortchanging Education: How U.S. Spending on Grades K–12 Lags Behind Other Industrial Nations* (Washington, D.C.: Economic Policy Institute, 1990), p. 11.

35. UNDP, *Human Development Report, 1995*, pp. 88–89.

36. Schor, *The Overworked American*, p. 29.

37. Bureau of Labor Statistics [online], ftp://ftp.bls.gov/pub/special.requests/ForeignLabor/supptab.txt.

38. Edward Dolnick, "Why German Autoworker Brigitte Dunst Loves Her Four-Day Workweek," *UTNE Reader*, May–June 1995, p. 65.

39. Oregon Public Broadcasting, *Running Out of Time*, 1994.

40. United Nations, *Human Development Report, 2001,* pp. 214–17.

41. UNDP, *Human Development Report, 2002*, p. 149.

42. UNDP, *Human Development Report, 1995*, p. 8.

43. Celestine Bohlen, "Where Every Day Is Mother's Day," *New York Times*, May 12, 1996.

44. United Nations, *Human Development Report, 2001*.

45. *Statistical Abstract of the United States, 2001*, p. 838.

46. Bill McKibben, *Hope, Human and Wild: True Stories of Living Lightly on the Earth* (St. Paul, Minn.: Hungry Mind Press, 1995).

47. Tamar Gabelnick, "The United States Is Still #1 in Arms Sales," *Common Dreams News Center* [online], www.commondreams.org/views02/0810-02.htm.

48. Sources for the United States/Canada comparison include *Social Policy* (summer 1992); the *Statistical Abstract of the United States*, various years; the United Nations, *Human Development Report, 1999, 2001*, and *2002*; and the International Institute for Democracy and Electoral Assistance [online], www.idea.int/vt/index.cfm.

49. Walden Bello, with Shea Cunningham and Bill Rau, *Dark Victory: The United States, Structural Adjustment, and Global Poverty* (London: Pluto Press, 1994), esp. pp. 95–104; Kevin Danaher, "Is the U.S. Becoming a Third World Country?" *Global Exchange* (fall 1995); Takis Fotopoulis, "Development or Democracy?" *Society and Nature* 3, no. 1 (1995): esp. 88–89.

7

THE SOCIOLOGY
OF DEVELOPMENT

The study of development in the Third World today cannot be undertaken without recognizing the imbalance of power that exists between the more-developed countries and the less-developed ones. Development in the Third World, or the lack of it, is deeply affected by decisions made in the First World. The patterns of economic growth, stagnation, and political and economic power that exist in developed nations such as the United States have gradually been extended beyond national borders, helping to create the intricate web of international relations that currently exists.

This chapter looks at a variety of theories of development and analyzes their contributions to our understanding of development (as well as global polarization) in the Third World today. We will consider their ability to answer such questions as Why are some nations more "advanced" than others? How do nations "develop"? What forces are responsible for the great poverty that exists in the world today? And is the relationship between the advanced nations and the less-developed nations one of helpful assistance or of exploitation? In particular, we will focus on the role of the United States, which is the leading political, economic, and military force on the international scene.

On the most basic level one might suppose that the key ingredients to development are the resources available to a people and the ability of these people to take advantage of them. Thus, a group of people living on the edge of a desert region far from any major body of water might not be expected to develop much in the way of transportation and trade. Their economic and social development might progress very little over long periods of time. In contrast, a people living in a fairly rich environment, on the shores of an ocean or great river, may progress very quickly. If their environment is rich enough, they will be able to produce enough for subsistence rather easily, and this could free up a significant amount of time or perhaps a whole class of people who could devote their energies to exploration and experimentation. Such activity will most likely bring new advances and increased development to that society.

Likewise, another group of people living on a trade route in a physical terrain that provides natural fortification may be inclined to use this advantage for extracting tolls or tariffs from various traders, or even for outright piracy. If a group of people happen to live in an area where trading is relatively easy, and they also happen to have a natural resource that is highly desired, they may find themselves in a very advantageous bargaining position and use their good fortune to build a wealthy nation. If their trading partners are inclined to use force in pursuit of these valuable resources, this hypothetical nation may be compelled to develop militarily and may be able to do so with great success because of its trading advantage.

Jared Diamond, in his masterly book *Guns, Germs, and Steel*, identifies the broad factors underlying historical patterns in the development of civilization.[1] Attempting to answer the question of why civilizations advance in certain parts of the world and not others, and why European civilization had the upper hand in most of its contacts with other civilizations, Diamond cites the importance of several environmental factors.

Archaeologists generally recognize six *nuclear areas*: the Indus River Valley in present-day Pakistan; parts of present-day China; Mesopotamia—the area between the Tigris and Euphrates Rivers in Iraq; Egypt in the area around the Nile River; the highlands of Mexico (Mesoamerica); and the Peruvian Andes.[2] A nuclear area is a region where civilization is thought to have risen more or less spontaneously, that is, without being influenced by other civilizations.

Among the key factors underlying the development of civilization that Diamond emphasizes is the presence of many suitable species of plant and animal life. Large-seeded grasses, such as wheat, rice, corn, barley, are especially important since they supply a fair amount of protein, they can be saved and transported for planting, and one can select the finest seeds for planting thereby improving the quality of the next generation of crops (many early farming societies practiced this form of primitive genetic engineering).

The presence of domesticable animals was also crucial to the development of civilization. Animals that could be herded or penned in could supply a regular source of food. Other large animals that could be domesticated were used for transporting supplies and people, plowing fields, and other burdensome tasks. One of the reasons the nuclear areas of Mesoamerica and the Peruvian Andes were more limited in their expansion was the almost total dearth of beasts of burden. The llama is the largest of domesticable beasts of burden in South America but its load-bearing capacity is rather low. The lack of draft animals, as well as the rugged terrain, is one of the reasons the Inca and other South American peoples never developed wheeled transportation.

The availability of suitable species of plant and animal life permitted the development of large, dense, sedentary, stratified societies. These societies were able to produce a surplus, which is a necessary condition for the growth of leisure and specialization. As a society became more productive, fewer people were needed in the production of necessities. This freed labor for other activities. In early civilizations, this surplus of production often led to the development of a parasitic leisure class, protected by a military caste, and advised by a priestly caste that also served to justify the system of stratification to the toiling masses. But often there was at least a small class of people who used their relative freedom from labor to pursue intellectual interests that resulted in significant advances in science and technology. Societies today continue to fight an often unacknowledged battle over how the surplus gets used—for the whims of the wealthy, or for undertakings that reduce the toil and suffering of the laboring classes.

The spread of nuclear, or original, civilizations was dependent on some additional factors. One of the more interesting ones that Diamond identifies is the lack of geographic barriers along the east/west axis. Consistent amounts of sunlight are important for any species of plant to survive, and along the same latitude plants will receive the amount of sunlight in which they evolved to thrive. But moving north or south changes the amount of sunlight that, along with changes in temperature and precipitation, can jeopardize a species' ability to exist. Therefore, claims Diamond, ease of movement from east to west is much more important for the spread of civilization than is ease of movement from north to south. Other more obvious factors, such as the barriers posed by oceans, mountains, and deserts, are also factors in the spread of civilization.

The development of densely populated societies, particularly in Europe and Asia, created some problems along with the benefits. One was the spread of diseases that, at times, threatened the very existence of the civilization. The evolution of dense human settlements that were also populated by large numbers of domesticated animals, without the development of proper sanitation systems and with very primitive medical practices, created fertile conditions for diseases to cross over from the animal population to the human one, and then to rapidly spread from person to person. This proved to be a curse and a blessing for Europeans. The curse was the death and suffering it caused. The Black Plague in the 1300s, for example, is estimated to have killed more than ten million people, perhaps a third of Europe's total population. But the survivors of epidemic diseases such as smallpox, measles, and typhoid passed some immunity on to future generations. Europeans then, became protected carriers of some of the world's most deadly diseases—one of the reasons that in the great encounter between Europe and the indigenous populations of North and South America, the Europeans emerged as victorious conquerors.

Diamond's work provides great insight into the development of early civilizations, but the uneven development that exists in the world today is a more complicated matter. In the modern world we are dealing with sophisticated societies, each with a complex history of its own, and each acting on the others in complex ways. Often it is hard to make generalizations about nations, but as we shall see, there are certain discernible patterns of development that help shed light on the questions for which we seek answers.

MODERNIZATION THEORY

One of the earliest and most rudimentary theories of modern development was proposed by Walt Rostow (1916–2003). Known as the "theory of modernization," Rostow claimed that a society's development evolved through a set series of stages. He outlined these five stages as follows.

1. The traditional society: Societies in this stage are characterized by limited production, as the advantages that science and technology have to offer are not yet available on any significant scale. According to Rostow, "The value system of these societies [is] generally geared to what might be called a long-run fatalism." The common feature of traditional societies is that they share "a ceiling on the productivity of their economic techniques."

2. Preconditions for takeoff: In this stage the insights of modern science begin to result in greater productivity in agriculture and industry. A

decisive feature of this transitional phase is often the "building of an effective centralized state."

3. The takeoff: During this stage resistance to growth is overcome, and growth becomes the normal condition. New production techniques spread in agriculture, and new industries expand rapidly. Incomes increase for those who save and invest, and the new class of entrepreneurs grows quickly.

4. The drive to maturity: This is a long period of sustained progress. According to Rostow, a country enters into maturity "some sixty years after take-off begins." Maturity is "the stage in which an economy demonstrates the capacity to move beyond the original industries which powered its take-off."

5. The age of high mass consumption: In this stage the leading economic sectors shift toward the production of durable consumer goods and services, and rising incomes allow vast numbers of people to buy these things. At the beginning of the 1960s, Rostow saw only eight countries as having entered this stage: the United States, Canada, Great Britain, Australia, Sweden, Germany, France, and Japan.[3]

Rostow's theory of modernization is similar to the various evolutionary theories that have infused the social sciences ever since Darwin's theory of evolution made its mark on the biological sciences. From the early sociological work of Auguste Comte and Emile Durkheim, evolutionary theory and the neat taxonomy of functionalism have provided a comfortable and scientific-sounding theory of human societies. The problem is that these approaches often don't explain very much. And this is part of the problem with Rostow's work. Critics have complained that Rostow's categories are vague and some of his assumptions (particularly those concerning societal values) are unfounded. But perhaps the most important criticism of Rostow's theory of modernization is that he has generalized too much based on one specific case: Rostow's stages are derived mainly from an analysis of the British Industrial Revolution, but today's developing nations face a very different world than the British did 200 years ago.[4]

Rostow deliberately chose to ignore the unique situations faced by the contemporary developing nations he studied. In fact, many have argued that Rostow's work is very politically motivated. It may have been that Rostow, deeply affected by the cold war, was more concerned with showing the superiority of capitalism than he was with understanding the real problems of development. His work asserts that contact between the advanced and the undeveloped nations is beneficial to the latter since there is bound to be a transfer, or diffusion, of technology and scientific knowledge to the undeveloped nations.

Rostow's main work is titled *The Stages of Economic Growth: A Non-Communist Manifesto*, and it seems primarily concerned with convincing people that Third World nationalism, Marxism, and socialist revolution have nothing to offer the nations of the Third World. Unfortunately, Rostow's work has little to offer those who seek to understand development. Nevertheless, because of Rostow's status as a spokesperson for the government, his work received a great deal of attention in academia and was used to justify many government policies toward the Third World. Whatever validity Rostow's stages of development have in explaining and understanding development in the "advanced" nations, little of it is applicable to what is now happening in the less-developed nations.

Rostow's work had some empirical justification rooted in the work of economist Simon Kuznets (1901–1985). In 1955, Kuznets's study of development in the Western world revealed that early economic growth was accompanied by increased inequality, but after a certain level of per capita income had been achieved, the income gap began to narrow. This pattern of

Walt Rostow

Walt Whitman Rostow was born in 1916 in New York City. He had a distinguished academic career, studying in England as a Rhodes scholar and receiving his Ph.D. in economics from Yale University in 1940. Rostow served in the Office of Strategic Services (a precursor to the CIA) during World War II and went on to serve in a variety of capacities in the federal government, including as deputy assistant for national security affairs and special assistant to the president on national security.

Rostow was one of President Lyndon B. Johnson's chief advisers on economics as they pertained to foreign affairs and was considered by many to be one of the architects of the Vietnam War. Rostow had recommended the introduction of U.S. troops in Vietnam and advocated their use to block the Ho Chi Minh Trail. He also recommended a naval blockade and bombing assaults against North Vietnam and that U.S. troops be used in Laos.

Rostow maintained a lively optimism about the U.S. war in Vietnam and took pains to convey a positive outlook to government officials and to the American public via the press. According to *New York Times* columnist Anthony Lewis, Rostow "systematically interpreted intelligence reports for President Johnson in ways most likely to make the war seem to be going well. . . . As far as possible he kept dissenting views from the President."

Senate investigations in the mid-1970s uncovered the fact that the CIA had a hand in publishing some 250 books, among which was Walt Rostow's *The Dynamics of Soviet Society*.[5]

decreased inequality was assumed to apply to the Third World and is known as *Kuznets' principle*. Two faults in Kuznets' principle are now clear. One is that Kuznets assumed that changing patterns of income distribution were automatic, rather than seeing them as a result of a conscious struggle on the part of the working class in the developed world for a bigger slice of the income pie. The second problem is that income inequality has been on the rise again in many developed nations for several decades. Despite its scientific shortcomings Kuznets' principle gave First-World policymakers moral justification for ignoring the problem of inequality in the developing world.

Rostow's works on the economics of development were paralleled in the field of politics by the writings of political scientist Samuel P. Huntington. In 1968, Huntington published *Political Order in Changing Societies*, in which he argued that the problems of developing societies were not economic but political, in the sense that developing nations lacked the political structure to carry out modern development. Huntington felt, above all else, that governments in the Third World needed to be stabilized and that this stability, not democracy, should be the goal of U.S. policymakers. Huntington argued that democracy was a luxury that developing states could not afford and he supported the modernization efforts of dictators such as the Shah of Iran (see chapter 8).[6]

Huntington's writings, like Rostow's, were widely accepted among the U.S. political elite and used to justify support for anticommunist military dictatorships. Also like Rostow, Huntington played a role in advising the U.S. government on its policy toward Vietnam.

HOW IS DEVELOPMENT MEASURED?

Traditionally, development analysts relied solely on economic statistics to measure development. Specifically, the GNP (more recently the GDP, or the GNI—Gross National Income) was simply divided by the population to obtain the GNP or GDP per capita. Countries were then ranked according to this figure. There are four main problems with this method. The first is that GNP figures measure all types of economic activity in which there is an official payment transaction, but many of these do not add to the quality of life. Second, the GNP does not reflect a great deal of activity that is productive but for which no payment is exchanged. This shortcoming tends to leave out much of women's work, particularly in less-developed nations. Third, per capita GNP is a mathematical average that does not take into account inequality and therefore gives no indication of the extent and depth of poverty in a particular country. The fourth problem is that strict economic figures do not measure other aspects of human development such as literacy, life expectancy, job satisfaction, and the degree of political freedom.

The first two shortcomings create a paradox whereby GNP per capita may rise but actual living standards drop. For example, imagine a situation where a woman takes on a factory job or a job as a field laborer due to her family's need for cash. The job may take so much of her time that productive activity she had previously done, such as transporting water, making clothes, cooking, teaching the children, watching over someone else's children, is now neglected, and her family, as well as others in the community, suffer. This illustrates why claims of development by many economists must be greeted with skepticism. The introduction of a factory or an agrarian development project almost always cause per capita GNP to rise, but these things do not always result in real improvements in people's lives.

In 1990, the United Nations published its first attempt at an alternative measure of development. As discussed in the previous chapter, the Human Development Index is based on life expectancy, literacy, and average income. Although still falling short as a complete measure of human well-being, the HDI is an improvement over measures of development that rely strictly on income and production. In practice, many Third World nations score higher on the HDI than on a rating system based solely on GNP per capita.

The Gross National Product includes air pollution and advertising for cigarettes, and ambulances to clear our highways of carnage. It counts special locks for our doors, and jails for the people who break them.

The Gross National Product includes the destruction of the redwoods and the death of Lake Superior. It grows with the production of napalm and missiles with nuclear warheads. . . .

And if the Gross National Product includes all this, there is much that it does not comprehend. It does not allow for the health of our families, the quality of their education, or the joy of their play. It is indifferent to the decency of our factories and the safety of streets alike. It does not include the beauty of our poetry or the strength of our marriages, the intelligence of our public debate or the integrity of our public officials. . . .

The Gross National Product measures neither our wit nor our courage, neither our compassion nor our devotion to country. It measures everything, in short, except that which makes life worthwhile; and it can tell us everything, about America—except whether we are proud to be Americans.

—Robert F. Kennedy[7]

IS ONE WORLD ENOUGH?

Before proceeding further, a word or two regarding terminology may help avoid some confusion. Some of the words used to describe the less-developed nations of the world are often used interchangeably, but often they have their origins in different schools of thought and have different theoretical implications. The term "Third World," for instance, is generally synonymous with the notion of a less-developed nation. The term was coined in France in 1952 by a French demographer who drew a connection between the poor and powerless in the contemporary world with the "tiers etat"—the poor and powerless in France prior to the 1789 revolution.[8] The term "Third World" is used today almost interchangeably with the term "peripheral nation" or just "periphery." However, these two latter terms come out of a different theoretical perspective, as we shall see shortly.

Traditionally, the term "First World" has been applied to the center or metropolitan nations of world capitalism. These include the United States, Canada, most of Europe, Japan, Australia, New Zealand, and possibly Israel. The term "Second World" has been used to refer to the socialist countries of the world: the former Soviet Union, the nations of Eastern Europe, China, North Korea, Vietnam, Cuba, and several others. The term "Third World" is generally used as a label for any nation on the periphery of world capitalism: Central and South America, the Caribbean (except Cuba), most of Africa, Asia (excluding the socialist nations and Japan), and Oceania (except for Australia and New Zealand).[9]

Irrespective of their popularity, these categories have come under criticism for two reasons. First is the chauvinism inherent in referring to the developed, capitalist, predominantly white nations of the world as the *First* World and the poorer nations populated mostly by people of other races as the *Third* World. The second is a more complex criticism based on one's theoretical model of how the world's economic and political systems work. This criticism points out the shortcomings of thinking about the world as being three somewhat distinct entities. Scholars such as Immanuel Wallerstein and Samir Amin, for instance, have repeatedly emphasized how intricately tied the Third World nations are economically, and often politically, to the core capitalist nations. They are all part of one world system. Some nations are closer to the core, or heart, of world capitalism, and some are farther away toward the periphery.

While theorists such as Wallerstein and Amin were more concerned with understanding development processes on the periphery, other analysts came to find the three worlds point of view a hindrance to understanding those nations that claimed to be socialist. In fact, the "Second World" did not evolve or function free from First World interference, and its political and economic forms were highly influenced by the power of the leading capitalist nations and by the world economic system as a whole. For those who came to believe that the nations of the Second World were not really socialist but some sort of transitional or historically specific form, the understanding of the character of these nations was aided by the recognition that they were still a part of a world system whether they wanted to be or not. This position has even greater validity now that the Soviet Union and the eastern bloc nations have "disintegrated."

Lastly, in recent years, the terms *north* and *south* have been used more and more to distinguish the wealthier core capitalist nations from the poorer exploited nations of the world. However, these terms imply some sort of geographic determinism, and there are many exceptions to the north (rich)–south (poor) dichotomy.

ALTERNATIVE THEORIES OF DEVELOPMENT

How do we best explain the differences that exist between rich and poor nations in the world today? Why are there such great disparities in living standards throughout the world? Are there common factors that can help us understand how nations develop? What forces are responsible for the great poverty and deprivation, not to mention environmental destruction, that exist in the present world?

We have already seen that modernization theory is unable to answer these sorts of questions and offers little as an explanatory model. The best theoretical framework for understanding development is one that starts out with an understanding that world trade and politics are dominated by the developed nations and that the system of relations among nations is very unequal. Furthermore, much of the motivation for the international policies of the developed nations can be found in the problem of falling profit rates or in the accumulation crisis that was discussed in chapter 2.

The Theory of Imperialism

The recognition by Karl Marx that the relationship between the more- and the less-developed nations is one of exploitation dates back to the mid-1800s and was elaborated in the works of many people since. Both V. I.

Lenin and Rosa Luxemburg wrote extensively in the early 1900s on the subject of imperialism. Lenin and Luxemburg each felt that imperialism was the logical extension of capitalism when capitalism faced an accumulation crisis due to falling domestic profit rates. Luxemburg argued that imperialism was absolutely essential for advanced capitalism since the only way that capital accumulation could continue was through overseas expansion.[10] In the words of sociologist Al Szymanski: "Indeed, Luxemburg predicts that the final economic crisis and collapse of capitalism will occur once there are no more non-capitalist areas into which capitalism can expand. Consequently, capital must be exported to the less-developed areas of the world to avoid a cataclysmic economic depression that would be produced by the absence of investment possibilities within the system."[11]

The essence of the imperialist theory of development is that due to saturated markets and a falling rate of profit, and the attraction of cheap labor and resources, capital from the developed nations is "exported" and used to develop new nations. The prime beneficiaries of imperialism are, of course, the capitalists of the developed nations. According to this perspective, development does take place in the new nations, but there is a clear and consistent relationship of exploitation.

Dependency Theory

Dependency theory grew out of the early twentieth-century Marxist approach advanced by Lenin and Luxemburg and as a response to modernization theory. By the 1960s, a number of analysts had come to the realization that development in the Third World was severely lacking. These theorists, most notably Andre Gunder Frank, "argued that the massive and persistent poverty that existed in countries like Argentina, Peru, Chile and Brazil was *caused* by exposure to the economic and political influences of the advanced countries."[12] In fact, Frank declared unhesitatingly that "the absolute standard of living of the majority of Latin Americans is going down."[13] In Andrew Webster's words, "The view that the impact of advanced society is progressive, whether in the form of the diffusionism thesis of modernization theory or in the form of the imperialist thesis of classical Marxism, was completely rejected."[14]

The essence of dependency theory revolves around the notion that during the early stages of imperialism certain relationships were established that led to a long-term pattern of production that was designed to suit the needs of the developed nations. This established a dependency on the developed nations from which it is extremely difficult to break free. The picture is complicated by what Frank labeled the *comprador class*—local elites who benefit from the system of exploitation and whose interests become very closely tied to their counterparts in the *metropolitan* (developed) countries. Thus the comprador class is complicit in the exploitation of its own nation and dependent on the metropolitan elites for its income and sometimes great wealth, and ultimately for military equipment and support. The masses, however, experience dislocation and chronic deprivation. The end result of the relationships between the metropolitan nations and the Third World nations is one of great exploitation and the production of underdevelopment (or in the words of Teresa Hayter, "the creation of world poverty").

World System Theory

The analysis of development has increasingly led more theorists to conclude that in the modern world national economies are very closely linked. A variety of terms have sprouted that emphasize this reality: the *global assembly line*, *globalization*, *multinational* and *transnational corporations*, *global division of labor*, and Immanuel Wallerstein's *capitalist world economy*. Wallerstein claims that there is presently a single-world economic system; it is one unit with a single division of labor and multiple cultural systems. This system has been developing since the 1500s (the era of mercantile capitalism) and is primarily characterized by market trade.[15]

Wallerstein introduces three very useful terms to replace the old concepts of First, Second, and Third Worlds. In Wallerstein's model, there are three structural positions in the world economic system: *core*, *periphery*, and *semiperiphery*. The core nations are, for the most part, those that are most frequently referred to as the First World or developed nations, but they also include the developed "socialist" nations that were often referred to as Second World. The core nations are characterized by diversified production, higher technology, and relatively high profit rates and wages. The peripheral nations, as the name suggests, are on the fringes of the world economy, but they are still tied in to it through the world market system. The peripheral nations are characterized by low profits in many domestic industries (foreign-owned corporations often have high profits), labor-intensive production, less-advanced technology, and low wages and less-diversified production. Semiperipheral nations fall between the two and act as core nations to the periphery. Some examples are Brazil, Mexico, South Korea, and Israel. The relationships among these three sectors are characterized by *unequal exchange* enforced by strong states over weak ones. Wallerstein envisions the relationship among the core nations and the other nations as being parallel to the relationship between a capitalist and a worker: "Thus capitalism involves not only the appropriation of the surplus value by an owner from a laborer, but an appropriation of surplus of the whole world economy by core areas."[16]

The manner in which core nations exploit the less-developed nations is illuminated by the concepts of *uneven and combined development*. In analyzing ecological problems in the underdeveloped world, James O'Connor states that these problems are exacerbated by uneven and combined development. *Uneven development* simply refers to the historically produced, uneven spatial distribution of industry, banking, commerce, technology, wealth, and the like. *Combined development* refers to the combination of economic, social, and political forms characteristic of developed regions with those found in undeveloped regions. In seeking to maximize profit, modern capitalism combines the advanced technology and industrial organization of the core nations with low-paid, unorganized, and politically powerless labor in the semiperiphery and the periphery. It is a combination of nineteenth-century labor conditions with twenty-first-century technology, and it is ultimately supported by the most advanced military.[17]

ARE THIRD WORLD NATIONS DEVELOPING?

One might think that the simple accumulation of knowledge and technology would automatically lead to development and an increased standard of living (as Rostow suggests). However, in spite of the great diffusion of modern technology and production techniques, much of the world still experiences severe poverty and starvation. In fact, one could argue that these things have made life worse for many people.

Clearly, development takes place at an uneven pace, but does the interaction of the core nations and the less-developed nations actually cause a decrease in productivity and living standards leading to greater poverty, widespread hunger, environmental degradation, increased mortality, and other social problems? The evidence suggests that this is very often the case. Critics of U.S. policy in Central America, for example, have pointed out that during the 1970s and 1980s, U.S. corporate investment increased by roughly 500 percent, but the increased presence of U.S. technology and capital caused trade deficits and external debts to skyrocket for the nations of the region. Likewise, infant mortality rates increased in El Salvador, Honduras, and Panama. Overall per capita food production in Central America decreased, and terror and repression, sanctioned by the local elites and the U.S. government, became endemic to daily life.[18]

In the long view of history, the gap between the rich and the poor nations widened due to the fact that the richer nations were getting richer faster than the poorer ones. But at certain times world economic growth slowed and poor nations became poorer. One such setback occurred from the mid-1970s until the early to mid-1990s. During that time the gap between the rich and poor nations increased due in large part to a decline in living standards in many poorer nations. Alan Durning of the World-watch Institute estimated that in the 1980s more than forty of the world's less-developed nations finished the decade poorer than they started it. In fact, the situation was so bad that Durning declared, "The term developing nation has become a travesty; many countries are no longer developing as much as disintegrating."[19]

During the 1980s in particular many nations experienced a rise in malnutrition, a decrease in life expectancy, and a drop in per capita income. Among the hardest hit were Brazil and Nigeria, the most populous nations on their respective continents. Many other nations regressed including Madagascar, Malawi, Bangladesh, Sri Lanka, Pakistan, and Haiti.[20] In most parts of the world the poor most likely live in rural areas. This is not the case for much of Latin America, a phenomenon I will discuss later. Very often the poor are members of ethnic minorities, such as the indigenous Indians of Central and South America or the Kurds in southwest Asia.

The increasing poverty rates in the so-called developing nations have, to some extent, ended the debate between the proponents of modernization theory and those of the various theories of underdevelopment, for modernization theory has little to offer in terms of explaining the deteriorating conditions in much of the Third World in the 1980s and 1990s.

THE LEGACY OF COLONIALISM

One of the major reasons for the development problems that exist in much of the world today is the destruction of indigenous social relationships and productive economic practices, as well as the evolution of various patterns of relationships that were established during the era of colonialism. Generally, colonies fall into two categories. First, there are those colonies established primarily as a new homeland for settlers from the mother country, such as the British colonies in North America in the 1600s and 1700s; or in Rhodesia and the Cape of Africa, as well as Australia and New Zealand, in the nineteenth century; or the case of the Dutch in parts of southern Africa and, to some degree, the French in Algeria. Second, there are colonies that are procured for the enrichment of the mother country, especially the exploitation of natural resources but also for their labor. The prime example of this type is the Spanish conquest of much of the Americas. In the second type, the relationship is more purely one of political and economic domination for the enrichment of the colonial power; however, this may also be a factor in the first type of colony, a fact that has often led to sharp conflicts between colonies and their mother country. The second type of colonialism is more common, and it is the type that we will examine here.

Colonialism may be best described as the formal political domination of one country by another in which the relationship between the two nations is always one of economic exploitation, although the dominant nation may pretend otherwise. The era of modern colonialism started shortly after the great boom in global exploration that is symbolized by the travels of Christopher Columbus, and it is generally agreed to have peaked in the late 1800s and the beginning of the twentieth century, although some European countries held on to their colonies for many decades after. However, the end of colonialism did not mean the end of exploitation. While many countries were granted formal political independence, the economic relationships did not necessarily undergo drastic change. This reality gave rise to the term *neocolonialism*, which designates a situation of formal independence coupled with continued economic exploitation by an external power.

The effects of colonialism are felt very strongly today in both the economic development of the Third World and its political development. Let us begin a somewhat detailed examination of colonialism by taking a look at the methods used to subjugate the people in an array of colonies and the long-lasting consequences these have had. A classic example of colonial domination and its brutality can be seen in the methods used by King Leopold II of Belgium in colonizing the Congo Free State, the portion of Africa now encompassed by the nation of the Democratic Republic of the Congo.

King Leopold's Congo

Using the services of the great explorer Sir Henry Morton Stanley (1841–1904) in the late 1870s, Leopold saw the potential for wealth that the

Congo region of Africa held. But in order to secure control of the Congo, Leopold had to not only subjugate the native populations but defeat an Anglo-Portuguese attempt to colonize the Congo River basin. In 1885, Leopold consolidated his control over the region and gained the recognition of the major European powers and the United States as the sovereign of the Congo Free State, an area eighty times larger than Belgium itself.

The Congo was rich in natural rubber reserves, a fact that would quickly become a curse rather than a source of wealth for the native people in the region. For quite some time native Africans had been trading ivory, tin, palm oil, and other goods with the Europeans, but the invention of the rubber tire for bicycles, carts, and automobiles dramatically increased European demand for rubber. One of the first steps in securing the rubber for European interests was a decree by King Leopold that native rights were restricted to the actual sites of the towns and villages and a small area around them that was under cultivation. Other land was ruled "vacant" and property of the state, that is, of King Leopold. Of course, natives had used this land for hunting and other purposes, but this was of no concern to the king. The decree gave Leopold control over perhaps 90 percent of the land, and commercial activity in the king's territory would be permitted only after a tax was paid to the king's officials. Leopold also weakened the local economies and simultaneously strengthened his own position by forbidding the natives to trade with other Europeans. Exploitation of the Congo's resources was facilitated by the establishment of Belgian-owned concessions that used native labor to extract rubber and other resources. Official representatives of the Belgian king were rewarded through a system of sliding-scale bonuses for increased production of rubber and ivory in their districts.

The entire system of exploitation was enforced by the Belgian military and by the establishment of a native army. These soldiers were also rewarded if production increased in their districts. Enforcement of the system of exploitation became barbaric and, for the most part, people in Belgium and the rest of Europe were shielded from knowledge of the cruelty. As part of the system of control, women and children were often taken away to "hostage houses" where they were held to ensure the cooperation of the men in meeting rubber and ivory quotas. Soldiers sent out to get rubber and ivory often found that the most effective method was to raid villages, seize prisoners, and have them redeemed afterward for set quantities of ivory and rubber. In the late 1890s, a Swedish missionary disclosed that Belgian officers were requiring the native soldiers to bring in as "trophies" the hands and sexual organs of males, as proof that they had performed their missions to punish villagers for noncooperation. Belgian soldiers also took part in this barbarism. One wrote home telling how he had killed 150 men, cut off 60 hands, and crucified women and children.[21] Baskets of hands that had been smoked in order to keep them from rotting in the warm, moist climate would often be presented to the Belgian officials.

Occasionally, Congo courts—really no more than a tool of Belgian rule—would find a soldier guilty of crimes of cruelty but few, if any, ever served time in jail. The courts generally accepted the defense that the soldiers acted under orders of their superiors, but the courts never chose to initiate proceedings against the superiors.

The system of exploitation was also enforced by forbidding the natives to clear the ground for farming or to go hunting and fishing, because these activities took time from rubber extraction. Consequently, their villages deteriorated, their food supply diminished, and starvation ensued. The Congo River, to which Henry Morton Stanley had traveled just two decades earlier and seen large areas teeming with vibrant, productive human life, had become depopulated and, in places, reduced to desert-like conditions. Travelers' accounts in 1903 and afterward told of walking for weeks without seeing another human being. After twenty years of King Leopold's rule, an estimated ten million inhabitants of the Congo had died either directly at the hands of Belgian or native soldiers, or from starvation and disease brought about by colonial exploitation. Many had fled the Congo as well, but their fate may not have been much better. The French, seeing the economic advantage of King Leopold's system, constructed its likeness in the neighboring French Congo with similar results. It is likely that some Congo natives managed to flee as far as Rhodesia or South Africa only to work and perhaps die in the gold or diamond mines there. By 1900, almost every square mile of Africa had been colonized.

French West Africa

French colonialism in West Africa, while not taking quite the barbaric form of Leopold's rule in the Congo, may in the long run have had more severe consequences. It offers a very instructive lesson for understanding the roots of a variety of problems that exist in the Third World today.

In 1659, the French established a colonial outpost in what is now known as Senegal, and French traders made a steady profit dealing in slaves, ivory, animal skins, and gold.[22] By 1865, the area of modern Senegal had come under French colonial control, and later, along with Mauritania, Mali, and Niger, it became part of French West Africa. The

French recognized that the area was suitable for growing peanuts and that this could benefit their slave trade. Peanut seeds were brought from Brazil by the slave ships, planted in Africa, and used as provisions for slaves on the journey to the Americas. As time went on, peanuts and peanut oil became more and more important commercially, and French colonial authorities were able to establish the peanut as the dominant cash crop in the Sahel region, the dry grasslands in western Africa.

Before the peanut became so dominant, the local people had grown a variety of crops and an ecologically sound system of crop rotation had been practiced. But the French, who had essentially imposed this crop on the people, had little interest in the consequences that the peanut would have on the local populations. Peanuts take a lot of nutrients from the soil, and farmland used for growing peanuts generally needs a long fallow period to recuperate. If peanuts are grown year after year on the same land, the organic material in the soil is sharply diminished, crop output consequently drops, the soil's ability to grow anything and hold water is reduced, and the region's susceptibility to drought and *desertification* increases.

It should be noted that the average West African peasant had little intrinsic incentive to grow peanuts. This is something that was forced on them, and the method of coercion provides an interesting lesson in the economics of colonialism. The French, after declaring the region their own, levied taxes on the peasants that had to be paid in cash. One of the few ways that peasants could come up with the cash was to produce crops that the French were willing to buy. In a sense, the peasant was exploited twice, first by selling his crop and then by handing over a part of the money made from the sale to the French government as tax payments. The reader should note how crucial the introduction of a money-based system of trade is to the development of a worldwide system of capitalism. West Africans were reduced to laboring on their own land for someone else's benefit.

This system of relationships set the stage for future economic and ecological problems. Over time, West Africans were producing less food for themselves. The soil was being farmed too intensely in an attempt to keep up the tax payments and earn money for other things they now had to buy. Overall food production was reduced, leaving less food available to be stored for emergency use. Periodic droughts and locust infestations led to numerous famines in the 1900s. By the time the French West African colonies received their independence in 1960, the region was on the verge of ecological disaster. A major drought and famine took place in the Sahel from 1969 to 1974, resulting in one of the great tragedies of the twentieth century.

Disease and starvation were rampant, but a pattern of dependency had been established that required the continued production of cash crops for export. So although every single nation in the region was producing enough grain to feed its population, many people were dying of hunger and the region was exporting large amounts of food to feed foreigners.[23] From 1970 to 1974, the region exported approximately $1.25 billion worth of food. Even though formal colonialism had ended, the region was clearly tied to a world market system of unequal exchange. Colonialism in the past had laid the foundation for famine and environmental disaster in the present and future.

Colonialism in Indochina and India

Colonial policies similar to those in French West Africa were implemented by the French in Southeast Asia. From 1860 to 1931, France was able to convert approximately 40 percent of the potential food-producing land in Indochina (Laos, Cambodia, and Vietnam) to production for rubber, coffee, tea, and rice for export. Ironically, much of the rice was being exported to West Africa to help compensate for lower food production for domestic consumption among West Africans. Both regions, however, experienced a decrease in available food. Famines struck West Africa seven times between 1900 and 1930. In Vietnam, the colonial system of production for export, combined with Japanese occupation and war, resulted in two million deaths due to starvation between 1943 and 1945.[24]

British colonialism in India had a similar effect. A system of land revenue (essentially a tax) imposed on India meant that more production had to be shifted to exchange crops—crops that the British were willing to buy. For the most part this meant cotton. As Indian agriculture shifted more and more to cotton production, less land was used for food production, and the food that was produced also shifted more toward cash crops to suit British needs. British economic policy also took on extremely coercive forms:

> From the beginning of the 19th century, the British systematically destroyed the Indian textile industry by economic means (prohibition of imports into England) and also extra economic means (destruction of the industrial towns of Surat, Dacca, Murshidabad, and others). They imposed agricultural specialization, by creating from scratch a pattern of large landed property, reinforced by the exemption of the cotton fields from the tax.[25]

In essence, the British had industrialized their own textile production, destroyed the Indian textile industry, forced India to produce cotton and sell it at a low rate, shipped the raw materials to England where they were manufactured into clothes and other textiles, and then sold these goods back to the people of India who could afford them and to other markets around the world. British colonial policy was hardly benevolent to its colonial subjects or to the local economic systems. In fact, it went as far as forbidding "the establishment of modern industry in the colonies after having destroyed the crafts."[26]

In the mid-1800s, one of the world's chief exporters of cotton was the United States, which exploited an enslaved population of stolen Africans to harvest crops at minimal cost. During the 1860s, though, the American Civil War caused cotton production and exports to drop. The British attempted to fill the void in the world market by forcing greater production out of their Indian colony. The resulting increase in land used for growing cotton led to decreased food production; this, coupled with increased rice exports from India to Australia, caused a major famine in 1866. It has been estimated that one million people were victims of starvation in the region of Orissa alone.[27]

British rule in India had far-reaching effects. At first, the British appointed *revenue-farmers*, who were responsible for collecting the land taxes. Gradually, the revenue-farmers developed into large landlords. This followed the English pattern because, as India's first prime minister, Jawaharlal Nehru (1889–1964), pointed out, "It was far easier to deal with a few individuals than with a vast peasantry."[28] Under the British system, "The balance between industry and agriculture was upset, the traditional division of labor was broken up and numerous stray individuals could not be easily fitted into any group activity."[29] The British carefully cultivated their allies within Indian society and exploited existing differences, thereby worsening various rivalries. According to Nehru: "A new class, the owners of land, appeared; a class created by, and therefore to a large extent identified with, the British government. The breakup of the old system created new problems, and probably the beginnings of the new Hindu-Moslem problem can be traced to it. . . . British rule . . . consolidated itself by creating new classes and vested interests who were tied up with that rule and whose privileges depended on its continuance."[30]

Nehru went on to discuss how the British pursued policies deliberately designed to create divisions among sectors of Indian society and to encourage "one group at the cost of the other."[31] He also claimed that "nearly all of our major problems today have grown up during British rule and as a direct result of British policy."[32]

Colonialism in Ireland and China

British colonial policy had similar results in Ireland as the Irish were forced into an overdependency on the potato as a staple crop. In the 1800s, a high percentage of Irish land was being used to grow crops and raise livestock for export to England. Since the potato was a high-yield crop and a fairly nourishing and filling food source, it became popular for families to grow potatoes on the small amount of land available for domestic production. When the potato blight struck in 1845, the result was a devastating famine directly caused by colonialism. Out of a population of eight million, approximately one million people died of starvation, and about 1.5 million emigrated, mostly to the United States, as refugees from the devastation that the potato blight caused.[33]

British and other colonial powers also attempted with varying degrees of success to colonize China. China is one of the world's oldest civilizations and prior to its extensive contact with Europe in the 1700 and 1800s, China was more advanced in many ways. Chinese porcelain, silk, tea, and other products were highly desired in Europe, but the demand for European products in China was minimal. The British, in order to stimulate trade, embarked on a concerted policy of drug dealing in order to create a need for British currency. The British brought opium from India for sale in China, and when the Chinese authorities tried to put a stop to the drug trade the British declared war in the name of free trade. The first *opium war* was fought from 1839 to 1842, and victorious England was able to extract a number of concessions from China. England was awarded the territory of Hong Kong and granted access to five port cities.

The drug addiction that resulted from the opium trade contributed to the impoverishment of China and created an economic and chemical dependency from which Great Britain was able to benefit. A second opium war, in which France joined in on the side of the British, was fought from 1856 to 1860, and resulted in a further loss of Chinese sovereignty. China suffered a third major defeat at the hands of foreigners in 1895 when Japan overtook part of the Korean peninsula and the island of Taiwan.

The late 1800s witnessed a series of rebellions in China against the West, including the *Boxer Rebellion* in 1898–1900, which was put down by joint British, Russian, German, French, Japanese, and U.S. expeditions. The country was then divided into spheres of influence by the imperial powers. Nationalist sentiment continued to grow in China, as did the appeal of communist economic and political philosophy. The Chinese communist revolution eventually cast off foreign domination and established a communist government in China in 1949 that nationalized all foreign holdings, instituted extensive land reform, and initiated widespread education and health programs.[34]

These are just a few examples of how colonialism disrupted indigenous development and caused past and recent famines. The general relationship between the core nations and the Third World or peripheral nations is summed up nicely by the Indian scholar Ranjit Sau:

> To the extent there was any exchange of goods between the outer periphery and the metropolitan center of world capitalism throughout the four centuries, it had always been an unequal exchange to the detriment of the former. . . . They are poor partly because this natural wealth has been, and still is being, plundered by imperialism for the needs of its own industrialization at the expense of those countries from which it slips away in its raw state.[35]

THE AUTHORITARIAN STATE: A COLONIAL LEGACY?

Colonialism has not only contributed to economic and environmental problems, it has also contributed to the prevalence of authoritarian regimes in the Third World. In his book *The Rise of the Authoritarian State in Peripheral Societies*, Clive Thomas notes that in the Third World today there is a prevalence of repression, political assassination, disappearances, and installed dictatorships. According to Thomas, these authoritarian features have developed, in part, due to the "absence of internal democratic practices."[36] Interestingly, Thomas makes the claim that "the source of that oppression is not, and never has been, located in the composition of the existing government; it is rooted in the structure of social relations, classes, and the organization and levels of development of the productive forces."[37]

Thomas's point is that the colonial experience was that of an economic and a political system that was essentially imposed from the outside, and it was tailored to suit the interests of the colonizers. The political system did not include democratic participation or representative politics. Adding to the problem was the fact that social groups capable of forming a counterbalance to the power and interest of the local elites had not yet emerged. In European capitalism, the working class developed gradually and in such concentrations that it was able to organize into political groups. There were also classes of intelligentsia and others who were capable of acting as critics of the ruling groups, or as a voice for the oppressed. The relatively gradual development of capitalism enabled the working class and various middle strata to exert pressure on the ruling groups and slowly expand democratic rights. This basic pattern held true for the United States as well. Peripheral societies, however, might be said to have fallen victim to *political* uneven and combined development. Not only were methods of production imposed on these societies, but so were some aspects of modern political forms, including an advanced military apparatus, which overwhelmed the social forms that existed in everyday life.

Thomas explains that the type of state structure that existed in colonial nations was "instrumental" in the sense that the dominant classes used it for their own purposes; but to view it in only that way would be an oversimplification. The state in peripheral societies is the product of complex factors and, to a large degree, is shaped by the need to "promote the growth of commodity relations" in the context of international political and economic systems.[38]

Racism is an additional factor that has contributed to the rise of authoritarianism in peripheral societies. Very often the occupational and class structures of colonial nations were, and still are, clearly delineated along racial lines. The main lines of demarcation may have been between the white colonizers and the nonwhite colonized, but the colonizers were usually adept at exploiting cultural, ethnic, and racial divisions among the colonized. Racial and other differences were turned into various layers of privilege and deprivation. After independence the bitter legacy of these differences has helped pave the way for authoritarianism, internal strife, and even civil war.[39] The experience of Haiti is a good example of this, as we will see in chapter 9.

HUNGER AND POVERTY

The abstract problems of underdevelopment and exploitation manifest themselves concretely as poverty, hunger, illness, and death in much of the Third World. It is estimated that 700 million people suffer from hunger, many of whom die from hunger-related causes including diseases that result from low resistance due to malnutrition. The vast majority of these deaths occur among children. Upward of twelve million children die yearly from hunger-related causes.[40] In addition, up to two billion people have vitamin and mineral deficiencies in their diets, which can lead to serious health problems.[41]

The poverty and hunger that are so rampant in much of the world today are a direct consequence of an unequal distribution of resources, wealth, and power. The most obvious inequality related to the problem of hunger is an unequal distribution of land. According to the international relief organization Oxfam, in eighty-three countries of the world, 3 percent of the landowners control almost 80 percent of the land. In some places the distribution is even more unequal. In Argentina, for instance, it is estimated that 2 percent own 75 percent of the land. The Worldwatch Institute has calculated land distribution inequality using the Gini index, which, as we will recall, is a statistical index that measures the degree of inequality. The higher the index, the greater the inequality. Worldwatch figures from a 1989 study are reproduced in Table 7.1.

Unequal distribution of land leads to a variety of problems that we will discuss shortly, but first we should note two points. First, there is still room for expanded production since a great deal of the world's cultivatable land is not being farmed. Oxfam estimates that in Asia and Africa less than 20 percent of the potentially cultivatable land is being farmed. Most of that land is controlled by large landowners or is open country.[42]

Second, according to the Institute for Food and Development Policy, it is a myth that there isn't enough food to feed all the world's inhabitants. The world produces enough grain to provide everyone with 3,500 calories a day. If we add to this the amount of other commonly eaten foods such as vegetables, nuts, fruits, beans, tubers, free-range livestock, and fish, we've got to wonder where all the excess food is going. The world produces enough food to provide each person with nearly four and a half pounds of food daily, and in recent decades the rate of growth in food production has been higher than the rate of population growth.[43] The hunger problem ought not to be as bad as it is. One of the reasons it is such a problem is because many of the world's poorest nations are net exporters of food. According to Oxfam, thirty-six of the world's forty poorest nations export food to North America. Africa, where more than half the population suffers from malnutrition, exports millions of dollars worth of protein foods to Europe each year. Likewise, India and Brazil are two of the top Third World food exporters, while tens of millions in each country lack sufficient food.[44]

The world's food-consumption patterns are grossly out of balance. The richest 25 percent of the world's population consumes two-thirds of the world's food production.[45] This is a pattern that exists within individual countries and also on a worldwide scale. It has been estimated that in Brazil the rich consume seventeen times more than the poor; and under the

Table 7.1. Concentration of Landownership[46]

Country	Share of Landowners (%)	Share of Arable Land Owned (%)	Gini Index
Latin America			
Venezuela	1	67	92
Colombia	1	48	86
Brazil	1	45	84
Honduras	1	44	78
Mexico	2	47	58
Asia			
India	1	4	64
Indonesia	1	14	62
Pakistan	1	9	52
Philippines	1	12	51
Africa			
Kenya	1	40	55
Cameroon	4	16	44
Congo	1	35	37
Malawi	2	9	36

apartheid system in South Africa, the rich were consuming twenty-nine times more than the poor. The problem of hunger in the world today is clearly not a result of underproduction: It results from unequal distribution that stems from poverty and economic and political inequality. Rich countries, including the United States, Canada, Australia, Japan, and those of Western Europe, consume 70 percent of the world's food grains. How is such massive consumption possible? Most of the grains "consumed" by the rich are actually used to feed beef and dairy cattle. The average American consumes about 2,000 pounds of grain per year, mostly in the form of milk, eggs, meat, and alcoholic beverages. The average American in the course of a year consumes sixty-five pounds of beef, and it is commonly estimated that it takes about twenty pounds of grain to produce one pound of beef.[47] Only about 150 pounds of grain are consumed directly as grain or flour. In contrast, the average Asian consumes only about 400 pounds of grain, most of that in its original form.[48]

Is Overpopulation the Cause of Hunger?

Some of the world's problems, such as hunger, pollution, and desertification, are often blamed on "overpopulation," and although it is true that there is a limit to what the earth can sustain and that there may be profound psychological consequences from overcrowding, explaining these problems in terms of overpopulation can obscure more significant political and economic causes. A quick comparison of a few different countries shows that there is no consistent correlation between population density and hunger. China, for instance, has only half the cropland per person as India, but India has had much more of a hunger problem over the past few decades. Great Britain has nearly the same population density as India. There are densely populated countries with intense hunger, such as Bangladesh, and there are countries such as Brazil or Senegal where there are great food resources, relatively low-population densities, yet severe hunger. And there are countries such as the Netherlands that have very little land per person, yet have no hunger problem and manage to export large amounts of food year after year.

One point that is often overlooked is that population growth is often a *response* to hunger and poverty rather than a *cause*. This point is well made in Mahmood Mamdani's *The Myth of Population Control*, which critiques some of the population studies and birth control programs sponsored by the Rockefeller Foundation and other upper-class foundations. In agricultural societies children are usually viewed as economic assets and not economic burdens, as they are in industrial societies. Children undertake many chores in the fields that help their families survive. In poor societies undergoing a transition to industrialization, many people are forced off the land, but children are stilled viewed as potential assets since they may be able to get jobs at an early age, plus there is always the hope that one child may be able to get a good education and eventually a decent job in the city that can support the remaining family members. In fact, economic security seems to be the major factor that contributes to the slowing of population growth in any society under normal conditions (that is, disregarding extreme circumstances such as war, famine, etc.). Countries with higher standards of living tend to have significantly lower population growth rates. Likewise, within individual countries, social classes that are more economically secure tend to have fewer children (the very rich are often an exception to this), and the poorer classes more. Children represent both a hope for future security and, for many of society's poorest members, the one thing that they can call their own and of which they can be proud. Birth rates fall as inequality lessens, poverty is reduced, education increases, and women gain greater rights. This has been the case in China, Colombia, Cuba, the state of Kerala in India, Costa Rica, and elsewhere.[49]

The issue of economic security lies at the heart of the whole question of population control. One might wonder, for instance, what changes would take place in the population growth rate in the industrialized nations if Social Security, Medicare, retirement pensions, and similar programs did not exist.

Does the Free Market Contribute to Hunger?

Unequal distribution of land and other resources has intensified poverty and hunger in much of the world. Inequality and market economies combine to drive small farmers out of business. Take, for example, a period of low crop yield due to drought or insect infestation. During such a time the larger farms can get by, for they generally have more reserves they can use for themselves or sell for cash to buy the things they need. In fact, during times of bad harvest larger farmers may find themselves doing better economically because the decrease in food production has caused effective demand to increase, thereby causing prices to rise. Larger farmers may also benefit because they can loan out money at high interest rates (once again, because of the demand), and they may be able to hire labor at reduced costs because so many people are desperately looking for work. However, for poor farmers a decrease in total production makes things worse. If poor farmers suffer several years of these conditions, they may be forced to sell part or all of their land in order to pay back loans or feed their families. In addition, the more well-off farmers are in a better position to take advantage of technology, hybrid seeds, improved fertilizers, and advanced irrigation systems, all of which may be made available by the developed nations. These advantages may allow them to increase their yields, which can cause market prices to fall, but because of their higher productivity large farmers will still make higher profits. The smaller farmers, unable to take advantage of these advances, suffer a drop in income because of deflated prices.

Overall then, inequality and the market system lead to a polarization of society into a relatively small class of large landowners versus a large class of small landowners and landless peasants. The problem is exacerbated by the international market, which, in effect, dictates what Third World farmers can produce, and by the investment patterns, development policies, and consumption patterns of the core nations.

Probably the most effective single solution to world hunger is land reform. Land reform can take many forms, but when instituted in a just manner with the needs of the small landowners and agricultural laborers in mind it can make a tremendous difference. The redistribution of land held by large landlords or foreign corporations to people who need land can make the most substantial improvements. Often, much of the land owned by large landowners is not even being used for production. This was true in the case of Guatemala's nationalization of a portion of United Fruit Company's land in the 1950s. In Nicaragua, shortly after the Sandinista revolution in 1979, the new government distributed land to forty thousand previously landless peasants; and by 1985, over seventy thousand land-poor families had received land. In six years, nearly four million acres of land had been redistributed to those who needed it most.[50]

Other types of land reform can also make a significant impact. In the Indian state of Kerala, for instance, the abolition of tenancy probably did more to ease hunger in the region than any other initiative. Prior to the reforms made in 1969, many tenant farmers paid over 50 percent of the return on their production to the landlords.[51]

Successful land reform has taken place in such diverse countries as Japan, South Korea, Taiwan, China, Zimbabwe, and Nicaragua. But there have also been phony land-reform programs in such countries as Mexico and El Salvador that have made problems worse. Each program must be evaluated on its own merits and not by its name.[52]

Environmental Issues

People often make the connections among food production, overpopulation, and environmental destruction, but in a way that omits the primary causal factors of inequality and exploitation. Logic might suggest that since food production takes nutrients from the soil and the expansion of farming and grazing threatens delicate grasslands and the environments of wild animals, then increased production will necessarily make matters worse. This train of thought, however, overlooks the fact that enough food is being produced to feed everyone—as we noted earlier. The problem is that it is not being justly distributed because, for the most part, distribution takes place according to the ability to pay. Many people are simply too poor to buy what they need, so the system neglects them and they starve.

Much of the earth's surface is being turned into desert, and much of the earth's ecologically irreplaceable rain forests are being destroyed. These are serious concerns that must be understood properly in order to be rectified. The truth regarding environmental destruction is that it is not caused by increased food production per se, but by the present method of food production. The immensity of these land-use problems is staggering. According to Frances Moore Lappé and Joseph Collins, about one-quarter of U.S. farmland is losing topsoil faster than nature can restore it; at the current rate of destruction, the Brazilian rain forest will be gone in thirty-five years; and for every ten acres of Central American rain forest in 1961, only six were left by the late 1970s.[53]

Major environmental threats in the Third World today come from marginalized peasants forced to eke out a living on the least productive land and from large-scale economic development projects, including logging. Peasants who have been forced off their land, for one reason or another, sometimes try to farm or graze their livestock on fragile land, sometimes turning it into a virtual desert within a few years. Rural farmers may also use slash-and-burn techniques to clear away patches of forest and make new farmland. *Deforestation* can upset delicate ecosystems and reduce the soil's ability to hold water, inhibit nature's ability to cleanse the air of carbon dioxide and other pollutants (thereby accelerating the greenhouse effect), and cutback on the planet's capacity to produce oxygen.

However, it is not poor Third World farmers whom we should hold responsible for this situation. We must recognize that these farmers' options have become very limited and that they are coerced by circumstances into making decisions that can harm the environment. This is exactly the sort of thing that happened in the Sahel region of Africa. History shows that small-scale agriculturalists are often aware of the impact that their actions have on the environment, and if they are dependent on that environment, they have an obvious stake in its preservation. However, when external forces upset the social balance, the fragile environmental balance is the next thing to go. As Durning has pointed out: "Nothing incites people to deplete forests, soils, or water supplies faster than fear they will soon lose access to them."[54]

The responsibility for today's environmental crisis lies with economic interests, whose concern is short-term production for profit. These interests also lie at the heart of various development projects that clear land for large agribusiness (often owned by foreign conglomerates) to produce crops for export. Other projects, such as the construction of dams, can result in large-scale destruction of forests and the wholesale displacement of many indigenous people. Additional forces at work include mining and lumber industries. Strip-mining is often practiced in parts of the Third World where there is less political opposition to it than there is in the United States or in other developed nations. The same can be said of forestry practices. Rain forest hardwoods such as teak and mahogany are highly valued for their beauty and durability. The timber industry often cuts down areas of rain forests with little regard for the ecological consequences. Timber practices in Third World nations are an example of uneven and combined development. The latest timber removal techniques are often unchecked by any type of socially and ecologically conscious regulatory agency. In Third World rain forests there are few social groups or institutionalized ways of checking the onslaught of the timber companies.

The deterioration of the environment in the Third World is, of course, also the result of industrialization that spews tremendous quantities of pollutants into the atmosphere. This pollution problem is especially troublesome when combined with the shrinkage of the rain forests, for the forests are able to "recycle" some of the pollutants. Another contributing factor to air pollution, and to land-use problems, is the automobile. In the United States there are an estimated 1.7 people per auto. In the Third World the people-to-car ratio is not nearly as low, but it is in the Third World where the number of passenger cars is rising most rapidly. The developed nations are increasingly relying on the Third World to take up the slack in passenger car demand. The growth rate in auto consumption has been increasing at an annual rate of 15 percent in Asia, 14 percent in Latin America, and 7 percent in Africa, compared to 6.5 percent in North America and 3.5 percent in Europe.[55] The increased number of cars in the Third World may make it appear as though people are becoming better off (in fact, Rostow used the automobile as an indicator of development), but as sociologists George Martin and Peter Freund argue in *The Ecology of the Automobile*, automobile ownership and use often increase the social and physical distance among classes and races, and an auto-centered society has tremendous social costs. In addition to intensifying various social inequalities, the automobile is one of the major contributors to air pollution and its resulting health problems. Presently, automobile use is overwhelmingly concentrated in Third World urban centers, which is causing massive traffic congestion and increased pollution. Mexico City has more cars than New York City, and Sao Paolo, Brazil, has more than London. Air pollution in Mexico City is worse than in Los Angeles. According to Freund and Martin, "World Bank data show that in 1989 Mexico City was exposed to 4.4 million tons of all man-made pollutant emissions and that 76 percent were attributable to motor vehicles. In

1985, Los Angeles was exposed to 3.5 million tons of pollutants, 63 percent of which were produced by motor vehicles."[56]

Part of the reason for the increased auto-caused air pollution in the Third World relative to the developed nations is that the cars may be older and their owners may not be able to afford proper maintenance. However, there is a structural reason that has to do with the effects of uneven and combined development. Whereas when the developed nations gradually shifted to auto use and democratic processes allowed some space for organized citizens' groups to exert pressure for stricter emission standards (or for other forms of transportation), this has not been the case in the Third World. Cars often lack rudimentary air pollution controls, catalytic converters are not required, leaded gas is still in widespread use, and governments may not have imposed any miles-per-gallon guidelines on manufacturers.[57]

NEOLIBERALISM

U.S. policymakers and many international investors currently favor an international system of trade and investment and a model of development, known as neoliberalism. Neoliberalism, in its current incarnation, was championed by the 1974 Nobel Prize–winning Austrian economist Friedrich von Hayek (1899–1992). Hayek claimed that state intervention in the economy made people too dependent on the state. Hayek cited slowing economic growth in many developed countries, along with the fiscal crisis (debt) confronting many national governments as reasons to return to the free market.[58] Hayek's neoliberal philosophy was readily adopted by Margaret Thatcher in Great Britain, and Ronald Reagan in the United States. Hayek's followers helped implement a wide variety of neoliberal reforms in many Third World countries. The Third World versions of neoliberalism are often more extreme since many less-developed nations have underdeveloped democratic organizations and mediating institutions.

Among the major principles of neoliberalism are the deregulation of industries or economic sectors; the elimination or reduction of tariffs and other barriers to trade; reduced government spending for social services; *privatization*—the selling of state-owned enterprises to private interests; and a greater emphasis on production for export rather than for domestic need.

One of the products of neoliberalism is the reduction of the protective functions of the national government. Citizens in a neoliberal nation are less able to count on the government to look out for their common interests.

According to neoliberal philosophy, citizenship is expressed in the marketplace through decisions about whether or not to purchase certain products or to pay for certain services. A government that puts an effort into ensuring product safety, protecting the environment, or providing services to the poor, the elderly, or the disabled is regarded as a hindrance to the free market, which is the ultimate judge of what is good or bad, right or just, worthy or unworthy.[59] Neoliberalism, according to some, means a lack of accountability and a lack of transparency. It means hiding the truth about what is actually happening and protecting profit makers who are responsible for environmental destruction, hunger, poverty, and other social ills. The neoliberal model is largely based on the free market principles espoused by Adam Smith and other philosophers of early capitalism, principles that were largely rejected through much of the twentieth century because of the great inequality, war, and economic depression with which they were associated. One of these principles is that of *comparative advantage*. This was a theorem put forth by the English economist David Ricardo (1772–1823). Ricardo was an advocate of free trade (and a very wealthy man) who felt that economic prosperity resulted from national economic specialization. Each country would develop best if it relied on its natural advantages; advantages in human skills as well as its geographic advantages. According to Ricardo, nations should produce what they are best at producing. Through trade, goods and services would then be transformed into income that could be used to satisfy needs unmet by domestic production. One of the implications of the theory of comparative advantage is that the world's distribution of wealth is largely natural and not the result of powerful political, military, and economic institutions. In criticizing the theorem, sociologist Philip McMichael wrote "the concept of comparative advantage presents itself as an efficient allocation of global resources and benefits based on ecological and cultural endowments, but it is in reality a corporate, rather than a geographical, property."[60]

Neoliberalism exists because it is supported by the privileged. In the words of Susan George: "Starting from a tiny embryo at the University of Chicago with the philosopher-economist Friedrich von Hayek and his students like Milton Friedman at its nucleus, the neoliberals and their funders have created a huge international network of foundations, institutes, research centers, publications, scholars, writers and public relations hacks to develop, package and push their ideas and doctrine relentlessly."[61] In meeting basic needs, neoliberalism has failed neomiserably, and nations that adopted it most readily are now among the most troubled economically (e.g., Chile). Neoliberalism has become a secular fundamentalism for many of the leaders of the western developed nations—a set of dogmatic beliefs to which they stubbornly cling in spite of the negative impact of its policies and the passionate backlash it provokes.

THE WORLD BANK AND THE INTERNATIONAL MONETARY FUND

Probably no other institutions have had a greater effect on the development of Third World economic strategies than the World Bank and the International Monetary Fund. Both the World Bank and the IMF were established at the Bretton Woods Conference in New Hampshire following World War II. The goals of the World Bank were to rebuild global infrastructure and assist the development of member countries. The IMF's purpose was to promote currency convertibility and exchange rate stabilization. Initially, for the World Bank, Europe's infrastructure was the main priority and Third World development took a backseat.

Both the World Bank and the IMF have had strong ideological principles that worked against the socialist nations of the world and attached all sorts of strings to the money lent in the Third World.[62] The role played by the World Bank and the IMF in development should not be underestimated. They are, as Robert Browne has claimed, the "gatekeepers to whatever stock of development capital the world community is willing to make available for the Third World"; and this role has given them tremendous leverage.[63] The lending policies of both institutions have created numerous problems, not the least of which is what Susan George has called the *debt treadmill*. Most debtor nations are simply unable to pay off their loans and are in positions where they must pay out millions or even billions of dollars to the IMF, the World Bank, or the core nations, without making a dent in the principal that they owe.

In 1982, Mexico was the first Third World country to officially default on its international debt, and since then numerous other countries have followed suit.[64] The IMF and the World Bank responded by forcing borrowers to take extreme austerity measures that would ensure that payments would continue to be made to the banks. The World Bank now routinely makes loans called *structural adjustment loans* (SALs) or advises nations to impose *structural adjustment programs* (SAPs). The precise terms of individual SAPS are generally kept secret, but according to Juliette Majot, a policy analyst for the International Rivers Network, a San Francisco-based environmental group, they usually include: "shifting domestic food production to production of food for export; devaluing the currency (to further encourage exports); cutting social spending (including health and education); restricting credit and suppressing wages; privatizing national industries; and, finally, liberalizing trade."[65]

It is no coincidence that during the 1980s (known as the World Bank's decade of adjustment) absolute poverty in the Third World rose substantially.[66] Approximately 1.2 billion people in the Third World live in poverty, a figure that doubled during the 1980s. Scathing criticism of the twin powers came in the early 1990s when the United Nations International Children's Emergency Fund (UNICEF) and its Economic Commission for Africa estimated that at least six million children under the age of five died each year since 1982 in Africa, Asia, and Latin America as a result of SAPs imposed by the World Bank and the IMF.[67]

Aside from the transfer of wealth through debt payments, the "development" projects sponsored by the World Bank and the IMF have also come under sharp criticism. These projects are often of questionable value to the poor of the Third World; instead, they frequently seem to be geared toward the economic interests of First World corporations and their Third World compradors.

The World Bank's policies on transportation development illustrate how it favors the interests of multinational corporations over the needs of the local populations:

> Of the amount that the World Bank loaned for urban transport projects in the Third World in 1972–1985, 49% went to roads, 17% to buses, 16% to rail systems, 12% to road traffic management, 5% percent to road and rail technical assistance, and 1% to pedestrian facilities. Non-motorized forms of travel such as . . . bicycles . . . have received virtually no subsidy. Thus, alternative transport, which is viewed as "backward," is sacrificed to the auto.[68]

Likewise, shipping ports, railroads, highways, dams, and electrification have often displaced much of the local population, deprived them of their traditional means of support, harmed the environment, and facilitated the extraction of raw materials and the export of goods out of the peripheral nations.

Such policies also serve to further the advantage that the "haves" have over the "have-nots." From 1984 to 1990, debt collection by the World

Bank and the IMF resulted in a net transfer of $155 billion from poor nations to rich nations. It is estimated that today the richest fifth of the world receives about 150 times more income than the poorest fifth. Part of the reason for this great imbalance is that wages of many Third World workers have been falling. To make matters worse, social services in many Third World nations have deteriorated. Some of these trends are directly attributable to the lending policies of the World Bank and the IMF. Expenditures on health in countries undergoing structural adjustment guided by the IMF or the World Bank in Africa were cut by 50 percent in the 1980s, and educational spending was reduced 25 percent.[69]

One of the requirements typically made by the IMF is that recipient nations dismantle their restrictions on foreign exchange. This deregulation makes it easier for the comprador class to export its money overseas, thereby encouraging capital flight and corruption that further weaken the nation. Moreover, when the IMF forces a currency devaluation to encourage exports, those whose holdings are in foreign currencies automatically profit. The devaluing of their nation's currency means that foreign money can purchase much more. Thus, devaluing currency serves to help ensure the allegiance of the comprador class to the overall program of the IMF.

Seen in this light, it is clear that the Third World debt crisis is better understood from a class perspective than as a national problem. Different classes within the Third World nations stand to lose or gain based on their relationship to the power- and wealth-holding classes of the core capitalist nations. One scandalous example of this involves Raul Salinas, the eldest brother of former Mexican president Carlos Salinas (1989–94), who transferred more than $80 million from Mexico to Swiss banks with the direct aid of Citibank officials. Mr. Salinas opened the accounts under false names, and much of the money is regarded as "illicit earnings."[70]

In addition to accelerating the ruthless exploitation of much of the world, officials at the World Bank and the IMF have shown an alarming contempt for human rights and democratic principles. For example, in 1947, the Dutch sent 145,000 troops to suppress the Indonesian independence movement. The effort was undertaken despite the fact that the Dutch economy had not fully recovered from World War II and was in fact operating at a lower level than it had been eight years before. The World Bank came to Holland's aid with a $195 million reconstruction loan. The United Nations condemned the World Bank for providing the government with resources that, in effect, subsidized the cost of its war against the people of Indonesia. The bank, however, chose not to respond to the UN's condemnation.[71]

Likewise, in 1966, the World Bank lent money to South Africa in spite of a UN General Assembly resolution calling on all UN-affiliated institutions to cease financial support of South Africa because of its policy of apartheid. The bank also lent money to Portugal in spite of a UN resolution that denounced Portugal's continued colonial control of Angola and Mozambique.[72] The World Bank and the IMF are officially part of the UN's Economic and Social Council, but in reality the UN exercises no control over them.

In the early 1970s, the World Bank cut off funds to the democratically elected government of Chile and then began lending money to the extremely repressive Ceausescu regime in Romania. In 1979, Senator James Abourezk denounced the World Bank on the floor of the U.S. Senate and pointed out that a disproportionate amount of the bank's loans were going to some of the world's most repressive dictatorships. At the time, the bank was expanding its loans to four newly repressive governments.[73]

Some have argued that World Bank money doesn't go so much for development for the world's poor as it does for contractors and consultants, most of whom are from the world's wealthiest nations. According to one World Bank official, "Most of our money doesn't go to the South, it goes straight from Washington to Pennsylvania, where they manufacture the turbines, or Frankfort, where they produce the dredging equipment."[74]

Researcher Catherine Caufield found that the Bank's top five financial contributors (the United States, Japan, Germany, France, and the United Kingdom) "are also the top five beneficiaries of World Bank expenditures . . . together they receive more that half the money the Bank spends. . . ."[75] Caufield also notes that "over the years, American firms alone have received $24 billion in business from the World Bank—exactly what the Bank spends on foreign procurement."[76]

Many of the World Bank's projects are considered failures, but private investors who buy the Bank's bonds are in a no-lose situation. The bonds are guaranteed by the Bank's member nations, so even if a World Bank project fails miserably on economic terms bond holders still receive their dividend payments—tax payers in wealthy nations foot the bill. One could make a strong case that World Bank and IMF development projects don't exist to help the poor, they exist to help the rich, and that is why they are so poorly planned and why so many people in the Third World are adversely affected.

In recent years shockingly arrogant statements by World Bank officials have added to its tarnished reputation. Lawrence Summers, the World Bank's chief economist, wrote a memo to another staff member claiming that "the economic logic behind dumping a load of toxic waste in the

All the world's bank robbers combined have not done one-tenth of one percent of the harm that the World Bank has done in just fifty years.
—Jim Hightower, radio commentator and
former Texas agricultural commissioner

lowest wage country is impeccable, and we should face up to that." Summers was thinking that since incomes are lower in the Third World, work time lost due to illnesses is less costly. Funeral expenses are no doubt lower too. Summers also wrote, "Just between you and me, shouldn't the World Bank be encouraging more migration of the dirty industries to the LDCs [less-developed countries]?" And, "I've always thought . . . that the under-populated countries in Africa are vastly underpolluted; their air quality is probably vastly inefficiently low compared to Los Angeles or Mexico City."[77] Summers went on to say that pollutants in the Third World would not cause much of a problem since child mortality is high and life expectancy is low there. Summers eventually left his post at the World Bank to take a position in the Clinton administration as the top international economist in the Treasury Department, and later became president of Harvard University. Unfortunately, hard-pressed for foreign currency, Third World nations have indeed been importing toxic wastes. For example, northern developed nations have been paying just a few dollars per ton to dump their waste in Africa. This is just a fraction of what it costs to dispose of it within their own borders, where it is usually disposed of more safely.

THE MEXICAN DEBT CRISIS

IMF and World Bank lending policies have not solved the development problems of the Third World, nor have they lessened the financial crisis that increased lending is often intended to alleviate. Numerous countries have acquired debt problems reaching critical proportions. Brazil, the earth's fifth most populous nation, for example, followed neoliberal prescriptions for reform advocated by U.S. policymakers for the past few decades, but by 2002 its economic system reached a breaking point and had to be rescued with a $30 billion loan from the IMF. The loan comes with many strings attached and threatens Brazil's sovereinty.[78]

How have so many nations reached the breaking point like Brazil? Mexico provides a prime example of the forces at work. Risky lending to

Mexico in the period from 1974 to 1982 (fueled by *petrodollars*—vast sums of capital accumulated in First World banks as a result of the rise in petroleum prices), led to a debt crisis in that country that caused Mexico to default on its loans. At the time (1982), Mexico owed U.S. banks about $25 billion, and despite the fact that Mexico's upper class probably had enough funds *in foreign banks* to pay off much, if not all, of this debt, they were not forced to pay.[79] Instead, new loans with structural adjustment provisions were given to Mexico, which further impoverished the poor and the working class. During the 1980s, real wages in Mexico fell by 50 percent. Half the population is below the official poverty line, and 20 percent live in extreme poverty.[80] At the other end of the class spectrum, massive wealth has been accumulating quite rapidly. From 1991 to 1995, the number of billionaires in Mexico grew from just two to at least twenty-eight. Mexico has more billionaires than all but three of the world's nations.[81]

Poverty, displacement, inequality, and corruption are some of the conditions responsible for the series of rebellions that have taken place in the Chiapas region of southeast Mexico since 1994 and have threatened the authority of the government in that region. Foreign investors tied the 1995 Mexican loan bailout to "stability" in Chiapas. Representatives from U.S. financial giants Goldman Sachs and Merrill Lynch told the Mexican government that it needed to do something about the Zapatista uprisings in the Chiapas region of Mexico in order to restore investor confidence. An internal Chase Manhattan Bank memo declared, "The [Mexican] government will need to eliminate the Zapatistas to demonstrate their effective control of the national territory and security policy."[82] Within days of President Clinton's announcement for a new bailout plan for Mexico, the Mexican Army initiated combat operations against the Zapatistas.

Overall, the Clinton plan provided Mexico with $50 billion in bailout money. The United States provided $20 billion from the Treasury Department's Exchange Stabilization Fund, $17.8 billion came from the IMF, $2.5 billion from the World Bank, and $10 billion from European banks. Mexico, in turn, had to make relatively high interest payments on the loans, it had to show a balanced budget(!), and, to ensure repayment, the Mexican national oil company Pemex was required to have its foreign customers deposit their payments in a special U.S. bank account. In case of default, the account would have been seized by the Federal Reserve Bank of New York and turned over to the U.S. Treasury.[83]

The arrangements made with Mexico have a number of consequences that demonstrate the functions of institutions such as the IMF and the World

> We thought we were on the path to the First World and suddenly something went wrong. One minute the World Bank and IMF were saying that Mexico was the best example. Now we are the worst example. . . . We are losing control. If we don't find another type of development, we are finished.
> —Enrique del Val Blanco, Mexico's Human Service Ministry[84]

Bank, and they illustrate the lopsided relationships between the core capitalist nations and the rest of the world. First, the bailout saves foreign investors who made risky decisions in the years leading up to the crisis. Second, it leaves the wealth of Mexico's upper class untouched. Third, it increases the rate of exploitation of Mexico's workers to the benefit of multinational corporations. Fourth, it raises much of the money for the bailout from the American public, who end up paying either through higher taxes or reduced government services.

An additional possible outcome is an increase in illegal immigration to

The Zapatista Uprising in Chiapas, Mexico

The following are excerpts from Subcommander Marcos, "A Tourist Guide to Chiapas," *Monthly Review* (May 1994):

Chiapas loses blood through many veins: through oil and gas ducts, electric lines, train cars, bank accounts, trucks and vans, boats and planes, through clandestine paths, gaps, and forest trails. This land continues paying tribute to the imperialists: petroleum, electric energy, cattle, money, coffee, banana, honey, corn, cacao, tobacco, sugar, soy, melon, sorghum, mamey, mango, tamarind, avocado, and Chiapan blood flows as a result of the thousand some teeth sunk into the throat of southeastern Mexico. Primary materials, thousands of millions which flow to Mexican ports, and railroad, air, and truck transportation centers headed towards different part of the world: The United States, Canada, Holland, Germany, Italy, Japan; but with the same fate: imperialism.

Every day they suck 92,000 barrels of petroleum and 516,000,000 cubic feet of gas. They take the petroleum and gas away and leave the stamp of capitalism as change: ecological destruction, agricultural scraps, hyper-inflation, alcoholism, prostitution, and poverty. The beast is not satisfied and extends its tentacles to the Lacandon Forest: eight petroleum deposits are under exploration. The paths are made with machetes by the same peasants who were left without land by the insatiable beast. The trees fall and dynamite explodes on land where peasants are not allowed to cut down trees to cultivate the land. Every tree that is cut down costs the United States, as a further devaluation of the peso in 1995 caused wages in Mexico to fall even lower. Multinational corporations with facilities in Mexico stand to gain from this, but if the increased exploitation results in more illegal immigration, tensions in border states like California and Texas will be heightened. In addition, corporations in the United States may feel an even greater incentive to move some of their operations south of the border. Meanwhile, the possibility of Mexico climbing out of the cycle of debt is nil. Mexico simply does not make enough money from exports to raise the money it needs to pay off the debt. For example, in 1995, Mexico faced interest payments and a maturing principal in the neighborhood of $70–80 billion, but total exports raised only $30–35 billion.[85]

Devaluing the currency is especially problematic. Currency devaluation makes the peso worth less in relation to foreign currencies. Consequently, if you are a foreigner you can now buy Mexican goods for a lower price or take greater advantage of the even lower price for Mexican labor. If you are a wealthy Mexican and some of your wealth is held in overseas banks, domestic

---

them a fine of ten minimum wages and a jail sentence. The poor cannot cut down trees while the petroleum beast, every day more in foreign hands, can. The peasant cuts them to survive, the beast to plunder.

Chiapas also bleeds coffee. Thirty-five percent of the coffee produced in Mexico comes from the area . . . 53 percent is exported abroad, principally to the United States and Europe.

The second most important export after coffee is beef. The cattle are sold for 400 pesos per kilo by the poor farmers and resold by the coyotes and introducers for up to 10 times the price they paid for them.

The tribute that capitalism demands from Chiapas has no historical parallel. Fifty-five percent of national hydro-electric energy comes from this state along with 20 percent of Mexico's total electrical energy. However, only one-third of the homes in Chiapas have electricity.

Honey which is produced in 79,000 beehives in Chiapas goes entirely to U.S. and European markets. Some 2,756 tons of honey produced annually in the Chiapas countryside is converted into dollars which the people of Chiapas never see.

What does the beast leave behind in exchange for all it takes away?

Half the people of Chiapas have no potable water and two-thirds have no sewerage. Education is the worst in the country. One and a half million people have no medical services at their disposal. Fifty-four percent of the Chiapan population suffers from malnutrition and in the highlands and forests this percentage increases to 80 percent.

currency devaluation makes your foreign money worth much more. This is one reason why comprador elites often accede to IMF demands for currency devaluation. The nation's working class suffers, but the local elite profit.

Neoliberal economic measures, such as forced currency devaluation and unregulated foreign investment, along with the control of currency exchange rates by institutions such as the IMF, facilitate the exploitation of nations and continents by corporate interests.

In the words of Joseph Stiglitz:

> The billions of dollars which it [the IMF] provides are used to maintain exchange rates at unsustainable levels for a short period, during which the foreigners and the rich are able to get their money out of the country at more favorable terms (through the open capital markets that the IMF has pushed on the countries). For each ruble, for each rupiah, for each cruzeiro, those in the country get more dollars as long as the exchange rates are sustained.[86]

POPULATION DISPLACEMENT AND URBANIZATION

Over the course of world history three massive migrations of people have taken place. The first was the great urban implosion that took place in Europe during the transition from feudalism to capitalism. The second was the great migration of people to the Americas, particularly during the late 1800s and early 1900s. The third is taking place today in the Third World as millions of people are being uprooted from the countryside and moving to the urban centers. The population of Mexico City and its surrounding metropolis, for example, is now over twenty million; Sao Paolo, Brazil, is nearly nineteen million; and over a quarter of El Salvador's population lives in the city of San Salvador.[87]

Three major forces are contributing to this latest migration. One is the routine functioning of the market, which we have already examined, that is driving people from their farmlands. The second is war. And the third consists of a variety of development projects such as those run by the World Bank. All these factors are not only displacing people but they are making them poorer.

It is estimated that development projects run by the World Bank alone have forcibly displaced more than two million people, and that number could be doubled within just a few years if the World Bank proceeds with its currently scheduled projects.[88] In addition, according to the World Bank's own analysis, "There is not a Bank project in the world where resettled people have managed to regain their prior level of income."[89]

CONCLUSION

Colonialism and neocolonialism (formal political independence but a continued system of economic exploitation by other nations) have had three major effects on the world today:

1. They have set back development and helped create the groundwork for intense and prolonged poverty and hunger.
2. They have built the foundation for the development of authoritarian states, which restrict basic human rights and thereby keep people from creating solutions to these problems.
3. They have hastened environmental degradation by forcing overuse of farming and grazing land and by the extraction and use of raw materials for the needs of industrialization.

Today many Third World authoritarian states are propped up with money, military equipment, and training from the developed nations for a wide variety of reasons. We now turn to an examination of the various types of conflicts that are all too frequent in the current world, and we'll see how these conflicts are in some ways the legacy of colonialism and in other ways the result of present policies of the core nations.

NOTES

1. Jared Diamond, *Guns, Germs, and Steel: The Fates of Human Societies* (New York: W. W. Norton, 1999).

2. Ted C. Lewellen, *Dependency and Development: An Introduction to the Third World* (Westport, Conn.: Bergin and Garvey, 1995), p. 31.

3. Walt W. Rostow, *The Stages of Economic Growth: A Non-Communist Manifesto* (Cambridge, England: Cambridge University Press, 1964), pp. 5–10.

4. Andrew Webster, *Introduction to the Sociology of Development*, 2d ed. (Atlantic Highlands, N.J.: Humanities Press, 1991), p. 52.

5. *Contemporary Authors*, New Revision Series, vol. 8, pp. 427–29; William Blum, *Killing Hope: U.S. Military and CIA Interventions Since World War II*

(Monroe, Maine: Common Courage Press, 1995), p. 117; David Halberstam, *The Best and the Brightest* (New York: Penguin Books, 1972), pp. 193–200, 772–76.

6. Mike Mason, *Development and Disorder: A History of the Third World Since 1945* (Hanover, N.H.: University Press of New England, 1997), pp. 21–23.

7. Quoted in Ronald Colman, "Measuring Real Progress," *Genuine Progress Index Atlantic* (Canada) [online], www.gpiatlantic.org/realprog.pdf.

8. Lewellen, *Dependency,* p. 3.

9. Ranjit Sau, *Unequal Exchange, Imperialism, and Underdevelopment* (Oxford, England: Oxford University Press, 1978), p. 3.

10. Albert Szymanski, *The Logic of Imperialism* (New York: Praeger, 1981), p. 31.

11. Ibid.

12. Webster, *Introduction to the Sociology of Development,* p. 85.

13. Andre Gunder Frank, *Capitalism and Underdevelopment in Latin America* (New York: Monthly Review Press, 1969), p. 318.

14. Webster, *Introduction to the Sociology of Development,* p. 85.

15. Immanuel Wallerstein, *The Capitalist World Economy* (Cambridge, England: Cambridge University Press, 1979), pp. 5–6.

16. Ibid., p. 18.

17. James O'Connor, "Capitalism, Uneven Development, and Ecological Crisis," in *Critical Perspectives in Sociology,* ed. Berch Berberoglu (Dubuque, Iowa: Kendall/Hunt Publishing, 1993), pp. 256–64.

18. Tom Barry et al., *Dollars and Dictators: A Guide to Central America* (New York: Grove Press, 1983), p. 112 and elsewhere; see also "Challenging the Leadership of the Global Economy," *Global Exchange* (fall 1994).

19. Alan B. Durning, *Poverty and the Environment: Reversing the Downward Spiral* (Washington, D.C.: Worldwatch Institute, 1989), p. 14.

20. Ibid., p. 19.

21. Much of the information on Leopold's rule in the Congo comes from E. D. Morel, *The Black Man's Burden* (New York: Monthly Review Press, 1969). Morel's book was first published in Great Britain in 1920; see esp. chaps. 9 and 10. See also Leften S. Stavrianos, *Global Rift: The Third World Comes of Age* (New York: William Morrow, 1981), pp. 301–303; and Adam Hochschild's superb and moving *King Leopold's Ghost* (Boston: Houghton Mifflin, 1999).

22. Richard W. Franke and Barbara H. Chasin, *Seeds of Famine* (Montclair, N.J.: Allanheld, Osmun, 1980), pp. 64–65.

23. Frances Moore Lappé and Joseph Collins, *World Hunger, Twelve Myths* (New York: Grove Press, 1986), p. 17.

24. Richard W. Franke, "Why Hunger? An Anthropologist's Viewpoint," paper presented at the Victor Johnson Symposium on World Hunger, Amherst College, Amherst, Massachusetts, December 3, 1981, p. 8.

25. Samir Amin, *Unequal Development* (New York: Monthly Review Press, 1976), p. 299.

26. Ibid., p. 199. This analysis of British colonialism's impact on India's development also applies to the nation of Bangladesh, which by the mid-1850s had become part of British India.

27. Marx, *Capital* (New York: International Publishers, 1967), 2:140–41; and Franke, "Why Hunger?" p. 6.

28. Jawaharlal Nehru, *The Discovery of India* (Garden City, N.Y.: Anchor Books, 1959), p. 219.

29. Ibid., p. 217.

30. Ibid., p. 219.

31. Ibid., p. 221.

32. Ibid.

33. The number of deaths and the immigration statistics come from *Encyclopedia Britannica*, vol. 17 (Chicago: Encyclopedia Britannica, 1985), p. 359.

34. James DeFronzo, *Revolutions and Revolutionary Movements*, 2d ed. (Boulder, Colo.: Westview Press, 1996); see chap. 3, "Revolution in China." See also *The World Guide 2001/02* (Oxford: New Internationalist Publications, 2001), pp. 165–67.

35. Sau, *Unequal Exchange, Imperialism, and Underdevelopment*, pp. 40–41.

36. Clive Thomas, *The Rise of the Authoritarian State in Peripheral Societies* (New York: Monthly Review Press, 1984), p. xiii.

37. Ibid., p. 136.

38. Ibid., p. 20.

39. The Horn of Africa, for instance, has suffered numerous civil wars and famines in recent decades. The conflicts and the development problems are the heritage of differential treatment by the colonial powers. For example, John Prendergast and John Fierno comment, "The roots of the civil wars lie in the colonial rule of the British and the Italians and the monarchical rule in Ethiopia until 1974. Instead of promoting social harmony, colonial administrators and Ethiopian monarchs intensified ethnic and religious tensions by favoring some groups at the expense of others. As this strategy divided the local population and allowed for dictatorial rule, economic and political inequities linked to ethnic origin or religion endure and undermined these modern nation-states" ("Crisis in the Horn of Africa," in *Altered States*, ed. Phyllis Bennis and Michel Moushabeck [New York: Olive Branch Press, 1993], p. 345). This was typical of colonial policies throughout the world. In the case of the Horn of Africa, the situation was worsened by postcolonial cold war policies: "Since independence, government armies across the Horn of Africa have been the main beneficiaries of foreign aid programs. During the Cold War, the Horn's dictators were assets to the superpowers, and military aid was the most facile instrument for the cooptation of African leaders" (ibid.).

40. Food First (Institute for Food and Development Policy), *12 Myths About Hunger* [online], www.foodfirst.org/pubs/backgrdrs/1998/s98v5n3.html.

41. Dinyar Godrej, "Hunger in a World of Plenty," *New Internationalist* (May 1995): 8.

42. Durning, *Poverty and the Environment*, p. 26.

43. Food First, www.foodfirst.org/pubs/backgrdrs/1998/s98v5n3.html.

44. According to Lappé and Collins, *World Hunger*, p. 12, 300 million Indians are going hungry. The world's second-largest food exporter is Brazil, but eighty-six million Brazilians are suffering from hunger.

45. Susan George and Nigel Paige, *Food for Beginners* (Oxford, England: Oxford University Press, 1982), p. 68.

46. Durning, *Poverty and the Environment*, p. 26.

47. Frances Moore Lappé and Anna Lappé, *Hope's Edge* (New York: Tarcher/Putnam, 2002), pp. 38–39.

48. Oxfam, *Facts for Action*.

49. Lappé and Collins, *World Hunger*, pp. 26, 27; and Richard W. Franke and Barbara H. Chasin, *Kerala: Radical Reform as Development in an Indian State* (San Francisco: Institute for Food and Development Policy, 1989).

50. *Food First Action Alert: Nicaragua: Give Change a Chance* (San Francisco: Food First and Institute for Food and Development Policy).

51. Franke and Chasin, *Kerala*, pp. 54–56.

52. Lappé and Collins, *World Hunger*, pp. 74–75. For an informative discussion of land reform and development in South Korea and Taiwan, see Stephen Rosskamm Shalom, "Capitalism Triumphant?" *Z Magazine*, April 1989.

53. Lappé and Collins, *World Hunger*, pp. 36–37.

54. Durning, *Poverty and the Environment*, p. 42.

55. Peter Freund and George T. Martin, *The Ecology of the Automobile* (Montreal, Canada: Black Rose Press, 1994), p. 65.

56. Ibid., p. 67.

57. Hillary French, "Clearing the Air," in *State of the World, 1994*, ed. Lester Brown et al. (New York: W. W. Norton, 1994).

58. Mason, *Development and Disorder*, pp. 27–28.

59. Susan George, *A Short History of Neoliberalism*, presented at the Conference on Economic Sovereignty in a Globalizing World, Bangkok, March 24–26, 1999. See [online], www.millennium-round.org/. See also Elizabeth Martinez and Arnoldo Garcia, *What Is "Neo-Liberalism"? A Brief Definition for Activists* [online], apctax.igc.apc.org/envjustice/neolib.html.

60. Philip McMichael, *Development and Social Change: A Global Perspective* (Thousand Oaks, Calif.: Pine Forge Press, 2000), p. 241.

61. George, *A Short History*, 1999.

62. Robert S. Browne, "The IMF and the World Bank in the New World Order," in *Altered States*, ed. Bennis and Moushabeck, pp. 117–19.

63. Ibid., p. 124.

64. Ibid., p. 120.

65. Juliette Majot, "Brave New World Bank," *Global Exchange* (winter 1994): 6.

66. Ibid., p. 2.

67. Davison Budhoo, "IMF/World Bank Wreak Havoc on Third World," in *Fifty Years Is Enough: The Case Against the World Bank and the International Monetary Fund*, ed. Kevin Danaher (Boston: South End Press, 1994), pp. 21–22. Budhoo is an economist from Grenada who resigned from the IMF in 1988 in protest of what he called its "increasingly genocidal policies."

68. Freund and Martin, *The Ecology of the Automobile*, p. 69.

69. "Challenging the Leadership of the Global Economy," *Global Exchange* (fall 1994): 2; Budhoo, "IMF/World Bank," p. 21.

70. Anthony DePalma, with Peter Truell, "A Mexican Mover and Shaker Got the Red Carpet at Citibank," *New York Times,* June 5, 1966.

71. Bruce Rich, "World Bank/IMF: Fifty Years Is Enough," in *Fifty Years Is Enough*, ed. Danaher, p. 8.

72. Ibid.

73. Ibid., p. 10.

74. Catherine Caufield, *Masters of Illusion: The World Bank and the Poverty of Nations* (New York: Henry Holt, 1996), p. 242.

75. Ibid., p. 243.

76. Ibid.

77. Vandana Shiva, "International Institutions Practicing Environmental Double Standards," in *Fifty Years Is Enough*, ed. Danaher, p. 102.

78. Larry Rohter, "Brazilians Find Political Cost for Help from I.M.F.," *New York Times*, August 8, 2002.

79. Walker F. Todd, "Bailing Out the Creditor Class," *Nation*, February 13, 1995.

80. "The Contract with Mexico," *Left Business Observer,* March 14, 1995.

81. Medea Benjamin and Kevin Danaher, "Killing Mexican Peasants to Restore Investor Confidence," *Global Exchange* (spring 1995): 3.

82. Ibid., p. 1. See also *Dollars and Sense*, May–June 1995, p. 4.

83. "The Contract with Mexico," *Left Business Observer*, p. 3.

84. Quoted in Kevin Danaher, ed., *Mexico's Economic Crisis* (San Francisco: Global Exchange, 1995).

85. Ibid., p. 7.

86. Joseph E. Stiglitz, *Globalization and Its Discontents* (New York: W. W. Norton, 2002), p. 209.

87. *World Almanac and Book of Facts, 1993* (New York: Pharos Books), pp. 818, 751.

88. Majot, "Brave New World Bank," p. 5.

89. Ibid., p. 6.

8

THE COLD WAR AND U.S. INTERVENTIONISM

When the Soviet Union went through a series of rapid changes that started in the mid-1980s and culminated in the breakup of the union in 1991, it marked the end of an era not only for the people of the Soviet Union and the eastern bloc nations of Europe but for world politics as well. The end of the two-superpower era and the reshuffling of strategic national alliances led to the common use of the term the *new world order*. To understand this era we must first distinguish it from its predecessor, the old world order. How do these two eras differ?

Perhaps the most outstanding feature of the old world order was the polarity represented by the United States and the Soviet Union. Openly hostile to each other for decades, the two superpowers faced each other in a standoff backed by the most advanced military capabilities in the world and by nuclear arsenals that were theoretically capable of destroying the people of the earth many times over. Some strategists argued that these weapons actually ensured a relative state of peace because any attack by one country on the other would bring a retaliation that would result in the destruction of both nations. This steady state came to be known as MAD, *mutually assured destruction*; it represented the animosity and anxiety that loomed over entire generations of the world's people. By the 1980s, disarmament movements (in Europe, the United States, and the Soviet Union), economic constraints on the two superpowers (particularly the Soviets), and popular pressure for democratic reforms in the Soviet Union all combined to bring an end to the nuclear arms race and to the relative hegemony of military priorities in the Soviet Union.

However, the old world order consisted of much more than the Soviet-U.S. dichotomy. At times the whole of the twentieth century has been referred to as the "American century" and the period after World War II as "Pax Americana." What these terms attempt to capture is the ascendancy of the United States in the realms of world politics, military might, industrialization, science, and other areas. One of the most salient components of the old world order was the ability of the United States to impose its will on many of the nations of the Third World in spite of opposition from the Soviet Union, or from anyone else for that matter. In fact, much of the cold war hostility between the United States and the Soviet Union can be better understood as a ploy to rally support for U.S. Third World policies.

This was obviously the case when the United States claimed that a conspiracy to take over Guatemala was being orchestrated by the Soviet Union and then manufactured evidence to show to the media, offering "proof" of a totally unfounded accusation. The threat of Soviet expansionism was also used to justify and gain support for the war in Vietnam. As Noam Chomsky has stated, "The cold war framework was scarcely more than a pretext to conceal the standard refusal to tolerate third world independence."[1]

The old world order can be defined by the following characteristics: (1) a division of the world into two competing ideological and economic systems headed by the United States on one side and the Soviet Union on the other; (2) a European continent physically and ideologically divided—a reminder of the causes of two world wars and the hegemony of the Soviet Union and the United States; (3) a Third World in turmoil due to the rebellion against the imperialism of the United States and the European capitalist powers, and also due to the geopolitical strategies of the Soviet Union and the United States; and (4) perhaps most significant, the continued expansion of the capitalist world economy into all corners of the globe (including those nations calling themselves socialist) led by U.S. capital, arranged through the world's political and financial institutions, and ultimately supported by the threat or actual use of military force.

OLD WORLD ORDER INTERVENTIONISM

The intervention by the United States in many countries around the world is a key element of the old world order and is important to understand in order to illuminate the causes of many contemporary world problems. In the decades following World War II, U.S. military, political, and economic aims were pursued almost unchecked in the Third World. This was true particularly in Latin America. The United States often interfered in the affairs of various countries in order to help a particular candidate or political party succeed. Sometimes this interference consisted of channeling money to those whom it supported, sometimes it meant sending weapons or providing military backup, and sometimes it meant an outright invasion by U.S. military troops.

Europe after World War II

Immediately after World War II, the United States was involved in many efforts to stop the "spread of communism" in Europe. These efforts were often led by the CIA, which had been established by the National Security Act of 1947, which also established the National Security Council. The CIA, for example, spent $65 million over a twenty-year period to influence elections in Italy.[2] In the years following the war, the Italian Communist Party (PCI) had developed a large following. Membership in the party totaled about 2.5 million people in 1947, and the party had a good chance of winning the elections scheduled for 1948.[3] U.S. Secretary of Defense James Forrestal undertook efforts to raise money from his wealthy friends and Wall Street colleagues to run some operations to undermine the PCI. Allen Dulles, who had been an Office of Strategic Services chief in Switzerland during the war and had been asked by President Truman to help oversee the early years of the CIA, felt that prospects of a PCI victory in Italy were too serious for these operations to be left in private hands. Dulles urged the government to take on Forrestal's project, and so began decades of U.S. meddling in Italian elections.[4]

Once the federal government became involved, a wide variety of resources were called upon to aid the anticommunist cause. Voice of America radio programming began to emphasize the generosity of the United States toward Italy, and anti-Soviet propaganda increased. Radio programs used such Italian-American celebrities as Frank Sinatra to warn against a PCI victory. The first announcement of the Marshall Plan was made just before the elections. Two weeks prior to the elections, the United States insisted that Italy be allowed entrance as a member of the United Nations. These and other means of leverage helped defeat the PCI in the April 1948 elections.[5]

In Greece, as World War II came to a close, British troops moved in to crush Greek resistance fighters who had fought valiantly against the Nazi occupation. Anxious to regain their influence in Greece, the British were determined to restore the Greek king to power. In their determination the British used ex-members of the Nazi Security Battalion in active service in the Greek Army. The United States aided Great Britain in its efforts and gradually became more and more involved. Even before World War II had officially ended, the U.S. Navy and Air Force transported more than two British divisions into Greece to suppress the People's Liberation Army (ELAS). As D. F. Fleming asserts in *The Cold War and Its Origins*: "Greece was the first of the liberated states to be openly and forcibly compelled to accept the political system of the occupying Great Power. It was Churchill who acted first and Stalin who followed his example, in Bulgaria and then in Romania, though with less bloodshed."[6] By late 1946, guerrilla warfare was being waged in Greece, but within months Great Britain informed the United States that it could not bear the burden, militarily and economically. The Greek government then requested aid from the United States via an official letter that was actually drafted by officials in the U.S. State Department. By the end of 1947, the Greek military was entirely supported by American aid, and at least one fighting unit was composed primarily of ex-members of the Nazi Security Battalion.

During this period human rights in Greece deteriorated, and the Greek Left was finally defeated in 1949, having lost tens of thousands of lives. U.S. influence in Greece became very far-reaching. Andreas Papandreou, eventually Greece's premier from 1981 to 1989, declared that the United States "exercised almost dictatorial control during the early fifties."[7] In 1947, the American Mission to Aid Greece informed the State Department that they had "established practical control . . . over national budget, taxation, currency issuance, price and wage policies, and state economic planning, as well as over imports and exports, the issuance of foreign exchange and the direction of military reconstruction and relief expenditures."[8] In addition, the Greek government created the CYP, a virtual clone of the American CIA, which made further contributions to the deterioration of human rights in Greece.

The United States was to intervene again in Greek internal affairs in 1967. At that time, a coup was led by five military officers, four of whom reportedly had CIA or U.S. military connections. The coup led to the installation of George Papadopoulos as prime minister. Americans at the U.S. military mission in Greece privately joked that Papadopoulos was "the first CIA agent to become Premier of a European country."[9] Papadopoulos had been a captain in the Nazi Security Battalion and was on the CIA payroll for fifteen years. Under his rule human rights eroded to the point that Greece was forced out of the Council of Europe because of torture, murder, and other human rights violations. Later, in an interesting act of solidarity, the Papadopoulos junta made a $500,000 contribution to the 1968 Nixon-Agnew presidential campaign.[10]

Iran

One of the earliest and most successful CIA operations took place in Iran in the early 1950s. Iran at that time was controlled by Premier Mohammad Mosaddeq (1880–1967), who was a progressive nationalist. Mosaddeq's government had nationalized the British-owned oil company that monopolized Iran's petroleum industry, and the United States and Great Britain, in particular, took exception to Mosaddeq's actions. The British, along with the U.S. government and the major American oil companies, led a worldwide boycott of Iranian oil. However, the boycott and the economic problems it caused did not succeed in toppling the government. So the CIA, along with British Intelligence, embarked on its first campaign to overthrow a government. The coup was led by Kermit "Kim" Roosevelt (the grandson of former president Theodore Roosevelt), and it successfully ousted Mosaddeq and established Shah Mohammad Reza Pahlavi as the unchallenged autocrat in Iran. It also established a major foothold in the region for American oil companies. Under a new agreement, Gulf Oil, Standard Oil, Socony-Mobil, and Texaco were to have a 40 percent share in Iran's oil.[11] Not coincidentally, Kim Roosevelt was made a vice president of Gulf Oil in 1960.[12]

But the coup planted the seeds for decades of repression, exploitation, and growing hatred of the West—especially the United States. The shah's Iran developed a reputation as one of the most repressive governments in the world and perhaps the world's worst human rights violator. Under the shah's rule the secret police (the SAVAK) grew to enormous proportions and wielded great power. In the late 1970s, before the shah was overthrown, there were estimates of 25,000–100,000 political prisoners being held in Iran's jails. But this tells only part of the story. According to one Amnesty International official, Iran at that time had the "highest rate of death penalties in the world, no valid system of civilian courts and a history of torture which is beyond belief. No country in the world has a worse record in human rights than Iran."[13]

Unbeknownst to much of the American public, the U.S. government was providing a great deal of the training for the SAVAK and was supplying the

Iranian military with the most advanced military equipment available. In fact, the SAVAK was set up by the CIA in 1957. The military officers who ran the SAVAK received their training "at the Marine base in Quantico, VA, and attended orientation programs at CIA headquarters in Langley, VA."[14] The U.S. Agency for International Development (AID) also financed police training programs in which SAVAK officers took part.[15]

U.S. actions in Iran from the 1950s to the late 1970s were undoubtedly the prime cause behind the great animosity the Iranian people showed toward the United States in the late 1970s and early 1980s when they overthrew the shah and took over the U.S. embassy, holding fifty-two Americans hostage for 444 days.

Indonesia

Like Iran, Indonesia was the victim of a U.S.-sponsored coup that overthrew a relatively progressive government and led to decades of repression and increased foreign exploitation. Long a Dutch colony, Indonesia gained formal independence in 1945. Indonesia is rich in oil, and its major exports are petroleum products, wood, and rubber. U.S. corporate interests have been present since the early 1900s when Standard Oil, Goodyear Tire and Rubber, and the U.S. Rubber Company began operating there. At the end of World War II, Indonesia declared its independence and began taking increasingly nationalistic positions. Numerous foreign companies were nationalized, and U.S. corporate interests were threatened. In 1958, the CIA supplied arms and a small air force to right-wing rebels who attempted to seize control of the government. The attempted takeover was unsuccessful, although it did provoke a civil war.[16] The CIA continued its efforts, and, after repeated attempts to bribe President Sukarno (1902–1970) had failed, it organized the Council of Generals, which was to lead a military coup in 1965. The council's existence and purpose was exposed, but the CIA kept up its efforts by supporting General Suharto, who eventually led an army takeover of the government in late 1965. Suharto ruled Indonesia until 1998 when he was overthrown in the midst of a severe economic crisis.[17]

The bloodshed that followed the 1965 coup remains one of the most devastating tragedies in human history, yet it is not a widely known one. Between 500,000 and 1 million people were killed by the new government and its armed supporters. Officially, 750,000 people were arrested, very few of whom were ever tried for any crimes. Furthermore, according to Amnesty International, not a single person tried for a crime was found not guilty.[18] The coup in Indonesia was talked about in much kinder terms by the U.S. government and the American press, and the "changes" that took place were generally hailed as being favorable ones. In fact, a look at Rand McNally's popular reference book *World Facts in Brief* reveals this sanitized version of these crucial events: "Economic and political instability led to an attempted Communist coup in 1965, after which the government outlawed communism, cut its ties with China, and strengthened relations with Western powers."[19]

U.S. involvement in the bloodbath was finally acknowledged by the United States in 1990. Former CIA and U.S. embassy officials revealed that over a period of several months the CIA handed over lists with the names of thousands of suspected communists to the Indonesian military. U.S. personnel in Indonesia and Washington, D.C., would later check off the names of those executed based on information received from Indonesian officials in Jakarta.[20]

The changes in Indonesia were a boon to Western financial interests. In 1967, Indonesia established a Foreign Investment Law that provided generous incentives to foreign companies. Goodyear, Uniroyal (formerly U.S. Rubber), Union Carbide, National Cash Register, Eastern Airlines, Mobil Oil, Freeport Sulphur, and many others moved in to reap the profits.[21] According to Noam Chomsky and Edward Herman, "By 1973 foreign interests controlled 59% of the capital invested in forestry, 96% in mining, 35% in industry, 47% in hotels and tourism, and 33% in agriculture and fisheries."[22] The new government clearly acted as a comprador class, selling its nation's resources and its citizens' rights for the money and arms that the core nations were willing to give. In addition, the new Indonesian government was intensely corrupt. Government officials often pocketed much of the tax money collected from the public and absconded with a great deal of the aid money that foreign governments contributed. Bribery also become widespread along with mismanagement of many government-run or regulated programs and industries.[23]

Repression, corruption, violence, massive foreign investment and profit making are still the prime characteristics of Indonesia today. In addition, Indonesia turned its aggression outward as it conducted an occupation of the former Portuguese colony of East Timor. Indonesia invaded East Timor in 1975 just hours after a cordial visit from President Gerald Ford and Secretary of State Henry Kissinger.[24] Roughly 150,000 East Timorese people lost their lives (a quarter of the total population) as a result of the invasion. According to Philip Liechty, an ex-CIA official, General Suharto was "explicitly given the green light to do what he did." Liechty also says that the United States supplied most of the weapons, ammunition, and even food for the Indonesian troops.[25] From the mid-1970s to the late 1990s, Indonesia kept up its occupation of East Timor with U.S. support, and continued its repression of the people with nary a word of criticism from the U.S. government or the American media.[26] East Timor finally became fully independent on October 25, 1999.

Chile

In 1970, Dr. Salvador Allende, a socialist, was elected president of Chile. The new government was a mixed coalition of political forces and contending viewpoints, but Allende was able to institute a variety of measures that were clearly designed to improve the quality of life for the people of Chile. These reforms placed the Allende government in direct opposition to foreign conglomerates and the U.S. government. Allende nationalized the copper mines, which previously had made enormous profits for two American companies—Kennecott Copper and Anaconda Copper. From 1955 to 1970, Anaconda Copper's annual profits averaged 21.5 percent in Chile compared to a 3.6 percent average in other countries. Kennecott's profits were even higher—52.8 percent per year, and there were several years when its profits exceeded 100 percent. The company's profits in Chile generally ran about five times greater than in other countries.[27]

Allende also began implementing a land reform program that had been passed in 1967 by a previous administration. Under this program the government began taking unused land owned by big landlords and corporations and distributing it to landless peasants.[28] Allende's programs were making a significant impact on the quality of life for many Chilean people. Michael Parenti sums up these changes:

> Through a variety of government programs, agricultural production showed a dramatic upsurge, the inflation rate dropped by half, construction was up 9 percent and unemployment down to less than 5 percent, the lowest in a decade. Beef and bread consumption increased by 15 percent in the 1971–72 period. A government program sought to provide every Chilean child with a half-liter of milk daily. During Allende's first year, the economy enjoyed an 8.5 percent growth in GNP, the second highest in Latin America. Generally, Allende pursued policies that threatened the prerogatives of the rich, cut into profits while increasing wages, and brought a modest redistribution of goods and services in favor of the poorer strata.[29]

One of the American-based companies that actively opposed Allende was ITT—International Telephone and Telegraph. Chilean officials had been negotiating to purchase ITT's share of the Chilean Telephone Company, but ITT refused to accept Chile's monetary offer that was based on an evaluation made by experts from other countries. ITT had previously recognized the threat that Allende represented to its financial and ideological interests. Prior to Allende's election in 1970, ITT had offered to make a $1 million contribution to the CIA to help prevent Allende from winning the election. (The CIA and other agencies had spent about $20 million in 1964 to keep Allende from getting elected then.) The financial offer was refused, but the State Department and the CIA had been making plans to derail Allende. ITT also began to make plans.[30]

Reminiscent of numerous personnel connections among the CIA, the State Department, and the United Fruit Company when the CIA did its dirty work in Guatemala, ITT, the CIA, and the State Department also shared personnel. ITT's director, John McCone, was the director of the CIA from 1961 to 1965, when he became director of ITT but secretly continued to work as a consultant to the CIA.[31] Likewise, Jack Neal, a high-ranking ITT employee described as an "anti-communist workhorse," had thirty years' experience in the State Department.[32] It was Neal who prepared an eighteen-point plan to bring about Allende's downfall. These plans included economic pressure through the cutoff of international credit (no doubt facilitated by the fact that ITT's president, Eugene Black, had been president of the World Bank) and aid to various opposition groups within the country.[33] Much of what ITT proposed was put into action by the CIA and the U.S. State Department. The United States put up an economic blockade around Chile, credit was cut off, and the CIA spent an estimated $8 million for right-wing activities in Chile. The thinking of the U.S. power elite is captured in the words of the U.S. ambassador to Chile at that time, Edward Korry: "Not a nut or a bolt will reach Chile under Allende. We will do everything in our power to condemn the Chilean people to utmost poverty and deprivation." President Nixon declared that we would "make the economy scream," and Secretary of State Henry Kissinger proclaimed: "I don't see why we need to stand by and watch a country go Communist due to the irresponsibility of its own people." Meanwhile, although aid and credit to the Chilean government was cut off, the United States increased its aid to the Chilean military to the tune of $47 million.[34]

In September 1973, the military seized power and killed Salvador Allende, ending a brief era of hope and progress for the Chilean people and throwing the country into a long period of suffering and continued pillage by foreign economic interests. The new government was headed by General Augusto Pinochet. The liberal rights of free expression enjoyed by the Chilean people under Allende, as well as many progressive government reforms such as the milk program for children and various health services, came to an abrupt and painful end. An estimated twenty thousand to thirty thousand people were killed (estimates vary widely), and many more were imprisoned by the new regime. Post-Allende Chile became infamous for its brutality toward Allende sympathizers and toward those who spoke out against Pinochet's crimes. Amnesty International declared, "Many people were tortured to death by means of endless whipping as well as beating with fists, feet and rifle butts. Prisoners were beaten on all parts of the body, including the head and sexual organs. The bodies of prisoners were found in the Rio Mapocho, sometimes disfigured beyond recognition."[35]

Victor Jara, Chile's most popular folksinger/guitarist was tortured to death. His body was found outside the stadium in Santiago that was used as a prison after the coup. Jara's hands had been broken and his body badly mutilated.[36]

Parenti described some of the grotesque viciousness of the Pinochet junta:

> The tortures delivered upon Pinochet's victims included application of electric shock to different parts of the body, particularly the genitals; forcing victims to witness the torture of friends and relatives; raping women in the presence of other family members; burning sex organs with acid or scalding water; placing infected rats into the vagina; mutilating, puncturing, and cutting off various parts of the body, including genitalia, eyes, and tongue; injection of air into women's breasts and veins (causing slow, painful death); shoving bayonets and clubs into the vagina or anus, causing rupture and death.[37]

After solidifying its power, the Chilean military junta (through Operation Condor) extended its terrorism to Chilean refugees in other countries, often with the cooperation of those similarly repressive states. Allende's former commander in chief, General Carlos Prats, for example, was killed by a bomb in Argentina. Orlando Letelier, another high-ranking official from the Allende administration, was assassinated in 1976, along with American Roni Moffit, right in Washington, D.C. The CIA, despite being aware that operatives sent by DINA (the Chilean secret police) had entered the country to do a job, did nothing to prevent the assassination. In fact, U.S. government officials later undertook an effort to create a false trail of evidence implicating Cuba in the killings. The head of the CIA at that time was George H. W. Bush, who, with partial credit to an uncritical press, later went on to become president without being tarnished by this potential scandal.[38] International pressure forced Chile to pursue the men behind the Letelier assassination and ultimately resulted in the conviction of General Manuel Contreras Sepulveda and Brigadier General Pedro Espinoza Bravo. Contreras and Espinoza were each given six-year sentences in 1995, which they served in a $2.7 million prison built at the request of General Pinochet. At the time of their incarceration, the prison in Punta de Peuco had no other prisoners.[39] Revelations made in 2002 disclosed that the day before Letelier's assassination a senior U.S. State Department official canceled an order that U.S. ambassadors approach South American dictators about ending their use of death squads.[40]

Dominican Republic

The full extent of U.S. intervention and interference in other countries may never be fully disclosed, but what we do know about it shows that it is very extensive. In addition to the cases of Italy, Iran, Guatemala, Indonesia, and Chile, which we have already discussed, there are many others. In Africa, for example, the CIA plotted to assassinate Patrice Lamumba of the Congo, and in January 1961, Lamumba was beaten to death by Congoese men who had a close relationship with the CIA.[41]

In 1965, President Johnson sent twenty-five thousand U.S. Marines into the Dominican Republic to block the return to office of Juan Bosch, who had been duly elected. The stated purpose of the intervention was to stop the spread of communism and protect lives. To help justify the invasion, Johnson told reporters at a press conference that "some 1,500 innocent people were murdered and shot, and their heads cut off." The decapitations were 99 percent fiction, but they served the purpose of mustering support for a military invasion.[42] The U.S. military action prevented Bosch's return to office and helped fortify a system of economic dependence and political exclusion.

In *The Washington Connection and Third World Fascism*, Chomsky and Herman point out the historical importance of the U.S. invasion. According to the authors, there are five main characteristics that marked the Dominican model of development in the years following Johnson's intervention. I summarize them here since they are applicable to many other U.S. *client states* (governments that are largely dependent on the United States and show great loyalty to it):

1. Extensive and systematic terror: As in Guatemala and elsewhere, the government of the Dominican Republic was brought into being by the power of the United States, and, "by a strange coincidence," paramilitary "death squads" came into being and terrorized much of the population.[43]
2. Corruption: Officials of the U.S.-backed government have shown a widespread willingness to be bought off. Corruption is commonplace, and U.S. corporations have shown an open willingness to bribe politicians.
3. A favorable investment climate: A variety of investment laws have given foreign corporations privileged status, exempting them from a whole plethora of tariffs and taxes.
4. Effective government pacification of the labor force: This refers to the implementation of various laws that make it difficult for trade unions to operate. In fact, government troops and police are regularly used to break up independent unions. The repression of workers' rights to strike or organize for better pay and working conditions goes hand in hand with the third point above. Like the tax laws, laws regulating the labor force are created or enforced for the benefit of foreign corporations.
5. A deterioration in the well-being of the population: Except for the elite and perhaps a small upper-middle class, the daily conditions of life in the Dominican Republic have deteriorated markedly. Since the living standards were not very high to begin with, this means that abject, life-threatening poverty has become even more commonplace.

Whereas these five characteristics represent a step backward in human rights and the material quality of life for the great majority of people in the Dominican Republic, to U.S. investors they represent stability and profit making—an ideal so emblazoned in the consciousness of U.S. officials that the U.S. embassy in the Dominican Republic referred to the nation as "one of the brightest spots in Latin America."[44] These characteristics also apply to many, if not all, of the nations where the United States has helped topple one government in favor of another.

Cambodia

The tragedy of Cambodia represents one of the low points of the twentieth century and has its roots in U.S. policy in Southeast Asia, particularly the latter stages of the Vietnam War. In Cambodia, on March 18, 1970, the government of Prince Norodum Sihanouk was overthrown by a coup d'etat led by CIA-trained Cambodian defense minister General Lon Nol. Lon Nol's forces included special commando units trained, armed, financed, and officered by the CIA. For fifteen years preceding the coup, the CIA had attempted to get Prince Sihanouk to change his neutralist policies and take a stronger role in "combating communism" in the region. These attempts included visits by Allen Dulles while he was head of the CIA, who offered "proof" that Cambodia was about to be taken over by communists. The "proof," however, directly contradicted Prince Sihanouk's own intelligence reports.

Sihanouk was intent on maintaining a high degree of independence from the United States, and he had a good deal of support in his efforts. In 1963, the Cambodian National Congress voted "to end all aid granted by the United States in the military, economic, technical and cultural fields." Sihanouk felt that the aid corrupted Cambodian officials and business-people who ended up "constituting a clientele necessarily obedient to the demands of the lavish bestower of foreign funds." Sihanouk felt Cambodian independence was compromised because the aid could only be used for private enterprise and not state institutions; nor could it be used for the defense of Cambodia in case of attacks by U.S. allies.[45]

After the 1970 coup, people around the country rose up to protest the new Lon Nol government, but they were violently suppressed by Nol's troops and CIA commandos.

These events, along with Nixon's secret war in Laos and Cambodia and the official U.S. invasion of Cambodia in 1970, left the region in turmoil and set the foundations for the Pol Pot regime that ruled Cambodia from 1976 to 1979. Under Pol Pot human rights disintegrated and upward of one million people were killed. The number of people killed by Pol Pot's Khmer Rouge is subject to debate, and some have suggested that it was convenient for the U.S. government and the media to exaggerate the casualties.[46] The United States clearly used the Pol Pot regime as an example of how bad communist governments can be and also as a means of shifting blame for the great turmoil in the region. For example, many of the dead attributed to the Khmer Rouge's terror may have been victims of the U.S. bombings that struck the country for four years. U.S. B-52 sorties reached a frequency as high as eighty-one per day—more than in Vietnam. Over 500,000 tons of bombs were dropped, destroying ancient irrigation systems, blackening the land, killing hundreds of thousands of Cambodians, and creating four million refugees.[47] With the countryside in ruins and the

In his farewell press conference in September 1973, Emory Swank, the American ambassador to Cambodia, called the war in Cambodia "Indochina's most useless war."

U.S. congressman Pete McClosky, following a visit to Cambodia, declared that what the United States had done to the country "is a greater evil than we have done to any country in the world, and wholly without reason, except for our own benefit to fight against the Vietnamese."

Others have called it Nixon's greatest crime.[48]

traditional social structure crippled, starvation and disease caused hundreds of thousands of more deaths. It is in this context that Pol Pot's regime came to power, and, in that sense, its creation was the doing of the United States.

Vietnam

U.S. involvement in Vietnam spanned several decades dating back to when Vietnam was still a French colony. By the end of France's war with Vietnam in 1954, the United States was paying 80 percent of the cost of the war.[49] At the end of the war, as the French faced an ignominious defeat at Dien Bien Phu, officials in the Eisenhower administration considered U.S. intervention and the use of nuclear weapons, but rejected the option when Congress and Britain balked. (According to former State Department official Daniel Ellsberg, U.S. Secretary of State John Foster Dulles went so far as to offer the French nuclear weapons to use against the Vietnamese.)[50]

After the defeat of the French, the United States moved to subvert the Geneva Accords, which called for the withdrawal of French troops and elections to be conducted in 1956. There is little question that Ho Chi Minh, the leader of the Vietnamese revolutionary movement, would have won these elections handily and the nation would have been unified. President Eisenhower was well aware of this and said so in his memoirs: "I have never talked or corresponded with a person knowledgeable in Indochinese affairs who did not agree that had elections been held at the time of the fighting, possibly 80 percent of the population would have voted for the Communist Ho Chi Minh as their leader rather than Chief of State Bo Dai."[51]

The view that Vietnam was two countries, North Vietnam and South Vietnam, was an ideological fabrication of the U.S. government. The Geneva Accords were quite specific that the seventeenth parallel was a "provisional demarcation line" to aid in some of the practical aspects of

Robert S. McNamara, one-time president of Ford Motor Company, secretary of defense under John F. Kennedy and Lyndon Johnson, and later the president of the World Bank, was one of the main architects of the U.S. war in Vietnam during the 1960s, so much so that the Vietnam War has sometimes been referred to as "McNamara's war." In his 1995 book *In Retrospect: The Tragedy and Lessons of Vietnam*, McNamara acknowledges that "we were wrong, terribly wrong" about Vietnam. McNamara also sheds some light on the Tonkin Gulf incident, noting that CIA commandos, acting as part of OPLAN 34-A, had conducted raids on two islands in the gulf just two days before the North Vietnamese made the alleged attack on the U.S. destroyers. McNamara points out that top officials in the White House, the Pentagon, and the CIA were all aware of the commando mission.

French withdrawal and in the transition to self-rule. The accords stated unambiguously that the seventeenth parallel "should not in any way be interpreted as constituting a political or territorial boundary."[52] The Geneva Accords also prohibited "the introduction into Vietnam of any reinforcements in the form of all types of arms, munitions and other war material, such as combat aircraft, naval craft, pieces of ordnance, jet engines and jet weapons, and armored vehicles."[53] But the United States did just that. It helped arrange for Ngo Dinh Diem to be the premier of the mythical nation of South Vietnam and backed him up with over $1 billion in military and economic aid between 1955 and 1960.[54] But Diem's regime was so corrupt and unpopular that the State Department and the CIA decided Diem was too much of a political liability and sponsored a generals' coup in November 1963 that assassinated Diem and his brother Ngo Dinh Nhu, who headed the secret police.[55]

Major intervention was finally authorized in 1964 by the Gulf of Tonkin Resolution, which "gave the president unlimited authorization to conduct war in southeast Asia."[56] The resolution was based on an event of questionable origins, a confrontation between two U.S. destroyers and several Vietnamese PT boats, which history has shown either never occurred or was the result of a U.S. provocation.[57] In either case, the Tonkin Gulf incident became the pretext for wider U.S. involvement in a war that should have ended ten years before it did.

The CIA's successes in the 1950s and 1960s undoubtedly led to a false confidence that mired the nation more and more deeply into the war with Vietnam. The CIA ran a number of covert actions in Vietnam. One was the agency's Counter Terror program, which started in 1965. According to one

U.S. official who served as an adviser to South Vietnamese internal security officials, the Counter Terror teams and their successor, the Provincial Reconnaissance Units, used techniques of terror including assassination, physical abuse, kidnaping, and intimidation.[58] A later program was called Operation Phoenix. While ostensibly a program to counter Vietnamese "terrorists," the program really served to suppress opposition to the Saigon government and to the United States. Under the ultimate authority of CIA director William Colby, Operation Phoenix was responsible for the deaths of over twenty thousand suspected Vietcong (according to Colby's testimony to Congress) in its first two and a half years of operation. The South Vietnamese government placed the death toll higher, at forty-one thousand. By the end of Operation Phoenix, at least thirty-five thousand Vietnamese had been murdered.[59] According to Robert F. Gould, Colby's legal adviser in Saigon, "everybody there accepted torture as routine." Another Phoenix agent said he "never knew an individual to be detained as a 'Vietcong' suspect who ever lived through an interrogation."[60]

U.S. involvement in Southeast Asia gradually grew to include a secret air and ground war in Laos and a secret air war in Cambodia. When these became public the intensity of protest by Americans increased, particularly on college campuses. The extent of public protest was one of the factors that led Nixon to initiate COINTELPRO (see chapter 5) and also to assemble the team of "plumbers" who broke into Democratic headquarters and started the whole Watergate scandal. The plumbers were originally formed to stop information leaks about the war and broke into the office of Daniel Ellsberg's psychiatrist to obtain material damaging to Ellsberg. Ellsberg had worked in the State Department and had leaked the famous *Pentagon Papers* to the press.[61] On April 30, 1970, Nixon announced the invasion of Cambodia, and this triggered demonstrations across the country including the infamous one at Kent State University in Ohio, where four students were shot to death by National Guard troops.

As the light at the end of the tunnel grew dimmer, the actions of the U.S. government became more senseless and reached a point of desperation. Nixon escalated the bombings in Vietnam to horrific proportions, and U.S. military activities became less directed at winning the war and more at punishing the Vietnamese and making the country unlivable. The idea that the U.S. government had held back and fought with one hand tied behind its back (as portrayed in the film *Rambo* and a host of Hollywood's other Vietnam War movies) is, for the most part, untrue. The scale of the bombings inflicted on Vietnam is staggering:

During all of World War II, the United States dropped about 2,000,000 tons of bombs in all theaters, including the strategic bombing of Europe and Japan, and the tactical bombing in all campaigns throughout the Pacific and European theaters. By the end of 1971, the United States had dropped 6,300,000 tons of bombs on Indochina. In just two years, 1968–1969, the United States dropped over one-and-a-half times more tonnage on South Vietnam alone than all the Allies dropped on Germany throughout World War II. By 1969, North Vietnam was being hit each month with the explosive force of two atomic bombs. The 1972 Christmas bombing alone ravaged Hanoi and Haiphong with more tonnage than Germany dropped on Great Britain from 1940 through 1945. The total firepower used by the United States on Vietnam probably exceeded the amount used in all previous wars combined. Bombs dropped on Vietnam between 1965 and 1969 equaled "500 pounds . . . for every man, woman, and child in Vietnam."[62]

By the end of the war some three million Vietnamese were dead, the countryside was scarred by millions of bomb craters (twenty-one million in South Vietnam alone), and South Vietnam had been sprayed with eighteen million gallons of poisonous chemicals.[63] These numbers, of course, do not come close to capturing the human suffering, nor can they help us to measure how much Vietnam's future development—economically, politically, and socially—was set back.

For the United States, the cost of the war was much less, but it still had a dramatic impact on the nation. Fifty-eight thousand Americans lost their lives in the Vietnam War, and many more were wounded or disabled. The nation split over the war and, perhaps most important, trust in government plummeted. The consensus on American foreign policy ended, and the nation suffered the effects of what many people called the *Vietnam syndrome*. The syndrome referred to the reluctance of politicians and/or the population at large to support foreign intervention or commit U.S. troops anywhere where they might get involved in a prolonged conflict. The United States did not want another costly war.

Nicaragua

"We have never interfered in the internal government of a country and have no intention of doing so, never had any thought of the kind."

—Ronald Reagan

With the bitter taste of defeat in Vietnam still fresh, the U.S. government slowly edged toward another entanglement in Central America, this time against smaller nations much closer to home. U.S. intervention in Nicaragua had been long-standing, but in the 1980s, the strength of the Sandinista government frustrated U.S. government officials in a way that was similar to the situation in Vietnam. It was partly the inability to impose the will of U.S. policymakers on Nicaragua that led to more talk of the Vietnam syndrome. For years the United States viewed Central and South America as its "backyard," and the Caribbean was frequently referred to as "the American Lake"; these were places where the United States could do as it pleased and where other imperial powers were excluded.[64]

One of the earlier cases of U.S. military intervention in Nicaragua helped to set the stage for the tensions between the United States and Nicaragua in the 1980s. In 1912, the U.S. Marines were sent to Nicaragua to back a conservative party revolt against the existing nationalist government. The marines stayed intermittently for twenty years, and they established the National Guard under the leadership of Anastasio Somoza Garcia (1896–1956). Somoza was responsible for assassinating Cesar Augusto Sandino in 1934. Sandino had been the leader of a popular and powerful antiimperialist army of peasants.

Somoza increased his power in 1936 when he ousted President Juan Bautista Sacasa, and with the blessings of the U.S. government Somoza initiated the longest, most corrupt dictatorship in Latin America. In 1956, Somoza's son Luis Somoza Debayle (1923–1967) became president, and in 1967 his other son, Anastasio Somoza Debayle (1925–1980), became president.

An indication of the power and corruption of the Somoza regimes is illustrated by the fact that in 1934 the Somoza family had practically no land, but by the 1950s, the family was the country's largest landowner. By the 1960s, the family owned the country's only airline, one television station, a newspaper, a cement plant, textile mills, sugar refineries, breweries and distilleries, and a Mercedes Benz dealership.[65] To renew the struggle begun by Sandino and his followers, the Sandinista National Liberation Front was founded in 1961. After a prolonged struggle against the U.S.-backed Somoza dictatorship, the Sandinistas finally succeeded in deposing Somoza on July 19, 1979. As a parting shot, Samoza ordered his air force to bomb the capital city of Managua. He also ran off with nearly the entire national treasury, making himself one of the richest men in all the world, and was given refuge in the United States.

Somoza left his nation in a state of poverty and deprivation. At the time of the Sandinista victory, infant mortality in Nicaragua was 120 per 1,000 live births, and life expectancy was just fifty-three years. At least 57 percent of the population was illiterate, and unemployment was officially 22 percent. But all were not poor; those in the comprador class had profited immensely. The top 5 percent of the population received 30 percent of the GDP, but the bottom 50 percent received just 15 percent of it.[66]

The Sandinista government instituted a variety of reforms that reflected its commitment to the Nicaraguan people. Among these were some exemplary health and education programs. During the first five years that the Sandinista government was in power, illiteracy was reduced from 57 percent to 13 percent, infant mortality dropped from 120 to 75 per 1,000, unemployment was cut in half, and 40,000 previously landless families received land. There were also major health campaigns to eradicate measles, polio, malaria, and diphtheria. In fact, improvement in healthcare was so impressive that Nicaragua received an award from the World Health Organization for the greatest achievement in health by any Third World nation.[67] Nicaragua was also unanimously chosen by UNESCO in 1980 for its grand prize in recognition of the country's national literacy campaign. Food production and distribution also improved markedly. After three years Nicaraguans were eating 30 to 40 percent more rice and corn than before 1979.

The U.S. reaction to the Sandinistas was one of increasing hostility, which brought the two nations to the verge of war and caused the Reagan administration to wage a furious misinformation campaign designed to sway U.S. public opinion. It also led to a whole variety of actions on the part of administration officials that violated national and international laws. In the early 1980s, the CIA began covert operations against Nicaragua, and President Reagan became more and more obsessed with overthrowing the Sandinistas, though at first he denied this was his aim. He even went so far as to declare, "We have never interfered in the internal government of a country and have no intention of doing so, never had any thought of the kind."[68] The programs instituted by the Sandinistas became the targets of attacks by U.S.-backed opposition groups known collectively as the *contras*. President Reagan referred to the contras as the moral equivalent of our nation's founding fathers, thereby besmirching our nation's heritage, since the contras were anything but moral. Contra forces regularly assassinated literacy teachers and burned down health clinics and schools. Their atrocities were widely documented by a variety of international human rights organizations. Americas Watch, for example, reported that the contras engaged in kidnapings, torture, and murder of unarmed civilians. Likewise, a 1984 report by the Council on Hemispheric Affairs condemned the contras as being one of "the worst human rights violators" in Latin America.[69] Edgar Chamorro, a former member of the directorate of the Fuerza Democratica Nicaraguense (FDN)—the principal U.S.-funded contra group—confirmed these reports, "During my four years as a 'contra' director, it was premeditated policy to terrorize civilian noncombatants to prevent them from cooperating with the government. Hundreds of civilian murders, mutilations, tortures and rapes were committed in pursuit of this policy, of which the 'contra' leaders and their CIA superiors were well aware."[70]

In support of the contras, the U.S. government went to great extremes. It supplied them with tens of millions of dollars in arms. It attempted to create a conflict between Nicaragua and its neighbors. It even went so far as to mine Nicaragua's harbors, damaging a dozen merchant freighters from six different countries.[71] The U.S. government also permitted the existence of ten to fifteen illegal military training camps within U.S. borders that operated as bases for contra terrorist activities.[72]

During the 1980s, Nicaragua made numerous overtures to the United States in order to bring about a peaceful settlement. For instance, Nicaragua proposed border inspections by international officials in order to refute claims that Nicaragua was arming rebels in El Salvador (Nicaragua served to gain by this since these inspections would undoubtedly show that it was the contras who were crossing the borders in order to wage the war and then find refuge in Honduras or Costa Rica). Nicaragua was the only country in the region that was willing to ban arms imports and remove foreign military advisers from the region.[73] Nicaragua also brought its case to the UN's World Court in The Hague, Netherlands, which found the United States in violation of a multitude of international laws.

In December 1982, Congress passed the *Boland Amendment*, which prohibited the use of funds to support the contras and any efforts to overthrow the government of Nicaragua. The Boland Amendment was held in little regard by the Reagan administration, and various efforts were undertaken to circumvent it. Violation of the Boland Amendment by Reagan's staff eventually led to the biggest government scandal since Watergate. In spite of the law, the Reagan administration attempted to continue funding the contras by soliciting donations from private sources and by diverting money from illegal arms sales to Iran. Private citizens such as Joseph Coors (of Coors Brewing) donated money to a fund-raising network directed by Marine Lieutenant Colonel and National Security Council member Oliver North. The money was laundered through several Panamanian companies,

Nicaragua v. *The United States*
Excerpts from the World Court Ruling, June 27, 1986

- The Court, by 12 votes to 3, rejects the justification of collective self-defense maintained by the United States of America in connection with the military and paramilitary activities in and against Nicaragua, the subject of this case.
- By 12 votes to 3, decides that the United States of America, by training, arming, equipping, financing and supplying the contra forces or otherwise encouraging, supporting and aiding military and paramilitary activities in and against Nicaragua, has acted against the Republic of Nicaragua, in breach of its obligations under customary international law not to intervene in the affairs of another state.
- By 12 votes to 3, decides that the United States of America, by certain attacks on Nicaraguan territory in 1983–84 has acted, against the Republic of Nicaragua, in breach of its obligation under customary international law not to use force against another state.
- By 12 votes to 3, decides that, by laying mines in the internal or territorial waters of the Republic of Nicaragua during the first months of 1984, the United States of America has acted, against the Republic of Nicaragua, in breach of its obligations under customary international law not to use force against another state, not to intervene in its affairs, not to violate its sovereignty and not to interrupt peaceful maritime commerce.
- By 14 votes to 1, decides that the United States of America, by producing in 1983, a manual entitled "Operationes sicologicas en guerra de guerrillas," and disseminating it to contra forces, has encouraged the commission by them of acts contrary to general principles of humanitarian law; but does not find a basis for concluding that any such acts which may have been committed are imputable to the United States of America as acts of the United States of America.
- By 12 votes to 3, decides that the United States of America is under a duty immediately to cease and to refrain from all such acts as may constitute breaches of the foregoing legal obligations.
- By 12 votes to 3, decides that the United States of America is under an obligation to make reparation to the Republic of Nicaragua for all injury caused to Nicaragua by the breaches of obligations under customary international law enumerated above.
- By 14 votes to 1, decides that the form and amount of which reparation, failing agreement between the parties, will be settled by the Court, and reserves for this purpose the subsequent proceedings in the case.
- Unanimously, recalls to both parties their obligation to seek a solution to their disputes in accordance with international law.[74]

deposited in Swiss bank accounts, and used to buy arms for the contras. The entire operation violated a variety of laws including the Boland Amendment and the Intelligence Oversight Act. However, to some the most appalling part of the Iran-contra scandal, or *contragate* as it became known, was the fact that North arranged for weapons to be sold to Iran during a time when the United States was hostile to Iran. In exchange Iran would help obtain the release of American hostages held in Lebanon.[75] The sale of missiles to Iran contradicted forceful statements made by Reagan during his election campaign against Jimmy Carter in 1980 to the effect that the U.S. government should never bargain for hostages. It also violated the Arms Export Control Act. Efforts to get at the truth behind the Iran-contra scandal were blocked by many administration officials, and a number of them were convicted of obstructing Congress and other charges. Very few of these individuals were sent to jail. After losing to Bill Clinton in the 1992 election, George H. W. Bush pardoned Secretary of Defense Caspar Weinberger and several others. Numerous other convictions were overturned because they were judged to be "tainted" by Oliver North's lengthy testimony to Congress years before, for which he was granted immunity from prosecution.

The trail of evidence also led to suspicions that Reagan officials may have made a deal with the Iranian government much earlier, which helped Reagan defeat Carter in the 1980 elections. Iran, at the time, had been holding fifty-two American hostages since taking over the U.S. embassy when the shah was overthrown. President Carter's inability to gain the release of the hostages was hurting him in his efforts to be reelected. Some have charged that Reagan officials made a deal with Iran, promising to provide them with weapons in order to avoid an *October surprise*—that is, a preelection release of the hostages that might have swung the vote to Jimmy Carter.[76] Adding weight to these charges is the fact that the hostages were released the very day that Reagan was inaugurated and the further revelations in 1991 that the U.S. government "secretly and abruptly" changed its policy shortly after Reagan took office and allowed Israel to sell billions of dollars of arms and ammunition to Iran. The flow of arms to Iran through Israel continued during Operation Staunch, which was a public campaign aggressively promoted by the Reagan administration as a worldwide effort to cut off the supply of military goods to Iran.[77]

The Iran-contra scandal shows how limited the U.S. Congress has become in its constitutionally defined responsibility of having the sole power to declare war. For decades Congress and the executive branch have struggled over the capacity of the president to use U.S. troops to intervene in other nations, or to fund military and political operations overseas. For the most part, Congress has surrendered much of its responsibility in this regard. It has done this not because it does not believe in a separation of powers and a series of checks and balances but because members of Congress tend to come from the upper levels of the American class structure and the majority of them see their class interests as being best served by an executive branch that is able to readily intervene overseas when corporate and political-ideological interests call for it.

The U.S. government was unable to expand the war on Nicaragua due to a variety of reasons. Unlike the early 1960s when the United States gradually increased its presence in Vietnam without much domestic opposition, in Nicaragua U.S. policy was challenged by many activists right from the start. Those who opposed U.S. intervention in Central America were a prime factor in influencing public opinion. Polls throughout the 1980s consistently showed that most Americans were opposed to aiding the contras. The proximity of Nicaragua, and El Salvador, to the United States permitted many people to get a firsthand look at what was actually happening in these two countries. Tens of thousands of Americans traveled to Nicaragua and were able to counteract the anti-Sandinista proclamations of the Reagan administration. Between 1980 and 1988, some 80,000 to 100,000 North Americans visited Central America, many through study groups and various types of peace delegations.[78] Likewise, various direct aid programs, such as those sponsored by the numerous sister city projects set up throughout the nation, were able to provide medical and other supplies and to help nullify the economic sanctions that the administration had established against Nicaragua.

In spite of public opposition, the Reagan administration, and later the Bush administration, was able to continue various sorts of aid to the contras, sometimes using third-party nations in the process.[79] Weary of the immense cost and the physical and psychological burden of the war, the Nicaraguan people elected the U.S.-backed candidate, Violeta Chamorro, in the 1990 presidential election. The Sandinistas, however, retained a great deal of control over the military and are the leading force behind many of the local health and educational programs that are being run in the country.

As the 1990s progressed, Nicaragua's economic condition deteriorated. The country fell further into debt and became one of the latest victims of IMF and World Bank structural adjustment. By 1994 Nicaragua's per capita foreign debt had become the highest in the world. Foreign debt amounted

"Reagan Is Repeating Eisenhower's Error"
by Philip C. Roettinger[80]

As a CIA case officer, I trained Guatemalan exiles in Honduras to invade their own country and unseat the elected president, Jacobo Arbenz. Our liaison officer with the Honduran military was Nestor Sanchez, now an assistant secretary of defense and a key policymaker in the current war against Nicaragua.

I now consider my involvement in the overthrow of Arbenz a terrible mistake, one that this administration seems bent on reenacting in Nicaragua.

In March 1954, three months before we toppled Arbenz and installed our handpicked liberator, Colonel Carlos Castillo Armas, CIA Director Allan Dulles convened his Guatemalan operatives at Opa-Locka Marine Air Base in Miami for a pep talk. Dulles told us exactly what Reagan is telling the American people now: that U.S. support for the rebels will foil the spread of communism.

Later I learned that Dulles had lied to us. Communism was not the threat we were fighting at all; land reform was.

When I authorized Castillo Armas to return to Guatemala and assume the presidency that we had prepared for him, I had no idea of the consequences of the CIA's meddling. Our success in Guatemala led to 31 years of repressive military rule and the deaths of more than 100,000 Guatemalans. The overthrow of the Arbenz government destroyed vital social and economic reforms, including land distribution, mandatory universal Social Security and trade-union rights.

Support for the Nicaraguan contras portends the same bloodshed. Even if the contras are able to unseat the Sandinista government, with or without the help of U.S. troops, can anyone sincerely believe that they will be able to govern? Hundreds of thousands of Nicaraguans have been beneficiaries of land, healthcare and education programs under the current government; they are hardly likely to acquiesce to rule imposed by the United States.

The coup I helped engineer in 1954 inaugurated an era of unprecedented military rule in Central America. Generals and colonels acted with impunity to wipe out dissent and garner wealth for themselves and their cronies. Their days became numbered in 1979 with the overthrow of Nicaraguan dictator and U.S. ally Anastasio Somoza.

I am 70. I have lived and worked in Latin America for more than 30 years. Done with skullduggery, I devote my time to painting some of the region's beautiful scenery. It is painful to see my government repeat the same mistake in which it engaged me 32 years ago. I have grown up. I only wish my government would.

to 800 percent of the nation's GNP, per capita income in the mid-1990s was about half of what it had been ten years earlier, and unemployment in some regions climbed to a staggering 60 percent.[81] Today the nation exists in a delicate state of balance. Many of the conflicts of past decades have not been resolved, and the people are acutely aware that the decisions they make may ultimately bring about renewed U.S. aggression.

El Salvador

Throughout the 1980s, the situation in Nicaragua received a great deal of press attention and was the subject of numerous presidential addresses and press conferences. In contrast, the war in El Salvador was largely ignored. The major difference between the two, from a U.S. government public relations standpoint, was that the Nicaraguan government was supposed to be our enemy and the El Salvadoran government was supposed to be our friend. However, measured on any objective scale, the war in El Salvador was worse, and our "friends" in San Salvador were much more to blame for the violence than our "enemies" in Managua were. In Nicaragua an estimated thirty-five thousand people lost their lives as a result of the contra war in the 1980s. In El Salvador the death toll was probably close to seventy-five thousand.[82] Most of the deaths in Nicaragua can be attributed to our allies, the contras. But in El Salvador most of the deaths are attributable either directly to U.S.-trained and supplied government forces or to government-backed death squads. (Note: The coup orchestrated by the United States in Guatemala in 1954 set off decades of civil war that resulted in approximately 200,000 deaths. Most of the victims were indigenous people killed by the Guatemalan military or death squads with military connections. See chapter 5 herein for a brief description of the events around the 1954 coup.)

El Salvador is a nation of great inequalities. Two percent of the population owns approximately 60 percent of the land and receives one-third of the nation's income. In recent decades poverty has been on the rise and landlessness has been increasing: In 1961, 12 percent of the rural population was landless; by 1971, 30 percent was landless; by the 1980s, the figure had risen to an astounding 65 percent.[83] At the other end of the spectrum, less than 1 percent of the landowners owned 77.8 percent of the land. In the early 1980s, 2 percent of the population was receiving nearly half of the nation's income, and almost half of those in rural El Salvador who die from natural causes are children less than five years old who die of starvation.[84] It is these conditions that gave rise to a determined movement for social change that reached its peak of power in the late 1970s and early 1980s. At that time the Democratic Revolutionary Front (FDR) controlled one-third of the territory in El Salvador and was recognized by some foreign powers as the legitimate government. Robert White, the former U.S. ambassador to El Salvador, once estimated that the FDR was supported by more than 80 percent of the Salvadoran people.[85]

The United States, however, sided with the government in San Salvador and contributed financial and military support. The government of El Salvador took some very heavy-handed measures in order to ensure its control. These included bombing its own population in the countryside and either sponsoring or allowing right-wing death squads to terrorize the population. Reputable eyewitnesses denounced the policies of the Salvadoran government, but still U.S. support continued. An owner of a coffee farm testified before a U.S. Subcommittee on InterAmerican Affairs:

> The vast majority of killings are made in sweeps in the countryside by the armed forces engaging in indiscriminate killings or by death squads that operate under the formal or informal direction of the regional or local army commanders. If these types of killings were to be brought under control, there would still be scores of death squad killings, ordered by the radical right in the oligarchy. But, there would not be over 5,000 innocent deaths at the hands of the army as there were last year in my country.[86]

A former undersecretary at the Ministry of Agriculture also claimed that it was the government that was responsible for most of the killings: "I resigned from my position . . . because I believed that it was useless to continue in a government not only incapable of putting an end to violence, but a government which itself is generating the political violence through repression."[87]

During the time that the Salvadoran government was inflicting untold violence against its own people, the United States consistently portrayed it as an exemplary democracy worthy of support. In contrast to Nicaragua, where the United States denounced the 1984 elections (which gave the Sandinistas about two-thirds of the vote) as fraudulent (but foreign observers found little to fault), the 1984 elections in El Salvador were fraught with problems, yet the U.S. government and the press celebrated them as meritorious and valid. At the time of the 1984 elections the army was still in the practice of publishing a "death list" of people it opposed. It would be hard for a true opposition candidate to come through a campaign with his life still intact. In addition, all opposition newspapers and radios had either been shut down by government forces or destroyed by bombs planted by right-wing terrorists. The CIA spent $2 million to aid the campaign of the candidate it supported, Jose Napoleon Duarte. Outside observers also reported a wide range of fraudulent election-day practices.[88]

In March 1993, the United Nations Truth Commission released a report on El Salvador that implicated the U.S. government in many of the atrocities that had taken place in that country over the previous decade. The report named over sixty officers of the Salvadoran military who had either ordered, executed, or concealed major atrocities there. At least forty-five of these officers had received training at the U.S. Army School of the Americas, which was established by the United States in Panama in 1946. According to Vicky A. Imerman, a codirector of the School of Americas Watch, the school has taught counterinsurgency techniques, psychological operations, and intelligence gathering to "some of the worst dictators, war criminals, and violators of human rights in the hemisphere."[89]

The School of the Americas (SOA) gradually lost favor in Panama, where it became known as the School of the Assassins, and was forced out of Panama in 1984 and relocated to Fort Benning, Georgia. Among the luminaries who received their training at the SOA was General Hugo Suarez, dictator of Bolivia from 1971 to 1978. Suarez came to power in a violent coup and was one of the leading architects of repression in Bolivia. The SOA was proud enough of Suarez, however, to induct him into its Hall of Fame in 1988. Panama's ex-president and onetime CIA liaison Manuel Noriega was also trained at the SOA. Haitian police chief Joseph-Michel Francois, who played a role in the coup that forced President Aristide out of power, was another trained at the SOA. Among the many Salvadorans trained there were Colonel Jose Mario Godinez Castillo and Colonel Dionisio Ismael Machuca. Godinez was cited by the Salvadoran Non-Governmental Human Rights Commission (NGHRC) for his involvement in 1,051 summary executions, 129 tortures, and 8 rapes. Machuca was a director of the National Police and was cited by the NGHRC for involvement in 318 tortures and 610 illegal detentions.[90]

Under a steady barrage of criticism from human rights activists, and several close votes in the U.S. House of Representatives that threatened to cut off its funding, the SOA reopened on January 7, 2001, as the Western Hemisphere Institute for Security Cooperation. Critics of the SOA have expressed deep scepticism of the "new" Institute. The U.S. branch of the United Nations Association, for example, pointed out that the new "Board of Visitors, appointed by the Pentagon for supervision and accountability . . . consists of members of the Department of Defense who had previously stalwartly endorsed the discredited School of the Americas."[91] SOA Watch described the changes as "cosmetic."[92]

Later, in 1993, the U.S. State Department released more than twelve thousand documents that helped to shed more light on U.S. relations with the Salvadoran government. Between 1980 and 1991, when the United States was aiding the Salvadoran government with $1 billion in military aid, the military was dominated by officers who either ordered or took part in death squad activities.[93] Among the most well known of these was Roberto d'Aubuisson, whom even the CIA under Reagan described as the "principal henchman for wealthy landowners and a coordinator of the right-wing death squads" that murdered several thousand people in El Salvador. The documents also showed that the CIA had informed George H. W. Bush in 1984

School of the Americas or School of the Assassins?

On March 15, 1993, the United Nations Truth Commission Report on El Salvador was released, citing dozens of Salvadoran officers for involvement in atrocities committed during a decade of war. The School of Americas Watch compared the commission's findings with lists of SOA graduates obtained from the National Security Archive in Washington, D.C., and discovered numerous SOA graduates cited in the UN report.

Some of the soldiers involved in the worst atrocities had the most SOA training, and many received additional training *after* being involved in an atrocity. The findings included the following:

- Of the three officers cited in the assassination of Archbishop Oscar Romero in 1980, two were SOA graduates.
- Of the five officers cited in the 1980 murder of three U.S. nuns and a Catholic layworker, three were SOA graduates. The four women were forced out of their van by members of the Salvadoran National Guard, raped, and killed.
- Three officers, all SOA graduates, were cited in the assassination of three labor leaders at the Sheraton Hotel in San Salvador.
- Three officers, two of them SOA graduates, were cited in the massacre at El Junguillo. Salvadoran soldiers raped women and children and killed the inhabitants of the village.
- Twelve officers, ten of them SOA graduates, were cited for their role in the El Mozote massacre in 1981. Hundreds of unarmed civilians were killed.
- Of the six officers cited for the 1983 Las Hojas massacre, three were SOA graduates. Soldiers of the Jaguar Battalion murdered sixteen civilians and burned their corpses.
- Seven officers were cited for the San Sebastian massacre in 1988; six were SOA graduates.
- Twenty-seven officers were cited in the murder of six Jesuit priests, their housekeeper, and her daughter. The murders took place at the priests' residence in San Salvador in 1989. Nineteen of the officers cited were SOA graduates.[94]

that allegations linking d'Aubuisson to the killing of Archbishop Oscar Romero in 1980 were "credible." The documents released by the government also contained allegations that d'Aubuisson was "egocentric, reckless and perhaps mentally unstable." In spite of its awareness that d'Aubuisson trafficked in drugs, smuggled arms, and directed the meeting that planned the assassination of Romero, the U.S. government continued to supply him with arms and other support. D'Aubuisson was even invited to lunch with the American ambassador to the UN, Jeane Kirkpatrick, and to a Fourth of July party at the U.S. embassy in San Salvador. In addition, the Reagan administration routinely withheld important information about d'Aubuisson from the U.S. Congress and the public.[95]

One of the more violent and controversial episodes of El Salvador's civil war was the massacre that took place at El Mozote in 1981. Hundreds of people—men, women, and children—were savagely killed by the U.S.-trained Atlacatl Battalion. Many had their throats cut or were hanged from trees. One witness described a soldier throwing a small child into the air and catching him on his bayonet. Other children as young as two years old were hanged. Although the massacre was reported in some of the U.S. press, the Reagan administration, determined to get congressional approval for more military aid, denounced the reports as false, and the *Wall Street Journal* attacked the reporters as victims of communist propaganda.[96] Such stonewalling kept the truth of El Mozote in question and helped deflect criticism of U.S. policy.

Throughout the 1980s, and even into the 1990s, the U.S. government was willing to ally itself and give billions of dollars in aid to some of the cruelest and most antidemocratic forces in the hemisphere. Is such action simply the outcome of zealous anticommunism or does it spring from something deeper and more complex? Repeatedly, U.S. officials have shown much too much willingness to ally themselves with the most barbaric elements of a nation as long as those elements are sympathetic to U.S. development policies and the financial interests of U.S.-based capitalism.

Grenada

Unable to force the Sandinistas out of office in Nicaragua and struggling to subdue the rebel movement in El Salvador, the Reagan administration made a quick and decisive strike at Grenada, a much easier target, in an operation that many contended was a dress rehearsal for an invasion of Nicaragua. Grenada is a small island nation in the Caribbean, which, at the time of the U.S. invasion, had a population of about eighty-five thousand people. It is about one-tenth the size and population of Rhode Island. The invasion was preceded by a coup that overthrew the prime minister, Maurice Bishop, executing him and several of his ministers. The new government declared martial law and proceeded to solidify its power. On October 25, 1983, the United States invaded with seven thousand troops accompanied by several hundred troops supplied by six Caribbean nations.[97]

Three primary reasons were given for why the Reagan administration felt compelled to invade Grenada. Initially, the official line was that we needed to go in to protect American lives. The second major reason given was the standard U.S. goal of "restoring democracy." The third reason was actually a set of beliefs involving the presence of several hundred Cubans on the island and the possibility of an expanding Soviet influence.

At the time of the invasion, there were about 1,000 Americans in Grenada, including about 800 at St. George's University Medical School.[98] Just prior to the invasion, White House spokesperson Larry Speakes declared that there was no indication of any danger to Americans. After the invasion, however, he reversed field and said the Americans had been in danger. He also stated that the airport was closed the day before the invasion and people couldn't leave the country. Later, after witnesses contradicted him and pointed out that at least four charter planes left the day before the invasion, Speakes admitted that his original claim was not true. In fact, a few American students actually had left that day. The chancellor of the medical school, Charles Modica, also contradicted the official line when he came to New York City and disputed Washington's portrayal of the dangers the students faced. Modica insisted that the U.S. ambassador to Barbados told him to lie when he was asked about the students' safety. Later, after extensive "debriefing" by the State Department, Modica recanted his previous assertions. But Modica was not the only school administrator to contradict Washington on this point. The dean of preclinical studies arrived in South Carolina declaring that the coup had not put his students in any danger. According to the *Nation*, sources in Jamaica confirmed the dean's position and Modica's original statements. Much later on, declassified Defense Department documents also showed that the medical students were not in any danger.[99]

The fact is the students were never physically threatened until U.S. troops landed and the shooting began. In any event, if the primary objective of the U.S. invasion was to secure the safety of the students, why didn't the marines get the students off the island? A rescue operation does not require the overthrow of the government. Furthermore, there are Americans all over the world who have at times faced similar dangers, but we have rarely responded with an invasion. In the case of the Chilean coup of 1973, there is evidence that some Americans faced real dangers and that the U.S. embassy could have helped them quite easily but instead turned its back. In fact, some have charged that the U.S. government may have provided the Chilean military with information on Americans who supported the Allende government.[100] In contrast to the U.S. response to Grenada, consider that after three American nuns and a lay church worker were stopped at a roadblock by Salvadoran National Guard troops, taken from their van, raped, brutally murdered, and buried in a shallow grave, the United States made no parallel moves against the government of El Salvador.[101] The United States continued its support and deliberately played down the connections between its clients and the many atrocities that occurred in El Salvador.

The second set of reasons given for the invasion fall under the category of "restoring democracy." By this logic, we would have invaded Chile after Allende had been overthrown, or we would have fought against the contras in Nicaragua rather than supplying them with arms. The fact of the matter is that the U.S. government has been instrumental in overthrowing democracies in many parts of the world, and it has supported some very antidemocratic governments. Furthermore, there is evidence that the United States had been considering an invasion before the coup had even taken place. The United States had been training for a Caribbean island invasion for at least two weeks before General Austin's men had deposed Maurice Bishop. Others have contended that military exercises going back to 1981 were conducted in preparation for an invasion of Grenada.[102]

The third set of charges had to do with the presence of Cubans on the island who were helping to enlarge the airport at Port Salinas. The Reagan administration charged that the airport was being developed for military purposes, perhaps for the use of the Soviet Union. These charges are easily refuted. Michael Manley, the former prime minister of Jamaica, had this to say: "As for the menacing airport at Port Salinas, the British construction firm that designed it has categorically denied that it was intended for military purposes. It was built to accommodate wide-body jets carrying tourists, and three other airports in the Caribbean have longer runways."[103]

In addition, a spokesperson for the Plessey Company, a major contractor for the new airport, rejected assertions that the airport was constructed to serve as a military base for Cuba and the Soviet Union. "The airport was being built to purely civilian specifications," said spokesperson Tony Devereaux. The airport did not have any of the features of a modern military air base. It did not have underground fuel dumps. It did not have special bays to protect parked aircraft from bombs. And it did not have a protected control tower. Furthermore, the airport development project was encouraged by the World Bank in order to promote tourism, and at least half of the financing for the airport came from West European countries.[104]

The U.S. invasion of Grenada was clearly a violation of the charter of the Organization of American States (OAS), which unambiguously states that "no state or group of states has the right to intervene, directly or indirectly, for any reason whatever, in the internal or external affairs of any other state." The UN General Assembly passed a resolution condemning the invasion by a vote of 108 to 9.[105] The resolution was ignored by the U.S. government and received very little attention in the U.S. media.

The real purposes of the U.S. invasion were threefold. First, it was an effort to prevent Grenada from following a course that was too independent of Washington's will and the model of development favored by the international corporate community. The United States routinely opposes any government that could serve as an alternative model of development to other Third World nations. For years the New Jewel movement in Grenada had been showing its dedication to the people of Grenada and exercising independence from foreign control. Under the New Jewel government, elementary and secondary education were free for the first time. Free healthcare clinics were opened in the countryside. Free milk and other goods were being distributed to the needy. Unemployment had been dropping steadily, and the government encouraged food cooperatives and production for self-sufficiency rather than export.[106]

Second, the invasion of Grenada served as a warning to the Sandinista government in Nicaragua that its lack of responsiveness to U.S. wishes could cause it to suffer the same fate.

Third, the more conservative sectors of the U.S. ruling class used Grenada as a small antidote to the Vietnam syndrome. Shortly after the invasion occurred, Reagan exclaimed, "Our days of weakness are over . . . our military forces are standing tall."[107] Henry Kissinger no doubt recognized this as an antidote also. When he was selected by President Reagan to chair a special commission on Central America, he asserted that the commission had to have as one of its primary goals the stifling of all meaningful debate regarding U.S. policy in Central America. Kissinger felt that strong domestic opposition to the U.S. policy on Vietnam was responsible for the U.S. failure there. According to the *Guardian* (London), Kissinger's aim "was to create a national consensus to avoid a similar outcome in Central America."[108] The quick and easy victory in Grenada with a minimum of American casualties (nineteen dead) was a way of convincing the American public that the United States could win wars in the Third World without paying a heavy price—a theme that would be replayed on a bigger scale in the Persian Gulf in 1991.

Afghanistan

Meanwhile, on the other side of the globe, the United States was engaged in a cold war sparring match with the Soviet Union. Afghanistan was the battlefield and the long-term consequences of U.S. policy would leave a deep scar on that nation and also play a part in the *blowback* that took the form of a terrorist attack that killed more than 3,000 people at the World Trade Center in New York City and the Pentagon in Washington, D.C., on September 11, 2001.

Afghanistan is a relatively sparsely populated country, and much of its terrain is rocky and dry. Historically, Afghanistan's value lay not in any of its natural resources but in its strategic location in terms of Russian and British colonial designs. The Russians had long had an interest in the area in order to gain access to the seaports of the Persian Gulf. British concerns revolved around gaining access to its colonial empire in India through the Kyber Pass and in repressing anti-British Indian rebels who sought sanctuary in the region. The British fought three wars in Afghanistan. The second of these wars (1878–80) resulted in the overthrow of the Afghan shah, and in much greater British influence. The British redrew Afghanistan's borders to bolster their own strategic interests, creating a buffer between the Russian empire and their own. In 1919, after the third British-Afghan war, Afghanistan was freed from British "protection."[109] Afghanistan's national government was never very strong; local leaders often exercised substantial power, and the areas they controlled didn't correspond to the borders drawn by the British.

Important to understanding recent events in Afghanistan is understanding its role in the cold war. Torn by internal power struggles for many decades, Afghanistan began to take strides in a positive direction under Hafizulah Amin in 1979. Amin introduced a compulsory literacy campaign, abolition of the dowry system and other traditional customs, and radical land reform. However, by the end of the year, Amin was assassinated. The new government was headed by Babrak Karmal, who had the backing of Soviet troops. The Soviet support elicited a hostile reaction from the United States and from Islamic fundamentalists. The United States began supporting a movement known as the *mujahedin*, with arms and intelligence. Many of these Islamic militants were trained in Pakistan at religious schools called *madrases*, and they served as a surrogate for U.S. troops as the United States hoped to "bleed" the Soviet Union, making it their Vietnam. Much as he did with the Nicaraguan contras, President Reagan praised the mujahedin, stating that "the resistance of the Afghan freedom fighters is an example to all the world of the invincibility of the ideals we in this country hold most dear, the ideals of freedom and independence."[110] The U.S strategy succeeded as the Soviet Union stopped sending aid and the Karmal government collapsed. By the time the Soviets withdrew they had lost an estimated fifteen thousand troops, and a million Afghans had died.[111]

The consequences for many of the Afghan people were severe as the mujahedin fought with each other for six years after Soviet withdrawal and a new armed faction, the *Taliban* (students), gained strength. The Taliban were primarily trained in Pakistan, and they aimed to create a united Islamic government in Afghanistan. By 1996, they had succeeded and instituted a variety of strict laws. Women were forced to wear the chador or burqa, which covered them from head to toe, they were banned from attending school, and hospitals in Kabul (the capital city) were told not to treat women.[112] The U.S. government notably showed little concern. One diplomat stated, "The Taliban will probably develop like the Saudis did. There will be . . . pipelines, an emir, no parliament and lots of Shari'a law. We can live with that."[113] Senators as disparate as Republican Orrin Hatch and Democrat Bill Bradley proclaimed their support for the mujahedin. (Bradley urged that they be recognized as "the sole legitimate representatives of the Afghan people.")[114]

The development of the Al Qaeda terrorist network is, in part, a result of U.S. policies in Afghanistan that placed a priority on opposing the Soviet Union, no matter what the consequences. It also is a result of U.S. aid to Pakistan, which provided intelligence and other support to the mujahedin. During the 1980s, the United States sent $2–3 billion in weapons and supplies through the CIA and ICS (Pakistan's Inter-Service Intelligence Agency).[115] The blowback resulting from U.S. policies in Afghanistan was anticipated by many people. One U.S. diplomat in Pakistan stated, in 1996, "You can't plug billions of dollars into an anti-Communist jihad, accept participation from all over the world and ignore the consequences. But we did. Our objectives weren't peace and grooviness in Afghanistan. Our objective was killing Commies and getting the Russians out."[116]

Cuba

Another notable Third World intervention campaign is the long-term U.S. aggression against Cuba. This includes the infamous 1961 Bay of Pigs invasion, which failed miserably and proved to be a long-running embarrassment to many government officials and right-wing activists. The CIA also

---

U.S. Acts of Aggression Against Cuba

- Bombing and strafing raids by airplanes based in the United States in 1959 and 1960. Among the targets were sugarcane fields and sugar mills that were firebombed.
- In April 1961, the CIA-organized Bay of Pigs invasion took place. Over 100 Cuban exiles died in the attack and 1,200 were taken prisoners. At least four pilots flying for the CIA lost their lives.
- Throughout the 1960s, there were countless sea and air raids by Cuban exiles financed and trained by the CIA. They damaged oil refineries, chemical plants, sugar mills, railroad bridges, and other targets.
- From the early 1960s to the present, the United States has conducted a trade and credit embargo against Cuba and persuaded other nations to participate.
- The United States has sabotaged goods destined for Cuba from other nations. Chemicals were added to lubricating fluids in order to cause rapid wear to engines. A manufacturer in Germany was paid by the CIA to make off-center ball bearings to be shipped to Cuba. Another manufacturer was paid to ship Cuba defective wheel gears.
- The British Leyland Company did business with Cuba in spite of American pressure. So in 1964, the CIA arranged an at-sea collision that beached a cargo ship carrying British Leyland buses destined for Cuba. British Intelligence cooperated in the operation.
- The CIA put contaminants in sugar being exported from Cuba.
- A Canadian agricultural technician was paid $5,000 to infect Cuban turkeys with a virus that probably resulted in the deaths of 8,000 turkeys.
- In 1971, the CIA gave a virus to Cuban exiles that causes African swine fever. Within two months the Cuban government was forced to slaughter 500,000 pigs to prevent a nationwide animal epidemic.
- In 1980, Cuban exiles brought germs to Cuba that may have caused a dengue fever epidemic. The U.S. Army had experimented with a type of mosquito that carries dengue fever, and the United States government had done research on dengue fever as a potential agent of biological warfare.
- Since the revolution, the United States has maintained a military base at Guantanamo Bay in Cuba over the harsh objections of the Cuban government. The base amounts to an occupation of Cuban territory by a foreign power.[117]

Some Major Events in Recent Cuban History

1953. *July 26:* Fidel Castro and others launch an armed attack on Cuba's second-largest military barracks, the Moncada Garrison, Santiago de Cuba.

1956. *December 2:* Castro and eighty-one other revolutionaries sail from Mexico for Cuba in the yacht *Granma*, marking the beginning of the guerilla struggle in the Sierra Maestra mountains.

1959. *January 1, New Year's Day:* Cuban dictator Fulgencio Batista flees the island.
January 8: Castro makes triumphal entry into Havana.
March 17: President Eisenhower orders CIA to begin training Cuban exiles to overthrow Castro.
May 17: First agrarian reform law is decreed, giving land to 100,000 peasant families and eventually nationalizing 44 percent of the land.

1960. *March 14:* Cuba and the Soviet Union sign major trade agreement.
June 29: Cuba nationalizes U.S.-owned oil refineries for refusing to refine Soviet crude oil.
July 6: Eisenhower cancels Cuba's sugar quota.
July 10: The Soviet Union agrees to buy the sugar affected by the quota cancellation.
August 7: Cuba nationalizes all U.S.-owned industrial and agrarian enterprises.
October 14: Urban Reform Law drastically cuts rents and provides for renters to become owners.
October 19: First U.S. embargo prohibits exports to Cuba, except for nonsubsidized foodstuffs and medicines.

1961. *April 17–19:* Bay of Pigs invasion—1,500-man army invades Cuba, but Cubans do not join them in an uprising against Castro. Over 1,200 are captured. Castro declares the socialist nature of Cuba's revolution.
May: Literacy campaign begins. Within four months, illiteracy is reduced from 24 percent to 7 percent.

1962. *February 7:* An embargo on U.S.-Cuban trade (except medical supplies) goes into effect.
October 22: President Kennedy announces the presence of Soviet nuclear missiles in Cuba and establishes a naval blockade of the island.
October 27: Kennedy proposes that the Soviets remove weapons from Cuba in exchange for an end to the blockade and assurances that the United States will not invade Cuba.
November 8: United States announces that all Soviet missile bases in Cuba have been dismantled.

attempted to assassinate Fidel Castro at least six times over a two-year period in the early 1960s.[118] Included in this chapter is a partial list of U.S. attempts to destabilize Cuba and bring down the revolutionary government. In spite of these attempts, the Cuban revolution stands firm and Fidel Castro remains in power. What these acts of aggression have accomplished is only to make life more difficult for the people of Cuba, and they have forced the Cuban government to be more cautious and restrictive than it would otherwise be.

The hardships that exist in Cuban society and the tensions between Cuba and the United States are primarily a result of U.S. actions. This was recognized as far back as 1960 by John Kennedy when he was campaigning for the presidency:

> We refused to help Cuba meet its desperate need for economic progress. . . . [W]e used the influence of our government to advance the interests and increase the profits of the private American companies which dominated the island's economy. . . . [A]dministration spokesmen publicly hailed Batista . . . as a staunch ally and a good friend at a time when Batista was murdering thousands, destroying the last vestiges of freedom and stealing hundreds of millions of dollars from the Cuban people. . . . [T]hus it was our own policies, not those of Castro, that first began to turn our former neighbor against us.[119]

Killing Hope

One other U.S. Third World intervention ought to be mentioned because its failure to achieve U.S. goals has resulted in long-term conflict and the loss of tens of thousands of lives: In Angola the U.S. government (and especially the CIA) lent its support to two unpopular political organizations rather than the popular MPLA (Popular Movement for the Liberation of Angola), which would have easily won elections after the Portuguese granted Angola its independence in 1975.[120] The case is very similar to Vietnam in that in both situations the United States backed the colonial government for years and then supported less popular political factions after the colonialists withdrew and an agreement was hammered out to provide for a transfer of power. In both cases, a prolonged and destructive conflict was created where a relatively smooth transition to a new nationalist government could have taken place.

The United States has a very long history of military intervention in the affairs of other countries. From 1789 to the beginning of World War II, U.S. troops were sent to foreign countries 145 times without authorization from

Congress.[121] The cases of intervention described in this chapter are from the period since the end of World War II, and it is far from a comprehensive list. What these cases illustrate is that interventions are rarely undertaken with the best interests of the U.S. public in mind, nor with the interests of the recipient nations at heart. Overwhelmingly, they are the result of a political and economic bias that ends up being destructive to many people. This is true of both the pre– and the post–World War II eras. One of the most comprehensive works on U.S. interventions since World War II is *Killing Hope: U.S. Military Interventions since World War II*, written by former State Department official William Blum. Blum documents U.S. intervention in at least forty-six nations since the end of the war. These interventions often included assassination attempts, as indicated in the accompanying "Hit List."

HIT LIST[122]

The following is a list of prominent foreign individuals in whose assassination (or planned assassination) the United States has been involved since the end of World War II. The list does not include several assassinations in various parts of the world carried out by anti-Castro Cubans employed by the CIA and headquartered in the United States.

1949	Kim Koo, Korean opposition leader
1950s	CIA/Neo-Nazi hit list of numerous political figures in West Germany
1950s	Zhou Enlai, prime minister of China, several attempts on his life
1950s, 1962	Sukarno, president of Indonesia
1951	Kim Il Sung, premier of North Korea
1953	Mohammed Mossadegh, prime minister of Iran
1950s (mid)	Claro M. Recto, Philippines opposition leader
1955	Jawaharlal Nehru, prime minister of India
1957	Gamal Abdul Nasser, president of Egypt
1959, 1963, 1969	Norodom Sihanouk, leader of Cambodia
1960	Brig. Gen. Abdul Karim Kassem, leader of Iraq
1950s–1970s	José Figueres, president of Costa Rica, two attempts on his life
1961	François "Papa Doc" Duvalier, leader of Haiti
1961	Patrice Lumumba, prime minister of the Congo

1961 Gen. Rafael Trujillo, leader of Dominican Republic
1963 Ngo Dinh Diem, president of South Vietnam
1960s Fidel Castro, president of Cuba, many attempts and plots on his life
1960s Raúl Castro, high official in government of Cuba
1965 Francisco Caamaño, Dominican Republic opposition leader
1965–66 Charles de Gaulle, president of France
1967 Che Guevara, Cuban leader
1970 Salvador Allende, president of Chile
1970 Gen. Rene Schneider, commander-in-chief of army, Chile
1970s, 1981 General Omar Torrijos, leader of Panama
1972 General Manuel Noriega, chief of Panama Intelligence
1975 Mobutu Sese Seko, president of Zaire
1976 Michael Manley, prime minister of Jamaica
1980–86 Moammar Qaddafi, leader of Libya, several plots and attempts upon his life
1982 Ayatollah Khomeini, leader of Iran
1983 Gen. Ahmed Dlimi, Moroccan Army commander
1983 Miguel d'Escoto, foreign minister of Nicaragua
1984 The nine comandantes of the Sandinista National Directorate
1985 Sheikh Mohammed Hussein Fadlallah, Lebanese Shiite leader (eighty people killed in the attempt)
1991 Saddam Hussein, leader of Iraq
1999 Slobodan Milosevic, president of Yugoslavia
1998, 2001–2002 Osama bin Laden, leading Islamic militant

NOTES

1. Noam Chomsky, "Introduction: World Orders, Old and New," in *Altered States*, ed. Phyllis Bennis and Michel Moushabeck (New York: Olive Branch Press, 1993), p. 6.

2. Alan Wolfe, *The Seamy Side of Democracy*, 2d ed. (New York: Longman, 1978), p. x.

3. Ibid., p. 150.

4. David Wise and Thomas B. Ross, *The Invisible Government* (New York: Vintage Books, 1974), pp. 95–98.

5. Wolfe, *The Seamy Side*, pp. 150–51. See also William Blum, *Killing Hope: U.S. Military and CIA Interventions Since World War II* (Monroe, Maine: Common Courage Press, 1995), p. 30. For details regarding Operation Gladio, which used many anticommunist zealots and Mussolini-era fascists to disrupt the Left and popular movements for socialism and democracy in Italy, see Arthur E. Rowse, "Gladio: The Secret U.S. War to Subvert Italian Democracy," *Covert Action Quarterly* (summer 1994). Rowse argues that the CIA worked with right-wing forces to implement propaganda, intelligence, and terror campaigns, which played a large role in creating the instability, political violence, and corruption in Italy that lasted for decades.

6. D. F. Fleming, *The Cold War and Its Origins, 1917–1960* (Garden City, N.Y.: Doubleday, 1961), 1:182. The information on Greece comes primarily from two additional sources: William Blum, *Killing Hope: U.S. Military and CIA Interventions Since World War II* (Monroe, Maine: Common Courage Press, 1995); and Todd Gitlin, "Counter-Insurgency: Myth and Reality in Greece," in *Containment and Revolution*, ed. David Horowitz (Boston: Beacon Press, 1967).

7. Blum, *Killing Hope*, p. 38.

8. Ibid.

9. Ibid., p. 218.

10. Ibid., p. 220.

11. Wise and Ross, *The Invisible Government*, p. 113.

12. Ibid., p. 110.

13. Noam Chomsky and Edward S. Herman, *The Washington Connection and Third World Fascism* (Boston: South End Press, 1979), p. 13.

14. Ibid., p. 49.

15. Ibid.

16. See Audrey R. Kahin and George McT. Kahin, *Subversion as Foreign Policy* (New York: New Press, 1995), especially for U.S. involvement in destabilizing Indonesia in the late 1950s.

17. *The World Guide, 2001/2002.*

18. Chomsky and Herman, *The Washington Connection*, p. 209.

19. Rand McNally, *World Facts in Brief* (New York: Rand McNally, 1986), p. 181.

20. Kathy Kadane, "U.S. Officials' Lists Aided Indonesian Bloodbath in '60s," *Washington Post,* May 21, 1990.

21. Dierdre Griswold, *Indonesia: The Bloodbath That Was* (New York: World View Publishers, 1970).

22. Chomsky and Herman, *The Washington Connection*, p. 210.

23. Ibid., pp. 212–13.

24. Richard W. Franke, *East Timor: The Hidden War* (New York: East Timor Defense Committee, 1976); Anthony Lewis and John Pilger, "Abroad at Home: The Hidden Horror," *New York Times,* August 12, 1994.

25. Lewis and Pilger, "Abroad at Home."

26. For more on the media's lack of coverage, or biased reportage, on East Timor, see Michael Parenti, *Inventing Reality* (New York: St. Martin's Press, 1993), pp. 193, 203–204; and Edward S. Herman, *The Real Terror Network* (Boston: South End Press, 1982), pp. 141–44.

27. Dr. Salvador Allende, from a speech delivered at the UN, December 4, 1972; printed in *The Human Factor*, vol. 12, nos. 2–3 (summer–fall 1974): 8 (published by the Graduate Sociology Student Union, Columbia University, New York).

28. Parenti, *Inventing Reality*, p. 143.

29. Ibid., pp. 143–44.

30. Anthony Sampson, *The Sovereign State of ITT* (Greenwich, Conn.: Fawcett Publications, 1974).

31. Ibid., p. 263; and Victor Marchetti and John D. Marks, *The CIA and the Cult of Intelligence* (New York: Dell, 1974), pp. 53, 109.

32. Sampson, *The Sovereign State*, p. 256.

33. Ibid.

34. Korry's quote comes from the film *Controlling Interests* by California Newsreel; Nixon's and the U.S. military aid figures from Parenti, *Inventing Reality*, p. 144; and Kissinger's from Wolfe, *The Seamy Side*, p. xi.

35. Chomsky and Herman, *The Washington Connection*, p. 9.

36. Ibid. In *Assassination on Embassy Row* (New York: Pantheon, 1980), John Dinges and Saul Landau describe Victor Jara's murder: "In a smaller Santiago stadium, Chilean folksinger Victor Jara tried to keep up the prisoners' spirits. He kept talking, though the guards forbade it, and when they punched him he began to lead the entire stadium in song. The guards broke his guitar. He went on singing. In full view of thousands of prisoners, the guards broke Jara's hands and wrists and then beat him to death."

37. Parenti, *Inventing Reality*, p. 146.

38. Herman, *The Real Terror Network*, pp. 66, 71–73. See also Dinges and Landau, *Assassination*.

39. Calvin Sims, "Two in Chile Get Jail Terms in U.S. Killing," *New York Times*, May 31, 1995; Calvin Sims, "Chilean Jail for Officers Is Gracious, but Still Jail," *New York Times*, November 24, 1995.

40. Diana Jean Schemo, "Latin Death Squads and the U.S.: A New Disclosure," *New York Times*, October 23, 2002.

41. Ralph W. McGehee, *Deadly Deceits* (New York: Sheridan Square Press, 1983), p. 60; and John Stockwell, *In Search of Enemies* (New York: W. W. Norton, 1978), p. 237.

42. David Wise, *The Politics of Lying* (New York: Vintage Books, 1973), p. 60.

43. In Guatemala, for instance, more than 110,000 civilians were killed by the Guatemalan army (according to Amnesty International) between 1978 and 1995. In spite of occasional reprimands publicly voiced by U.S. officials, and even sporadic cuts in military aid, for the most part U.S. funds have continued to sup-

port very repressive regimes. The United States has trained many Guatemalan military officers at the School of the Americas, and Guatemalan military personnel have been on the CIA payroll for years. Colonel George Hooker was the U.S. Defense Intelligence Agency chief in Guatemala from 1985 to 1989. Hooker told reporter Allan Nairn that "it would be an embarrassing situation if you ever had a roll call of everybody in the Guatemalan Army who ever collected a C.I.A. paycheck." According to Hooker, the CIA's payroll encompasses most of the upper echelon of the army. One of Guatemala's dictators, General Oscar Humberto Mejia Victores (1983–86), told Nairn that the country's death squads were started in the 1960s by the CIA. See Allan Nairn, "C.I.A. Death Squad," *Nation,* April 17, 1995; Eric Schmitt, "School for Assassins, or Aid to Latin Democracy?" *New York Times,* April 3, 1995; Tim Weiner, "Long Road to Truth about Killings in Guatemala," *New York Times,* March 24, 1995; Tim Weiner, with Sam Dillon, "In Guatemala's Dark Heart, C.I.A. Lent Succor to Death," *New York Times,* April 2, 1995; and Tim Weiner, "Guatemalan Agent of C.I.A. Tied to Killing of American," *New York Times,* March 23, 1995.

44. Chomsky and Herman, *The Washington Connection*, pp. 242–51.

45. Blum, *Killing Hope*, p. 136.

46. Noam Chomsky, *The Culture of Terrorism* (Boston: South End Press, 1988), p. 46; and much of *After the Cataclysm*, by Noam Chomsky and Edward S. Herman (Boston: South End Press, 1979).

47. Helen Caldicott, *Missile Envy* (New York: Bantam Books, 1986), pp. 215–16; and Chomsky and Herman, *After the Cataclysm*, pp. 154, 165.

48. Blum, *Killing Hope*, p. 139.

49. Marvin E. Gettleman, Jane Franklin, Marilyn Young, and Bruce H. Franklin, *Vietnam and America: A Documented History* (New York: Grove Press, 1985), p. 50.

50. [Online] www.ellsberg.net/weblog/1_27_03.htm. See also Blum, *Killing Hope*, p. 124.

51. Gettleman et al., *Vietnam and America: A Documented History*, p. 69.

52. Ibid., pp. 70, 79.

53. Ibid., p. 75.

54. Wise and Ross, *Invisible Government*, p. 158.

55. Ibid., pp. 163–64; and Gettleman et al., *Vietnam and America*, pp. 223–34.

56. Gettleman et al., *Vietnam and America*, p. 239.

57. For an in-depth discussion of the Tonkin Gulf incident, see Wise, *The Politics of Lying*, pp. 61–67; and Gettleman et al., *Vietnam and America*, pp. 238–39, 246–50. Former CIA official Ralph McGehee called the incident a series of U.S. provocations (McGehee, *Deadly Deceits*, p. 139). For McNamara's admissions concerning commando raids just prior to the Tonkin Gulf incident, see Tim Weiner, "Once Commandos for U.S., Vietnamese Are Now Barred," *New York Times,* April 14, 1995.

58. Marchetti and Marks, *The CIA and the Cult of Intelligence*, pp. 236–37.

59. Herman, *The Real Terror Network*, p. 184.

60. Chomsky and Herman, *The Washington Connection*, pp. 322–28; Blum, *Killing Hope*, p. 132.

61. Gettleman et al., *Vietnam and America*, p. 422.

62. Ibid., p. 461.

63. Ibid., pp. 461, 464.

64. Ronald Fernandez, *Cruising the Caribbean: U.S. Influence and Intervention in the Twentieth Century* (Monroe, Maine: Common Courage Press, 1994), pp. 136, 290, 406.

65. Tom Barry and Deb Preusch, *The Central American Fact Book* (New York: Grove Press, 1986), p. 272.

66. Jenny Pearce, *Under the Eagle* (Boston: South End Press, 1982), p. 19.

67. Oxfam, *Facts for Action,* no. 8; and *United Nations Population and Vital Statistics Report.*

68. In Joshua Cohen and Joel Rogers, *Inequity and Intervention: The Federal Budget and Central America* (Boston: South End Press, 1986), p. 50.

69. Barry and Preusch, *The Central American Fact Book*, p. 277.

70. Edgar Chamorro, "Terror Is the Most Effective Weapon of Nicaragua's 'Contras,'" *New York Times,* January 9, 1986.

71. Institute for Policy Studies, *In Contempt of Congress* (Washington, D.C.: Institute for Policy Studies, 1985), p. 12.

72. *Parade*, March 15, 1981; and *Village Voice*, July 23, 1985.

73. Chomsky, *The Culture of Terrorism*, p. 120.

74. *Case Concerning Military and Parliamentary Activities In and Against Nicaragua (Nicaragua v. United States)*, International Court of Justice, judgment of June 7, 1986 [online], www.icj-cij.org/; and *Military and Paramilitary Activities In and Against Nicaragua (Nicaragua v. United States of America)*, International Court of Justice, 1986 [online], www.gwu.edu/~jaysmith/ nicus3.html.

75. The hostages were being held by Islamic Fundamentalists in Lebanon. They were taken captive in retaliation for U.S. intervention in Lebanon on behalf of the fascist Phalange movement in August of 1982. See Doug Vaughan, "Too Good to Be True: Special Prosecutor's 'Final Report' on Iran-Contra," *Covert Action Quarterly* (spring 1994): 15, 57.

76. This is the argument made by Gary Sick in *October Surprise: America's Hostages in Iran and the Election of Ronald Reagan* (New York: Times Books, 1991), and by Robert Parry in *Trick or Treason: The October Surprise Mystery* (New York: Sheridan Square Press, 1993).

77. Seymour Hersh, "U.S. Said to Have Allowed Israel to Sell Arms to Iran," *New York Times,* December 8, 1991.

78. Medea Benjamin and Andrea Freedman, *Bridging the Global Gap* (Washington, D.C.: Seven Locks Press, 1989), p. 17.

79. Jonathan Marshall, Peter Dale Scott, and Jane Hunter, *The Iran Contra*

Connection: Secret Teams and Covert Operations in the Reagan Era (Boston: South End Press, 1987), see chap. 5, "Israel and the Contras."

80. Excerpted from the *Los Angeles Times*, March 26, 1986.

81. Charles Brazier, "State of the World Report," *New Internationalist*, January/February 1997, p. 5; Compas de la Primavera, *Deadly Embrace: Nicaragua, the World Bank and the International Monetary Fund* (Washington, D.C.: Nicaragua Network Education Fund, 1996), p. 10.

82. David Gonzalez, "Fighters' Demands Open Old Wounds in Central America," *New York Times*, August 19, 2002.

83. Pearce, *Under the Eagle*, pp. 209–10.

84. Jeff McMahan, *Reagan and the World* (New York: Monthly Review Press, 1985), p. 125.

85. Ibid., p. 131.

86. Pearce, *Under the Eagle*, p. 225.

87. Ibid., p. 232.

88. Committee in Solidarity with the People of El Salvador, *Would You Buy a Used Dictatorship from This Man?* (Washington, D.C.). See also Edward S. Herman and Frank Broadhead, *Demonstration Elections* (Boston: South End Press, 1984).

89. Vicky A. Imerman, "School of the Americas/Assassins," *Covert Action Quarterly* (fall 1993): 5.

90. Ibid.

91. "Policy Positions on Substantive Issues: Resolution on the Western Hemispheric Institute for Security Cooperation," United Nations Association of the USA, 2001 [online], www.unausa.org/.

92. [Online], www.soaw.org/new/.

93. Clifford Krauss, "U.S., Aware of Killings, Kept Ties to Salvadoran Rightists," *New York Times*, November 9, 1993.

94. Imerman, "School of the Americas/Assassins."

95. Ibid.

96. Anthony Lewis, "The Whole Truth," *New York Times*, December 6, 1993; Mark Danner, "The Truth of El Mozote," *New Yorker*, December 6, 1993.

97. McMahan, *Reagan and the World*, p. 197; and Steven Holmes, "Less Strategic Now, Grenada Is to Lose American Embassy," *New York Times*, May 2, 1994.

98. McMahan, *Reagan and the World*, p. 197.

99. *Nation*, November 5, 1983; Holmes, "Less Strategic Now, Grenada Is to Lose America Embassy," *New York Times*, May 2, 1994; and Stuart Taylor, "In Wake of Invasion, Much Official Misinformation by U.S. Comes to Light," *New York Times*, November 6, 1983, p. 20.

100. This is charged in Thomas Hauser's book *The Assassination of Charles Horman* (New York: Avon, 1978), which was made into a very moving film (*Missing*) by the renowned director Costa-Gavras. The book was also released under the title *Missing*.

101. Krauss, "U.S., Aware of Killings, Kept Ties to Salvadoran Rightists." Also see: "Jusice and the Generals" on the PBS Web site, www.pbs.org/wnet/justice/elsalvador_people.html and The Religious Task Force on Central America and Mexico, www.rtfcam.org/martyrs/women/women.htm.

102. McMahan, *Reagan and the World*, pp. 205–206; Alexander Cockburn and James Ridgeway, "The Making of a Counterrevolution," *Village Voice*, November 8, 1983; and Alexander Cockburn, "Press Clips," *Village Voice*, November 8, 1983.

103. "Who Is Next?" *Nation*, November 12, 1983.

104. McMahan, *Reagan and the World*, p. 213; Cockburn and Ridgeway, "Making of a Counterrevolution"; and Stephen Rosskamm Shalom, *Imperial Alibis* (Boston: South End Press, 1993), p. 100.

105. McMahan, *Reagan and the World*, pp. 207, 221.

106. Parenti, *Inventing Reality*, p. 150.

107. Holmes, "Less Strategic Now."

108. McMahan, *Reagan and the World*, p. 196.

109. *The World Guide, 2001/2002* (Oxford: New Internationalist Publications, 2001).

110. The Center for Economic and Social Rights, *Afghanistan Fact Sheet #1* [online], www.cesr.org.

111. Ibid.

112. Physicians for Human Rights, *The Taliban's War on Women: A Health and Human Rights Crisis in Afghanistan* [online], www.phrusa.org/research/exec.html.

113. The Center for Economic and Social Rights, *Afghanistan Fact Sheet #1* [online], www.cesr.org.

114. For more on U.S. support for the mujahedin, and a good synopsis of the British colonial influence in Afghanistan, see Jim Ingalls, *U.S. Foreign Policy in Afghanistan,* May 2001 [online], www.sonaliandjim.net/politics/talk.pdf.

115. The Center for Economic and Social Rights.

116. William Blum, *Rogue State: A Guide to the World's Only Superpower* (Monroe, Maine: Common Courage Press, 2000), p. 37.

117. This list is a summary of some of the actions described by William Blum in *Killing Hope,* pp. 184–93.

118. Ralph W. McGehee, *Deadly Deceits* (New York: Sheridan Square Press, 1983), p. 58.

119. Felix Greene, *The Enemy: What Every American Should Know About Imperialism* (New York: Vintage Books, 1971), p. 140.

120. John Stockwell, *In Search of Enemies* (New York: W. W. Norton, 1978).

121. Wolfe, *The Seamy Side*, pp. 166–67.

122. Blum, *Killing Hope*, p. 453; with later additions provided by Blum to the author.

9 A NEW WORLD ORDER?

With the end of the cold war in 1989 the United States lost one of its prime justifications for Third World intervention—the alleged threat of Soviet expansionism. It also lost a major justification for continuing its huge expenditures on the military. The potential Soviet threat and massive military spending had complemented each other well for decades and helped form the basis for some ideological agreement about the U.S. role in the world and the federal government's spending priorities.

In the post–World War II era, military spending had become an indispensable part of the American economic machine. Although there are many other ways of spending money that would be more effective at increasing employment, military spending led to the direct employment of millions of people either in the armed forces itself or in industries that produced goods for the military. In addition, many millions more are employed in industries that are indirectly bolstered by military spending. More important, from the perspective of the corporate elite, profits in "defense" industries run much higher than the average for all other industries.[1]

The cold war was a very important factor in stimulating some sectors of the U.S. economy, thereby helping to stave off the problem of falling profits. On this point Paul Sweezy has written, "The relative prosperity of U.S. capitalism since the Great Depression of the 1930s has depended first on world war and after that on cold war."[2] According to Sweezy, the U.S. ruling class, in the period immediately following the collapse of the Soviet Union, was in a quandary as to what could possibly take the place of the cold war as a justification for maintaining a massive military apparatus. "And then out of the blue came Saddam Hussein—a godsend if ever there was one."[3] And while others might argue that the United States has rarely had a difficult time conjuring up vicious enemies to parade before the American public (think of Iran's Ayatollah Kohmeini, Panama's Manuel Noriega, Nicaragua's Sandinistas, Libya's Muammar al-Qaddafi, Iraq's Saddam Hussein, etc.), there is no denying that for many decades the Soviet Union served this function most consistently. (Former CIA task force chief John Stockwell argued, well before 1989, that the CIA and the U.S. government routinely exaggerated the threats presented by all sorts of foreign governments, individuals, and social movements in order to maintain public support for the billions of dollars spent yearly for "defense" purposes.)[4]

Of course, in addition to justifying the military, the attack on Iraq served another purpose. As Sweezy notes, "What could be more useful than repairing the tarnished image of a giant with feet of clay that the United States had received as a legacy of the Vietnam war?"[5] So as George Bush was proudly rallying the country in his State of the Union Address declaring that "we stand at a defining hour . . . what is at stake is more than one small country, it's a big idea—a new world order," the U.S. government was going to battle not just with Iraq but with a much bigger foe— the Vietnam syndrome.[6]

THE GULF WAR OF 1991

Iraq is an oil-rich country just slightly larger than the state of California. Once known as Mesopotamia, Iraq is the site of one of the earliest human civilizations. At the time of Operation Desert Storm—the name given to the U.S.-led military intervention into Iraq that was officially brought on by Iraq's invasion of Kuwait in August of 1990—Iraq had a population of about nineteen million. Iraq's attack on Kuwait was precipitated by a number of factors, and a brief historical sketch is needed in order to understand Iraq's actions.

The borders of present-day Iraq and Kuwait were established by British colonialists with little input from, or regard for, the indigenous populations in the region. Great Britain had colonized the area of present-day Kuwait in 1899 and the area known as Iraq in 1920. Under the terms of the San Remo Conference in 1920, territories of the Arab Middle East, formerly part of the Ottoman Empire, were divided up between England and

France. In 1921, Great Britain established the nation of Iraq; and in 1922, the British high commissioner, Sir Percy Cox, established the borders of present-day Iraq, Kuwait, and Saudi Arabia. In doing so, he gave Kuwait 310 miles of coastline on the Persian Gulf compared to just 36 for the much larger Iraq.[7] Needless to say, the Iraqis were not happy about this, but there was little they could do, being under British control as they were.

Iraq achieved its independence from Great Britain in 1932, the monarchy that headed Iraq at that time was set up by the British and was hardly a progressive nationalist force. By the time Kuwait received its independence in 1961, Iraq had become a republic much more willing to challenge the neocolonial policies of such core nations as Great Britain. Immediately following Kuwait's independence, Iraq's leader, Major General Abdul Karim Kassem, laid claim to Kuwait and threatened to annex it by force, but was prevented from doing so by the British who had rushed to Kuwait's defense.[8] In sum, the territorial boundaries established by foreign colonial powers may be the single most important factor that led to war between Iraq and Kuwait, and, for that matter, between many contending groups and nations in the region.

There were other factors that from the Iraqi viewpoint justified the war against Kuwait. Among the foremost of these is the dispute regarding the Rumaila oil field. The oil field is approximately fifty miles long and is estimated to hold thirty billion barrels of oil. Ninety percent of the field lies within the borders of Iraq. Iraq charged that in the 1980s Kuwait had pumped billions of dollars of oil out of the Rumaila field and should have compensated Iraq in some way. Compounding this charge was the fact that Iraq had fought a war with Iran for much of the 1980s that had left Iraq with a huge debt it hoped to pay through the sale of oil. It also hoped to have some of the debt forgiven by those countries that had sided with Iraq during the war. The extraction of oil from the Rumaila field by Kuwait hurt Iraq in two respects. First, it meant that less oil was available for Iraq to sell on the open market. Second, it contributed to the overproduction of oil by Kuwait, which caused the price of oil to drop.

In addition to flooding the world market in apparent violation of OPEC (the Organization of Petroleum Exporting Countries) agreements, Kuwait refused to forgive Iraq's debt and also refused to lease two islands it controlled in the Persian Gulf that Iraq wanted to use as deep-sea ports. Perhaps peaceful solutions to these problems could have been found, or Iraq could have suffered in silence, but Saddam Hussein chose the military option. In all likelihood, Hussein miscalculated the support he would get from other Arab nations and also the intensity of international condemnation that his actions would evoke. He was also misled regarding how the United States would respond.

Nevertheless, Iraq's invasion of Kuwait was a success in military terms. Within just seven hours of crossing the border into Kuwait, Iraqi troops and tanks occupied Kuwait City, the nation's capital.[9]

The U.S. response to the invasion was one of official condemnation and outrage, but many wondered if the United States had not encouraged the war in some ways. Throughout the 1980s, Israel had an interest in keeping the war between Iraq and Iran going, and the United States supplied Iraq with weapons while Israel secretly supplied Iran on behalf of the Reagan administration.[10] In addition, Oliver North's Iran-contra network illegally sent arms to Iran while the Reagan administration was (illegally) allowing Saudi Arabia, a major U.S. arms customer, to transfer large quantities of U.S. arms to Iraq.[11] In sum, the United States had been giving significant military aid to Iraq in the years preceding its attack on Kuwait.

Furthermore, on July 24, 1990, Margaret Tutweiler, a spokesperson for the U.S. State Department, declared that "we [the United States] do not have any defense treaties with Kuwait, and there are no special defense or security commitments to Kuwait." The very next day, just one week prior to the Iraqi invasion, April Glaspie, the U.S. ambassador to Iraq, told Saddam Hussein that the United States has "no opinion on Arab-Arab conflicts like your border disagreement with Kuwait." This basic line was repeated on July 31 by U.S. Undersecretary of State John Kelly at a meeting of the Foreign Affairs Subcommittee of the U.S. House of Representatives. Kelly stated, "We have no defense treaty relationship with any Gulf country. That is clear. . . . We have not historically taken a position on border disputes."[12] These statements could have easily been interpreted by Iraq as an indication that the United States would not take a position on an Iraqi invasion of Kuwait. If the United States were truly interested in stopping the invasion, why would its highest officials in the area of Persian Gulf relations be making statements such as those made by Tutweiler, Glaspie, and Kelly? U.S. officials could have stated clearly and definitively the U.S. government's opposition to an Iraqi invasion of Kuwait.

On the matter of the statements made by Ambassador Glaspie and others, Samir Amin has commented, "We know almost certainly now that this invasion was a trap set by Washington into which Saddam Hussein, encouraged by the U.S. Ambassador to Baghdad, had fallen."[13] Former U.S. Attorney General Ramsey Clark has documented claims that the

United States was preparing for war with Iraq for at least a year before Iraq invaded Kuwait. In 1989, the U.S. Central Command (CENTCOM) replaced the Soviet Union with Iraq in its War Plan 1002 as the main enemy in the region. CENTCOM was headed by U.S. Army General Norman Schwarzkopf Jr., who was uniquely qualified for the position: He had spent a great deal of time in the Middle East, and his father had played an instrumental role in overthrowing the government of Iran in 1953 (see chapter 8). In 1990, CENTCOM conducted at least four war games with Iraq designated as the enemy; some of these games were premised on an Iraqi invasion of Kuwait.[14] Clark's investigation of the circumstances leading up to Operation Desert Storm caused him to conclude that "the U.S. government used the Kuwait royal family to provoke an Iraqi invasion that would justify a massive assault on Iraq to establish U.S. dominion in the Gulf."[15]

The hypothesis that the United States had been intent on a military attack on Iraq before the invasion of Kuwait would tend to explain why the United States did not pursue numerous peaceful options more vigorously. In the time between the invasion that started on August 2, 1990, and the start of the U.S. air war against Iraq on January 16, 1991, a number of proposals were made that could have prevented thousands of deaths, but these proposals were summarily rejected by the Bush administration. For example, in December, Algeria and Jordan had arranged to bring Saddam Hussein and Saudi Arabia's King Fahd together for negotiations. Hussein met with Algeria's President Ben-Jedid Chadli, but Fahd, under pressure from the United States, refused to meet with Chadli. Afterward, former U.S. national security adviser Zbigniew Brzezinski expressed his feelings that the war could have been avoided if the United States had not sabotaged the efforts of the Algerian government.[16]

Later that same month, Iraq was willing to drop its claims concerning the Rumaila oil field and the Gulf islands and to withdraw its troops from Kuwait if the United States pledged not to attack, if it removed its troops from the region, and if it agreed to an international conference on the Palestinian question. Another plan proposed by France with the support of numerous other countries was rejected by the United States. UN Secretary-General Perez de Cuellar expressed his frustration with U.S. intransigence at the UN and noted Iraq's willingness to withdraw from Kuwait under certain conditions.[17]

Nevertheless, the United States seemed determined to use its military force to settle the Iraq-Kuwait dispute. When the United States held an emergency session of the Security Council on August 2, 1990, there was little disagreement among the participants that Iraq's actions ought to be condemned. However, in the succeeding two months, a number of resolutions pertaining to the Gulf conflict were passed, and the United States sought to get as much backing as it could for the use of force to end the conflict. The way in which the United States obtained this backing is a lesson in UN politics in the new world order. According to Phyllis Bennis:

> Virtually every developing country on the Security Council was offered new economic perks in return for a vote in favor of the U.S. war: Colombia, impoverished Ethiopia, and Zaire (already fully in thrall to the U.S.) were all offered new aid packages, access to World Bank credits or rearrangements of International Monetary Fund grants or loans. . . . Military deals were cut as well. Ethiopia's government was given access to new military aid after a long denial of arms to that civil war-racked nation. Colombia was also offered a new package of military assistance.[18]

The United States, in order to prevent a possible veto by China, began to reopen diplomatic relations that had been cut since the Tiananmen Square massacre. One week after the UN vote that authorized the use of force against Iraq, the World Bank announced that China would be given over $100 million in economic aid.[19]

Those nations that did not go along with the U.S. position were subject to retribution. Cuba, already the subject of an economic blockade and diplomatic isolation, had little to lose and voted against the resolution. The small Arab republic of Yemen also opposed the resolution. Yemen's ambassador was told by a U.S. official just after the vote, "That will be the most expensive 'no' vote you ever cast." Within days the United States cut its $70 million aid package to Yemen.[20]

Throughout the U.S. attack on Iraqi troops in Kuwait and the U.S. Air Force bombings of Iraq itself, the U.S. public was rarely exposed to pictures or stories depicting the misery of the war, nor were figures on the number of dead easy to come by. Operation Desert Storm was portrayed as an exercise in technical wizardry and military efficiency. The war was given a great deal of television coverage that emphasized the precision of the missiles and fighter planes. The coverage resembled a series of commercials for U.S.-made military hardware, and some referred to the war as "operation desert stage." The press, just as it had failed to report on the hypocrisy of U.S. actions at the United Nations, was also negligent in investigating many of the claims made by both sides during the war.[21] The uncritical reportage was not entirely the fault of the press since the government had imposed a press blackout of the war and even practiced outright censorship in many cases. *New York Times* correspondent Malcolm Browne declared, "I've never seen anything that can compare to it, in the degree of surveillance and control the military has over the correspondents." Browne went on to say that the military had so restricted the press that it was functioning much like the Nazi propaganda corps. Pools of reporters were carefully controlled, and U.S. military officials had right of approval over the final copy and footage. Reporters who tried to cover the war outside the Pentagon's officially sanctioned press pools were sometimes detained or even threatened by U.S. soldiers. One wire-service photographer was held for six hours by U.S. Marines who threatened to shoot him if he left his car. He was told, "We have orders from above to make this pool system work." Likewise, a French television crew was forced at gunpoint to turn over film to the marines. Government control of the media brought on a federal lawsuit filed by nine news organizations and four journalists, but the lawsuit was not joined by the major networks or wire services and had little practical consequence.[22]

In general, media executives were happy to toe the line on the Gulf War. NBC president Michael Gartner refused to air footage obtained by Jon Albert, a twelve-year NBC employee, that showed civilian areas damaged by U.S. aerial attacks. In fact, Gartner prohibited Albert from working for NBC ever again.[23] Publisher William Randolph Hearst III suspended columnist Warren Hinckle for three months for an article he wrote for the *San Francisco Examiner*. Elsewhere in the American media establishment, editors were fired and radio talk show hosts forced to resign, all for being critical of the war. Clerks at the major wire services were even instructed to destroy any photographs showing dead bodies.[24]

The American people were sheltered from the knowledge that the United States violated the Geneva Conventions by bombing civilian areas—including a bomb shelter that resulted in approximately 1,600 deaths—by unrestrained attacks on fleeing troops and by destroying facilities that are necessary to civilian life and health (hydroelectric plants, water treatment facilities, etc.).[25] During the war, the United States dropped napalm, fuel-air explosives, and cluster bombs, and their targets were not always military ones. Among the civilian targets hit were storage dams, pumping stations, food warehouses, and grain silos. Iraq's irrigation system was severely damaged, and its food-production capability was cut in half. The destruction of Iraq's agricultural superstructure ensured that the civilian population would suffer the effects of the war long after it had officially ended. And their suffering would not easily be ameliorated, as the United States had also bombed an estimated twenty-eight civilian hospitals and fifty-two community health centers.[26] Many observers commented that the air war bombed Iraq back into a preindustrial era. The devastation undoubtedly ensures that Iraq will not present any significant challenge to Western powers for many years to come and that its future development will be greatly dependent on (or perhaps more accurately, at the mercy of) the United States and other core nations. But one has to wonder what the future price will be and who will pay it, for the United States has certainly sewn the seeds for future economic and health problems for the people of Iraq and has given them a memorable reason for hating the United States.

To gain support for the war against Iraq, the U.S. government and the press were quick to tell stories that weren't true or to exaggerate possible threats. President Bush repeated a story several times that claimed Iraqi troops were taking Kuwaiti babies out of incubators and leaving them on the floor to die. Bush claimed that 312 babies died from this exercise in cold-blooded brutality. But the story was simply untrue. It was repeated so many times that although there was some evidence contradicting it at the time, the truth didn't come out for months, and even then it was pretty much ignored.[27]

Also in order to rally public support for the coming U.S. attack, and to convince Saudi Arabia to permit the United States to station hundreds of thousands of troops there, the government repeatedly claimed that the Iraqis had amassed over 100,000 soldiers near Kuwait's border with Saudi Arabia in preparation for an invasion of that country. All evidence, however, pointed to the contrary. The ultimate proof that the Bush administration was lying came in the form of satellite photographs obtained by a Florida journalist, which showed no buildup of Iraqi forces. This evidence, like so much additional evidence that countered the U.S. government's official line, was virtually ignored by the U.S. press.[28]

In spite of a large-scale propaganda effort by the government, public opinion polls showed that the public was not highly supportive of a war against Iraq. But in the fall of 1990, a *New York Times/CBS News* opinion poll found that 54 percent of the respondents felt that military action would be justified in order to keep Iraq from acquiring nuclear weapons. After this poll was published, President Bush began to claim that Hussein was on the verge of developing the bomb and that "he has never possessed a weapon he didn't use."[29] (Of course, no one suggested that the United States should have invaded South Africa after it developed the bomb, even though South Africa was committing acts of aggression against its neighbors. Parallel cases can be made regarding Israel, India, and Pakistan, but the United States has chosen not to act in these cases. Such cases are only made against nations that are at variance with the United States on key issues.) In sum, Bush's claims were clearly exaggerated and politically motivated.

The Real Reasons for the Gulf War

There are many reasons why the U.S. government chose such a violent and inflexible "solution" to the Persian Gulf problem. Some of these reasons weigh more heavily than others, and some are easier to substantiate. One reason that should be mentioned is that the war helped to boost George Bush's popularity. In the fall of 1990, Bush's approval rating reached its lowest point. Later polls showed his popularity climbing as he made increasingly belligerent statements regarding Saddam Hussein, and by the end of the Gulf War, Bush's approval rating reached a record 88 percent.[30] It seemed that much of the nation was looking for someone or something upon which to take out its frustrations.

Undoubtedly, the war was waged in such a destructive manner as to reassert U.S. dominance in the region with the area's great oil reserves in mind. This goal requires either a willing client state to act as a surrogate for U.S. interests or a direct presence capable of advancing U.S. goals. From the mid-1950s to the late 1970s, the role of surrogate was played by the nation of Iran headed by its shah, installed and heavily armed by the United States. With the fall of the shah, however, U.S. hegemony was directly weakened and the United States was forced to rely more heavily on Israel, which is a liability in certain respects due to its conflicts with many Arab nations. The destruction of competing powers such as Iraq serves to enhance U.S. influence in the Middle East, and the subversion of Arab solutions such as those proposed by Jordan was necessary because they could have undermined U.S. power by recognizing the authority of other Arab nations. As some have pointed out, accepting an Arab solution would have meant sharing the power to set the agenda.[31] Not coincidentally, the rescuing of the Kuwait autocracy had nothing to do with the restoration of democracy, since most of Kuwait's population does not have basic citizenship rights; rather, it kept in power an autocracy that has been closely allied with the political and economic interests of the Western core nations.

U.S. influence in the Middle East is partly ensured by promoting differences among the nations of the region and by undermining Pan-Arabian solidarity. This perspective helps explain why the United States can work to arm both sides of a conflict, such as it did in the Iran-Iraq War, or why the United States privately sends signals encouraging a war that it publicly opposes.

The purposes served by U.S. actions in the Persian Gulf were many, but foremost among them were conquering the Vietnam syndrome, reestablishing a strong U.S. influence in the region, and sending a signal to the rest of the world that the United States was willing and able to take military action on matters of global importance. In short, the United States was showing that it was prepared to continue its old world order interventionist policies.

Buried Alive

"The U.S. Army division that broke through Iraq's defensive front line used plows mounted on tanks and combat earthmovers to bury hundreds or thousands of Iraqi soldiers—some still alive—in more than 70 miles of trenches. 'For all I know, we could have killed thousands,' said Col. Anthony Moreno. 'I came through right after the lead company,' Moreno said. 'What you saw was a bunch of buried trenches with people's arms and things sticking out of them.' A thinner line of trenches on Moreno's left flank was attacked by the 1st Brigade, commanded by Col. Lon Maggart. Maggart estimated that his force buried about 650 Iraqi soldiers."[32]

A heavy price was paid by Iraq in order for the United States to attain the aforementioned objectives. Before the war was over, U.S. military sources were estimating that 100,000 Iraqi soldiers had been killed.[33] Reliable estimates of the number of civilians killed are difficult to find, but it probably numbers in the tens of thousands. The destruction of much of the nation's infrastructure and the continuation of sanctions after the war resulted in malnutrition, the spread of disease, and the subsequent death of hundreds of thousands more. In fact, within a year of the war's end, an estimated 150,000 additional civilians had died; and by early 1994, the total number of Iraqi dead as a result of the bombings and the sanctions had risen to 300,000. Most of those who die as a result of the continuing sanctions are children. UNICEF estimated that the sanctions resulted in the death of up to 100,000 children in 1994 alone. At the end of 1995, the results of a UN Food and Agricultural Organization study were published. The study found a twofold increase in infant mortality, a fivefold increase in mortality of children under the age of five, and a total of 567,000 child deaths in Iraq since August 1991—all attributable to UN-imposed sanctions.[34]

Long after the official end of the war, the United States conducted frequent bombing raids in northern Iraq, and continued to charge with Iraq with developing weapons of mass destruction. From 1991 to 1998, the UN conducted weapons inspections in Iraq, but the inspections were stopped after accusations that the United States was using the inspections for purposes other than the officially sanctioned purpose. Specifically, it was charged that the United States was attempting to gather intelligence about Iraqi security services and the whereabouts of Saddam Hussein. Swedish diplomat Rolf Ekeus, who headed the UN weapons inspection mission (Unscom) said that as time went on the purpose of the mission was changed by the United States for purposes clearly outside the Unscom mandate. Ekeus claimed that attempts were made to provoke crises that could "form the basis for direct military action."[35] In 1999, the United States acknowledged that it monitored radio communications of Sudam Hussein's innermost security forces using equipment it secretly installed under the cover of the UN inspections.[36]

The implication of U.S. actions should be made clear. The diversion of the Unscom weapons inspections by the United States jeopardized a process that could have promoted regional security. Multilateral agreements that would permit weapons inspections could have a lot to offer to the cause of global peace and security. That groudbreaking possibility suffered a serious setback due to the actions of the United States.

Tensions between Iraq and the United States increased again in 2001 and 2002, when President George W. Bush declared that Iraq was part of an axis of evil. Bush worked to build support for a "regime change" in Iraq, arguing that it was necessary because of Iraq's support of terrorism and its development of "weapons of mass destruction." However, investigations had determined that there was no connection between Iraq and the Al Qaeda bombing of September 11, 2001, or the subsequent incidents of anthrax being sent through the U.S. mail. Conveniently, the Bush Administration and the mainstream press ignored the role the United States may have played in biological and chemical weapons development in Iraq. Throughout much of the 1980s, private U.S. suppliers, licensed by the U.S. Department of Commerce, exported toxic biological substances that could be used as weapons of mass destruction. According to a U.S. Senate Committee in 1994, some of these biological materials were "identical to those the United Nations inspector found and removed from the Iraqi biological warfare program" after the Gulf War.[37] Among the biological materials exported to Iraq were

- Bacillus anthracis, which causes anthrax.
- Clostridium botulinum, a source of botulinum toxin.
- Histoplasma capsulatam, which causes a disease that attacks the lungs, brain, spinal cord, and heart.
- Brucella melitensis, a bacteria that can damage major organs.
- Clostridium perfringens, a highly toxic bacteria that causes systemic illness.
- Clostridium tetani.
- Escherichia coli (E. coli).[38]

The American public was also not reminded of revelations made in 1969 that for years the United States had instructed foreign specialists in chemical and biological warfare. Hundreds of foreigners from thirty-six nations had been trained at the Army's Chemical School at Ft. McClellan, Alabama. Among those receiving training were officials from South Vietnam, Iraq, Egypt, Israel, and Yugoslavia.[39]

The case of Iraq illustrates what has become an increasing problem commonly referred to as blowback, in which U.S. economic, political, and military policies result in unintended consequences that come back like an unexpected boomerang. Economic exploitation, reckless military action, and short-sighted political alliances often sow seeds of resentment and hostility that manifest themselves years later as violent attacks on U.S. civilian and military targets.[40]

Gulf War Syndrome

Of the 700,000 U.S. soldiers who fought in the Persian Gulf War, roughly 45,000 developed "Gulf War syndrome"—a variety of symptoms including rashes, asthma, incontinence, hair loss, memory loss, pneumonia, and chronic pain. In addition, concerns have been raised about the offspring of Gulf War veterans.

The question of whether these symptoms, and this proportion of illness, signifies a genuine syndrome connected to Gulf War service is still disputed and raises important concerns about toxic hazards posed by modern warfare. Soldiers in the Gulf War were exposed to twenty-one "reproductive toxicants" that could have harmed them as well as their future offspring. These toxins include fumes from diesel fuel, smoke from burning wells, insect repellant, radiation from the nearly one million depleted uranium-tipped shells fired during the war, potentially harmful vaccinations administered by the military, and chemicals released by the U.S. bombing of Iraq's chemical plants. (Much of Iraq's chemical arsenal was equipped by U.S. companies, eighty of which were sued by ailing Gulf War veterans.)

Most Americans who served in the Gulf War were given pyridostigmine bromide, or PB. PB was thought to offer some protection from nerve gas. In its haste to use PB, the Pentagon persuaded the Food and Drug Administration (FDA) to abandon the usual safeguards on testing a drug for a new purpose. PB was known to cause serious side effects, including impaired breathing, vision, stamina, and short-term memory. After the war a Department of Agriculture study found that the toxicity of PB is multiplied when used in conjunction with the common insect repellant DEET.

Other vaccines were also used by some Gulf War soldiers. A vaccine against "weapon-borne anthrax" was administered to 150,000 American soldiers, 43 percent of whom experienced immediate side effects. A vaccine against botulism that was not approved by the FDA was given to 8,000 soldiers.

The Pentagon regularly tried to stymie investigation into the problem or simply denied its existence. In 1994, a U.S. Senate committee disclosed that Persian Gulf veterans were ordered "under threat of Article 15 or court-martial" to discuss their vaccinations with no one, not even with medical professionals who need the information to treat adverse reactions to the vaccines.

Civilians are also victims of toxic warfare. The radioactive waste left behind by depleted uranium weapons poses a health risk to civilians long after the fighting has stopped. DU was used in large quantities in the Gulf War and also in the war in Yugoslavia in 1999. Often the threat posed by these toxins are underestimated, misunderstood, or officially denied.

For decades the U.S. military refused to acknowledge the claims of soldiers whom it ordered to march into A-bomb test sites in the 1950s. These veterans fought the Veterans Administration for thirty years before winning compensation. Likewise, Vietnam veterans finally won a $180 million settlement from Agent Orange manufacturers in 1984, after years of government denial and intransigence.[41]

This is only a test
In May of 2002, the Defense Department disclosed that it had sprayed U.S. ships and sailors with chemical and biological agents during cold war–era testing. Later, in October, it released more details acknowledging the use of chemicals and live biological agents in tests conducted from 1962 to 1971 on its own troops, on American soil.[42]

On March 19, 2003, the United States began a major military assault on Iraq. The assault was initiated in spite of progress made by a new round of international weapons inspections and in spite of U.S. inability to win approval for war from the United Nations Security Council. It also took place in the face of unprecedented mass demonstrations for peace, which took place in many cities throughout the world on February 15 and involved an estimated eight to ten million people.

The basis for the new war against Iraq was outlined in a major new defense strategy statement issued by the U.S. government in September of 2002.[43] The new strategic plan includes several original principles that have major implications for U.S. power and world peace. Among these are (1) An explicit statement that the United States reserves for itself the right to wage preemptive war; (2) A willingness to act unilaterally, i.e., "to act alone" without support of the UN or major coalitions of nations; (3) To maintain and even fortify its unmatched military power; and (4) To make no distinction between terrorists and the nations that harbor them.

The notion of preemptive war is particularly disturbing. In essence, the United States has declared that it may attack another nation even if that nation has made no concrete aggressive move toward any other nation. Such a notion violates United Nations agreements and other international laws that have taken decades to achieve and may signal the start of an era where diplomacy and other means of conflict resolution completely give way to the rule of might. The willingness to act alone further weakens the United Nations' ability to evaluate the credibility of any U.S. claims against another nation.

A Brookings Institution paper summed up some of the problems with the preemptive doctrine:

> Elevating the preemptive option to a policy has serious negative consequences. For one, it reinforces the image of the United States as too quick to use military force and to do so outside the bounds of international law and legitimacy. This will make it more difficult for the United States to gain international support for its use of force, and over the long term, may lead others to resist U.S. foreign policy goals more broadly, including efforts to fight terrorism. Elevating preemption to the level of a formal doctrine may also increase the Administration's inclination to reach for the military lever quickly, when other tools still have a good chance of working.
>
> Advocating preemption warns potential enemies to hide the very assets we might wish to take preemptive action against, or to otherwise prepare responses and defenses ... advocating preemption may well embolden other countries that would like to justify attacks on their enemies as preemptive in nature.[44]

It was largely due to the George W. Bush administration's insistence on a military solution to its issues with Iraq, regardless of the sentiment of many of its allies and potential allies (whom the Bush administration began to call "irrelevant"), that the United States lost much of the international sympathy and support it had gained after the September 11, 2001, attack on the World Trade Center. By early March of 2003, public opinion polls were finding strong popular opposition to the United States in many nations long regarded as allies. The Pew Research Center for the People and the Press, for example, found that while 59 percent of Americans supported a war to remove Saddam Hussein from power in Iraq, only 39 percent of Britons and 13 percent of Spaniards favored military action. The Pew Center also found that opinions about the United States were becoming more negative. Only 25 percent of Germans had a favorable opinion of the United States, down from 61 percent nine months earlier. Likewise, in France, the percent with favorable views of the United States fell from 63 percent to 31 percent. And in Italy, favorable opinions fell from 70 percent to 34 percent.[45]

OPPORTUNITIES IN THE NEW WORLD ORDER

If the advent of the new world order is marked by the collapse of the Soviet Union and, in turn, the end of its nefarious plans to spread totalitarian

(Reprinted by permission of Jeff Danziger)

socialism throughout the world, then it ought to mean that now there is a new opportunity to encourage democracies to flourish. It ought to mean that the United States doesn't have to support repressive governments or right-wing terrorists just because they represent the only viable opposition to communism. However, as we have already seen, U.S. foreign policy, especially in the Third World, was not really aimed at stopping Soviet expansionism but at promoting capitalist expansion. If the United States were genuinely interested in the new opportunity for promoting democracy and human rights, its policies regarding Iraq and Haiti, for example, would be much different. In the case of Iraq, after its withdrawal from Kuwait, the United States, in spite of its verbal encouragement for Iraqis to rise up against Hussein, did nothing to aid the democratic opposition within Iraq. In fact, since the United States had supplied Saddam Hussein with weapons, technology, and money, and since his regime routinely used torture and violence to crush its opposition, there is probably a more convincing case in arguing that the United States has opposed the development of democracy and human rights in Iraq. The same can be said of the case of Haiti, which we will look at in detail now.

Haiti

The nation of Haiti represents a unique case study of U.S. policy in the new world order. It also represents a classic example of the way in which colonialism and neocolonialism can underdevelop a nation economically, politically, and socially.

Haiti is situated on the western half of the island of Hispaniola (the Dominican Republic is on the eastern half). Haiti's miseries started shortly after Columbus first visited the island in 1492. At that time as many as eight million indigenous people lived on the island, and Columbus described them as "lovable, tractable, peaceable, gentle, decorous Indians."[46] Soon they became the victims of slavery, disease, and slaughter, and within fifty years of Columbus setting foot on the island of Hispaniola, there were probably fewer than 1,000 Indians remaining.[47]

The loss of the Indian population caused the Spanish settlers to resort to "importing" African laborers. The slaves were worked hard, and it is estimated that up to one-third of them did not survive more than three years of intense exploitation.[48] In 1677, Haiti became a French colony, and the nation's class structure, to a large extent, continued to be formed on the basis of skin color. A series of slave rebellions led by Toussaint l'Ouverture

(1746–1803) succeeded in gaining independence for Haiti in 1804. Haiti became the first and only nation in which black slaves were able to rise up and defeat their oppressors and form an independent nation. As such, Haiti represented an early case of "the threat of a good example" and became the object of much Western hostility; it was often blamed for inciting or inspiring slave rebellions elsewhere.

After Haiti's independence the nation faced political isolation, and colonial powers were able to dictate terms of trade that put the small, young nation at an extreme disadvantage. The legacy of colonialism, international animosity, and the lack of any comparable model to follow led to the development of an authoritarian state much along the lines discussed by Clive Thomas in his book *The Rise of the Authoritarian State in Peripheral Societies* (see chapter 7 herein). In sum, despite its independence, Haiti remained a neocolony of Western core nations that continued to plunder Haiti for its coffee, sugar, cotton, hardwoods, and cheap labor. The United States and the Western European powers gradually came to recognize the legitimacy of the Haitian government and were willing to provide aid or better terms of trade in exchange for certain concessions. The United States finally recognized Haiti in 1862, perhaps due to the "enlightened" attitude toward blacks at the time or, more likely, due to the fact that "President Lincoln and others saw Haiti as a place that might absorb blacks induced to leave the United States (Liberia was recognized in the same year, in part, for the same reason)," as Noam Chomsky has claimed.[49]

Military interventions by foreign powers were rather commonplace in Haiti throughout the 1800s, and they no doubt contributed to Haiti's lack of development and to the growth of an authoritarian state. The United States undertook twenty-four armed interventions in Haiti between 1838 and 1914.[50] However, the most significant intervention, which set the basis for the problems in contemporary Haiti, took place in 1915 when the U.S. Marines invaded Haiti and occupied the country until 1934. Thousands of Haitians were killed as a result of the invasion. In the first recorded instance of coordinated air-ground combat, the U.S. Marines killed 3,250 rebels, 400 of whom were executed outright. The 1915 invasion forced a new Constitution on Haiti, one that allowed foreign ownership of land, which had been banned for the previous 100 years. (The U.S. Marines disbanded the National Assembly for refusing to ratify the Constitution and rigged a plebiscite vote to make its adoption official.) The United States also prohibited elections because it was certain that anti-American candidates would win.[51]

U.S. corporations hungry for sugar, bananas, rubber, and other resources moved in for the feast. New laws were enforced by the Haitian police, now officially trained and controlled by the U.S. Marines, and thousands of Haitians were forcibly conscripted to do corvee labor for the good of the new government, the marines, and foreign corporations.[52] Haitians did not accept the new order passively, but their rebellions were relatively futile against the well-armed occupying forces and resulted in the death of thousands of Haitians. When the marines departed Haiti in 1934, they left behind a system of established structures, including a well-armed and powerful military and an entrenched comprador class, which helped to ensure the future openness of Haiti to U.S. investment dollars.

In 1957, Dr. Francois Duvalier (1907–1971), commonly known as "Papa Doc," became president. Papa Doc Duvalier quickly established his own personal security force, the Volunteers for National Security, which eventually became known as the "Tontons Macoutes" and which terrorized Haiti for decades. In 1964, Duvalier was named president for life; and upon his death in 1971, he passed the presidency on to his son, Jean-Claude ("Baby Doc"). While Papa Doc Duvalier ruled Haiti, his notorious Tontons Macoutes killed tens of thousands of Haitians, yet he was given a great deal of aid by the U.S. government. In his first four years as president Duvalier received over $40 million from the U.S. government, and he was able to get away with using AID vehicles for his own purposes.[53] The U.S. Marines returned to Haiti one time during the 1960s, not to intervene on behalf of Haiti's beleaguered citizens but in support of Duvalier. The justifications for U.S. support of Haiti's dictator ring a familiar bell, as indicated from the following rationales contained in U.S. government documents written in the 1960s: (1) The overriding objective is to deny Haiti to the communists; (2) In short-term political terms, the United States desires to ensure Haiti's support of the United States on matters of importance in the OAS, UN, and other international organizations; and (3) The United States has the continuing objective of protecting private American citizens and property interests in Haiti.[54]

The true reason for U.S. support of Duvalier undoubtedly lies primarily in the third point. Haiti has long been a source of profits for U.S. corporations, as both its natural resources and its cheap labor have been highly prized. In 1969, Duvalier, acutely aware of his role in the world capitalist system, welcomed Nelson Rockefeller to Haiti by suggesting that "Haiti could be a vast reservoir of manpower for Americans establishing reexportation industries closer, safer, and more convenient than Hong Kong."[55] By the late 1970s, goods assembled in Haiti surpassed coffee as the nation's number one export. By 1980, there were 200 assembly plants in the capital city of Port-au-Prince, and they employed sixty thosuand people. By the mid-1980s, Haiti had become the world's ninth-largest assembler of goods destined for U.S. consumption.

It may be unnecessary to say it at this point, but the proliferation of these offshore assembly plants in Haiti did little to improve the well-being of the population.[56] Haiti followed the course of an authoritarian state's development outlined in chapter 7: At least 75 percent of the population was poverty-stricken, political dissent was forbidden, and the Tontons Macoutes operated as death squads against any possible opposition. In addition, deforestation and the loss of fertile topsoil from much of the arable land was setting the basis for future ecological problems and continued poverty and dependency. These are the conditions that breed resistance and rebellion in a country's population, and Haiti is no exception.

In spite of the Duvaliers' terror network, the Haitian people were able to organize a resistance that developed momentum and finally ousted Baby Doc Duvalier in February of 1986. It was not until Baby Doc's future seemed certain that the United States finally cut its support for the dictator in order to facilitate the smooth transition to another pro-U.S. regime. This pattern of support and denial has become de rigueur in U.S. policy circles. It happened with Anastasio Somoza Debayle in Nicaragua in 1979 and with Ferdinand Marcos in the Philippines in 1986. Unfortunately, the new Haitian government, led by a man who had served as a loyal general under two generations of Duvaliers, did not offer any positive change for Haiti; General Henri Namphy proved as repressive as the Duvaliers had been.[57] Nevertheless, the U.S. government and the press seemed quite satisfied. A State Department spokesperson remarked that "the government is off to a good start," and among the initial aid given to Haiti was $384,000 worth of riot control equipment.[58]

Demonstrations and general strikes continued throughout Haiti. In spite of setbacks, which included the murders of two presidential candidates and several massacres of people coming to vote in the 1987 elections, the movement for change continued to gain momentum.[59] In the late 1980s, Father Jean-Bertrand Aristide became more and more widely known as an outspoken critic of the Haitian government. He was also known for his seemingly uncanny ability to avoid death, for in Haiti, any well-known leader of the opposition who had not been murdered was a rare find. But Aristide survived; and in December 1990, he was elected president of Haiti, defeating the U.S.-backed candidate (and former World Bank official) Marc Bazin in the nation's first democratic elections. Aristide collected 67 percent of the votes compared to just 14 percent for Bazin.[60]

But the victory of a government's opponent in a national election is just a small part of taking power away from privileged and corrupt elites. As history has shown many times over, ruling elites are reluctant to relinquish their power and privileges. And when they feel their power slipping away, they often refuse to abide by the rules of fair play. Thus, Aristide's election in 1990 was a short-lived exercise in democracy for Haiti. In less than a year, his government was overthrown by the military and Aristide was expelled from the country.

The progressive nature of Aristide's government, however, was clearly illustrated during the short time it held power: His government instituted a program to distribute unused land to peasants, credit to small farmers was increased, efforts were under way to curtail erosion and desertification, a major public works program to create jobs was announced, and movement had begun to increase the minimum wage. Some of Haiti's problems that affected the United States also saw some remediation. First, there was a dramatic decrease in the number of "boat people" leaving Haiti. Second, the U.S. Drug Enforcement Agency (DEA) reported that the amount of cocaine being shipped out of Haiti had dropped. Aristide's government had been making definite progress against drug dealers and corrupt police officials who were an integral part of the drug trade.[61]

Given the history of U.S. relations in the Caribbean and Central America, the pertinent questions here are: Was the United States involved in overthrowing the Aristide government? Did the United States genuinely pursue an efficacious course of action to restore Aristide to the presidency? Charges that people working in the Bush administration were responsible for the coup were made by at least one of Aristide's advisers, Reverend Attoine Adrien.[62] At the time of this writing, however, there appears to be no direct evidence linking any part of the U.S. government to the actual coup that took place in September 1991. Nevertheless, it should be noted that some of the individuals who took part in the coup had been trained and supported by the U.S. government. In addition, the progressive policies of the Aristide government were contrary to those traditionally favored by the U.S. State Department and such organizations as AID. AID opposed Aristide's proposed increase in the minimum wage, and it sponsored a "democracy project" that gave money to various political organizations that opposed the Aristide government. Conservative organizations also received money from the National Endowment for Democracy, which had been instrumental in providing funds for right-wing groups opposed to the Sandinista government in Nicaragua.[63]

This sudden concern for a so-called democratic opposition stands in stark contrast to U.S. concerns during the most repressive years of Haiti's past. According to an observer of Haiti, Amy Wilentz:

> During the four regimes that preceded Aristide, international human rights advocates and democratic observers had begged the State Department to consider helping the democratic opposition in Haiti. But no steps were taken by the United States to strengthen anything but the executive and the military until Aristide won the presidency. Then, all of a sudden, the United States began to think about how it could help those Haitians eager to limit the powers of the executive or to replace the government constitutionally.[64]

Among the individuals with close ties to the U.S. power structure who clearly benefited from U.S. aid was Major Joseph-Michel François, chief of police in Haiti's capital of Port-au-Prince. François was trained at the SOA in Fort Benning, Georgia, was a prime force behind the coup that removed Aristide, and was a major architect of the repression in Haiti. He was also closely connected with the "attaches" who functioned much as the Tontons Macoutes had in earlier years.[65] And General Raoul Cedras was a CIA source for years before leading the coup and becoming the nation's latest in a long line of dictators.

In the years preceding the coup, the CIA created the Haitian Intelligence Service (SIN), which was staffed with corrupt Haitian Army officers and was supposedly designed to stem the flow of drugs through Haiti. Established in the mid-1980s, SIN was ineffective at achieving its official goal, and, in fact, many of its officers engaged in drug trafficking.[66] The United States provided SIN with millions of dollars in aid. Little of this went toward stopping the drug traffic, but much of it went toward terrorist acts against Aristide's supporters. The *New York Times* reported that SIN officials even threatened to kill the local chief of the DEA.

Shortly after the coup, stories were circulated in the U.S. press and statements were made by officials in the Bush administration to the effect that Aristide was psychologically unstable. The Bush administration was clearly attempting to alleviate some of the criticisms of Haiti's new government and cut off attempts to restore Aristide to the presidency. Much of the information that was distributed about Aristide, however, had come from intelligence sources inside the Haitian military. According to Senator Christopher Dodd of Connecticut, "A lot of the information we're getting is from the very same people who in front of the world are brutally murdering people."[67] In fact, one of the sources was General Raoul Cedras, who, in his capacity as a CIA intelligence source, provided the U.S. government with reports highly critical of Aristide. The CIA also circulated a story, later proven to be untrue, that Aristide was a manic-depressive who had been prescribed lithium by a Canadian doctor.[68] CIA official Brian Latell tried to whitewash the new regime by telling a congressional committee that General Cedras impressed him as a "conscientious military leader who generally wishes to minimize his role in politics." He also declared that during his own 1992 visit to Haiti he saw "no evidence of oppressive rule" and that there was "no systematic or frequent lethal violence aimed at civilians."[69] Latell described Aristide as "a murderer and a psychopath" while commenting that General Cedras and his associates were "one of the most promising group of Haitian leaders to emerge since the Duvalier family."[70]

In spite of these attempts to paint the Cedras government in a more favorable light, even the State Department had to acknowledge the human rights violations taking place in Haiti: "Haitians suffered frequent human rights abuses throughout 1992, including extra-judicial killings by security forces, disappearances, beatings and other mistreatment of detainees and prisoners, arbitrary arrests and detention and executive interference with the judicial process."[71]

During Aristide's seven months in office in 1991, there were relatively few human rights violations committed, and most of them were by the army, which was predominantly anti-Aristide. But after the coup, human rights abuses once again skyrocketed. By the end of 1992, nearly two thousand people had been killed, over five thousand illegal and arbitrary arrests had been made, and more than two thousand cases of beatings and shootings had been reported. And once again a steady stream of refugees started to flow out of Haiti.[72]

In the eight months following the coup, some thirty-four thousand Haitian boat people were intercepted at sea by the U.S. Coast Guard and sent back to Haiti. Similar numbers were sent back during the 1970s and 1980s.[73] In the late 1970s, the Carter administration had officially designated Haitian refugees as "economic refugees," a category that made it easier to deny them refuge in the United States. The policy of intercepting Haitian boats and sending the people on board back to Haiti has consigned many to die at the hands of the Haitian military and the attaches. The United States has also, at times, detained many of these boat people at its military base at Guantanamo Bay in Cuba—an area of land technically "leased" by the United States, but regarded more as a hostile occupation by the Cuban government. At Guantanamo, Haitians were denied legal counsel, and conditions at the camp drew severe criticism from human rights groups.[74] The policy of intercepting refugees at sea has been a way for the U.S. government to circumvent the *Principle of First Asylum*, which was established following World War II. This principle places an obligation on the nations surrounding the one in question not to return refugees but to instead admit them on at least a temporary basis.[75] Apparently, U.S. officials felt that the refugees' case for asylum was weaker if they never actually reached U.S. soil. Nevertheless, the U.S. policy of forced repatriation was condemned on several occasions by the UN High Commission on Refugees, although this was rarely acknowledged by the U.S. media.[76] Noam Chomsky pointed out the hypocritical differences between the way the United States deals with Haitian refugees as opposed to Cuban refugees: "Of the more than 24,000 Haitians intercepted by the U.S. Coast Guard [from 1981 to 1991], 11 were granted asylum as victims of political persecution, in comparison with 75,000 out of 75,000 Cubans. During Aristide's brief tenure, the flow of refugees dropped dramatically as terror abated and there were hopes for a better future. The U.S. response was to approve far more asylum cases."[77]

U.S. refugee policy is clearly influenced by political and ideological factors. Refugees from countries with governments that are disapproved of are encouraged, while refugees from governments that are approved of are denied entry. The policy is designed to undermine the governments we disapprove of and to reinforce anticommunist ideology among American citizens. The difference in the handling of refugees from Cuba and Haiti is a clear example of this, as was the handling of refugees from Nicaragua and El Salvador during the 1980s. Economic sanctions and embargoes are used in the same way. The United States was reluctant to support embargoes against Haiti and apartheid South Africa, but was pressured into it by other nations and popular opinion. Even after instituting or joining in these embargoes, the United States repeatedly claimed they were hurting the common folk and ought to be reconsidered. The United States took this position even though support for the sanctions was strong among the people of South Africa and Haiti. In addition, the United States often selectively enforced the sanctions and did not put pressure on other nations to join in. In contrast, sanctions were imposed on Iraq, Nicaragua, and Cuba, with little regard for, or even debate about, who would be hurt by them. If ordinary citizens suffered, this was tolerated because it might encourage them to revolt. Likewise, all sorts of arm twisting and deal making took place to make sure that other nations followed the U.S. line. And if the sanctions eventually become unpopular internationally, as they have in the case of Cuba with the UN General Assembly consistently voting to condemn the embargo, international opinion is disregarded and goes underreported in the U.S. news media.[78]

The position of the U.S. government on sanctions, aid, and refugees has little to do with human rights or political repression in the nations in question; rather, it is most often dependent on how agreeable the particular government is to U.S. political and military plans for the region and how open the government and the economy are to U.S. economic influence.

Initial efforts by the United States and the United Nations to restore Aristide to the presidency were ineffective and appear to have been half-hearted, to put it mildly. The embargo of Haiti is an example of this half-heartedness, for while the United States seemed to find every dinghy carrying a few Haitian refugees, it seemed unable to stop the shipment of all sorts of goods in and out of Haiti. The United States also allowed American companies to continue to do business with Haiti. According to the U.S. Department of Commerce, during the first nine months of 1992, trade with Haiti amounted to $265 million; and during the three years that Cedras ruled Haiti, profits for American companies doing business in Haiti increased.[79] Under the Bush administration certain American companies were permitted to export material to Haiti for assembly. Thus, despite the embargo organized by the OAS, U.S. apparel manufacturers and retailers imported over $67 million worth of clothing sewn in Haiti.[80] Critics of U.S. policy have pointed out that the Clinton administration could have seized the foreign assets of Haiti's wealthy elite and revoked their visas, blocking foreign travel. Steps like these were taken against Iraq in 1990, but not against Haiti. In addition, when the embargo was in effect, the U.S. press seemed intent on focusing on how it was hurting the poor of Haiti when, in fact, it appeared that the vast majority of Aristide supporters were in favor of continuing the embargo.[81] In a curious display of doublethink, the *New York Times* publicized a study of questionable validity that claimed that "Haiti sanctions kill up to 1,000 children a month," yet it offered little coverage of the mounting evidence that U.S. postwar sanctions against Iraq were killing tens of thousands of Iraqis.[82]

The U.S. invasion that took place in the fall of 1994 may have restored Aristide to power, but there are many reasons to believe that the changes that will be permitted are merely window dressing and, in fact, will strengthen the hold that foreign capital has on the nation. The agreement that former president Jimmy Carter worked out allowed many of the coup's leaders to remain in the country or live a very comfortable life in exile. The accord also permits the Haitian military to pick its own successors. Aristide also gave ground in regard to whom his cabinet members would be, agreeing to include some members of Haiti's small but very wealthy elite.[83] One wonders if the United States would have made its final moves against the Cedras regime if the World Bank had not hammered out an agreement with Aristide's advisers just one month before the U.S. invasion. The plan called for the World Bank to loan Haiti about $1 billion over the next five years. In exchange, Haiti was forced to make a number of structural adjustments designed to suit the interests of the bank. These adjustments included the privatization of many public services, increased tax collection, decreased tariffs, and reduced restrictions on imports.[84] According to University of Wisconsin scholar Patrick Bellegarde-Smith: "The Haitian delegation to the World Bank signed away the economic independence of the country. We're talking about the sale of 125 semi-private, semi-public agencies of the Haitian government—not to wealthy Haitians . . . but to foreigners, and the lifting of import duties."[85]

To make matters worse, U.S. support of right-wing paramilitary groups continued after the U.S. military came ashore. One of these groups was formed by Manuel Constant at the urging of the U.S. Defense Intelligence Agency. Originally called the Haitian Resistance League, the group later became known as FRAPH (Front for the Advancement and Progress of Haiti), and it received weapons from the United States and shared information with U.S. intelligence agencies. Before Aristide agreed to a variety of U.S. demands (including the World Bank's requirements), FRAPH had apparently stepped up its attacks on Aristide's supporters, thereby increasing the pressure on Aristide to make concessions.[86] When U.S. troops landed in Haiti, FRAPH members who were arrested by Haitian authorities or by U.S. troops were sprung from jail through the direct intervention of senior U.S. officials. Later, hundreds of pages of U.S. documents relating to FRAPH were released as a result of a lawsuit filed by the Center for Constitutional Rights. The documents revealed that although U.S. intelligence agencies regarded FRAPH as a gang of "gun carrying crazies" eager to "use violence against all who oppose it," American officers told their troops that FRAPH was a legitimate political party, "no different from Democrats or Republicans."[87]

No doubt FRAPH and others who inflicted so much violence and despair on Haiti have been protected by the refusal of the United States to hand over some 160,000 pages of documents seized from the headquarters

> "Haitian dictator Raoul Cedras left Haiti to live in Panama when Aristide was returned to power. He lives in a penthouse suite in a building called 'The Emperor.' The U.S. State Department alone pays him $5,000 a month in rent for his two properties in Haiti. Cedras jogs on the seafront each morning and his neighbors say they are surprised by how nice he is."
> —*New Internationalist*, January 1996

of the military and paramilitary groups in 1994. The documents likely contain information that would aid the rightful prosecution of corrupt officials, drug traffickers, human rights abusers, and the like. Instead, these groups have been shielded from justice. Meanwhile, the Lavalas movement that brought Aristide to power was severely weakened, and the image of the United States as a rescuing hero was projected to the average American and to much of the world.

The situation in Haiti, in the so-called new world order, is actually the product of old world order U.S. dominance in Latin America. It is the result of an imbalance of power through which the elite of the core capitalist nations have been able to extract the material wealth of nations outside the core and to exploit the labor of the people in these nations with little regard for the suffering inflicted or for the long-term environmental consequences. The fact that those who have suffered tend to be disproportionately dark skinned reflects a history of racism that has been inherent in the development of world capitalism. This does not mean that the core elite do not exploit "their own kind." In fact, for many contemporary Western investors, the possibility of restoring capitalism in Eastern Europe and taking advantage of new labor and product markets is regarded as an exciting opportunity. For the people of Haiti, however, a real new world order is a necessity. In the words of Yanique Joseph: "In countries of people of African descent, the need for a world order which allows societies to break free of the self-destructive policies of irresponsible elites, as well as an equally self-destructive strategy of economic development imposed by international forces, is immediate."[88]

Instead, the new world order, in all probability, means the continuation of vastly unequal relationships in the Third World, in conjunction with the accelerated penetration of capitalism into the former Soviet bloc nations.

EASTERN EUROPE: CAPITALISM REVIVED

For much of the twentieth century, the fate of Eastern Europe was closely tied to the actions of the Soviet Union. The advent of a new era began when Mikhail Gorbachev took office in 1985 and introduced a period of change marked by the policies of *glasnost* (openness) and *perestroika* (restructuring). These changes gradually eroded the power of the Soviet Communist Party and laid the groundwork for dismantling the state socialist economy. For the Soviet bloc nations of Eastern Europe, this meant a loosening of external control of which they took advantage by opening their economies to more private development and foreign investment.

One of the catalysts for change in Eastern Europe was the Polish labor union *Solidarity*. Leading a series of strikes by workers at the Gdansk Lenin Shipyard in 1980, Solidarity grew to be the largest independent workers' union in the world (in proportion to the size of the nation's workforce). Among Solidarity's demands were the acceptance of free trade unions independent of the Communist Party and the selection of managerial personnel on the basis of qualifications, not party membership. These demands threatened the domination of the Communist Party in Poland, but Solidarity's strength forced the government to acquiesce. Later, Solidarity called for a nationwide referendum on establishing a noncommunist government. The government, fearing possible Soviet intervention, took a strong stand against Solidarity, imposed martial law, and jailed Lech Walesa and other leaders of the union. International pressure and the persistence of the workers' movement eventually led to dramatic changes in Poland, including free elections and major economic reforms. In 1989, candidates backed by Solidarity swept the elections for Parliament; and in 1990, Lech Walesa became president.

The Solidarity movement tested Soviet willingness to intervene in support of communist governments in Eastern Europe to the point where the Soviet Union openly declared it would not do so. By 1989, many of the nations began instituting free-market economies and conducting their first free elections in decades. It was in that year that the Berlin Wall came down, followed shortly by German unification and an increase in the free movement of people throughout Europe.

Within the Soviet Union itself, many significant changes were taking place. In 1991, Gorbachev resigned as leader of the Communist Party and recommended that the Central Committee be disbanded. Several of the Soviet republics declared their independence, and by the end of the year, the Soviet Union had dissolved.

Solidarity, Yes! PATCO, No!

In 1981 President Reagan, an ardent supporter of Solidarity, fired 12,000 public air traffic controllers who had been striking for better working conditions and higher pay. This act prompted the proliferation of political buttons and bumper stickers that read "Right to strike? Only in Poland."

What was Solidarity asking for? How do you think Reagan would have responded to workers making these demands in the United States? Solidarity made twenty-one demands; some that workers in the United States might ask for include:

1. A guarantee of the right to strike and of the security of strikers and those aiding them.
2. Compensation of all workers taking part in the strike for the period of the strike.
3. Guaranteed automatic increases in pay on the basis of increases in prices and the decline in real income.
4. An increase in the minimum wage.
5. A full supply for the domestic market, with exports limited to surpluses.
6. Reduction in the age for retirement for women to fifty and for men to fifty-five, or after thirty years' employment for women and thirty-five years for men, regardless of age.
7. Improvements in the working conditions of the health service to ensure full medical care for workers.
8. Assurances of a reasonable number of places in day-care centers and kindergartens for the children of working mothers.
9. Paid maternity leave for three years.[89]

What has been the fate of the people of Eastern Europe and the former Soviet Union since the momentous changes of 1989–91? Let us look at two areas of life, the economic and the political, to assess the progress being made, then turn to the role that the West has played.

Economic Reform

At the start of 1990, the new Polish government instituted a series of economic reforms that would quickly be adopted by the other nations of Eastern Europe. Serious ruptures in the social and economic order were the immediate result.

In the first half of the year, Poles suffered a 40 percent drop in real wages. Food prices doubled in one month. Industrial sales plummeted. Social services were cut back. Unemployment rose dramatically, and Solidarity's popularity quickly dropped.[90] Contrary to the hopes of economic advisers and government officials, these effects were not short-lived. In Poland real wages were 33 percent lower at the end of 1992 than at the start of 1990. The effects were similar in other Eastern European nations. In Czechoslovakia real wages fell 21.5 percent, and in Hungary they dropped 14 percent over the same period. In Russia they fell 60 percent after the first six months of drastic reform in 1992.[91] Economists estimated that the economies of Eastern Europe would not return to their 1988 levels until the year 2010.[92]

Other data show that the economy of the Czech Republic shrank by 20 percent from 1989 to 1994, and in Hungary the five-year drop in GDP was about 18 percent. By 1994, 15 percent of all Poles were living in poverty compared to 5–10 percent in the previous decade, and unemployment had climbed to 15 percent. The restoration of capitalism brought about a sharp erosion in the ability of many people to provide themselves with basic necessities, although some are profiting and inequality is on the rise.[93]

The economic slide has had predictable effects on the well-being of the people of Eastern Europe. An October 1994 report by UNICEF stated that the economic changes had "provoked a deterioration of unparalleled proportions in human welfare."[94] According to the report, there was a tenfold increase in the number of families below the poverty line and some alarming trends in various health indicators. The overall mortality rate increased by 35 percent. Protein and calorie intakes were declining, and the rates of homicide and accidental death were rising.

UNICEF claims that the excess mortality in Russia, Ukraine, Bulgaria, Hungary, and Poland between 1989 and 1993 was 800,000. In Russia the crude death rate rose from 11.4 in 1991 to 14.4 in 1993 and to 16.2 in early 1994. Overall, the mortality rate was 35 percent higher than the pre-1989 rate. Life-threatening diseases have also risen in Russia. Typhoid and paratyphoid increased 13 percent in 1992 and 66 percent in 1993. Diphtheria increased 109 percent in 1992 and 290 percent in 1993. Deaths from tuberculosis rose 15 percent in 1992.[95]

Another consequence of the social transformation in Eastern Europe is the revival of all sorts of ethnic rivalries and the rebirth or strengthening of fascist movements in many of the European countries. In Lithuania, for example, the Constitution was rewritten to make non-Lithuanians (including Poles, Russians, and Ukrainians, who may have lived there for decades) second-class citizens. The new government also exonerated thousands of Lithuanians who had collaborated with the Nazis during World

War II.[96] Elsewhere in Eastern Europe there has been a resurgence of neo-fascist groups, some even holding state power.[97] Conflicts among groups vying for power left tens of thousands dead, with the worst violence occurring in Bosnia and other parts of the former Republic of Yugoslavia where the drive for ethnically pure states resulted in a policy of *ethnic cleansing*. In Western Europe, increased immigration and economic stagnation triggered a growth in postfascist nationalist groups in numerous countries including Italy, Germany, Austria, and France.[98]

All of this, however, has not been presented very clearly in the U.S. media. The media has tended to equate the "free market" and the newly created ability to invest profitably with political freedom, and it has tended to label as "democratic" only those factions (no matter how reactionary) that seek to expand capitalist economic reforms.[99] Thus when anticommunists are defeated in elections the Western press resorts to convoluted reasoning in order to avoid mentioning the people's dissatisfaction with the economic changes. A good example of this is the contrast between the favorable press given to the election of anticommunists in Hungary and the inability to explain sufficiently why that government was defeated in local elections in October 1990. According to Michael Parenti, the *New York Times'* explanation was as follows: "It was all because the voters were weary of frequent elections and felt 'distaste for the noise and confusion of unaccustomed political debate.' Furthermore, the anticommunist government was burdened by the 'legacy inherited from 40 years of Communist rule'—not by its own harsh free-market policies."[100]

Political Reform

Although the people of Eastern Europe have been able to participate in multiparty elections for the first time in many of their lives, the disastrous economic course that their leaders have taken gives one reason to question the ability of electoral politics to truly empower people. Whereas the people of Eastern Europe are free to vote for whichever candidates they choose, like citizens in Western-style democracies they are not free to exercise much influence over the economy. In fact, one might argue, under existing conditions even the government leaders have limited influence over the economic decision making.

In reality, much of the direction and control over the Eastern European economies has passed to the core capitalist nations, none of which seem overly concerned with the falling standard of living of the masses, or with encouraging democratic participation beyond electoral politics. In fact, at times Western leaders and economic advisers have encouraged actions that have undermined even limited democracy.

In discussing the influence of the core nations, let us consider the question of why nations such as Poland would inflict the hardship of immediate and vast changes on themselves. This is especially puzzling given the fact that many of the government officials who implemented these reforms were backed by, or were even members of, the Solidarity union. The answer is probably a combination of three general factors. First, people in Eastern Europe had grown so fed up with conditions under communism that they were willing to throw their support behind a movement that did not have clear answers but represented an alternative with the best possible chance of succeeding. Second, progressive reformers and much of the general public most likely had a romanticized vision of what capitalism would be able to provide. Knowing the wealth of Western Europe and the United States, and inundated with propaganda from Radio Free Europe, the Voice of America, and other sources, the people of Eastern Europe were choosing the capitalist road perhaps not very aware of the unemployment and poverty that typically accompany it. Perhaps, too, they thought they could preserve many of the social services such as free education and healthcare that they had come to take for granted. Third, unanticipated by many, a great deal of control over the economies in Eastern Europe, and indirectly over the social systems, has been assumed by Western advisers and Western political and economic institutions.

Although none of these three reasons has been given much consideration in the Western media, I would like to focus on the third since it ties in with the themes of globalization and polarization that have been developed throughout this book.

Western Influence and the Sachs Plan

Since 1989, the core capitalist nations have vigorously pursued plans to integrate Eastern Europe into the global economy and worked to cut off any alternative avenues that might tempt the Eastern European nations. Thus the West had forced an end to Comecon, the Eastern European trading unit, and taken steps to reduce Russia's influence. Along with various economic measures, the West pushed for extending membership in the North Atlantic Treaty Organization (NATO) to many Eastern European nations (excluding Russia), thereby isolating Russia even further.

The economic reforms that have been introduced in Eastern Europe since 1989 are part of a prescription for change drawn up in the United States by Harvard economist Jeffrey Sachs. The prescription has been labeled *shock therapy* due to its quick and painful results, and it consists of a number of significant reforms:

1. An end to government price controls and subsidies for wages.
2. Trade liberalization, especially with Western nations.
3. Convertible currency, to facilitate foreign trade.
4. Increased foreign investment by the West in Eastern Europe.
5. Privatization—the sale of state-run businesses to private citizens.

As we have seen, these measures have had a devastating effect on the standard of living of the people in Eastern Europe. The institution of these measures required a weakening of the working class, which, in spite of limited political freedoms under communism, had an advanced social wage—specifically, free healthcare, inexpensive housing and food, liberal maternity leave policies, and the like.

Industrial output in the Eastern European countries was not encouraged to any great extent by the West, probably due to the excess goods being produced in Western Europe. In other words, the nations of Eastern Europe were seen as new product markets for Western goods. For example, between 1989 and 1991, consumer goods imports into Hungary nearly doubled. The overall value of exports to the Czech and Slovak Republics and to Poland have also seen significant increases. Analyst Peter Gowan has labeled this an "export bonanza" for the West and notes that it has been strongly subsidized by Western governments through export credits and credit guarantees.[101] The imbalance in trade has been compounded due to a ban imposed by the World Bank on direct export promotion by the eastern nations.

One of the key elements in absorbing Eastern Europe into global capitalism has been privatization. The theory behind privatization, or at least the stated economic rationalization, is that state-owned enterprises are inefficient because they are protected from competition. Although there may be some truth to this, the bigger truths are that workers in state-run enterprises typically have better pay and benefits and that production can be geared more toward the social good than toward investor profit. Privatization, in reality, is a scheme to put state-run enterprises into private hands so they can enrich a segment of the population (often borrowing Western capital in the process). In the case of Eastern Europe, this overwhelmingly means

U.S. Chickens Invade Russia

As new markets opened up for Western goods, one industry that reaped a windfall is the U.S. poultry industry. From minimal sales in 1992, U.S. chicken exports to Russia climbed to $81 million in 1993, $303 million in 1994, and over $500 million in 1995.

U.S. poultry producers found the Russian market a convenient and profitable means to get rid of surplus dark meat not in high demand among American consumers. But some Russian producers claimed the chicken invasion was a Western plan to destroy Russian chicken production and capture the market.

One of the ironies of "chicken flight" is that it is subsidized by U.S. government loan guarantees, but Russian subsidies to chicken producers have been terminated. Meanwhile, American producers can hardly contain their glee. A spokesperson for the United States Poultry and Egg Export Council stated that American companies are "making money hand over fist." "It beats selling notebook computers," said another.[102]

concentrating more economic assets into the hands of Western capitalists—and, in many cases, at bargain prices.

In Poland and Hungary the overwhelming number of medium and large firms that have undergone privatization have been sold to foreign investors. In Hungary major sectors of the economy—brewing, cement, glass, bread, paper, and refrigerators—were sold to foreign corporations. In 1991, nine of the ten largest privatization sales were to Western multinationals. Among those who have made purchases are Electrolux, Unilever, and General Electric.[103] By the end of 1993, an astounding 55,000 enterprises had been acquired by Western companies.[104] Almost all East European automobile companies are now subsidiaries of Ford, GM, Mercedes, Volkswagen, Fiat, and a few other Western companies.[105] Whatever economic growth Eastern Europe experiences over the next few decades, it is bound to enrich Western financial interests perhaps more than anyone else.

It is quite evident that the economic interests of the West are outweighing the support of democratic principles. Other than supporting multiparty elections, the West has shown little interest in building real democracy. In fact, Western leaders want to avoid mass participation in decision making, and they have shown little concern for the impact economic restructuring has been having on people's lives. It is in part due to IMF and World Bank priorities that educational spending in Slovakia was reduced by 30 percent in 1993. Likewise, in the spring of 1995, the two Bretton Woods institutions required Hungary to charge fees for higher education and for medical treatment in order to obtain new loans.[106] The effects of these demands are to exclude many people from an advanced education and to create a growing divide between the privileged and the masses.

Polish sociologist Wlodzimierz Wesolowski has claimed that among the elite in Poland there was an "unvoiced assumption that people had to be demobilized in order to open the way for economic reforms" and that "the business of politics should be left to politicians and the emerging class of big capitalists."[107] In fact, after several years of the abysmal economic conditions brought about by shock therapy, people have voiced their dissatisfaction by showing former communists a good deal of support in national elections. In Poland, for example, Lech Walesa's party managed just over 5 percent of the vote in the 1993 parliamentary elections; and in 1995, Walesa lost the presidency to Aleksander Kwasniewski, founder of the Left Democratic Alliance and a former official of the Polish Communist Party. The success of such candidates has elicited some growing hostility on the part of the West toward Eastern Europe's democratic politics. Some of the hostility toward the electoral choices being made by Eastern Europe has been expressed in the journal *Foreign Affairs*, a publication of the highly influential Council on Foreign Relations. One writer called for a set of programs administered by the West to fund the mass media in the East, along with opposition parties, the courts, and police.[108] Suddenly, the philosophy of the new world order sounds a lot like the interventionism of the old world order.

Peter Gowan's explanation of the success of "postcommunist" parties sums up the situation very well: "The post communist parties have won support from electorates because . . . they are seen as seeking to rebuild the shattered social fabric by maintaining some minimal social commitments and by offering some protection to state enterprises which face political discrimination under World Bank tutelage."[109]

Hastening Russia's Demise

More of the West's shallow concern for democracy can be seen in its support of Boris Yeltsin, despite his violation of the Russian Constitution and his attack on the Parliament. Dismayed by Russia's dismal economic performance, particularly the 40 percent drop in real wages that occurred in 1992, the Parliament began to voice opposition to the shock therapy program. By the fall of 1993, Yeltsin could no longer tolerate their opposition, and he announced the dissolution of the Parliament, an act that clearly violated the Constitution. When the members of Parliament resisted by occupying the building, Yeltsin ordered a military assault on the Parliament. About 140 people were killed in the fighting and 150 arrested.[110] Yeltsin then closed down the Supreme Court and hostile newspapers and imposed censorship. In spite of these decidedly undemocratic actions, Yeltsin continued to receive strong support from President Clinton and other Western leaders.

Not only did support come after the fact, but prior to Yeltsin's actions against the Parliament, this course of action was advocated in an editorial in the influential British magazine the *Economist*. The editorial cried that Yeltsin "should abolish Parliament, introduce a new constitution, and call elections . . . [H]e has got to get rid of the present Parliament, which is blocking him at every turn."[111] The priorities of the West should be self-evident: Democratic ideals are worthy of support unless they conflict with Western economic interests.[112]

Yeltsin's antidemocratic tendencies are well documented in Jonathan Steele's book *Eternal Russia*, which presents a detailed account of the change that swept the Soviet Union particularly during the 1987–94 period. Steele claims that what occurred was much more a mirage of democracy than a true democratic transformation. He recounts how Russian prime minister Yegor Gaidar, one of the chief proponents of shock therapy, became a focal point of the conflict between Yeltsin and the Parliament. Gaidar was forced out of office by the Parliament in December 1992, but was then reappointed by Yeltsin in September 1993 after Western governments tied $24 billion in loans to Gaidar's continued role in the Russian government.[113]

Western interests continued to use money as a means of leverage when the IMF announced a $10 billion loan to Russia in February 1996. The loan was interpreted by many as an endorsement of Yeltsin and as a way of boosting his chances of winning reelection in June. The loan was scheduled to be paid out in monthly allotments; and the IMF made it clear that whether or not Yeltsin won the election the money would be cut off in the case of inappropriate government economic policies. In return for the loan, the Russian government agreed to abolish all export tariffs on oil and gas.[114]

Russia's economy was deeply jolted in the post-Soviet transformation period. After four years of shock therapy the GDP had fallen by 42 percent and industrial production by 46 percent. Average real monthly pay dropped from 94 rubles in 1991 to just 48 in 1995.[115] Inequality grew rapidly, poverty increased, and health services deteriorated. The effects of the transition included an increase in many communicable diseases. The number of cases of AIDS tripled in just three years (1997 to 1999); syphilis and tuberculosis increased for much of the 1990s; and life expectancy fell in six out of the decade's ten years.[116]

Meanwhile a wealthy national elite has been developing, crime has surged, and government corruption thrives. Boris Yeltsin resigned in 1999, but not before choosing his replacement, Vladimir Putin, a former KGB official. Putin's first act as president was to sign a decree giving Yeltsin immunity from prosecution.[117]

What the future holds for Russia, the former Soviet bloc nations, and the new republics of the former Soviet Union remains to be seen. But it is clear that what excites the interests of the Western elites is not the birth of Western-style political freedoms but the opening up of a vast portion of the world to renewed capitalist development. Prospects for the people of former socialist nations do not look good, however, for two reasons. First is the probability that the world has little room for more major capitalist powers. The existing core nations developed through the exploitation of their own populations, in conjunction with imperialist growth in the Third World.[118] The United States, Japan, France, Germany, and a few other countries so dominate production and markets throughout the world that there may be no space into which another world power can grow. If such a power were to develop, it would likely clash violently with the already established powers.

Second, it is not likely that the existing capitalist powers are going to view the new republics in Eastern Europe as newborns that need to be fed and nurtured. On the contrary, it is quite apparent that Western financial interests view them as new labor and product markets that can be exploited, and as a source of cheap raw materials. This can been seen in prescriptions that are driving wages down and in the rush to exploit the vast forests of Siberia.[119] Thus whatever room the core Western nations are willing to make in the global capitalist system, it is not likely to be for additional core nations that would threaten their wealth; rather, it would be for additional peripheral nations that would add to it. This, too, is likely to lead to greater conflict between the two areas of the world. In any event, the future holds a wide range of possibilities, and although the United States' ruling class may have a pretty clear idea of what it would like to happen, it should be obvious that the "new world order" is not by any means clearly established.

"In Eastern Europe, the death of communism had led the West to try to stamp out economic nationalism in favor of its own national and collective interests in the region. But this does not so much suggest a new era on the globe as something rather old-fashioned which, in the days of communism, used to be called imperialism."

—Peter Gowan[120]

THE CRISIS IN KOSOVO: U.S. GOALS AND MOTIVATIONS IN YUGOSLAVIA

The end of the cold war may have provided an opportunity for the United States to pursue a foreign policy more clearly guided by objective standards of justice and the promotion of human rights, but these were not the main reasons the United States and NATO intervened in Yugoslavia in the late 1990s.

In March of 1999, NATO began air strikes against Yugoslavia in order to force Yugoslav leader Slobodan Milosovic to stop his efforts to drive Albanians out of the Kosovo region of Yugoslavia. Kosovo's population is 90 percent Albanian and they are regarded as intruders by many of the Serbs who are the dominant ethnic group in Yugoslavia and who have claims to the region going back more than 600 years.

The most immediate effect of the bombing was that it forced the Organization for Security and Cooperation in Europe to remove the fourteen hundred civilian observers stationed in Kosovo. International civilian observers are one of the most powerful tools that the world has for preventing atrocities. In addition, the bombing had a major economic and environmental impact, the financial estimate of which is in the area of $30 billion.

While the ostensible reason for U.S./NATO military intervention was the protection of the lives and human rights of the Kosovars, the existence of many other more troubled regions calls that motivation into question. For example, in 1999 there were at least eight world "hot spots" suffering greater loss of life than Kosovo:

1. *Colombia.* In Colombia political killings had been taking place at the rate of three thousand to four thousand per year with an additional 300 to 400 disappearances. Nearly one million people have been turned into refugees as a result of the political violence there.[121]
2. *Turkey.* Since 1984, the Turkish military has bombed and depopulated more than three thousand Kurdish villages. As a result thirty thousand people have died, and two million Kurds have been turned into refugees. Furthermore even the U.S. State Department admits that torture is widely used against the Kurds.[122]
3. *East Timor.* From the time of the Indonesian invasion in 1975 to the implementation of sovereignty in the fall of 1999, approximately 200,000 Timorese lost their lives. During most of that time, Indonesia received U.S. military support and tacit approval for its actions. Most of 1999 was a time of intense violence in East Timor.

4. *Sudan.* Since the 1980s, a war has raged in the Sudan with little mention in the American media and little concern on the part of Washington. During the course of this time an estimated two million people have died and over four million have been turned into refugees.[123]

5. *Rwanda.* A half a million Tutsi were killed in a 1994 wave of genocide. By 1999, over 100,000 people were in jail on charges relating to the genocide and there was still fighting going on within the country. There is also a major refugee problem and Rwandan troops have been fighting in Burundi and the Congo.[124]

6. *Sierra Leone.* Civil war has raged for two decades, in large part due to a struggle for control of the nation's gold and diamond mines. The use of child soldiers is a key issue. Sixteen thousand UN peacekeepers were in Sierra Leone in 2001.[125]

7. *The Democratic Republic of the Congo.* A disastrous war has cost more than two million lives. According to a 2002 Human Rights Watch report, "During the four years of war, all parties routinely attacked civilians, killing, raping, and maiming thousands. Hundreds of thousands of civilians died of hunger, diseases, or exposure as a result of the war."[126]

8. *Iraq.* The combination of the U.S. bombing in 1991 of water storage facilities, grain silos, irrigation systems, hospitals, health clinics—facilities essential for the support of human life; the post-war sanctions; and the almost daily bombing raids that continue today have caused more than one million deaths. Dennis Halliday, a thirty-four-year United Nations official who headed the UN's humanitarian relief program in Iraq says the sanctions are "a form of warfare" and they are "producing 5,000 to 6,000 Iraqi deaths per month."[127]

To help understand why the United States acted to "save lives" in Kosovo but not in these other cases, it may help to ask what do these other nations have in common?

First, with the exception of Iraq, these global hot spots receive very little attention from the mainstream press. Iraq is often brought up by the media as a threat to the United States but the sanctions and their devastating toll on civilians are not. Second, U.S. policy is actively making things worse in many of the above cases.

In East Timor, the United States supplied aid to the Indonesian military and it maintained normal trade relations with Indonesia. Colombia, where the military has one of the worst—perhaps the worst—human rights record in the western hemisphere, is the largest recipient of U.S. military aid in the western hemisphere and the third-largest recipient of U.S. military aid in the world (in 1999, after Israel and Egypt). Turkey's main military supplier is the United States. Over 80 percent of Turkey's weapons come from the United States. During the 1990s, the United States provided Turkey with more than $12 billion in military assistance. Indirect aid by the United States also increased after Israel and Turkey signed a military training agreement in 1996, followed shortly thereafter by an arms industry cooperation pact.[128] In the Sudan, the United States bombed a pharmaceutical plant in August of 1998, destroying Sudan's ability to produce and distribute much needed medicines in a nation devastated by the two greatest threats to health: war and poverty. The bombing was in retaliation for terror bombings of two U.S. embassies in Africa and was based on erroneous intelligence reports that the factory was linked to Osama bin Laden and produced chemical weapons.[129]

The fact that U.S. policy is not guided by objective standards of human rights should be abundantly clear. So what were the real motivations behind the U.S.-led NATO action in Yugoslavia?

To understand what happened in Yugoslavia and to understand the consciousness of American policymakers it is necessary to take a look at the economic circumstances surrounding this intervention. And while there may be no obvious pot of gold in Yugoslavia, there are economic considerations that influence decision making. I'll return to the *economically conditioned* thinking of western policymakers. Let's first look at *economic conditions* in Yugoslavia.

Economic Conditions in Yugoslavia

The main force in establishing the Federal Republic of Yugoslavia were the communists who had fought Nazi occupation during WWII. These were led by Josip Broz Tito (1892–1980), a Croat, who was popularly known as "Tito." The proclamation of Yugoslavia as a republic took place in 1945.

Tito broke Yugoslavia's alliance with the Soviet Union in 1948 and was one of the founders of the *non-aligned movement*. One of Tito's most important economic innovations (and one I believe required a break with the Soviet Union) was the introduction of *self-management* in 1950. Its goals were to ensure workers direct, democratic participation in decision making concerning their living and working conditions, and to protect social democracy against the distortions and abuses of statism and bureaucracy. The system was based on social (not state) ownership of the means of production and natural resources, managed directly by workers in their own and the community's interests.[130] In 1953, most of agriculture was returned to private ownership and for the following two decades the combination of self-management and private production brought about substantial economic growth that attracted the attention of much of the European left.

Yugoslavia's multiethnic population required a balanced diplomatic juggling act to keep it all held together. This was compounded by the long history of each nationality in contrast to the short history of the Republic of Yugoslavia, and by uneven economic development. For example, Kosovo was the poorest region of Yugoslavia. In 1990, unemployment in Kosovo was 50 percent and per capita GNP $730 compared to $2,200 in Serbia.[131] Kosovo, of course, is populated predominantly by Muslim Albanians, a fact that extends back to the year 1690. (At that time, much of modern Yugoslavia was part of the Ottoman Empire. In 1690 there was a Serb revolt against the Ottomans that was defeated and ultimately tens of thousands of Serbian refugees left for other parts of Europe. The Ottomans then moved Albanian Muslims to the abandoned territory of Kosovo.)[132]

In the 1980s and early 1990s, economic problems intensified. It is important to put this in the context of the moves toward glasnost and perestroika that took place in the Soviet Union, as well as the economic and political reforms instituted in Poland and other Eastern European countries at that time. Briefly put, the political reforms, while ostensibly paving the way for greater democracy, allowed ethnic rivalries to surface more openly, brought forth open political agitation by neofascist groups, and created new possibilities for the fracturing of countries held together by sometimes weak social, economic, and political bonds. Compounding this was the fact that economic reforms were failing miserably.

Following the trend of the former socialist nations, Yugoslavia started to fracture, and in 1990, the Yugoslavian League of Communists renounced its constitutional single-party role and called on the parliament to draft a new constitution, eliminating the leading role assigned to the League in all spheres of Yugoslav life.

About that time Yugoslavia began pursuing more of a neoliberal model of economic development, especially under the regime of Prime Minister Ante Markovic. Neoliberal economic theory is the major unifying theme driving all U.S. foreign economic and military policy, as it is for many of the most economically advanced and politically dominant nations. Yugoslavia began to vigorously promote trade. In part this was necessary because Yugoslavia had fallen into the debt trap that is immiserating so many of the world's nations today. In 1989, Yugoslavia paid nearly $3.8 billion to foreign creditors but did not receive one single dollar in foreign aid.[133] As economic performance deteriorated in the following years, Croatia, Slovenia, Bosnia and Herzegovina, and Macedonia, all had incentives to withdraw from the Yugoslav Republic, as did Kosovo at the end of the 1990s. Bear in mind, having an incentive to secede isn't the same thing as having real solutions to the problems.

In 1989, Markovic traveled to the United States where he "negotiated" an aid package that required Yugoslavia to devalue its currency, freeze wages, cutback government spending, and privatize the socially owned enterprises. The cutbacks in government spending were required to redirect money to pay foreign creditors and this meant less money would be given by the central government to the various republics and autonomous provinces, thereby fueling secessionist movements. The privatization of socially owned industries resulted in massive layoffs and attempts to avoid privatization often meant nonpayment of wages. The nation's banking system was also dismantled under the guidance of the World Bank.[134]

The end result was that economic conditions deteriorated in Yugoslavia. History shows that whenever this happens existing differences among ethnic and/or religious groups can become volatile. They need to be handled very delicately. The response of the West was, in many ways, to worsen economic conditions through debt payment requirements and through UN economic sanctions that began in 1992. And later, through an attempt to impose a military "solution." All of these have made the situation worse.

ECONOMIC FACTORS INFLUENCING U.S. POLICYMAKERS

> [I]f this domestic policy is going to work, we have to be free to pursue it. And if we're going to have a strong economic relationship that includes our ability to sell around the world, Europe has got to be a key. And if we want people to share our burdens of leadership with all the problems that will inevitably crop up, Europe needs to be our partner. Now, that's what this Kosovo thing is all about . . . it's about our values.
>
> —Bill Clinton, March 23, 1999[135]

There are a variety of economic factors that are bound to influence American policymakers when it comes to issues of the sort being faced in the Balkans. For instance, parts of Yugoslavia are mineral rich, the nation has significant oil reserves, and there are proposed oil pipelines to be built from the Black Sea through Serbia to Italy. A more compliant Yugoslavian government is desirable for the pursuit of these interests.

In addition, at the time of U.S.-led NATO operations in Yugoslavia, the U.S. federal government was running a budget surplus for the first time in many years. The surplus amounted to more than $100 billion. The public, for the most part, preferred that the surplus be used to shore up the Social Security system or pay down the federal debt. The former conflicted with plans proposed by various factions of the American political and economic elite to reform Social Security through a multitude of plans calling for various forms of privatization. The existence of a surplus threatened Social Security privatization schemes that would have brought tens of billions of dollars in broker fees and profits. The war in Yugoslavia helped to increase military spending at the expense of other programs. After the demise of the Soviet Union military spending started to decrease, except for a blip at the time of the Persian Gulf War in 1991, and the Pentagon labored to find or manufacture new enemies to justify its budget. Its declared need to fight two wars simultaneously couldn't possible be met without a significant boost to the military budget.

Another economic factor that played into U.S. consideration regarding Yugoslavia was the transformation of NATO after the demise of the Soviet Union. By the late 1990s, NATO had added Poland, Hungary, and the Czech Republic to its ranks. As a condition of membership the three were told that they needed to upgrade their militaries at an estimated cost of $20–30 billion. The war in Yugoslavia was not likely the product of such cynical naked greed, but these sort of economic considerations along with some others put one in the frame of mind where military action doesn't sound like such a bad idea—a very different frame of mind than one might have if one was at risk of physical harm resulting from war. Some of the major military contractors in the United States were among the strongest lobbyists for the expansion of NATO. Their interests were the driving force behind NATO's expansion. Indicative of corporate America's love for NATO were reports in the *Washington Post* and elsewhere noting that a dozen corporations chipped in a quarter of a million dollars each to sponsor NATO's fiftieth anniversary celebration in Washington. They were part of a private-sector NATO support system that raised $8 million for the affair. The chief executives of the largest donors got to serve as directors of NATO's summit host committee. The whole affair was expected to give military contractors a unique chance to ingratiate themselves with leaders of the nineteen NATO member nations as well as leaders from the twenty-five nations that belong to the Partnership for Peace.[136]

The arms trade is big business and the United States is the world's leading arms dealer, controlling 55 percent of the world market share.[137] During 1993–94, 90 percent of the significant conflicts in the world involved at least one party that had received U.S. weapons or military technology prior to the outbreak of the conflict. And of the $59 billion in U.S. weapons transferred to nonindustrial countries from 1991 to 1995, 84 percent went to nondemocratic governments.[138]

Finally, the most significant motive was probably the general assimilation of Yugoslavia into the world market system. This is what neoliberal economic policy is all about and it might be better labeled the new imperialism. If one puts together the pieces one sees a series of steps doing just this. From the initial involvement of the International Monetary Fund that began in the 1950s and exploited the political differences between Tito and the Soviet Union. (Incidentally, for several decades Yugoslavia was the only "communist" country to be a member of the World Bank.)[139] To the 1984 National Security Decision Directive (NSDD) entitled "United States Policy towards Yugoslavia" and a 1982 NSDD on Eastern Europe both calling for "expanded efforts to promote a 'quiet revolution' to overthrow Communist governments and parties" while reintegrating the countries of Eastern Europe into the world market.[140] To the U.S.- and IMF-backed openly neoliberal regime of Ante Markovic beginning in 1989 and ending in 1992. In addition, the lessons of Bosnia no doubt were not lost on Slobodan Milosovic and the Serbian leaders. The constitution written for Bosnia at the Dayton accords in 1995 stipulated that the first Governor of the Central Bank of Bosnia and Herzegovina is to be appointed by the IMF and "shall not be a citizen of Bosnia and Herzegovina or a neighboring state."[141]

Assimilation into a world economic system occurs primarily through market trade, but it is a stacked deck with the United States, Great Britain, Germany, Japan, Canada, France, and perhaps a few others, acting as dominant partners in a global system of production, finance, trade, and military arrangements—a system of arrangements that is based on unequal exchange between the most advanced nations and everyone else.

And it is an arrangement in which the dominant partners rarely take responsibility for their roles in economic and social disasters. In Rwanda, between 500,000 and one million people were slaughtered. The seeds of these ethnic rivalries were sown and nurtured by German and Belgian imperialists and worsened by neoliberal structural adjustment imposed by western financial institutions in the early 1990s. In regard to Yugoslavia, Americans routinely heard the crying out of many outraged voices over ethnic cleansing that displaced hundreds of thousands of people, and our nation's leader were driven to war, seemingly by moral outrage. But why is so little said by U.S. government leaders about the suffering of millions of people who are displaced by World Bank projects?[142] Why were they so quiet when two highly respected international bodies declared that at least six million children under the age of five were dying each year in Africa, Asia, and Latin America as a direct result of Structural Adjustment Programs imposed by the Word Bank and the IMF? Where is the outrage and where is the simple U.S. technical assistance in defusing the tens of thousands antipersonnel bombs still exploding and maiming and killing people in Southeast Asia? And why do none speak out on the fact that of the most economically advanced nations the United States gives the lowest proportion of *genuine* foreign aid?

The fact of the matter is the United States has come to use human rights as a pretext for intervention when it suits its needs but is perfectly willing to overlook human rights when such considerations don't fit with other policy considerations. The United States uses foreign aid to promote narrow political aims and corporate interests above all else. Many of the crises existing in the world require negotiated political solutions; solutions that must also include economic considerations such as debt relief. Effective solutions require that many different voices are heard. And the process of developing these solutions should strengthen international agreements and the world's multilateral institutions. Too often these agreements and institutions are undermined by unilateral action, particularly by the United States. In the next chapter we will look closer at some of the global political and economic institutions, and assess their ability to resolve conflict and promote global welfare.

NOTES

1. "No Business Like War Business," *Defense Monitor* 16, no. 3 (1987): 5.

2. Paul M. Sweezy, "What's New in the New World Order?" *Monthly Review* (June 1991): 3.

3. Ibid.

4. See John Stockwell, *In Search of Enemies* (New York: W. W. Norton, 1978), and his conversation with Gil Noble on the ABC television show *Like It Is*, show no. 612, March 23, 1986.

5. Sweezy, "What's New," p. 4.

6. Phyllis Bennis and Michel Moushabeck, "Editor's Preface, Looking North: The New Challenge to the South," in *Altered States*, ed. Phyllis Bennis and Michel Moushabeck (New York: Olive Branch Press, 1993), p. xv. Although I have repeatedly

mentioned that the Soviet Union served as an excuse for many U.S. military interventions, it is also true that the existence of the Soviet Union as a formidable military power helped to keep U.S. interventionism somewhat in check and may have prevented U.S. victories in Southeast Asia, Angola, and elsewhere. For a detailed analysis of how the U.S. government has rationalized military intervention in the Third World and support for corrupt regimes that violate human rights (both during and after the cold war), see Stephen Rosskamm Shalom's *Imperial Alibis* (Boston: South End Press, 1993).

7. Bishara A. Bahhah, "The Crisis in the Gulf—Why Iraq Invaded Kuwait," in *Beyond the Storm*, ed. Phyllis Bennis and Michel Moushabeck (New York: Olive Branch Press, 1991), p. 50.

8. Ibid.

9. Steve Niva, "The Battle Is Joined," in *Beyond the Storm*, ed. Bennis and Moushabeck, p. 56.

10. See comments in chapter 8 in this book, and Seymour M. Hersh, "U.S. Said to Have Allowed Israel to Sell Arms to Iran," *New York Times*, December 8, 1991.

11. Ramsey Clark, *The Fire This Time* (New York: Thunder's Mouth Press, 1992), p. 7.

12. Bennis and Moushabeck, eds., *Beyond the Storm*, pp. 363–64.

13. Samir Amin, "The Real Stakes in the Gulf War," *Monthly Review* (July–August 1991): 15.

14. Clark, *The Fire*, pp. 10–11.

15. Ibid., p. 3. On the matter of whether Iraq was entrapped into invading Kuwait, see Edward Greer's excellent article "The Hidden History of the Iraq War," *Monthly Review* (May 1991).

16. Niva, "The Battle," p. 65.

17. Ibid., p. 66.

18. Phyllis Bennis, "Command and Control: Politics and Power in the Post–Cold War United Nations," in *Altered States*, ed. Bennis and Moushabeck, p. 41. See also Phyllis Bennis, "False Consensus: George Bush's United Nations," in *Beyond the Storm*, ed. Bennis and Moushabeck.

19. Bennis, "Command and Control."

20. Bennis, "False Consensus," p. 120.

21. See Michael Parenti, *Inventing Reality* (New York: St. Martin's Press, 1993); and Laura Flanders, "Restricting Reality: Media Mind-Games and the War," in *Beyond the Storm*, ed. Bennis and Moushabeck.

22. Bennis and Moushabeck, eds., *Beyond the Storm*, p. 371; and "Casualties at Home: Muzzled Journalists" and "Spin Control Through Censorship: The Pentagon Manages the News," *Extra!* (May 1991): 14–15.

23. Parenti, *Inventing Reality*, pp. 49, 167.

24. Ibid., pp. 167–68; *Extra!* pp. 14–15. See also Jim Naureckas and Janine Jackson, eds., *The Fair Reader: An Extra! Review of Press and Politics in the '90s* (Boulder, Colo.: Westview Press, 1996).

25. Parenti, *Inventing Reality*, p. 169.

26. Clark, *The Fire*, pp. 64–66.

27. Ibid., pp. 31–32; *Nation*, July 18, 1994, p. 94.

28. Clark, *The Fire*, pp. 28–29; Greer, "The Hidden History," p. 7.

29. Clark, *The Fire*, p. 30.

30. Robin Toner, "Casting Doubts: Economy Stinging Bush," *New York Times,* November 26, 1991.

31. Joe Stork, "Dinosaur in the Tar Pit: The U.S. and the Middle East after the Gulf War," in *Altered States*, ed. Bennis and Moushabeck, p. 234.

32. Excerpted from Patrick J. Sloyan, "Army Said to Plow Under Possibly Thousands of Iraqi Soldiers in Trenches," *Washington Post,* September 12, 1991.

33. Clark, *The Fire*, p. 43.

34. Ibid., pp. 208–10; Out Now, *War Watch,* no. 22 (February 1994): 2. See also Selma Al-Radi, "Iraqi Sanctions—A Postwar Crime," *Nation,* March 27, 1995. The figures for 1995 are from Sarah Zaidi and Mary C. Smith Fawzi, "Health of Baghdad's Children," *Lancet* (December 2, 1995): 1485. Related article by Barbara Crossette, "Iran Sanctions Kill Children, U.N. Reports," *New York Times,* December 1, 1995.

35. BBC News, world edition, July 30, 2002 [online], news.bbc.co.uk/2/hi/world/middle_east/2161552.stm.

36. Thomas W. Lippman and Barton Gellman, "U.S. Says It Collected Iraq Intelligence Via UNSCOM," *Washington Post* [online], www.washingtonpost.com/wp-srv/inatl/longterm/iraq/stories/unscom010899.htm [January 8, 1999].

37. William Blum, *Rogue State: A Guide to the World's Only Superpower* (Monroe, Maine: Common Courage Press, 2000), p. 122.

38. Ibid., pp. 121–22; Philip Shenon, "Iraq Links Germs for Weapons to U.S. and France," *New York Times*, March 16, 2003.

39. Blum, *Rogue State*, p. 120.

40. For a brilliant and prescient discussion of blowback, see Chalmers Johnson, *Blowback: The Costs and Consequences of American Empire* (New York: Henry Holt and Company, 2000).

41. Information on Gulf War syndrome comes primarily from *Life* magazine (November 1995); see also Dennis Bernstein, "Cover-Up: Chemical and Biological Agents and Gulf War Syndrome," *Covert Action Quarterly* (summer 1995).

42. Thom Shanker, "U.S. Troops Were Subjected to a Wider Toxic Testing," *New York Times*, October 9, 2002.

43. The White House, *The National Security Strategy of the United States of America*, September 2002.

44. Michael E. O'Hanlon, Susan E. Rice, and James B. Steinberg, "The New National Security Strategy and Preemption" (Washington, D.C.: Brookings Institution).

45. Alan Cowell, "A Worried World Shows Discord," *New York Times*, March 19, 2003.

46. Paul Farmer, *The Uses of Haiti* (Monroe, Maine: Common Courage Press, 1994), p. 60.

47. Ibid.

48. Ibid., p. 63.

49. Noam Chomsky, *Year 501: The Conquest Continues* (Boston: South End Press, 1993), p. 200. This recognition may have been a factor that enabled the Union to use Haitian ports as jumping-off points for some operations against the southern Confederacy during the Civil War.

50. Erwin Knoll, interview with Patrick Bellegarde-Smith, in *Progressive* (September 1994): 30; see also Chomsky, *Year 501*, p. 200.

51. Farmer, *The Uses of Haiti*, p. 93; and Chomsky, *Year 501*, p. 203.

52. Farmer, *The Uses of Haiti*, pp. 92–96.

53. Ibid., p. 108.

54. Ibid., p. 109.

55. Ibid., p. 115.

56. Ibid., p. 117.

57. Ibid., p. 127.

58. Ibid., pp. 127–28.

59. Ibid., pp. 138–42.

60. Yanique Joseph, "Haiti: At the Crossroads of Two World Orders," in *Altered States*, ed. Bennis and Moushabeck, pp. 456–57.

61. Farmer, *The Uses of Haiti*, pp. 167–69.

62. "Aristide Thanks Clinton but Won't Endorse Deal," *Star Ledger* (Newark, N.J.), September 2, 1994.

63. Farmer, *The Uses of Haiti*, pp. 172–73, 235. In addition to funding causes within Haiti, AID has vigorously promoted Haiti as a place for U.S. corporations to do business. AID has spent over $100 million on these efforts and has emphasized low wages and workforce pliability. See *War Watch*, no. 23 (May 1994): 3.

64. Quoted in Chomsky, *Year 501*, p. 211.

65. Vickey A. Imerman, "School of the Americas/Assassins," *Covert Action Quarterly* (fall 1993): 17.

66. Tim Weiner, "C.I.A. Formed Haitian Unit Later Tied to Narcotics Trade," *New York Times,* November 14, 1993.

67. Ibid.

68. Farmer, *The Uses of Haiti*, p. 192.

69. Weiner, "C.I.A."

70. Farmer, *The Uses of Haiti*, p. 192.

71. Weiner, "C.I.A."

72. Farmer, *The Uses of Haiti*, p. 222.

73. Ibid., p. 269; and Jenny Pearce, *Under the Eagle* (Boston: South End Press, 1982), p. 93.

74. Bill Frelick, "Closing Ranks: The North Locks Arms Against New Refugees," in *Altered States*, ed. Bennis and Moushabeck, p. 168; Farmer, *The Uses of Haiti*, pp. 263–64.

75. Frelick, "Closing Ranks," p. 167.

76. Chomsky, *Year 501*, p. 216.

77. Ibid., p. 206.

78. Raymundo del Toro, "U.S. Embargo of Cuba Violates U.N.'s Wishes," *New York Times*, November 3, 1994.

79. Farmer, *The Uses of Haiti*, p. 205; Chavannes Jean-Baptiste, "Tying Aristide's Hands," *Progressive*, September 1994, p. 26.

80. Farmer, *The Uses of Haiti*, pp. 198–99.

81. Ibid., p. 41.

82. Howard French, "Study Says Haiti Sanctions Kill up to 1,000 Children a Month," *New York Times*, November 9, 1993; see also French's article "Doctors Question Haiti Health Data," *New York Times*, November 24, 1993. For information regarding the effects of sanctions on Iraq, see Clark, *The Fire*, p. xxvii and elsewhere; and Al-Radi, "Iraqi Sanctions."

83. Dennis Bernstein, "Haiti: The Junta's Golden Parachute," *San Francisco Bay Guardian*, September 21, 1994, p. 19; John Kifner, "Aristide Vows to Include Wealthy in Haiti's New Cabinet," *New York Times*, October 20, 1994.

84. Betsy Reed, "Aristide's Financial Bind," *Dollars and Sense*, November–December 1994, p. 7.

85. Knoll, p. 32. Likewise, Jane Regan reports that "a month before the invasion, on August 26, in Paris, representatives of the Aristide government met with some of the major cogs in this U.S.-dominated machine: the World Bank, International Monetary Fund, Inter-American Development Bank and bilateral funders. The Aristide team verbally agreed to impose a neoliberal structural adjustment plan (SAP) that included the sale of public utilities and publicly owned businesses (euphemistically called 'the democratization of asset ownership'), liberalization of trade, and payment of debts." See "A.I.D.ing U.S. Interests in Haiti," *Covert Action Quarterly* (winter 1994–95).

86. Allan Nairn, "Our Man in FRAPH: Behind Haiti's Paramilitaries," *Nation*, October 24, 1994, esp. p. 464.

87. Allan Nairn, "Haiti Under the Gun," *Nation*, January 8 and 15, 1996; Nairn, "Our Man in FRAPH"; and Larry Rohter, "Cables Show U.S. Deception on Haitian Violence," *New York Times*, February 6, 1996.

88. Joseph, "Haiti," p. 460.

89. From "Understanding the Polish Revolt: An Interview with Daniel Singer and Marta Petrsewicz," *Radical America* (May–June 1981): 12.

90. Jon Weiner, "Capitalist Shock Therapy," *Nation*, June 25, 1990.

91. Peter Gowan, "Neo-Liberal Theory and Practice for Eastern Europe," *New Left Review* (September–October 1995): 20.

92. Ibid., p. 55.

93. Jane Perlez, "Fast and Slow Lanes on the Capitalist Road," *New York Times*, October 7, 1994.

94. Barbara Crossette, "U.N. Study Finds a Free Eastern Europe Poorer and Less Healthy," *New York Times*, October 7, 1994.

95. Gowan, "Neo-Liberal Theory," pp. 22–23.

96. Parenti, *Inventing Reality*, p. 129.

97. Paul Hockenos, "Uncivil Society: The Return of the European Right," in *Altered States*, ed. Bennis and Moushabeck.

98. Paul Hockenos, "Making Hate Safe Again in Europe," *Nation,* September 19, 1994.

99. Parenti, *Inventing Reality*, pp. 130–33.

100. Ibid., p. 133.

101. Gowan, "Neo-Liberal Theory," p. 24.

102. Michael R. Gordon, "U.S. Chickens in Russian Pots," *New York Times,* January 18, 1996.

103. Natalie Avery, "Stealing from the State (Mexico, Hungary, and Kenya)," in *Fifty Years Is Enough: The Case Against the World Bank and the International Monetary Fund*, ed. Kevin Danaher (Boston: South End Press, 1994), p. 98.

104. Gowan, "Neo-Liberal Theory," p. 45.

105. Matthew Brzezinski, "East Europe's Car Makers Feel Sting of Capitalism," *New York Times,* April 28, 1994.

106. Gowan, "Neo-Liberal Theory," p. 47.

107. Ibid., p. 49.

108. Ibid.

109. Ibid., p. 50.

110. *World Almanac and Book of Facts, 1996* (New York: Pharos Books, 1995), p. 812.

111. Gowan, "Neo-Liberal Theory," p. 51.

112. Parallels can be drawn to today's China: Western investment has increased dramatically since the late 1970s, and in the growing Chinese economy, this has meant large profits. Accordingly, the U.S. government has not pressed China very hard on its human rights policies. When China was closed to Western capital, U.S. condemnation was vehement.

113. Jonathan Steele, *Eternal Russia* (Cambridge, Mass.: Harvard University Press, 1994), pp. 38, 278, 282.

114. Darol J. Williams, "IMF Lends $10 Billion to Russia," *Star Ledger* (Newark, N.J.), February 23, 1996.

115. David Kotz with Fred Weir, *Revolution from Above: The Demise of the Soviet System* (New York: Routledge, 1997).

116. Michael Wines, "An Ailing Russia Lives a Tough Life That's Getting Shorter," *New York Times*, December 3, 2000; Abigail Zuger, "Russia Has Few Weapons as Infectious Diseases Surge," *New York Times,* December 5, 2000.

117. Jeffrey Tayler, "Russia Is Finished," *Atlantic Monthly* [online], www.theatlantic.com/issues/2001/05/tayler-p1.htm [May 2001].

118. This is a point made by Patrick Flaherty in his article "Privatization and the Soviet Economy," *Monthly Review* (January 1992).

119. Antony Scott and David Gordon, "The Russian Timber Rush," *Amicus Journal* (fall 1992); John C. Cushman Jr., "Siberian Logging Sets Off U.S. Battle," *New York Times,* January 30, 1996.

120. Gowan, "Neo-Liberal Theory," p. 60.

121. Coletta Youngers, "U.S. Entanglements in Columbia Continue," *NACLA Report on the Americas* (March/April 1998).

122. Jennifer Washburn, "Power Bloc: Turkey and Israel Lock Arms," *Progressive,* December 1998.

123. A. M. Rosenthal, "The Secrets of the War," *New York Times,* April 23, 1999.

124. Human Rights Watch [online], www.hrw.org/africa/rwanda.php.

125. Human Rights Watch [online], www.hrw.org/africa/sierraleone.php.

126. Human Rights Watch [online], *World Report 2002: Democratic Republic of the Congo* [online], www.hrw.org/wr2k2/africa3.html.

127. Jerry Kloby, *Inequality, Power, and Development* (Amherst, N.Y.: Humanity Books, 1997); Sid Shniad, "Former UN Official on Human Cost of Iraq Policy," *Guardian,* January 28, 1999.

128. Washburn, "Power Bloc."

129. Jeff Cohen, "Remembering the Last US Retaliation Against Terror," Common Dreams [online], www.commondreams.org/views01/0915-01.htm.

130. *The World Guide 1997/98*, p. 591.

131. Ibid.

132. Ibid.

133. Ibid., p. 592.

134. Michel Chossudovsky, "Dismantling Former Yugoslavia, Recolonizing Bosnia," obtained from *Z Magazine* [online], www. lbbs.org/yugoslvia.

135. Quoted in *Left Business Observer*, no. 89 (April 27, 1999).

136. Tim Smart, "Count Corporate America Among NATO's Staunchest Allies," *Washington Post,* April 13, 1999.

137. "U.S. Arms Sales," *Mother Jones* [online], www.mojones.com/arms/.

138. "Controlling U.S. Arms Sales," *Foreign Policy in Focus* 1, no. 4 (November 1996).

139. Doug Henwood in "This Kosovo Thing," *Left Business Observer*, no. 89 (May 1999), mentions the IMF's involvement in Yugoslavia in the 1950s. Catherine Caufield, *Masters of Illusion* (New York: Henry Holt, 1996), mentions the fact that the World Bank made loans to Yugoslavia in the 1950s for railroad and dam construction. She also briefly discusses loans made to state-run banks in the 1980s and their subsequent collapse.

140. Chossudovsky, "Dismantling Former Yugoslavia, Recolonizing Bosnia."

141. Ibid.

142. Juliette Majot, "Brave New World Bank," *Global Exchange* (winter 1994).

CONCLUSION

CHALLENGES TO POWER

Although the state is often said to have an exclusive right to use force, power is not a total monopoly of the state and force is not the only type of power. In today's world other bodies such as large corporations and supranational organizations exercise an ever-growing amount of power. But what forms of power are within the grasp of ordinary people? What alternatives do the masses of people throughout the world have other than to submit to the formidable coercive capabilities of corporations, governments, and supranational organizations like the World Bank, the WTO, and the IMF? How can the subversion of humane principles such as peace, justice, and equitable development by corporate interests and militarism be overcome?

In confronting the problems of the modern world some would have us believe that there is no need for mass action or more democracy, but simply a need to let the market work its magic. Under the banner of neoliberalism many conservatives and "reformed" liberals have united in the belief that the best of all possible worlds is attainable if we free the economic system of all restraints imposed on it by external forces, such as national governments. In the neoliberal model, characterized by deregulation of the economy, trade liberalization, the dismantling of the public sector (privatization), and the predominance of the financial sector of the economy over production and commerce, social problems, such as poverty, are not regarded as a consequence of the economic system and are not addressed systematically.[1] There is little or no room for government programs to address social problems.

How much of the neoliberal approach is rhetoric and how much of it is sincerely believed by its advocates is difficult to tell, for at the same time

341

that these market fundamentalists are advocating deregulation they are also setting up powerful new institutions to enforce their rules. For the wealthy, faith in neoliberalism comes easy since the rich clearly benefit. To better understand the current global economic order, let us take a look at one newly formed supranational organization that although ostensibly designed to promote trade and economic growth for the general good in reality has been contributing to accelerated polarization.

THE WORLD TRADE ORGANIZATION

The increased globalization of economic and political structures now taking place represents a form of uneven and combined development that is moving forward to the benefit of the elite of the core capitalist nations much more so than anyone else, and others may be devastated by its consequences. One of the most important organizations shaping globalization today is the World Trade Organization.

The WTO is the first multilateral organization with authority to enforce national governments' compliance with trade rules.[2] The WTO is part of the same heritage that began in Bretton Woods, New Hampshire, at the end of World War II, where the victorious major powers of the West created the IMF and the World Bank and established the General Agreement on Tarriffs and Trade (GATT). Representatives to GATT would meet every few years to iron out trade agreements. Eventually, the GATT meetings led to the creation of the World Trade Organization in 1995. As of February 2003, there were 145 member nations.[3]

Since its inception the WTO has been the subject of a great deal of criticism and angry, sometimes violent, protest. Criticisms of WTO include:

1. It is, in effect, trade legislation without representation. The WTO is not a democratic body, we don't elect representatives to it, yet it enacts laws that nations are expected to abide by and it has a mechanism for enforcing those laws.
2. The WTO operates in secret. It is difficult to find out what the WTO is doing or why it makes the decisions it does.
3. It subordinates all other considerations such as environmental issues, working conditions, and human rights, to the issue of trade.
4. The WTO has the power to institute sanctions against governments, thereby over-riding and undermining national sovereignty.

5. The is no mechanism for citizens to make appeals to WTO's dispute resolution process. It is a process without popular input.

The dispute resolution body of the WTO is one of its most controversial facets. The following WTO rulings illustrate how the WTO lowers standards, impinges on national sovereignty, and interferes with local decision making:[4]

- In the WTO's first ruling, the United States was forced to relax standards designed to limit gasoline contaminants after Venezuela won a WTO challenge against the Clean Air Act. Venezuela claimed the U.S. Clean Air Act was a violation of free trade.[5]
- The WTO ruled against provisions of the U.S. Endangered Species Act that required shrimpers to protect endangered sea turtles.
- The WTO ruled against Europe's ban on beef containing residues of artificial growth hormones. The European Union refused to back down and was hit with $116.8 million worth of WTO-authorized trade sanctions.
- Ten European nations have banned the use of asbestos. Canada, in turn, filed a WTO challenge that argued that such a ban provides more health protection than international standards and thus violates WTO agreements.
- The U.S. has threatened a WTO challenge if Denmark implements an intended ban on lead compounds in pigments and chemical processes to avoid lead's threat to child development.
- Japan changed its law promoting mom and pop neighborhood retail stores after the United States challenged it at the WTO. The law had required economic, traffic, environmental, and other impacts to be assessed before a megaretailer could open a facility.
- The European Union and Japan challenged the state of Massachusetts' preferential purchasing law, which penalizes companies doing business with Burma's military dictatorship. This policy of economically starving the ruling junta, based on the South Africa anti-apartheid strategy, has been called for by Burmese democracy leaders. However, WTO procurement rules forbid the consideration of noncommercial factors, such as human rights, in government purchasing decisions. They also require that all countries be treated the same regardless of their conduct.

The following example highlights a built in bias that virtually ensures that the rich nations will win:

- Guatemala implemented the UNICEF Code, which bans infant formula packaging with labels depicting healthy, fat babies to ensure that illiterate mothers do not associate formula with healthy infants and stop breast-feeding. Guatemala, faced with the prospect of a costly, lengthy fight, backed down and now exempts imported baby food products from its law.

The last example illustrates many problems rolled into one:

- After Chiquita Banana contributed a series of donations to both the Republican and Democratic Parties, the United States successfully attacked Europe's preferential treatment of bananas imported from former EU colonies. The United States implemented trade sanctions against the EU for not fully complying with the ruling. The EU says it will comply. Chiquita, Dole, and Del Monte are expected to be the big winners. Small independent farmers in the Caribbean will be the big losers.

As late as 1999, WTO critics were claiming that no democratically achieved environmental, health, or food safety law challenged at the WTO had ever been upheld. All of them were judged to be barriers to trade.

The WTO is not the only international agreement impinging upon national sovereignty. Chapter 11 of the North American Free Trade Agreement (NAFTA) empowers foreign investors to sue if public-policy decisions nullify their expectations of future profits.[6] In 1999, under the Chapter 11 provision, Methanex, a Canadian company, filed suit against the U.S. government in response to measures taken by California to phase out the use of MTBE, a gasoline additive. MTBE leaks from fuel storage tanks had contaminated Lake Tahoe, Shasta Lake, thirty public water systems, and thirty-five hundred ground water sites in California. MTBE is a carcinogen and even small amounts of it can render water unfit to drink. Methanex Corporation charged that banning MTBE violated the foreign-investment guarantee of NAFTA's Chapter 11. Methanex pleaded its case not to a government court but to a three-person arbitration panel created by NAFTA. The company argued that banning MTBE should be construed, in the wording of Chapter 11, as "tantamount to expropriation," and it demanded $970 million in compensation for damages the state of California would cause to Methanex's future profits.[7]

The World Trade Organization, as well as NAFTA's Chapter 11, undermines the ability of national governments to regulate business. The five hundred plus pages of the GATT agreement that established the WTO are not directed toward regulating trade so much as they are geared toward subordinating individual governments to the interests of private capital. The 145 nations that joined the WTO must "lower tariffs, end farm subsidies, treat foreign companies the same as domestic ones, honor all corporate patent claims," etc., and adhere to the judgments of the WTO, which has the power to enforce these agreements through trade sanctions.[8] The WTO undermines the ability of communities, states, and whole nations to upgrade their social and environmental standards. The tendency will be to pull down these standards to the level that exists where they are weakest.

Part of the rationalization for the WTO is the idea that the free market is the best mechanism for ensuring economic development and the wealth of nations. But it is a clearly demonstrable fact that free markets tend to benefit the economic interests of the more highly developed nations. In chapter 7, we saw that the well-being of much of the Third World has been degraded by its economic relationship to the First World, mostly through "free" trade. History shows that nations with protected economies, and those where the state takes an active role in the economy, often develop at a higher rate. Great Britain's economy was protected in the early stage of industrialization through tariffs and even by the use of military means to destroy competitors. As shown earlier, tariffs against imported textiles were important to the development of the British textile industry and, conversely, the British coerced India into lowering or abolishing tariffs thereby accelerating the decline of the Indian textile industry to the advantage of the British. The United States has also used tariffs and trade restrictions to strengthen domestic industries, not to mention the full coercive power of the state to enforce the system of slave labor prior to 1863. In the late 1800s tariffs against imported steel were important to the development of the U.S. steel industry (and to the wealth of Andrew Carnegie), as was the active role that the U.S. government played in establishing a national railroad network. Government subsidies to private industries also played a major role in the development of many countries, and they continue to be used by the most-developed nations today but, hypocritically, they are discouraged for the less-developed nations. The United States, Europe, and Japan spend $350 billion a year on agricultural subsidies and the United Nation's Development Program estimates that these subsidies cost poorer nations $50 billion in lost exports.[9] Nearly three billion people in the world live on less than $2 per day, yet the average cow in Europe receives about $2.50 per day in subsidies, according to the chief economist of the World Bank.[10]

In the twenty-first century the elite of the core capitalist nations, especially the owners of the major transnational corporations, know that their position is bound to be strengthened through free trade because of their superior resources. Likewise, GATT-like agreements including NAFTA, the proposed Free Trade Area of the Americas (FTAA), and *fast track* trade legislation (which gives the president power to bypass Congress and speed up trade negotiations), can be used to increase capital mobility and develop new legal agreements to lower the social costs of production.

The few less-developed countries that have avoided the worst aspects of dependency and exploitation have been able to do so due to some very exceptional circumstances. Some of them happen to be oil-rich nations in control (or partial control) of a highly valued commodity that has brought substantial wealth into the country and aided development, though there is often a consequential rise in inequality. Other nations happened to have gone through unique historical circumstances that allowed them to grow and develop. After World War II, Korea and Taiwan, for instance, were able to free themselves from their colonial relationship with Japan, and by confiscating Japanese assets were able to take advantage of the manufacturing industries that Japan had established in the two nations.[11] And, as opposed to countries such as Mexico and Brazil, U.S. corporations were not an active factor in the national economies.

Key industries in Korea and Taiwan were "protected by and nurtured behind a wall of tariffs, overvalued exchange rates, and other obstacles to foreign entry."[12] Their withdrawal from international markets was partly an accident of history and geography and partly a conscious effort by the governments of Taiwan and South Korea, and it contributed to their ability to develop domestic industries and enter into the world market on a much better footing than other Third World nations. In the 1980s, Korea's level of exports (measured on a per capita basis) was 100 times larger than India's, 50 times larger than Pakistan's, and more than 10 times greater than Mexico's or Brazil's.[13] Of course, in discussing the economic development of Korea and Taiwan we are looking at these two nations in a very narrow sense and are not commenting on issues such as economic inequality and democratic participation. Korea's economic progress, for instance, is partly built on the extreme exploitation of women workers. Women in manufacturing are paid at about half the men's rate and they are frequently the target of verbal and physical abuse.[14]

THE UNITED NATIONS

If organizations such as the WTO, the IMF, and the World Bank represent an extension of corporate power on the global level, are there other global institutions, such as the United Nations, capable of acting as a counterforce? In recent years, the United Nations has played a significant role in pressuring nations to undergo change and in negotiating peace agreements between warring parties. Changing coalitions of international powers have imposed sanctions and other forms of leverage against particular nations, often providing a critical boost to progressive forces within those nations. To many people, the one organization that represents the best possibility for resolving the world's conflicts is the United Nations. The UN's arms embargo and official condemnation of the Union of South Africa was instrumental in a bringing about an end to apartheid, and in ending South Africa's occupation of neighboring Namibia. The UN has also brokered peace agreements in El Salvador and Cambodia. It played a role in the Soviet Union's withdrawal from Afghanistan and in bringing about peace in Bosnia. It was also crucially important (but very slow) in ending Indonesia's repression of East Timor. However, most of these and other successes, are very limited and tenuous. In Afghanistan, for example, fighting between factions vying for power continued to take a heavy toll long after the Soviet withdrawal. In reality, the likelihood of the UN serving as a truly democratic institution of international reform is slim *under its present structure*. Historically, the key organs of the UN have been dominated by the United States. The United States has used the UN when it suited its interest and it has ignored the UN when it disagreed with the sentiment there.

The United States ignored UN condemnation of its invasion of Panama in 1989 (in a 75 to 20 vote the invasion was condemned as a "flagrant violation of international law") and in Grenada in 1983 (vetoing two UN Security Council condemnations).[15] It also ignored the World Court's ruling condemning U.S. aggression against Nicaragua (see chapter 8). The United States also continues to ignore UN sentiment regarding its embargo of Cuba. On November 27, 2001, the UN General Assembly, for the tenth consecutive year, passed a resolution calling for an "end to the economic, commercial, and financial embargo imposed by the United States against Cuba." The resolution passed by a vote of 167 to 3, with only the United States, Israel, and the Marshall Islands voting against it.[16] Not only are UN votes and rulings against the United States ignored by government officials but they receive little attention in the media so the American people are often unaware that the United States is acting in opposition to world opinion.

The structure of the UN gives the United States an advantageous position. The United States, along with France, the United Kingdom, China, and Russia, has a permanent position on the Security Council, which is responsible for matters of international peace and security. All together, there are fifteen nations on the Security Council. The remaining ten are elected for two year terms by the General Assembly and they may not serve consecutive terms. All decisions of the Security Council require a nine-member majority in order to be adopted. However, these decisions must have approval of all five of the permanent members. In practice this means that any one of the five permanent members may veto a resolution that could potentially have the endorsement of all the other member nations of the UN.

Thus the U.S. position as one of the five permanent members of the United Nations Security Council gives it authority to veto any Security Council resolution of which it disapproves. It has used its veto power many times, especially in regard to Security Council resolutions concerning Israel. During the UN's first fifty years, the United States used its veto power seventy times. It vetoed forty resolutions on the Middle East since 1967 and it vetoed twenty resolutions on Southern Africa.[17] Writing in *Monthly Review*, Norman Finkelstein noted that "during the past fifteen years, the Security Council has adopted eleven resolutions condemning Israeli aggression against Lebanon and other Arab countries. Four more such resolutions were vetoed by a lone U.S. vote."[18] Similarly, within a ten-year period, a lone U.S. veto blocked fourteen Security Council resolutions condemning Israeli human rights practices. Finkelstein points out that the Security Council has tried numerous times to authorize sanctions against Israel but has been blocked by the United States:

> In January 1982, the U.S. alone opposed a Security Council resolution calling for an arms and economic embargo against Israel for its annexation of the Golan Heights. In June 1982, the U.S. alone opposed a Security Council resolution threatening sanctions against Israel for its failure to withdraw from Lebanon. In August 1982, the U.S. alone opposed a Security Council resolution urging an arms embargo "as a first step" against Israel for its failure to withdraw from Lebanon. And in August 1983, the U.S. alone opposed a Security Council resolution threatening sanctions against Israel for its settlement policy.[19]

Regarding Israel, in addition to its Security Council vetoes, the United States has frequently been in the minority in General Assembly votes. In December 1982, a UN General Assembly resolution deploring Israel's invasion of Lebanon was passed 143 to 2, with only the United States and Israel voting against it. Similar resolutions have been adopted with votes as lop-sided as 153 to 2 and 151 to 3, with the United States once again dissenting.[20] Many of these resolutions were ignored by the U.S. media, in sharp contrast to the tremendous attention that the press gave similar resolutions concerning Iraq's aggression and human rights abuses. One of the lessons that should be learned from all this is that if the UN is going to be an effective body in resolving international disputes then either the United States must abandon the double standard it uses in judging various nations, or the power structure of the UN must be transformed in some way. However, making the UN more democratic is not a likely possibility for the near future. Even having a Secretary General who is able to promote the perspectives and interests of the less powerful nations is unlikely since the permanent five have veto power over nominations for the Secretariat. Likewise, any changes in the charter of the UN would require two-thirds approval by the General Assembly, but the permanent five can veto that as well.

The United States has also boycotted UN-sponsored events for selfish political reasons. For example, while Ronald Reagan was president the United States boycotted a UN disarmament conference (it was the only country to do so) held in New York City. The conference was originally proposed by France and it planned to "examine how money saved under future disarmament agreements could be used to stimulate economic development, particularly in the Third World."[21] The Reagan administration was concerned that the conference would give the Soviets a forum to discredit Reagan's "Star Wars" defense program and denounce Reagan's opposition to a nuclear test ban, while simultaneously pointing out that U.S. military expenditures were an obstacle to Third World development.[22]

The United States has also practiced other ways of subverting the work of the UN, such as denying visas to certain individuals so that they could not travel in the United States in order to attend UN hearings or conferences. The United States also has petulantly refused to pay its full membership dues to the UN and at, one point in 2001, owed $2.3 billion to the UN in back dues and peacekeeping fees.[23] To a great extent, the United States has been able to use the UN for its own purposes, and the media has played a supporting role in helping to get the public reaction that the government wants. This point of view is argued convincingly by author Phyllis Bennis in her book *Calling the Shots: How Washington Dominates Today's UN*. One of the points that Bennis makes is that the UN's peacekeeping role has expanded dramatically since the late 1980s, putting a serious burden on the UN's finances and this, coupled with the nonpayment of dues and peacekeeping fees by member nations (about half of the total debt is owed by the United States), has forced the UN to cut back many of its other projects.[24] In fact, in February of 1996 the UN announced that it was sliding toward bankruptcy and would cut about 10 percent of its permanent staff. The increase in the peacekeeping role of the UN has also increased the dominance of the United States within the organization due to the advanced military power and communications technology of the United States. These enable the United States to provide the field leadership and coordination that UN troops need, making peacekeeping operations dependent on the United States.

Another consequence of the expansion in peacekeeping is that less attention and fewer resources are given to the UN's social and economic development projects. Throughout the 1990s cuts in UN programs in health, education, development, culture, and democracy were taking place. This is a serious loss since the UN's Economic and Social Council (ECOSOC) offers a potentially more democratic alternative to the autocratic World Bank and International Monetary Fund. One might add that the need for UN peacekeeping missions means that social disorder and con-

The United Nations was established in 1945 in San Francisco at the Conference on International Organization. From its inception, the UN embodied a variety of antidemocratic characteristics that were designed to preserve the status quo of the world's balance of power. In particular, the organization was structured to ensure the dominance of the victor nations of World War II. The United States played a major role in shaping the UN to suit its needs.

Author Phyllis Bennis writes:

For the U.S., there was no question whether power or democracy would carry the day. And there would be no taking chances on decision-making. Recently released intelligence documents clearly demonstrate that for months prior to, as well as during, the San Francisco founding conference, U.S. intelligence agencies were bugging the offices and rooms of the other delegations, and intercepting and breaking coded diplomatic messages—including those of Washington's closest allies. . . .

According to historian Stephen Schlesinger, who has analyzed the long-classified files, the secret information allowed the U.S. team to indulge "not only in altruism but also in national self-interest. . . . The U.S. apparently used its surveillance reports to set the agenda of the UN, to control the debate, to pressure nations to agree to its positions and to write the UN Charter mostly according to its own blueprint."[25]

flict have already gone too far, while the UN's social and economic programs have the potential for ameliorating adverse conditions and preventing the outbreak of war. Other UN organizations have been severely cut back due to the UN's funding crisis. The Center on Transnational Corporations, for example, had been a key source of information on TNCs and had been working to establish a corporate code of conduct. The Center was abolished in 1992 in what some saw as a move to strengthen the World Trade Organization, the IMF. and the World Bank.[26]

THE INTERNATIONAL CRIMINAL COURT

For more than fifty years the International Court of Justice, more commonly known as the World Court, has been adjudicating disputes among nations. The court is understaffed and underused and, unfortunately, largely ineffective. Part of its ineffectiveness is due to a lack of support from the United States, and from the United States' flagrant disregard for World Court rulings (see chapter 8). (Interestingly, Libya, frequently referred to as an outlaw state by U.S. diplomats, did comply with a 1994 World Court ruling to withdraw from disputed territory in Chad.)[27] By the late twentieth century international momentum had built for the creation of a new court that would have the capacity to prosecute individuals for war crimes. Proponents felt that such a court would help create international cooperation for the capture and just prosecution of war criminals. By late 2002, the United States had delayed creation of the court by insisting that the United States have total immunity from the court. The United States' insistence that it be an exception only reinforces charges of hypocrisy and double standards made by many of its critics.

Regardless of the fate of the new International Criminal Court and the future of the UN, changes in international relations are continually occurring, as are significant changes within nations. Many of these changes are brought about not from above but from below—from the activities of ordinary people who under normal circumstances have very little power. In today's world there are many influential social movements and a growing number of *nongovernmental organizations* (NGOs) struggling to counterbalance corporate financial interests and the elite-oriented policies of national governments.

In today's world, confronting power that operates on an international scale is a very difficult matter. It is difficult for social movements to achieve much success in Third World countries, for example, even though the conditions for breeding social movements are so fertile there. The existence of a world power like the United States, which is so willing to support corrupt and repressive regimes, tends to make these regimes intransigent when dealing with forces in their own country that are seeking social change. These governments may simply feel that because they are supported by the United States or some other powerful core nation, they do not need to respond to any domestic pressure for change. History clearly shows that when peaceful avenues for change are denied, people often turn to violence. But the option of armed revolution is not an enticing one, since established military forces supported by the world's superpowers are not easy to defeat. Nevertheless, people do rise up, sometimes peacefully, sometimes in arms, and at times they are successful in forcing positive changes. In today's world there are many cases of resistance to exploitation and repression. Some are more violent and some are more successful, and some are woefully misdirected, but increasingly they seem to be recognizing that many local problems are the product of a global system of power.

RESISTANCE TO GLOBALIZATION AND POLARIZATION

Mexico, January 1994

On January 1, 1994, Mexico and much of the world was stunned by the takeover of several cities in the southern state of Chiapas by a poorly equipped but well organized army that became known to the world as the "Zapatistas."[28] The Zapatista National Liberation Army (EZLN) was comprised of peasants, mostly of Mayan descent, who put forth a series of demands and a show of force that shook up the Mexican government and gained the support of many people throughout Mexico and even the world. The Zapatistas explicitly tied their actions to the North American Free Trade Agreement, which went into effect on the very day of the uprising. Subcommandant Marcos declared that "to us, the free trade treaty is the death certificate for the ethnic peoples of Mexico."[29]

In the course of the rebellion about 145 people died, the Mexican government sent tens of thousands of its troops to Chiapas, a tense standoff ensued, and prolonged negotiations between the government and Zapatista leaders took place. Several factors prevented the Mexican military from recklessly attempting to exterminate the Zapatistas as some international banking interests had urged them to do. Among these were the international press attention that the Zapatistas received due to the dramatic nature of their actions, their reluctance to resort to violence, and the charisma (and even humor) of their leading spokesperson, Marcos. Another mitigating factor was the NAFTA agreement itself. Neither the Salinas government in Mexico nor its U.S. supporters wanted a bloody conflict that would give lie to the NAFTA image that was sold to constituencies in both countries. In addition, the presence of the press and many international observers (including the International Red Cross and many peace workers and human rights activists) who flocked to Chiapas in the succeeding months helped keep military abuses in check.

The Zapatista uprising shattered Mexico's image as a stable democracy with an industrial capacity and standard of living that made it worthy of the label of a "developed nation." Support for the Zapatistas uprising made it clear that many Mexicans felt their government was corrupt, that it had abandoned the aspirations of the 1910 revolution, that wages were too low, and that its large indigenous population was treated as second-class citizens. Several months into 1994, when the government declared that it had uncovered the identity of Marcos, demonstrators showed their solidarity by chanting "Todos Somos Marcos" (we are all Marcos). Over 100,000 people joined in support of the Zapatistas on numerous occasions in the Zocalo (la Plaza de la Constitucion) outside the National Palace in Mexico City.[30]

Since the January 1994 uprising the Zapatistas have continued to negotiate with the government and have won some small concessions. They have also been active in trying to build alliances that would strengthen the democratic opposition in civil society. On January 1, 1996, they announced the formation of an above-ground legal political organization called the Zapatista National Liberation Front (FZLN). In July of 1996, Mexico's newspapers announced that the FZLN had reached an agreement of mutual support with El Barzon, the National Union of Agricultural, Industrial and Service Providers.[31] El Barzon is a grassroots organization with one million members, seeking relief from the debt caused by high interest rates. It is the nation's largest protest group and has shown a flair for theatrical protest.[32]

Later that same month the Zapatistas sponsored an International Encounter for Humanity and Against Neoliberalism that drew 3,000 participants from five continents. The encounter was held in five villages in Chiapas and shows the perspicacity of the Zapatistas in making the connections between the new world economic order and the plight of people in remote villages.[33]

France, December 1995

It is not just people in the less-developed parts of the world who have been threatened by neoliberal policies. These policies, as we've seen earlier, are well under way in the United States and are also creeping forward in the social democracies of Europe. The availability of cheaper labor in Eastern Europe has given capital a relief valve and a means of leverage over the working classes of Western Europe. Thus, the economic elite in countries such as France and Germany have called for changes in state functions which, if enacted, would threaten the livelihood of many people in those nations. These reforms have engendered many protests. In France a three-week strike by the nation's rail and public transport workers sparked a much larger movement against the government's economic and social restructuring. Tensions had been building among certain sectors of French society prior to the strike. In October 1995, there was a massive national strike and demonstration of public sector workers who were protesting a wage freeze. That same month a nation-wide student strike took place in response to overcrowding, inadequate facilities, and the lack of job opportunities for graduates.

The transport workers went on strike in late November. Their immediate concerns were pension cuts and a proposed shutdown of nearly four thousand miles of railway lines. The shutdown would result in more layoffs—seventy-three thousand jobs had already been lost since the mid-1980s—as well as reduced services for the general public. Reduced rail services combined with general social service cutbacks in recent years and plans for reduced Social Security and health benefits set the stage for large-scale protest that France's daily newspaper *Le Monde* referred to as "the first revolt against globalization." The paper was wrong about it being the first revolt, but they were right that it was a revolt against globalization. According to journalist Raghu Krishnan, "Strikers and protestors made a direct link between the government's agenda and the demands of the European Union project . . . the infamous 'Maastricht criteria.' The Maastricht was an agreement signed by Western European nations that required 'high interest rates, a slashing of government deficts, the dismantling of public services, and an alignment of central bank policies.'"[34] The Maastricht agreement also sparked strikes and protests in other Western European countries.

When the strike began many cities experienced joint worker-student demonstrations. Numerous writers discussed the growing solidarity that quickly developed between different sectors of France's citizenry. The majority of the public supported the public transport workers strike. It was clear to many that the government's plans threatened not just the transport workers but others as well. Others, too, would eventually suffer layoffs, wage freezes, pension cuts, etc., and the nation's Social Security and healthcare systems would ultimately be dismantled.

Within a period of about one month the nation saw six days of nation-wide protests and each one was as big or bigger than the previous one. The largest protest involved over two million people, about half of whom were not even public sector workers. Ultimately, the government was forced to withdraw its plan to cut back on rail service and reduce pensions.

The strikes of December 1995 show the power of the working class and the general public when it has a high degree of unity. It was, in reality, a small victory in the battle against globalization, but it shows the potential that social movements have. It is especially instructive when we realize that the two major political parties that are, theoretically, closely allied with working class interests (the French Socialist Party and the French Commu-nist Party) did not play leadership roles and seemed to be supportive only out of a sense of obligation rather than out of a sincere realization of the importance and value of the movement.

Germany, May 1996

Perhaps inspired by the French working class, public workers in many German cities staged "warning strikes" in protest of Chancellor Helmut Kohl's efforts to cut back public spending. The strikes brought streetcars, buses, garbage disposal, mail, and other services to a halt. Workers expressed their opposition to wage freezes and proposals that public service employees work longer hours and accept reductions in unemployment ben-efits and sick pay.[35]

Russia

Declining living standards along with increased crime and mortality rates, led many Russians to question the free market economic reforms instituted by the Yeltsin government. This, in turn, sparked support for former Communist Party member Gennadi A. Zyuganov and put a scare into many western gov-ernment officials. In the United States the Clinton administration threw its support behind Boris Yeltsin in spite of his war against the rebellious Chechen Republic, which cost tens of thousands of lives. Yeltsin's campaign was aided by a staff of U.S. consultants who insisted on more negative ads with an anticommunist message.[36] In addition, IMF money was used as leverage to gain voter support for Yeltsin (see chapter 9).

Yeltsin's electoral victory did not mean that political conflict in Russia was over. The Russian government owes millions of dollars in back wages to many Russian workers. In February 1996, nearly half a million coal miners went on strike demanding their back pay, and the issue led to disruptions elsewhere. Some parts of Russia have simply refused to adapt to new ways. In describing the "mutinous" city of Tambov journalist Michael Specter wrote that it is a region "where people still spit when they hear the word privatization."[37]

Latin America

Throughout Latin America many battles against the new world economic order are taking place. In Ecuador, in June of 1994, a mobilization called by a coalition of indigenous people's organizations nearly paralyzed the country for over a week. Approximately 45 percent of Ecuador's twelve million inhabitants are indigenous. People set up roadblocks, boycotted marketplaces, workers struck, and there were large rallies and protest marches. In parts of the Amazon, indigenous communities occupied oil well sites to protest the privatization of the state-owned oil company. The indigenous movement was protesting neoliberal policies that have led to devaluation of the local currency, the elimination of subsidies and price controls, and the increased price of public services. More specifically, indigenous people were threatened by a new Agrarian Development Law that called for the elimination of communal lands. The law would have increased the concentration of land ownership in Ecuador and exacerbated the lack of access to land, which has been a growing problem that had sparked uprising in the past.[38]

Neoliberalism is also creating conflicts over land use and the environment, as neoliberal policies often facilitate the exploitation of natural resources. The Cofan Indians in Ecuador, a tribe of approximately twelve hundred indigenous people, have been fighting the Texaco Corporation and other oil companies because extraction of the region's resources have resulted in serious oil spills that led to toxins entering the food chain and threatening the health and livelihood of the local people. With the aid of an American missionary's son, who grew up with the Cofans, the tribe initiated a lawsuit in the U.S. District Court in Texas.[39] The Cofans' struggle led to a call to boycott Texaco. In a separate case, the Achuar Indians forced

British Gas to cease its exploration for oil in Ecuador's rain forests.[40] Like-wise, the Huaorani have been fighting Petroecuador and the transnational oil companies for years. Burdened by a high international debt Ecuador has boosted petroleum production and export to raise income. But the drilling operations have caused serious environmental damage and disrupted the local economies and traditions of indigenous groups. The impact on the Huaorani and others is likely to be permanent. But to what end? Ecuador has an estimated ten to twenty years of oil left in the Amazon, enough to pay off maybe a fifth of the current national debt.[41]

In Peru, similar struggles have been waged over environmental issues and neoliberal policies. One target of protests has been Southern Peru Copper, an American-owned company. The company's smelting plant in Ilo emits 2,000 tons of sulfur dioxide into the air daily causing respiratory problems for the area's residents.[42] And in 2002, violent protests erupted against the sale of two state-owned electric companies to a Belgian com-pany. Privatization scandals that cost the nation billions played a large part

---

Savages

"In 1967, Texaco discovered commercial oil in the Oriente (the Ecuadorean Amazon). In 1972 it had completed a 312-mile pipeline from the Oriente to Ecuador's Pacific coast. For the next seventeen years—until Petroecuador assumed operational control of the pipeline—the Texaco consortium shipped 1.4 billion barrels of oil over the Andes and accounted for 88 percent of the oil taken from the Oriente."[43] Ecuador had no environmental regulations for oil production, and almost no attempt was made to assess its environmental impact until 1989 when American Judith Kimmerling documented Texaco's careless-ness. Kimmerling discovered that the Texaco pipeline had ruptured at least twenty-seven times, spilling 16.8 million gallons of raw crude (in comparison, the *Exxon Valdez* spilled 10.8 million off the coast of Alaska). She calculated that the petroleum industry was spilling an additional 10,000 gallons of oil from secondary flow lines every week and dumping 4.3 million gallons of untreated toxic waste directly into the watershed every day.

More recently, the Dallas-based Maxus Energy Corporation began exten-sive operations in Ecuador's Oriente. Maxus in a previous incarnation had been known as Diamond Shamrock, a major producer of Agent Orange, a chemical defoliant used in the Vietnam war. In 1984, the Environmental Protection Agency declared Diamond Shamrock's Newark, New Jersey, production facility and a six-mile length of the Passaic River one of the nation's first envi-ronmental Superfund sites. The Passaic River had the highest level of dioxin of any river in the country. Dioxin is one of the deadliest toxins ever created.[44]

in fomenting political uprisings in Peru, which drove Alberto Fujimori out of power less than two years earlier.

In Bolivia, women have protested U.S. food aid because it undermines the ability of local farmers to sell their wheat at a high enough price to provide a basic income, and widespread protest forced a reversal of a World Bank-imposed privatization of water supply systems. Marcela López Levy, an Argentinian writer declared, "In a defining struggle against globalization, the people of Cochabamba, Bolivia took back their water from the hands of a corporate conglomerate."[45]

Elsewhere

In Nigeria the struggle of the Ogoni people against Royal Dutch Shell gained worldwide attention. Shell's environmental record resulted in protest and criticism within Nigeria. The issue came to the fore when Nigeria's military government executed playwright Ken Saro-Wiwa and eight other critics of Shell and the Nigerian government. Shell is the world's largest oil company and its participation in a $3.8 billion natural gas plant in Nigeria since the executions has prompted international condemnation.[46]

In India widespread protests against the Sardar Sarovar Dam forced the World Bank to cancel its funding.

GOING GLOBAL

The globalization of protest movements had been building for a few years before developing into a full-blown international "antiglobalization" movement in 1999. The "fifty years is enough" campaign, marking the fiftieth anniversary of the World Bank and the IMF in 1995, coupled with the birth of the WTO that same year, and an international church-based movement to forgive the debt owed by the Third World (Jubilee 2000), played an important role in raising consciousness about the new world economic order and these powerful institutions. Then, at the Third Ministerial Meeting of the WTO, held in Seattle in November–December 1999, tens of thousands of demonstrators attracted the attention of the world as they disrupted the city and prevented many of the delegates from making it to the meetings. The diversity of the protestors was notable. Students, trade unionists, farmers, environmentalists, religious activists, indigenous peoples, and others participated. The protests took many forms as well, from nonviolent rallies to street blockades, from teach-ins to property destruction that targeted retailers symbolic of unequal global exchange (Starbucks, GAP, McDonald's, etc.).

Similar international protests followed. In Melbourne, Australia, in September 2000, protestors blockaded the three-day World Economic Forum and kept more than 200 delegates from attending.[47] Other protests took place in Prague, Czech Republic, in the fall of 2000, at the annual meetings of the World Bank and IMF; then in Quebec City, in the spring of 2001, when thirty-four heads of state met to negotiate the Free Trade Area of the Americas; and then, at the G8 summit of the world's richest and most powerful nations in Genoa, Italy, in the summer of 2001. In each case, tens of thousands of protestors from all over the world came to confront the powers behind procorporate economic globalization, to demand that human rights, the environment, and the well-being of the poor be placed as higher priorities than "free trade" and corporate profit making. In some cases the confrontations turned violent, with tear gas and bullets used to disperse the demonstrators. In all cases the symbolism was strong, with heavily armed soldiers and police protecting the world's rich and powerful from the protestors who claimed to stand on the side of the world's environment and the poor, and who demanded that the world's leaders be held accountable.

But were they getting their point across? Or was the antiglobalization movement a hopeless cause? Were the protestors romantic idealists who had no realistic alternative? They've been denounced as modern-day Luddites, and one well-known editorialist referred to them as "ignorant protectionists."[48] Can the backlash against globalization have a positive effect? Do they have constructive alternatives to offer?

Partly in response to these questions the World Social Forum (WSF) was started in 2001. The first three Forums were held in Porto Alegre, Brazil, a city well known for its participatory budget process. The city's budget is prepared by a process involving mass participation through neighborhood meetings designed to prioritize needs and expenditures. The city is an appropriate location for the WSF, which bills itself as a democratic alternative to the gathering of the corporate elite attending the World Economic Forum. Since the early 1980s, the global corporate elite has been holding its World Economic Forum in Davos, Switzerland. Attendees pay $20,000 each to listen to the leading experts on regional economic conditions, and plot strategies for investing and reaping profits.[49] In contrast, the WSF promotes grassroots participation in efforts to share knowledge and strategies for building a better world—a world in which human rights, environmental sustainability, fair trade, gender rights, democracy, equitable development, and peace, overcome corporate power and profit making. In its first three years the WSF grew dramatically, the 2003 Forum had about 100,000 participants from 156 countries, and there were nearly 1,300 panel discussions and workshops.[50] Regional Social Forums have also been held.[51]

Resistance to the current form of globalization is not coming solely from on-the-street protestors but from an ever-growing number of influential nongovernmental organizations (NGOs). At the 2002 World Summit on Sustainable Development in South Africa, eight thousand NGOs were represented. (Noteworthy was the fact that, according to one report, the U.S. delegate, Secretary of State Colin Powell, was the only delegate to be jeered.)[52] Some of these organizations have presented sophisticated alternative plans. The International Forum on Globalization (IFG) is one such group.

The IFG has developed an alternative to economic globalization that places a much higher priority on environmental sustainability and democracy. The organization's ten principles, which form the basis for their larger alternative vision, are summarized below:

A Brazilian youth expresses his opposition to the Free Trade Area of the Americas (FTAA), at the 2003 World Social Forum. (Author's collection)

Ten Principles for Democratic and Sustainable Societies:[53]

1. *New Democracy.* The rallying cry of the amazing diversity of civil society that converged in Seattle in late 1999 was the simple word *democracy.* Democracy flourishes when people organize to protect their communities and rights and hold their elected officials accountable. For the past two decades, global corporations and global bureaucracies have grabbed much of the power once held by governments. We advocate a shift from governments serving corporations to governments serving people and communities, a process that is easier at the local level but vital at all levels of government.

2. *Subsidiarity* [favoring the local]. Economic globalization results first, and foremost, in de-localization and disempowerment of communities and local economies. It is therefore necessary to reverse direction and create new rules and structures that consciously favor the local, and follow the principle of subsidiarity, i.e., whatever decisions and activities can be undertaken locally should be. Whatever power can reside at the local level should reside there. Only when additional activity is required that cannot be satisfied locally, should power and activity move to the next higher level: region, nation, and finally the world.

3. *Ecological Sustainability.* Economic activity needs to be ecologically sustainable. It should enable us to meet humans' genuine needs in the present without compromising the ability of future generations to meet theirs, and without diminishing the natural diversity of life on Earth or the viability of the planet's natural life-support systems.

4. *Common Heritage.* There exist common heritage resources that should constitute a collective birthright of the whole species to be shared equitably among all. We assert that there are three categories of such resources. The first consists of the shared natural heritage of the water, land, air, forests, and fisheries on which our lives depend. These physical resources are in finite supply, essential to life, and existed long before any human. A second category includes the heritage of culture and knowledge that is the collective creation of our species. Finally, basic public services relating to health, education, public safety, and Social Security are "modern" common heritage resources representing the collective efforts of whole societies. They

are also as essential to life in modern societies as are air and water. Justice therefore demands that they be readily available to all who need them. Any attempt by persons or corporations to monopolize ownership control of an essential common heritage resource for exclusive private gain to the exclusion of the needs of others is morally unconscionable and politically unacceptable.

5. *Human Rights.* In 1948, governments of the world came together to adopt the United Nations Universal Declaration on Human Rights, which established certain core rights, such as "a standard of living adequate for . . . health and well-being . . . , including food, clothing, housing and medical care, and necessary social services, and the right to security in the event of unemployment." Traditionally, most of the human rights debate in the United States and other rich nations has focused on civil and political rights as paramount. We believe that it is the duty of governments to ensure these rights, but also to guarantee the economic, social, and cultural rights of all people.

6. *Jobs/Livelihood/Employment.* A livelihood is a means of living. The rights to a means of livelihood is therefore the most basic of all human rights. Sustainable societies must both protect the rights of workers in the formal sector and address the livelihood needs of the larger share of people who subsist in what has become known as the nonmaterial, or "informal sector" (including small-scale, indigenous, and artisanal activities) as well as those who have no work or are seriously underemployed. Empowering workers to organize for basic rights and fair wages is vital to curb footloose corporations that pit workers against each other in a lose-lose race to the bottom. And, the reversal of globalization policies that displace small farmers from their land and fisherfolk from their coastal ecosystems are central to the goal of a world where all can live and work in dignity.

7. *Food Security and Food Safety.* Communities and nations are stable and secure when people have enough food, particularly when nations can produce their own food. People also want safe food, a commodity that is increasingly scarce as global agribusiness firms spread chemical—and biotech-intensive agriculture around the world.

8. *Equity.* Economic globalization, under the current rules, has widened the gap between rich and poor countries and between rich and poor within most countries. The resulting social dislocation and tension are among the greatest threats to peace and sustainable

communities. Reducing the growing gap between rich and poor nations requires first and foremost the cancellation of the illegitimate debts of poor countries. And, it requires the replacement of the current institutions of global governance with new ones that include global fairness among their operating principles.

9. *Diversity.* A few decades ago, it was still possible to leave home and go somewhere else where the architecture was different, the landscape was different, the language, lifestyle, food, dress, and values were different. Today, farmers and film makers in France and India, indigenous communities worldwide, and millions of people elsewhere, are protesting to maintain that diversity. Tens of thousands of communities around the world have perfected local resource management systems that work, but they are now being undermined by corporate-led globalization. Cultural, biological, social, and economic diversity are central to a viable, dignified, and healthy life.

10. *Precautionary Principle.* All activity should abide by the precautionary principle. When a practice or product raises potentially significant threats of harm to human health or the environment, precautionary action should be taken to restrict or ban it even if scientific uncertainty remains about whether or how it is actually causing that harm. Because it can take years for scientific proof of harm to be established—during which time undesirable or irreversible effects may continue to be inflicted—the proponents of a practice or product should bear the burden of proving that it is safe, before it is implemented.*

WHAT CAN BE DONE ABOUT THE DEBT?

Creating a just and sustainable alternative to corporate-dominated economic globalization is a tremendous challenge, and it is compounded by the massive debt problem faced by Third World nations. Debt repayment has necessitated cutbacks in spending for social programs and local development that cripples many nations, and it causes poor nations to continually export their natural resources and manufactured products in order to

---

*This was excerpted from John Cavanagh, Jerry Mander, and the Alternatives Task Force of the International Forum on Globalization, *Alternatives to Economic Globalization: A Better World Is Possible* (San Francisco: Berrett Koehler, 2002). Reprinted by permission of the authors.

raise foreign currency to make debt payments. Does it need to be paid off? Can it be paid off? Can the debt be "forgiven"? The possibility of fully paying off the debt is bleak, and the loss of money it entails worsens local conditions. These facts make debt cancellation an option that has to be considered. Fortunately, there is precedent for debt cancellation and a strong international movement to do so, at least in part.

ODIOUS DEBT

The *Doctrine of Odious Debt* is an established international principle that justifies repudiation of debts that were not legitimately incurred. If, for example, a government borrowed money and used it for the personal enrichment of top officials, then it is an odious debt and the general public should not be required to pay it off. The debt should be paid by those who enriched themselves. Or, if money is borrowed for economically unsound or environmentally destructive programs without public input, then the public should not be held responsible.[54] When President Anastazio Somoza was overthrown by the Sandinista revolution in 1979, Somoza ran off with most of the national treasury. By the 1990s, Nicaragua had one of the highest per capita debts of any nation. The debt could have been declared odious since the money was not used for legitimate purposes that benefited the people of Nicaragua. The loans were used for the enrichment of Somoza, therefore, the debt payment should have been his responsibility. Likewise, in Zaire (the Democratic Republic of the Congo), dictator Mobutu Sese Seko enriched himself and his cronies at the expense of the general public. His corruption was well known to Western government officials, as well as to the World Bank and IMF, but he was regarded as a useful ally. In the late 1970s, one IMF official warned that there was "no (repeat no) prospect for Zaire's creditors to get their money back in the foreseeable future."[55] In spite of this warning, the IMF lent Zaire an additional $600 million, the World Bank lent $650 million, and Western governments lent another $3 billion. When Mobutu was overthrown in 1998, Zaire owed $13 billion to foreign creditors. Mobutu's repressive regime prevented public input into decision making, and citizens rarely benefitted from any of these loans. In fact, one could easily make the case that the foreign money propped up the dictatorship and facilitated domestic repression. If ever there was a clear-cut case of a debt being odious, Zaire certainly meets the criteria.

In reality, much international debt is odious. Apartheid South Africa, for example, was hardly a legitimate government of the people, but when apartheid ended the new government headed by Nelson Mandela was faced with more than $18 billion in debt. The IMF warned that failure to pay would result in economic isolation of South Africa. And in the Philippines, it was estimated that Ferdinand and Imelda Marcos, along with their cronies, pocketed a third of all loans made to the country, but the IMF insisted that the post-Marcos government pay the debt.

The United States, as the leading nation in the IMF, could lead the way in evaluating the legitimacy of national debts and encourage the IMF to abide by the doctrine of odious debts, but the United States has been very reluctant to forgive debt except in rare cases. Ironically, the doctrine of odious debt was first used by the United States after it took Cuba away from Spain in 1898 and Spain demanded that the United States pay Cuba's debts. The United States refused, claiming that the debt had been "imposed upon the people of Cuba without their consent and by force of arms . . . the creditors, from the beginning took the chance of the investment."[56] Occasionally the United States has provided debt relief but usually with an ulterior political motive, such as when it provided $7 billion in debt relief to Egypt to help build support for the Persian Gulf War in 1991.[57]

International pressure has resulted in some foreign debt being "forgiven" for some of the poorest nations. One of the most influential campaigns was Jubilee 2000 that started in the United Kingdom in 1990.[58] The work done by Jubilee 2000, Fifty Years Is Enough, and others, was vital in attaining public recognition that debt was crippling many of the world's poorest nations, sending them deeper into poverty. The debt is used to justify neoliberal reforms and austerity measures that extract a terrible toll on workers in debt-ridden countries. And, the debt has reached proportions that make it unlikely that many nations will ever pay it off. For example, between 1982 and 1996 the Latin American and Caribbean region made $739 billion in debt payments—more than the entire accumulated debt— but in spite of these huge payments the total debt continued to increase.[59]

In 1996, as a result of international pressure, the World Bank and the IMF initiated steps to provide debt relief for twenty-eight low human development nations.[60] Some nations were willing to go to greater lengths than the World Bank and the IMF. In 2000, Italy agreed to forgive $4 to $6 billion in debt owed by sixty-two impoverished nations, and several month later, Canada called for support of an immediate debt moratorium for the world's poorest nations.[61]

It's important to understand that much of the debt owed by the poor nations is in reality a result of a global system of unequal exchange in which natural and human resources have been exploited by core nations usually at rates far below their real value. In the overall picture, wealth has flowed from the poorer regions of the world to the richer ones. Oftentimes, investment capital that flowed from the rich nations to the poor was spent for development projects and services that facilitated the extraction of wealth to the benefit of foreign investors. It can be argued that by objective standards wealthy nations owe a great debt to the poor and that the current debt crisis faced by much of the Third World is a result of centuries of underpayment for resources and labor by core nations.

GLOBALIZATION FROM BELOW

One of the common threads that tie together alternative visions of globalization is the demand for greater local control. Local control (subsidiarity) is a key element in the IFG's statement of principles, and there are places where it has been put into practice. Michael Shuman, author of *Going Local*, has argued for a strategy called *progressive devolution*—the shifting of responsibility for many social services and aspects of decision making, from the federal government to states, and in some instances regions or municipalities.[62] Devolution of federal programs has been a trend in the United States for several decades, but too often it takes a regressive form in which responsibilities are devolved, or localized, but necessary resources are not provided.[63]

One of the most important alternatives to corporate dominated globalization, which may act as a model for many less-developed regions, is the Kerala people's campaign for democratic decentralization. In spite of a very low per capita income, the state of Kerala, India, has achieved an average life expectancy of over seventy years. The literacy rate is over 90 percent. Infant mortality is far below the average for all of India and is much closer to the average rate for high income countries than it is to the average for low income countries. The birth rate in Kerala is almost identical to the U.S., and much lower than the average for India as a whole. Childhood immunization rates for a number of illnesses are 100 percent.[64]

Kerala has attained admirable quality of life levels without dramatic economic growth in the conventional sense (GDP-driven). Anthropologist Richard Franke describes the Kerala "experiment" as an attempt to "make devolution large-scale, democratic, participatory, activist, egalitarian, empowering, self-reflective, self-reliant, and sustainable."[65]

In Kerala, authority has been transferred to autonomous and semi-autonomous local governments. The power to plan, raise revenues, and make decisions is done on the local level. And unlike the United States, the devolution of responsibilities and services was accompanied by devolving part of the national budget.

Kerala's decentralization included the mobilization of millions of people. According to Franke, "ordinary people were involved in as many of the stages as possible, including the discussions of grievances and needs, the gathering of information and publishing of local development reports, the development seminars, the task forces that drew up the projects, and the committees to implement and evaluate them. Both individuals and civil society organizations were drawn into the campaign."[66]

The Kerala People's Campaign for Democratic Decentralization has increased accountability of public officials and "appears to have brought about major reductions in corruption and a more effective delivery of public services." The campaign is also promoting self-reliant and self-sustaining production "encouraging local communities to . . . develop local production with local materials for local markets."[67] In short, Kerala shows that rich social capital, strong democracy, and local control are crucial factors in making a better world. Kerala is pursuing many of the strategies that the globalization from below movement has been advocating, and the outcome has been very positive.

Another hopeful example of democratic decentralization is that of the participatory budget process that is practiced in numerous cities in Brazil. Since 1989, Porto Alegre has been implementing a participatory budget that involves thousands of people in establishing the city's spending priorities. Porto Alegre's population is approximately 1.4 million, it was the host of the first three World Social Forums, and it actively promotes itself as a city that resists neoliberalism.[68] The participatory budget is credited with increasing government transparency and reducing corruption. It has also helped Porto Alegre make a significant increase in the quality of life for many of the city's residents. In the area of housing, to use just one example, from 1989 to 2000, more than eleven thousand housing units were built, a vast improvement over previous periods. The city does not merely provide funding for housing development but it assists with building social organizations that involve citizens in creating solutions. Roughly seventy-five self-managed housing cooperatives exist in Porto Alegre. The cooperatives combine resources to facilitate land purchases and the sharing of technical resources. The popular administration in Porto Alegre is guided by four main principles including (1) the expansion of democracy; (2) social inclusion, (3) sustainable development and technology, and (4) city organization and urban and environmental development.

Porto Alegre's participatory budget process has been adopted by numerous cities in Brazil. In Belo Horizonte, a city of 2.3 million people, thirty to forty thousand residents take part in various neighborhood meetings and municipal forums to discuss the municipal budget and determine spending priorities. Starting in 1996, Belo Horizonte's housing participatory budget has involved homeless families (organized in groups) in the decision-making process and has also encouraged the formation of self-managed cooperatives. Belo Horizonte not only involves its citizens but it bases the allocation of resources on an Urban Quality of Life Index (IQVU) that evaluates living conditions based on the local supply and demand of services. A region with a low IQVU and a large population receives a greater allocation of resources.[69] The participatory budget process has made a clear improvement in the quality of life in Belo Horizonte and Porto Alegre, the latter, in fact, has been rated the second most livable city in Latin America by the United Nations.

The examples of Kerala and Porto Alegre help make it clear that contrary to the neoliberal prescriptions of privatization and downsized government, the better strategy for improving the quality of life involves expanded government engagement of citizens. Participatory democracy and social inclusion should be key principles of every government and social movement.

In addition to the more localized alternatives to neoliberalism and corporate led globalization, national resistance may be making a comeback. In Brazil, for example, the landslide victory of Lula de Silva (the Workers Party candidate), in the 2002 presidential election surprised much of the world. The victory represented a major backlash to neoliberalism, but it is not the only sign of resistance on the part of national governments, particularly in Latin America. The government of Hugo Chavez in Venezuela, as of this writing, continues to maintain power in spite of internal attempts, especially by the comrador class, to undermine its authority, as well as open hostility from the U.S. elite (opposition groups have been funded by the National Endowment for Democracy).[70]

In Ecuador, the election of Lucio Gutierrez as president in the fall of 2002 also represented a blow to U.S.-led neoliberalism. Gutierrez's surge to victory was a clear result of the developing strength of various popular organizations, many of which explicitly target neoliberalism and the corruption associated with it, but it is also the result of popular resistance to foreign interference.

How well these national movements will be able to stay on course as they attempt a small degree of delinking from the elite-dominated world economic system is a critical question. Will they be able to maintain or improve the quality of life of their people? Will they continue to expand participatory democracy? Or will they be forced to retreat into a defensive posture due to external pressure from more powerful political and economic interests? In the future, many other worlds are possible.

NOTES

1. Carlos M. Vilas, "Neoliberal Social Policy: Managing Poverty (Somehow)," *NACLA Report on the Americas* (May/June 1996).

2. United Nations, *Human Development Report, 1999,* p. 30.

3. World Trade Organization [online], www.wto.org/english/thewto_e/the wto_e.htm.

4. WTO rulings are from Lori Wallach and Michelle Sforza, *Whose Trade Organization?* (Washington, D.C.: Public Citizen, 1999).

5. For additional information see David E. Sanger, "Trade Group Orders U.S. to Alter Law for First Time," *New York Times*, January 18, 1996; and David E. Sanger, "U.S. Defeated in Its Appeal of Trade Case," *New York Times,* April 30, 1996.

6. Jock O'Connell, "WTO, State Law on Collision Course," *Los Angeles Times,* January 23, 2000.

7. William Greider, The Right and U.S. Trade Law: Invalidating the 20th Century," *Nation*, October 15, 2001. See also "Bill Moyers Reports: Trading Democracy," PBS, February 5, 2002.

8. Michael Parenti, *Against Empire* (San Francisco: City Lights Books, 1995), p. 32. Other information from Ralph Nader's talk on Global Corporatism, available on tape from Global Exchange, San Francisco, Calif.

9. Nicholas D. Kristof, "Farm Subsidies That Kill," *New York Times,* July 5, 2002. See also Anuradha Mittal, "Giving Away the Farm: The 2002 Farm Bill," *Food First Backgrounder*, Institute for Food and Development Policy (summer 2002).

10. Edmund L. Andrews, "Rich Nations Are Criticized for Enforcing Trade Barriers," *New York Times*, September 30, 2002.

11. For a more detailed discussion of what made Taiwan's and South Korea's development unique, see Stephen Rosskamm Shalom, "Capitalism Triumphant" in *Z Magazine*, April 1989.

12. Bruce Cummings, quoted in Harry Magdoff, *Globalization: To What End?* (New York: Monthly Review Press, 1992), p. 36.

13. Magdoff, "Globalization," pp. 33–34.

14. Stephanie Seguino, "Trade Secrets: Sexism and Export-led Growth in South Korea," *Dollars and Sense*, January/February 1995.

15. See Michael Parenti, *Inventing Reality* (New York: St. Martin's Press, 1993), p. 195; and Noam Chomsky, *Year 501: The Conquest Continues* (Boston: South End Press, 1993), p. 7.

16. UN Press Release GA/9979 [online], www.un.org/News/Press/docs/2001/ga9979.doc.htm.

17. Phyllis Bennis, *Calling the Shots: How Washington Dominates Today's UN* (New York: Olive Branch Press, 1996), pp. 27, 52.

18. Norman Finkelstein, "Israel and Iraq: A Double Standard," *Monthly Review* (July–August 1991): 40.

19. Ibid., pp. 42–43.

20. Ibid., pp. 40–41.

21. Noam Chomsky, *The Culture of Terrorism* (Boston: South End Press, 1988), pp. 195–96.

22. Ibid.

23. Global Policy Forum [online], www.globalpolicy.org/finance/tables/index11.htm.

24. In 1988 the UN had 9,570 military personnel deployed around the globe and by 1994 the number had grown to 73,393. Bennis, *Calling the Shots*, p. 86.

25. Kevin Danaher, *Can We Democratize the UN?* (San Francisco: Global Exchange, summer 1995), p. 4.

26. Bennis, *Calling the Shots*, p. 4.

27. Ian Williams, *The UN for Beginners* (New York: Writers and Readers Publishing, 1995), p. 42.

28. The largest of these cities was San Cristobal with a population of 100,000.

29. John Ross, *Rebellion from the Roots* (Monroe, Maine: Common Courage Press, 1995), p. 21.

30. John Ross, *The Annexation of Mexico: From the Aztecs to the IMF* (Monroe, Maine: Common Courage Press, 1998), p. 208.

31. "Pacto de Apoyo Mutuo, Firman Barzon y EZLN," *Cuarto Poder* (July 23, 1996).

32. Dianne Solis, "In Mexico, a New Kind of Rebel Emerges," *Wall Street Journal*, September 1, 1995. See also the Guadalajara Declaration by El Barzon in *Mexico: A Current Issues Reader* (San Francisco: Global Exchange, 1996), p. 3.

33. On August 28, 1996, Mexican rebels (apparently not affiliated with the Zapatistas) conducted attacks on police stations and military posts in four southern Mexico states. The attacks were directed by the Popular Revolutionary Army, which had been active in the state of Guerrero previously. The PRA has called for revoking NAFTA and renegotiating Mexico's foreign debt. See Sam Dillon, "Rebels Strike in 4 Mexico States, Leaving 13 Dead," *New York Times,* August 30, 1996; and Julia Preston, "Stung by Attacks, Mexico Intensifies Search for Rebels," *New York Times*, August 31, 1996.

34. Raghu Krishnan, "December 1995: 'The First Revolt Against Globalization,'" *Monthly Review* (May 1996).

35. Alan Cowell, "Germany Is Tied Up by a 'Warning Strike'" of Public Workers," *New York Times,* May 21, 1996.

36. Alessandra Stanley, "The Americans Who Saved Yeltsin (Or Did They?)" *New York Times,* July 9, 1996; "Rescuing Boris," *Time,* July 15, 1996.

37. Michael Specter, "Red Flag Aloft, a Russian City Defiantly Upholds Soviet Ways," *New York Times,* February 3, 1996.

38. Nina Pacari, "Taking on the Neoliberal Agenda," *NACLA Report on the Americas* (March/April 1996).

39. Lawrence Lipman, "Ecuadorean Tribe Wields Unusual Weapons," *Record* (October 29, 1995).

40. *New Internationalist* (August 1996): 6.

41. Chris Jochnick, "Perilous Prosperity," *New Internationalist* (June 2001).

42. Calvin Sims, "In Peru, a Fight for Fresh Air," *New York Times* (December 12, 1995).

43. Joe Kane, *Savages* (New York: Vintage, 1996), pp. 70, 76.

44. Tina Traster, "Passaic River Listed as 'Endangered,'" *Record* (April 7, 1998).

45. Katharine Angiar, "A Culture of Life, a Culture of Death," *New Internationalist* (November 2001); and Marcela López Levy, "The Damn Water Is Ours," *New Internationalist* (September 2001).

46. Sims, *In Peru.*

47. Agence France Presse, "Anti-Globalization Protestors Claim Victory in Melbourne," *Common Dreams News Center* [online], www.commondreams.org/headlines/091100-02.htm [September 11, 2000].

48. The reporter was Thomas Friedman of the *New York Times*; see International Forum on Globalization, *A Better World Is Possible! Alternatives to Globalization* [online], www.ifg.org/alt_eng.pdf [spring 2002].

49. Francisco Whitaker, "World Social Forum: Origins and Aims" [online], www.forumsocialmundial.org.br/main.asp?id_menu=2_1&cd_language=2 [June 22, 2002]. See also: Rodney Bobiwash, "Report on the World Social Forum," Global Exchange [online], www.globalexchange.org/campaigns/brazil/news/ibin 020601.html. See also Katharine Ainger, "Other Possible Worlds," *New Internationalist*, www.newint.org/streets/brazil/ 070202/htlm [July 2, 2002].

50. [Online] www.forumsocialmundial.org.

51. For more on the WSF, see Jerry Kloby, *Another World Is Possible*, www.montclair.edu/pages/ics/wsf.html.

52. John Gershman, "Back to Earth," *Foreign Policy in Focus* [online], www.presentdanger.org/frontier/2002/0910earth.html [September 10, 2002].

53. International Forum on Globalization, *A Better World Is Possible! Alternatives to Economic Globalization* [online], www.ifg.org/alt_eng.pdf. A slight variation of the IFG's principles are included in Robin Broad, ed., *Global Back-*

lash: Citizen Initiatives for a Just World Economy (New York: Rowman and Little-field, 2002). Broad's book is a good survey of the visions and alternatives being presented by opponents of the current form of globalization.

54. Patricia Adams, interviewed by Juliette Majot, "The Doctrine of Odious Debts," in *Fifty Years Is Enough*, ed. Danaher.

55. Joseph Hanlon, "Odious Debts: Take the Hit," *New Internationalist* (May 1999).

56. Ibid.

57. Bennis, *Calling the Shots*, p. 31.

58. United Nations, *Human Development Report, 2002*, p. 102. The Jubilee USA Network is a good source of information on the continuing work of the Jubilee campaign [online], www.jubileeusa.org/.

59. Ecumenial Coalition for Economic Justice, *Jubilee Movement Shifts the Ground Under G7 Debt Plans* [online], www.ecej.org/ejrmay99.htm [May 1999].

60. United Nations, *Human Development Report, 2002*, p. 30.

61. Richard Boudreaux, "Taking Lead, Italy to Forgive Billions in Third World Debt," *Los Angeles Times*, July 15, 2000. Charlotte Denny, "Canada Calls for Immediate Halt to Debt Repayments by the World's Poorest States" *Guardian* (London), September 25, 2000.

62. Michael Shuman, *Going Local: Creating Self-Reliant Communities in a Global Age* (New York: Free Press, 1998). See also, "Going Local: Devolution for Progressives," *Nation,* October 12, 1998.

63. For a cautionary note on devolution, see Jerry Kloby, *The Devolution Solution* [online], www.montclair.edu/Pages/ICS/Viewpoint.htm.

64. Bill McKibben, *Hope, Human and Wild: True Stories of Living Lightly on the Earth* (St. Paul, Minn.: Hungry Mind Press, 1995). See also, Richard Franke's Kerala Web site [online], http://chss.montclair.edu/anthro/kerala.html.

65. Richard W. Franke, "Democratic Decentralization: The Kerala Experience in International Perspective," presented at the seminar "A Decade After the 73rd and 74th Constitutional Amendments," A. K. G. Centre for Research and Studies, Thiruvananthapuram, Kerala [online], http://chss.montclair.edu/anthro/FrankepaperAKGMay02.htm [May 18–19, 2002].

66. Ibid.

67. Ibid.

68. *Porto Alegre: Another World Is Possible.* A brochure published by the Porto Alegre municipal government.

69. *Participatory Budget: 10 Years of Experience in Belo Horizonte.* (A publication by the Belo Horizonte City Hall.) The city's Web site is www.pbh.gov.br.

70. According to an April 24, 2002, *New York Times* report. See [online], www.mediatransparency.org/recipients/ned.htm.

BIBLIOGRAPHY

"ACLU Says 'Veggie Libel' Laws Are Patently Unconstitutional." American Civil Liberties Union Press Release [online], www.aclu.org/news/n012298a.html [January 22, 1998].

Adams, Patricia. Interviewed by Juliet Majot. "The Doctrine of Odious Debts." In *Fifty Years Is Enough: The Case Against the World Bank and the International Monetary Fund*, edited by Kevin Danaher. Boston: South End Press, 1994.

Agence France Presse. "Anti-Globalization Protestors Claim Victory in Melbourne." Common Dreams News Center [online], www.commondreams.org/headlines/091100-02.htm [September 11, 2000].

Albeda, Randy. "Left in the Dust: U.S. Trails Other Nations in Support for the Poor." In *Real World Macro*. 5th ed. Somerville, Mass.: Economics Affairs Bureau, 1995.

Albeda, Randy, et al., eds. *Real World Macro*. 5th ed. Somerville, Mass.: Economics Affairs Bureau, 1995.

Ali, Tariq. *The Clash of Fundamentalisms: Crusades, Jihads and Modernity*. London: Verso, 2002.

Allende, Dr. Salvador. *The Human Factor*, vol. 12, nos. 2–3. New York: Graduate Sociology Student Union, Columbia University, summer–fall 1974.

Al-Radi, Selma. "Iraqi Sanctions—A Postwar Crime." *Nation*, March 27, 1995.

Amin, Samir. *Unequal Development*. New York: Monthly Review Press, 1976.

———. *Delinking: Towards a Polycentric World*. London: Zed Books, 1985.

———. "The Real Stakes in the Gulf War." *Monthly Review* (July–August 1991).

———. *Empire of Chaos*. New York: Monthly Review Press, 1992.

Anderson, Sara, John Cavanagh, Chris Hartman, and Betsy Leonard-Wright. *Executive Excess*. Boston: United for a Fair Economy, 2001.

Andrews, Edmund L. "Rich Nations Are Criticized for Enforcing Trade Barriers." *New York Times,* September 30, 2002.

Angiar, Katharine. "A Culture of Life, a Culture of Death." *New Internationalist* (November 2001).

Apple, R. W., Jr. "McNamara Recalls, and Regrets, Vietnam." *New York Times,* April 9, 1995.

———. "Poll Shows Disenchantment with Politicians and Politics." *New York Times,* August 12, 1995.

"Aristide Thanks Clinton but Won't Endorse Deal." *Star Ledger* (Newark, N.J.), September 1994.

Armstrong, David. "Dick Cheney's Song of America." *Harper's Magazine,* October 2002.

Arnove, Robert F., ed. *Philanthropy and Cultural Imperialism.* Bloomington: Indiana University Press, 1980.

Avery, Natalie. "Stealing from the State (Mexico, Hungary and Kenya)." In *Fifty Years Is Enough: The Case Against the World Bank and the International Monetary Fund,* edited by Kevin Danaher. Boston: South End Press, 1994.

'Bahhah, Bishara A. "The Crisis in the Gulf—Why Iraq Invaded Kuwait." In *Beyond the Storm,* edited by Phyllis Bennis and Michel Moushabeck. New York: Olive Branch Press, 1991.

Baran, Paul A., and Paul M. Sweezy. *Monopoly Capital.* New York: Monthly Review, 1996.

Barber, Benjamin. *Jihad vs. McWorld: How Globalism and Tribalism Are Reshaping the World.* New York: Ballantine Books, 1995.

———. *A Place for Us: How to Make Society Civil and Democracy Strong.* New York: Hill and Wang, 1998.

Barlett, Donald L., and James B. Steele. *America: Who Really Pays the Taxes?* New York: Touchstone, 1994.

Barry, Tom, et al. *Dollars and Dictators: A Guide to Central America.* New York: Grove Press, 1983.

Barry, Tom, and Deb Preusch. *The Central American Fact Book.* New York: Grove Press, 1986.

Barsamian, David. "Corporate Power: Profits Before People, An Interview with Ralph Nader." *Z Magazine,* February 1995.

Barzon, Firman. "Guadalajara Declaration." In *Mexico: A Current Issues Reader.* San Francisco: Global Exchange, 1996.

Batra, Ravi. *The Great Depression of 1990.* New York: Simon and Schuster, 1987.

———. "An Ominous Trend Toward Greater Inequality." *New York Times,* May 3, 1987.

Baxandall, Phineas. "The Privatization Myth." *Dollars and Sense,* January–February 1995.

Beaud, Michel. *A History of Capitalism, 1500–1980.* New York: Monthly Review Press, 1983.

Bello, Walden. "Global Economic Counterrevolution: How Northern Economic Warfare Devastates the South." In *Fifty Years Is Enough: The Case Against the World Bank and the International Monetary Fund*, edited by Kevin Danaher. Boston: South End Press, 1994.

Bello, Walden, with Shea Cunningham and Bill Rau. *Dark Victory: The United States, Structural Adjustment, and Global Poverty.* London: Pluto Press, 1994.

Bendix, Reinhard. *Work and Authority in Industry.* Berkeley: University of California Press, 1956.

Benjamin, Medea, et al. *Nicaragua: Give Change a Chance.* San Francisco: Institute for Food and Development Policy, 1986.

Benjamin, Medea, and Andrea Freedman. *Bridging the Global Gap.* Washington, D.C.: Seven Locks Press, 1989.

Benjamin, Medea, Joseph Collins, and Michael Scott. *No Free Lunch: Food and Revolution in Cuba Today.* New York: Grove Press, 1986.

Benjamin, Medea, and Kevin Danaher. *Killing Mexican Peasants to Restore Investor Confidence.* San Francisco: Global Exchange (spring 1995).

Bennet, Claudette E. *The Black Population in the United States: March 1994 and 1993.* U.S. Bureau of the Census, Current Population Reports, series P–20, no. 480. Washington, D.C.: Government Printing Office, 1995.

Bennis, Phyllis. "False Consensus: George Bush's United Nations." In *Beyond the Storm*, edited by Phyllis Bennis and Michel Moushabeck. New York: Olive Branch Press, 1991.

———. "Command and Control: Politics and Power in the Post-Cold War United Nations." In *Altered States*, edited by Phyllis Bennis and Michel Moushabeck. New York: Olive Branch Press, 1993.

———. *Calling the Shots: How Washington Dominates Today's UN.* New York: Olive Branch Press, 1996.

Bennis, Phyllis, and Michel Moushabeck, eds. *Beyond the Storm.* New York: Olive Branch Press, 1991.

———. *Altered States.* New York: Olive Branch Press, 1993.

———. "Editor's Preface, Looking North: The New Challenge to the South." In *Altered States*, edited by Phyllis Bennis and Michel Moushabeck. New York: Olive Branch Press, 1993.

Berberoglu, Berch, ed. *Critical Perspectives in Sociology.* Dubuque, Iowa: Kendall/Hunt, 1993.

Bernstein, Dennis. "Haiti: The Junta's Golden Parachute." *San Francisco Bay Guardian,* September 21, 1994.

———. "Cover-Up: Chemical and Biological Agents and Gulf War Syndrome." *Covert Action Quarterly* (summer 1995).

Bleifuss, Joel. "Know Thine Enemy: A Brief History of Corporations." *In These Times* (February 1998).

Block, Fred. *Revising State Theory.* Philadelphia: Temple University Press, 1987.

Bluestone, Barry, and Bennett Harrison. *The Deindustrialization of America.* New York: Basic Books, 1982.

Blum, William. *Killing Hope: U.S. Military and CIA Interventions Since World War II.* Monroe, Maine: Common Courage Press, 1995.

———. *Rogue State: A Guide to the World's Only Superpower.* Monroe, Maine: Common Courage Press, 2000.

Bohlen, Celestine. "Where Every Day Is Mother's Day." *New York Times,* May 12, 1996.

Bok, Derek. *The Cost of Talent.* New York: Free Press, 1993.

Bottomore, Tom. *Political Sociology.* New York: Harper and Row, 1979.

Boudreaux, Richard. "Taking the Lead, Italy to Forgive Billions in Third World Debt." *Los Angeles Times,* July 15, 2000.

Bowles, Samuel, David M. Gordon, and Thomas E. Weisskopf. *Beyond the Wasteland.* Garden City, N.Y.: Anchor Press/Doubleday, 1983.

Boyer, Richard O., and Herbert M. Morais. *Labor's Untold Story.* New York: United Electrical, Radio, and Machine Workers of America, 1955.

Brazier, Charles. "State of the World Report." *New Internationalist* (January/February 1997).

Breslow, Marc. "The Racial Divide Widens." *Dollars and Sense*, January–February 1995.

Breslow, Marc, and Mathew Howard. "The Real Un(der)employment Rate." *Dollars and Sense,* May–June 1995.

Brinkley, Joel. "C.I.A. Primer Tells Nicaraguan Rebels How to Kill." *New York Times,* October 17, 1984.

Broad, Dave. "Globalization Versus Labor." *Monthly Review* (December 1995).

Broad, Robin. *Global Backlash: Citizens for a Just World Economy.* New York: Rowman and Littlefield, 2002.

Bronfenbrenner, Kate. *Uneasy Terrain: The Impact of Capital Mobility on Workers, Wages, and Union Organizing.* Paper submitted to the U.S. Trade Deficit Review Commission, September 6, 2000.

Brown, Lester, et al. *State of the World 1994.* New York: W. W. Norton and Co., 1994.

Browne, Harry, and Beth Sims. *Runaway America.* Albuquerque, N.M.: Resource Center Press, 1993.

Browne, Robert S. "The IMF and the World Bank in the New World Order." In *Altered States,* edited by Phyllis Bennis and Michel Moushabeck. New York: Olive Branch Press, 1993.

Brzezinski, Matthew. "East Europe's Car Makers Feel Sting of Capitalism." *New York Times,* April 28, 1994.

Brzezinski, Zbigniew. *Out of Control: Global Turmoil on the Eve of the Twenty-first Century.* New York: Macmillan, 1993.

Budhoo, Davison. "IMF/World Bank Wreak Havoc on Third World." In *Fifty Years Is Enough: The Case Against the World Bank and the International Monetary Fund,* edited by Kevin Danaher. Boston: South End Press, 1994.

Bureau of Labor Statistics. *Household Data, Annual Averages* [online], ftp://ftp.bls.gov/pub/special.requests/lf/aat 39.txt.

———. *International Comparisons of Hourly Compensation for Production Workers, 1975–2001.* [online], ftp://ftp.bls.gov/pub/special.requests/Foreign Labor/supptab.txt.

———. *Monthly Labor Review* [online], www.bls.gov/data/home.htm [July 1986 and April 1988].

BusinessWeek. April 15, 2002.

———. April 26, 1993.

Byrne, John A., and Lori Bongiorno. "CEO Pay: Ready for Takeoff." *Business-Week,* April 24, 1995.

Byrne, John A., et al. "That Eye Popping Executive Pay." *BusinessWeek,* April 25, 1994.

Caldicott, Helen. *Missile Envy.* New York: Bantam Books, 1986.

Campen, Jim. "Lending Insights: Hard Proof That Banks Discriminate." *Dollars and Sense,* January–February 1994.

Canham-Clyne, John. "U.S. Policy on Haiti: Selling Out Democracy." *Covert Action Quarterly* (spring 1994).

Carnoy, Martin. *The State and Political Theory.* Princeton, N.J.: Princeton University Press, 1984.

Caufield, Catherine. *Masters of Illusion.* New York: Henry Holt, 1996.

Center for Economic and Social Rights. *Afghanistan Fact Sheet #1* [online], www.cesr.org.

Center for Responsive Politics. [online], www.opensecrets.org/industries/indus.asp?Ind=H04 [July 8, 2002].

Challenging the Leadership of the Global Economy. San Francisco: Global Exchange, fall 1994.

Chamorro, Edgar. "Terror Is the Most Effective Weapon of Nicaragua's 'Contras.'" *New York Times,* January 9, 1986.

Chasin, Barbara, and Gerald Chasin. *Power and Ideology.* Cambridge, Mass.: Schenkman, 1974.

Choderkoff, Daniel. "Redefining Development." *Society and Nature* 3, no. 1 (1995).

Chomsky, Noam. *The Culture of Terrorism.* Boston: South End Press, 1988.

———. *Necessary Illusions.* Boston: South End Press, 1989.

———. "After the Cold War: U.S. Middle East Policy." In *Beyond the Storm,* edited by Phyllis Bennis and Michel Moushabeck. New York: Olive Branch Press, 1993.

———. "Introduction: World Orders, Old and New." In *Altered States,* edited by Phyllis Bennis and Michel Moushabeck. New York: Olive Branch Press, 1993.

———. *Year 501: The Conquest Continues.* Boston: South End Press, 1993.

Chomsky, Noam, and Edward S. Herman. *After the Cataclysm.* Boston: South End Press, 1979.

————. *The Washington Connection and Third World Fascism.* Boston: South End Press, 1979.

————. *Manufacturing Consent.* New York: Pantheon Books, 1988.

Chossudovsky, Michel. "Dismantling Former Yugoslavia, Recolonizing Bosnia." *Z Magazine* [online], www.montclair.edu/Pages/ICS/DismantlingYugoslavia.htm.

Clark, Ramsey. *The Fire This Time.* New York: Thunder's Mouth Press, 1992.

Clarke, Renfrey. "U.S. Labor 'Missionaries.'" *Against the Current* (May–June 1994).

Cockburn, Alexander. "Press Clips." *Village Voice,* November 8, 1983.

Cockburn, Alexander, and James Ridgeway. "The Making of a Counterrevolution." *Village Voice,* November 8, 1983.

Cohen, Jeff. "Remembering the Last US Retaliation Against Terror." *Common Dreams* [online], www.commondreams.org/views01/0915-01.htm.

Cohen, Joshua, and Joel Rogers. *Inequity and Intervention: The Federal Budget and Central America.* Boston: South End Press, 1986.

Cohen, Stephen F. "Clinton's Yeltsin, Yeltsin's Russia." *Nation,* October 10, 1994.

Collier, Peter, and David Horowitz. *The Rockefellers.* New York: Signet, 1976.

Collins, Chuck. "Aid to Dependent Corporations: Exposing Federal Handouts to the Wealthy." *Dollars and Sense,* May–June 1995.

Collins, Chuck, Chris Hartman, and Holly Sklar. *Divided Decade: Economic Disparity at the Century's Turn.* Boston: United for a Fair Economy, 1999.

Collins, Glenn. "Coke Drops 'Domestic' and Goes One World." *New York Times,* January 13, 1996.

Colman, Ronald. "Measuring Real Progress." *Genuine Progress Index Atlantic.* Canada [online], www.gpiatlantic.org/realprog.pdf.

Commission on the Cities. *The Kerner Report Updated: Report of the 1988 Commission on the Cities, Race and Poverty in the United States Today.* 1988.

Committee in Solidarity with the People of El Salvador. *Would You Buy a Used Military Dictatorship from This Man?*

————. *Flying Death Squads.*

Contemporary Authors. New Revision Series, vol. 8.

"The Contract with Mexico." *Left Business Observer* (March 14, 1995).

Corporate Accountability Project. [online], www.corporations.org/system.

"Corporate Crime, Welfare and Influence." [online], www.spiritone.com/~gdy 52150/corplaw.html.

Cox, William. *Measures of Real Earnings Since 1970.* The Congressional Research Service, November 13, 1987.

Crossette, Barbara. "U.N. Study Finds a Free Eastern Europe Poorer and Less Healthy." *New York Times,* October 7, 1994.

————. "Iraq Sanctions Kill Children, U.N. Reports." *New York Times,* December 1, 1995.

————. "U.N., Facing Bankruptcy, Plans to Cut Payroll by 10%." *New York Times,* February 6, 1996.

Currie, Elliot, and Jerome H. Skolnick. *America's Problems.* 2d ed. Glenview, Ill.: Scott, Foresman and Company, 1988.

Cushman, John. "Industry Helped Draft Clean Water Law." *New York Times,* March 22, 1995.

———. "Siberian Logging Sets Off U.S. Battle." *New York Times,* January 30, 1996.

Danaher, Kevin, ed. *Fifty Years Is Enough: The Case Against the World Bank and the International Monetary Fund.* Boston: South End Press, 1994.

———. *Mexico's Economic Crisis.* San Francisco: Global Exchange (1995).

———. *Can We Democratize the United Nations?* San Francisco: Global Exchange (summer 1995).

———. *Is the U.S. Becoming a Third World Country?* San Francisco: Global Exchange (fall 1995).

Danner, Mark. "The Truth of El Mozote." *New Yorker,* December 6, 1993.

Davidson, Basil. *The African Slave Trade.* Boston: Little, Brown and Company, 1961.

"Deepening Cynicism Leaves Niche for Third Party." *Star Ledger,* August 1, 1995.

DeFronzo, James. *Revolutions and Revolutionary Moments.* 2d ed. Boulder, Colo.: Westview Press, 1996.

del Toro, Raymundo. "U.S. Embargo of Cuba Violates U.N.'s Wishes." *New York Times,* November 3, 1994.

Denny, Charlotte. "Canada Calls for Immediate Halt to Debt Repayments by the World's Poorest States." *Guardian* (London), September 25, 2000.

DePalma, Anthony, and Peter Truell. "A Mexican Mover and Shaker Got the Red Carpet at Citibank." *New York Times,* June 5, 1966.

De Witt, Karen. "Job Bias Cited for Minorities and Women." *New York Times,* November 23, 1995.

Diamond, Jared. *Guns, Germs, and Steel: The Fates of Human Societies.* New York: W. W. Norton and Co., 1999.

Dillon, Sam. "Rebels Strike in 4 Mexico States, Leaving 13 Dead." *New York Times,* August 31, 1996.

Dinges, John, and Saul Landua. *Assassination on Embassy Row.* New York: Pantheon, 1980.

Dollars and Sense, October 1985.

Dolnick, Edward. "Why German Autoworker Brigitte Dunst Loves Her Four-Day Workweek." *UTNE Reader,* May–June 1995.

Domhoff, G. William. *Who Rules America?* Englewood Cliffs, N.J.: Prentice Hall, 1967.

———. *The Higher Circles.* New York: Vintage Books, 1970.

———. *The Powers That Be.* New York: Vintage Books, 1978.

———. *Who Rules America Now?* Englewood Cliffs, N.J.: Prentice Hall, 1983.

———. *State Autonomy or Class Dominance.* New York: Aldine De Gruyter, 1996.

————. *Who Rules America? Power and Politics in the Year 2000.* Mountain View, Calif.: Mayfield Publishing, 1998.

Donziger, Steve R., ed. *The Real War on Crime.* New York: HarperCollins, 1996.

Durning, Alan B. *Poverty and the Environment: Reversing the Downward Spiral.* Washington, D.C.: Worldwatch Institute, 1989.

————. *Saving the Forests: What Will It Take?* Washington, D.C.: Worldwatch Institute, 1993.

Economic Policy Institute. [online], epinet.org.

Ecumenial Coalition for Economic Justice. *Jubilee Movement Shifts the Ground Under G7 Debt Plans.* [online], www.ecej.org/ejmay99.htm [May 1999].

Egan, Timothy. *The Good Rain.* New York: Random House, 1990.

————. "Alaska, No Longer So Frigid, Starts to Crack, Burn and Sag." *New York Times,* June 16, 2002.

————. "Owners of Malibu Mansions Cry, This Sand Is My Sand." *New York Times,* August 25, 2002.

Eichenwald, Kurt. "Could Capitalists Actually Bring Down Capitalism?" *New York Times,* June 30, 2002.

Encyclopedia Britannica. Vol. 10, 1985.

————. Vol. 17, 1985.

Engelberg, Stephen. "Business Leaves the Lobby and Sits at Congress's Table." *New York Times,* March 31, 1995.

Engels, Friedrich. "Socialism: Utopian and Scientific." In *The Essential Works of Marxism,* by Arthur P. Mendel. New York: Bantam, 1961.

"Enron and Campaign Finance Reform." *Public Citizen* [online], www.citizen. org/congress/campaign/legislation/shays-meehan/articles.cfm?ID= 6693 [January 24, 2002].

Fairness and Accuracy in Reporting. "Casualties at Home: Muzzled Journalists." *Extra!* (May 1991).

————. "Spin Control through Censorship: The Pentagon Manages the News." *Extra!* (May 1991).

Farb, Peter. *Humankind.* Boston: Houghton Mifflin Company, 1978.

Farmer, Paul. *The Uses of Haiti.* Monroe, Maine: Common Courage Press, 1994.

Federal Glass Ceiling Commission, U.S. Department of Labor. *Good for Business: Making Full Use of the Nation's Human Capital,* 1995.

Finkelstein, Norman. "Israel and Iraq: a Double Standard." *Monthly Review* (July–August 1991).

Flaherty, Patrick. "Privatization and the Soviet Economy." *Monthly Review* (January 1992).

Flanders, Laura. "Restricting Reality: Media Mind-Games and the War." In *Beyond the Storm,* edited by Phyllis Bennis and Michel Moushabeck. New York: Olive Branch Press, 1996.

Flavin, Christopher. Preface in *State of the World, 2002.* New York: W. W. Norton, 2002.

Fleming, D. F. *The Cold War and Its Origins, 1917–1960.* Vol. 1. Garden City, N.Y.: Doubleday, 1961.

Forche, Carolyn. "El Salvador: the Next Vietnam?" *Progressive,* February 1981.

Forbes. List of Wealthiest People [online], www.forbes.com [2002].

Foster, John Bellamy. *The Theory of Monopoly Capitalism.* New York: Monthly Review, 1986.

———. "Global Ecology and the Common Good." *Monthly Review* (February, 1995).

Fotopoulos, Takis. "Development or Democracy?" *Society and Nature* 3, no. 1 (1995).

Frank, Andre Gunder. *Capitalism and Underdevelopment in Latin America.* New York: Monthly Review, 1969.

———. "Development, Democracy, and the Market." *Society and Nature* 3, no. 1 (1995).

Franke, Richard W. *East Timor: The Hidden War.* New York: East Timor Defense Committee, 1976.

———. *Why Hunger: An Anthropologist's View.* Paper presented at the Victor Johnson Symposium on World Hunger, Amherst College, Amherst, Mass., December 3, 1981.

———. "Democratic Decentralization: The Kerala Experience in International Perspective." Presented at the seminar "A Decade after the 73rd and 74th Constitutional Amendments," A. K. G. Centre for Research and Studies, Thiruvananthapuram, Kerala, May 18–19, 2002, chss.montclair.edu/anthro/FrankepaperAKGMay02.htm.

Franke, Richard W., and Barbara H. Chasin. *Seeds of Famine.* Montclair, N.J.: Allanheld, Osmun, 1980.

———. *Kerala: Radical Reform as Development in an Indian State.* San Francisco: Institute for Food and Development Policy, 1989.

Frankel, Max. "McNamara's Retreat." *New York Times,* April 16, 1995.

Franklin, Jane. *The Cuban Revolution and the United States: A Chronological History.* Melbourne, Australia: Ocean Press, 1992.

Frazier, Kendrick. "The State of American Education." *Rethinking Schools* (winter 1993).

Frelick, Bill. "Closing Ranks: The North Locks Arms Against New Refugees." In *Altered States,* edited by Phyllis Bennis and Michel Moushabeck. New York: Olive Branch Press, 1993.

French, Hillary. "Cleaning the Air." In *States of the World,* edited by Lester Brown et al. New York: W. W. Norton, 1994.

French, Howard. "Study Says Haiti Sanctions Kill Up to 1,000 Children a Month." *New York Times,* November 9, 1993.

———. "Doctors Question Haiti Health Data." *New York Times,* November 24, 1993.

Freud, Sigmund. *Civilization and Its Discontents.* New York: W. W. Norton, 1961.

Freund, Peter, and George T. Martin. *The Ecology of the Automobile.* Montreal Canada: Black Rose, 1994.

Gaberlnick, Tamar. "The United States Is Still #1 in Arms Sales." *Common Dreams News Center* [online], www.commondreams.org/views02/0810-02.htm [August 10, 2002].

Gardner, Gary. "The Challenge for Johannesburg: Creating a More Secure World." Worldwatch Institution. *State of the World,* 2002.

Gaviglio, Glen, and David Raye. *Society As It Is.* 3d ed. New York: Macmillan, 1980.

George, Susan. "The Debt Boomerang." In *Fifty Years Is Enough: The Case Against the World Bank and the International Monetary Fund,* edited by Kevin Danaher. Boston: South End Press, 1994.

———. *A Short History of Neoliberalism.* Presented at the Conference on Economic Sovereignty in a Globalizing World. Bangkok [online]. www.millenium-round.org/ [March 24–26, 1999].

George, Susan, and Nigel Paige. *Food for Beginners.* Oxford: University Press, 1982.

Gershman, John. "Back to Earth." *Foreign Policy in Focus* [online], www.present danger.org/frontier/2002/0910earth.html [September 10, 2002].

Gerth, Hans H., and C. Wright Mills. *From Max Weber: Essays in Sociology.* New York: Oxford University Press, 1946.

Gettleman, Marvin E., Jane Franklin, Marilyn Young, and Bruce H. Franklin. *Vietnam and America: A Documented History.* New York: Grove Press, 1985.

Gilbert, Dennis, and Joseph A. Kahl. *The American Class Structure.* Homewood, Ill.: Dorsey Press, 1982.

Gitlin, Todd. "Counter-Insurgence: Myth and Reality in Greece." In *Containment and Revolution,* edited by David Horowitz. Boston: Beacon Press, 1967.

Glasberg, Davita Silfen, and Dan Skidmore. *Corporate Welfare Policy and the Welfare State.* New York: Adline De Gryter, 1997.

Glick, Brian. *War At Home.* Boston: South End Press, 1989.

Global Policy Forum. [online], www.globalpolicy.org/finance/tables/index11.htm.

———. *Ralph Nader Talks on Global Corporatism.* San Francisco, Calif.: Global Exchange.

Godrej, Alan. "Hunger in a World of Plenty." *New Internationalist* (May 1995).

Gold, David A., Clarence Y. H. Lo, and Erik Olin Wright. "Recent Developments in Marxist Theories of the Capitalist State." *Monthly Review* (October 1975).

Gonzalez, David. "Fighters' Demands Open Old Wounds in Central America." *New York Times,* August 19, 2002.

Gordon, Michael R. "U.S. Chickens in Russian Pots." *New York Times,* January 18, 1996.

Gowan, Peter. "Neo-Liberal Theory and Practice for Eastern Europe." *New Left Review* (September–October 1995).

Greene, Felix. *The Enemy: What Every American Should Know about Imperialism.* New York: Vintage Books, 1971.

Greenhouse, Steven. "A Potent, Illegal Weapon Against Unions." *San Francisco Chronicle,* October 24, 2000.

Greer, Edward. "The Hidden History of the Iraq War." *Monthly Review* (May 1991).

Greider, William. "The Right and US Trade Law: Invalidating the 20th Century." *Nation,* October 15, 2002.

————. "There Are More Enron's Out There: The Rot Is Systemic." *Nation,* February 4, 2002.

Griswold, Dierdre. *Indonesia: The Bloodbath That Was.* New York: World View Publishers, 1970.

Hakim, Danny. "For Flint, Mich., Takeover Adds to the List of Woes." *New York Times,* July 10, 2002.

Halberstam, David. *The Best and the Brightest.* New York: Penguin Books, 1972.

Handbook of Labor Statistics 1985.

Hanlon, Joseph. "Odious Debts: Take the Hit." *New Internationalist* (May 1999).

Harris, Louis. *BusinessWeek,* March 11, 1996.

Hartung, William C. *And Weapons for All.* New York: HarperCollins, 1995.

Hauser, Thomas. *The Assassination of Charles Horman.* New York: Avon, 1978.

Hayter, Teresa. *The Creation of World Poverty.* London: Pluto Press, 1983.

Headley, Bernard D. "Race, Poverty, Crime and Powerlessness in America's Inner Cities." In *Critical Perspectives*, edited by Berch Berberoglu. Dubuque, Iowa: Kendall/Hunt, 1993.

Henwood, Doug. "This Kosovo Thing." *Left Business Observer,* no. 28 (May 1999).

Herman, Edward S. *The Real Terror Network.* Boston: South End Press, 1982.

————. "The Income 'Counter Revolution.'" In *Crisis in American Institutions.* 3d ed. Edited by Jerome H. Skolnick and Elliot Currie. Boston: Little, Brown and Company, 1988.

————. "The Failure of Success." *Lies of Our Times* (December 1993).

Herman, Edward S., and Frank Broadhead. *Demonstration Elections.* Boston: South End Press, 1984.

Hersh, Seymour M. "U.S. Said to Have Allowed Israel to Sell Arms to Iran." *New York Times,* December 8, 1991.

Higham, Charles. *Trading with the Enemy.* New York: Delacorte Press, 1983.

Himmelstein, David U., and Steffie Woolhandler. *The National Health Program Book.* Monroe, Maine: Common Courage Press, 1994.

Hobsbawm, Eric. *The Age of Extremes.* New York: Vintage Books, 1996.

Hochschild, Adam. *King Leopold's Ghost.* Boston: Houghton Mifflin, 1999.

Hockenos, Paul. "Uncivil Society: The Return of the European Right." In *Altered States*, edited by Phyllis Bennis and Michel Moushabeck. New York: Olive Branch Press, 1993.

————. "Making Hate Safe Again in Europe." *Nation*, September 1994.

Holmes, Steven. "Less Strategic Now, Grenada Is to Lose American Embassy." *New York Times,* May 2, 1994.

———. "Income Gap Persists for Blacks and Whites." *New York Times,* February 23, 1995.

———. "Programs Based on Sex and Race Are Challenged." *New York Times,* March 16, 1995.

Honan, William H. "War Decoding Helped U.S. to Shape U.N." *New York Times,* April 1, 1995.

Horowitz, David. *Containment and Revolution.* Boston: Beacon Press, 1967.

Howe, Barbara. "The Emergence of Scientific Philanthropy, 1900–1920: Origins, Issues, and Outcomes." In *Philanthropy and Cultural Imperialism,* edited by Robert F. Arnove. Bloomington: Indiana University Press, 1980.

Human Rights Watch. *The Enron Corporation, Corporate Complicity in Human Rights Violations* [online], www.hrw.org/reports/1999/enron/index.htm [1999].

———. *World Report 2002: Democratic Republic of the Congo* [online], www. hrw.org/wr2k2/africa3.html.

———. www.hrw.org/africa/rwanda.php.

———. www.hrw.org/africa/sierraleone.php.

Huntington, Samuel P. "The Goals of Development." In *Comparing Nations and Cultures,* by Alex Inkeles and Masamichi Sasaki. Englewood Cliffs, N.J.: Prentice Hall, 1996.

Hurwit, Cathy. "A Canadian-Style Cure." *Dollars and Sense,* May 1993.

Imerman, Vicky A. "School of the Americas/Assassins." *Covert Action Quarterly* (fall 1993).

Inkeles, Alex, and Masamichi Sasaki. *Comparing Nations and Cultures.* Englewood Cliffs, N.J.: Prentice Hall, 1996.

Institute for Food and Development Policy. Food First. *12 Myths About Hunger* [online], www.foodfirst.org/pubs/backgrdrs/1998/s98v5n3.html.

———. *Food First Action Alert: Nicaragua: Give Change a Chance.* San Francisco: Food First and Institute for Food Development Policy.

Institute for Policy Studies. *In Contempt of Congress.* Washington, D.C.: Institute for Policy Studies, 1985.

International Forum on Globalization. *A Better World Is Possible! Alternatives to Economic Globalization* [online], www.ifg.org/alt_eng.pdf [spring 2002].

International Institute for Democracy and Electoral Assistance [online], www.idea.int/vt/index.cfm.

Jean-Baptiste, Chavannes. "Tying Aristide's Hands." *Progressive,* September 1994.

Jencks, Christopher. *Rethinking Social Policy: Race, Poverty, and the Underclass.* New York: HarperCollins, 1992.

Jochnick, Chris. "Perilous Prosperity." *New Internationalist,* June 2001.

Johnson, Chalmers. *Blowback: The Costs and Consequences of American Empire.* New York: Henry Holt, 2002.

Joint Center for Housing Studies. *State of the Nation Housing.* Cambridge, Mass.: Harvard University, 2003.

Joint Economic Committee of Congress. *The Concentration of Wealth in the United States.* July 1986.

Joseph, Yanique. "Haiti: At the Crossroads of Two World Orders." In *Altered States*, edited by Phyllis Bennis and Michel Moushabeck. New York: Olive Branch Press, 1993.

Jubilee USA Network [online], www.jubileeusa.org/.

Jubilee Movement Shifts the Ground Under G7 Debt Plans. Ecumenical Coalition for Economic Justice [online], www.ecej.org/ejmay99.htm [May 1999].

Kadane, Kathy. "U.S. Officials' Lists Aided Indonesian Bloodbath in '60s." *Washington Post*, May 21, 1990.

Kahin, Audrey R., and George McT. Kahin. *Subversion as Foreign Policy.* New York: New Press, 1995.

Kane, Joe. *Savages.* New York: Vintage, 1996.

Karlins, Marvin. *Psychology and Society: Readings for General Psychology.* New York: John Wiley and Sons, 1971.

Karnow, Stanley. "An Antiwar Protester Comes Out of the Closet." *New York Times,* April 16, 1995.

Kawachi, Ichiro, Bruce P. Kennedy, and Richard G. Wilkinson, eds. *The Society and Population Health Reader: Income Inequality and Health.* New York: New Press, 1999.

Kennickell, Arthur B. *An Examination of Changes in the Distribution of Wealth from 1989 to 1998: Evidence from the Survey of Consumer Finances.* Washington, D.C.: Federal Reserve Board, 2000.

Kerbo, Harold. *Social Stratification and Inequality.* New York: McGraw-Hill, 1991.

Kerner Report Update: Report of the 1988 Commission on the Cities, Race and Poverty in The United States Today.

Kidron, Michael, and Ronald Segal. *The State of the World Atlas.* New York: Penguin, 1995.

Kifner, John. "Aristide Vows to Include Wealthy in Haiti's New Cabinet." *New York Times,* October 20, 1994.

Kilborn, Peter T. "White Males and Management." *New York Times,* March 17, 1995.

Kitman, Jamie Lincoln. "The Secret History of Lead." *Nation*, March 2000.

Kloby, Jerry. "Increasing Class Polarization in the United States: The Growth of Wealth and Income Inequality." In *Critical Perspectives in Sociology*, edited by Berch Berberoglu. Dubuque, Iowa: Kendall/Hunt, 1993.

———. *Inequality, Power, and Development.* 1st ed. Amherst, N.Y.: Humanity Books, 1997.

Knoll, Erwin. Interview with Patrick Bellegarde-Smith. *Progressive,* September 1994.

Koning, Hans. *Columbus: His Enterprise.* New York: Monthly Review, 1976.

———. *The Conquest of America.* New York: Monthly Review, 1993.

Konner, Melvin. *Dear America.* New York: Addison-Wesley, 1993.

Kotz, David, and Fred Weir. *Revolution from Above: The Demise of the Soviet System.* New York: Routledge, 1997.

Krauss, Clifford. "U.S., Aware of Killings, Kept Ties to Salvadoran Rightists." *New York Times,* November 9, 1993.

Krishnan, Raghu. "December 1995: 'The First Revolt Against Globalization.'" *Monthly Review* (May 21, 1996).

Kristof, Nicholas D. "Farms Subsidies That Kill." *New York Times,* July 5, 2002.

Lacombe, John, and Joan Borum. "Major Labor Contracts in 1986 Provided Record Low Wage Adjustments." *Monthly Labor Review* (May 1987).

Lappé, Frances Moore, and Joseph Collins. *World Hunger: Twelve Myths.* New York: Grove Press, 1986.

Lappé, Frances Moore, and Anna Lappé. *Hope's Edge.* New York: Tarcher/Putnam, 2002.

Langman, Jimmy. "Enron's Pipe Scheme" [online], www.Corporatewatch.org [May 9, 2002].

Latane, Bibb, and John Darley. "Bystander 'Apathy.'" In *Psychology and Society: Readings for General Psychology,* compiled by Marvin Karlins. New York: John Wiley and Sons, 1971.

Left Business Observer. No. 89 (April 27, 1999).

"Left Turn." *Nation,* October 11, 1993.

LeGrande, Linda. *Who's Keeping Up in the 1980s? Compensation As an Indicator.* Washington, D.C.: Congressional Research Service, November 4, 1987.

Lenin, V. I. *Imperialism, The Highest Stage of Capitalism.* New York: International Publishers, 1939.

Lens, Sidney. "Socialism for the Rich." In *Society As It Is.* 3d ed. Edited by Glen Gaviglio and David Raye.

Leroy, Greg. "No More Candy Store: States Move to End Corporate Welfare as We Know It." *Dollars and Sense*, May–June 1995.

"Less Than Zero: Enron's Income Tax Payments, 1996–2001." Citizens for Tax Justice [online], www.ctj.org/html/enron.htm [January 17, 2002].

Levy, Marcela Lopeez. "The Damn Water Is Ours." *New Internationalist,* September 2001.

Lewellen, Ted C. *Dependency and Development: An Introduction to the Third World.* Westport, Conn.: Bergin and Garvey, 1995.

Lewis, Anthony. "The Whole Truth." *New York Times,* December 6, 1993.

Lewis, Anthony, and John Pilger. "Abroad at Home: The Hidden Horror." *New York Times,* August 12, 1994.

Lewis, Paul. "World Hunger Found Still Growing." *New York Times,* June 28, 1987.

Lichter, Daniel. "Racial Differences in Underemployment in American Cities." *American Journal of Sociology* (January 1988).

Lipman, Lawrence. "Ecuadorean Tribe Wields Unusual Weapons." *Record,* October 29, 1995.

Lyons, Richard D. "U.N. Approves Force to Monitor Yemen Truce." *New York Times,* June 30, 1994.

MacEwan, Arthur. "Markets Unbound: The Heavy Price of Globalization." *Dollars and Sense*, September–October 1994.

Magdoff, Harry. *Globalization: To What End?* New York: Monthly Review, 1992.

Mahler, Vincent A., and Claudio J. Katz. "Social Benefits in Advanced Capitalist Countries: A Cross-National Assessment." In *Comparing Nations and Cultures,* edited by Alex Inkeles and Masamichi Sasaki. Englewood Cliffs, N.J.: Prentice Hall, 1996.

Majot, Juliette. *Brave New World Bank.* San Francisco: Global Exchange (winter 1994).

Mamdani, Mahmood. *The Myth of Population Control.* New York: Monthly Review, 1972.

Mandel, Ernest. *The Place of Marxism in History.* Amherst, N.Y.: Humanity Books, 1994.

Marchetti, Victor, and John D. Marks. *The CIA and the Cult of Intelligence.* New York: Dell, 1974.

Marcos, Subcommander. "A Tourist Guide to Chiapas." *Monthly Review* (May 1994).

Martin, George T. *Social Policy in the Welfare State.* Englewood Cliffs, N.J.: Prentice Hall, 1990.

Martin, George T., and Mayer N. Zald, eds. *Social Welfare in Society.* New York: Columbia University Press, 1981.

Martinez, Philip, and Arnoldo Garcia. *What Is "Neo-Liberalism"? A Brief Definition for Activists* [online], www.apctax.igc.apc.org/envjustice.html.

Marx, Karl. "The Eighteenth Brumaire of Louis Bonaparte." In *Marx-Engels Reader*, edited by Robert C. Tucker. New York: W. W. Norton, 1972.

———. *Capital.* Vol. 1. New York: International Publishers, 1967.

Mason, Mike. *Development and Disorder: A History of the Third World since 1945.* Hanover, N.H.: University Press of New England, 1997.

Mauer, Marc. *Americans Behind Bars: One Year Later.* Washington, D.C.: Sentencing Project, 1992.

———. *Americans Behind Bars: The International Use of Incarceration, 1992–1993.* Washington, D.C.: Sentencing Project, 1994.

McCann, Thomas. *An American Company: The Tragedy of United Fruit.* New York: Crown Publishers, 1976.

McGehee, Ralph W. *Deadly Deceits.* New York: Sheridan Square Press, 1983.

———. "Back in the Saddle Again." *Progressive*, August 1985.

McKibben, Bill. *Hope, Human and Wild: True Stories of Living Lightly on the Earth.* Saint Paul, Minn.: Hungry Mind Press, 1995.

McLuhan, Marshall. *The Gutenberg Galaxy.* Toronto: University of Toronto Press, 1962.

McMahan, Jeff. *Reagan and the World.* New York: Monthly Review, 1985.

McMichael, Phillip. *Development and Social Change: A Global Perspective.* Thousand Oaks, Calif.: Pine Forge Press, 2000.

Mendel, Arthur P. *Essential Works of Marxism.* New York: Bantam, 1961.

Milgram, Stanley. "Behavioral Study of Obedience." In *Psychology and Society: Readings for General Psychology,* compiled by Marvin Karlins. New York: John Wiley and Sons, 1971.

Mills, C. Wright. *The Power Elite.* New York: Oxford University Press, 1956.

———. *The Sociological Imagination.* New York: Oxford University Press, 1959.

Minqi, Li. "China: Six Years After Tiananmen." *Monthly Review* (January 1996).

Mishel, Lawrence, and Jacqueline Simon. *The State of Working America.* Washington, D.C.: Economic Policy Institute, 1988.

Mishel, Lawrence, and Jared Bernstein. *The State of Working America, 1992–93.* Washington, D.C.: Economic Policy Institute, 1993.

———. *The State of Working America, 1994–95.* Washington, D.C.: Economic Policy Institute, 1994.

Mishel, Lawrence, Jared Bernstein, and John Schmidt. *The State of Working America, 2000/2001.* Washington, D.C.: Economic Policy Institute, 2001.

Mittal, Anuradha. "Giving Away the Farm: The 2002 Farm Bill." *Food First Backgrounder.* Institute for Food and Development Policy (summer 2002).

Montclair Committee on Central America. *A Critical Look at U.S. Policy in Central America,* 1986.

Moody, Kim. "U.S. Labor Wars: Bottom to Top." *New Politics* (winter 1996).

Moore, Stephen. "How to Slash Corporate Welfare." *New York Times,* April 5, 1995.

Morel, E. D. *The Black Man's Burden.* New York: Monthly Review Press, 1920, 1969.

Moyers, Bill. "Bill Moyers Reports: Trading Democracy." PBS Television, February 5, 2002.

Nader, Ralph. "Testimony of Ralph Nader Before the Committee on the Budget." U.S. House of Representatives [online], www.nader.org/releases/63099.html [June 30, 1999].

Nairn, Allan. "Occupation Haiti: The Eagle Is Landing." *Nation,* October 3, 1994.

———. "Our Man in FRAPH: Behind Haiti's Paramilitaries." *Nation,* October 24, 1994.

———. "C.I.A. Death Squad." *Nation,* April 17, 1995.

———. "Haiti Under the Gun." *Nation,* January 8/15, 1996.

Nash, Nathaniel. " Europeans Shrug as Taxes Go Up." *New York Times,* February 16, 1995.

Nation. November 5, 1983.

National Advisory Commission on Civil Disorders. *Report of the National Advisory Commission on Civil Disorders.* New York: Bantam Books, 1968.

Naureckas, Jim, and Janine Jackson, eds. *The Fair Reader: An Extra! Review of Press and Politics in the '90's.*

Navarro, Vincent. *Dangerous to Your Health*. New York: Monthly Review Press, 1993.

Nehru, Jawaharlal. *The Discovery of India*. Garden City, N.Y.: Anchor Books, 1959.

New Internationalist. August 1996.

Nichols, John. "Enron's Global Crusade." *Nation,* March 4, 2002.

Niva, Steve. "The Battle Is Joined." In *Beyond the Storm*, edited by Phyllis Bennis and Michel Moushabeck. New York: Olive Branch Press, 1993.

"No Business Like War Business." *Defense Monitor* 16, no. 3 (1987).

Nossiter, Bernard D. "U.S. As Whipping Boy." *New York Times,* October 5, 1981.

O'Connell, Jock. "WTO, State Law on Collision Course." *Los Angeles Times,* January 23, 2000.

O'Connor, James. *The Fiscal Crisis of the State*. New York: St. Martin's Press, 1993.

———. "Capitalism, Uneven Development and Ecological Crisis." In *Critical Perspectives*, edited by Berch Berberoglu. Dubuque, Iowa: Kendall/Hunt, 1993.

Oldenburg, Ray. *The Great Good Place*. New York: Marlowe and Company, 1999.

Orenstein, Catherine. "Haiti's Curse." *Lies of Our Times* (December 1993).

Orfield, Gary, and Carole Ashkinaze. *The Closing Door: Conservative Policy and Black Opportunity*. Chicago: University of Chicago Press, 1991.

Organization for Economic Cooperation and Development (OECD). *Income Distribution in OECD Countries*. Paris: OECD, 1995.

Ortiz, Roxanne Dunbar. "Aboriginal People and Imperialism in the Western Hemisphere." *Monthly Review* (September 1992).

Oxfam. *Facts for Action*, no. 8. London: Oxfam Publishing.

Pacari, Nina. "Taking on the Neoliberal Agenda." *NACLA Report on the Americas* (March–April 1996).

"Pacto de Apoyo Mutuo, Firman Barzon y EZLN." *Cuarto Poder* (July 23, 1996).

Parade, March 15, 1981.

Parenti, Michael. *Democracy for the Few*. 5th ed. New York: St. Martin's Press, 1988.

———. *Inventing Reality*. New York: St. Martin's Press, 1993.

———. *Land of Idols*. New York: St. Martin's Press, 1994.

———. *Democracy for the Few*. 6th ed. New York: St. Martin's Press, 1995.

———. "Popular Sovereignty vs. the State." *Monthly Review* (March 1995).

———. *Against Empire*. San Francisco: City Lights Books, 1995.

Parry, Robert. *Trick or Treason: The October Surprise Mystery*. New York: Sheridan Square Press, 1993.

Passell, Peter. "Race, Mortgage and Statistics: The Unending Debate over a Study of Lending Bias." *New York Times,* May 10, 1996.

Payer, Cheryl. *The World Bank: A Critical Analysis*. New York: Monthly Review, 1982.

Pearce, Jenny. *Under the Eagle*. Boston: South End Press, 1982.

Pechman, Joseph A. *Who Paid the Taxes*. Washington, D.C.: Brookings Institute, 1985.

Peres, Kenneth. "The Corporate Political and Economic Offensive and Its Impact on Labor." Communications Workers of America, District One. *The Economic Report of the President, 2002.*

Perlez, Jane. "Why Poland Swung to Left." *New York Times,* September 21, 1993.

———. "Fast and Slow Lanes on the Capitalist Road." *New York Times,* October 7, 1994.

———. "Out of Cash, Eastern European Health System Has a Relapse." *New York Times,* November 23, 1994.

———. "Ex-Communist Appears to Best Walesa for President of Poland." *New York Times,* November 20, 1995.

———. "Walesa's Nemesis: Aleksander Kwasniewski." *New York Times,* November 21, 1995.

Perlman, Selig. *A Theory of the Labor Movement.* Philadelphia: Porcupine Press, 1928.

Phillips, Kevin. "Reagan's America." *New York Times,* June 17, 1990.

———. *The Politics of Rich and Poor.* New York: Random House, 1990.

Physicians for Human Rights. *The Taliban's War on Women: A Health and Human Rights Crisis in Afghanistan* [online], www.phrusa.org/research/exec.html.

Piven, Frances Fox. "Is It Global Economics or Neo-Laissez-Faire?" *New Left Review* (September–October 1995).

Piven, Frances Fox, and Richard A. Cloward. *Regulating the Poor: The Functions of Public Welfare.* New York: Vintage Books, 1974.

———. *The New Class War.* New York: Vintage Books, 1985.

Plotkin, Sidney, and William E. Scheuerman. *Private Interest, Public Spending.* Boston: South End Press, 1994.

Poulantzas, Nicos. *State, Power, Socialism.* London: Verso, 1978.

"Pox Americana." *Monthly Review* (July–August 1991).

Prendergast, John, and John Fierno. "Crisis in the Horn of Africa." In *Altered States,* edited by Phyllis Bennis and Michel Moushabeck. New York: Olive Branch Press, 1993.

Proper, Carl. "Fighting for Fair Trade." *Dollars and Sense,* April 1986.

Putnam, Robert D. *Bowling Alone: The Collapse and Revival of American Community.* New York: Simon and Schuster, 2000.

Quinney, Richard. *Capitalist Society.* Homewood, Ill.: Dorsey Press, 1979.

Rand McNally. *World Facts in Brief.* New York: Rand McNally, 1986.

———. *World Facts and Maps.* New York: Rand McNally, 1994.

———. *World Facts and Maps.* New York: Rand McNally, 1996.

Ranney, Austin. "Poll Shows Disenchantment with Political Science." *New York Times,* August 12, 1995.

Raskin, Jamin B. "Gerrymander Hypocrisy: Supreme Court's Double Standard." *Nation,* February 6, 1995.

Reed, Betsy. "Aristide's Financial Bind." *Dollars and Sense,* November–December, 1994.

Regan, Jane. "A.I.D.ing U.S. Interests in Haiti." *Covert Action Quarterly* (winter 1994–95).

"Rescuing Boris." *Time,* July 15, 1996.

The Reshaping of New Jersey: The Growing Separation. New Jersey Council of Churches. February 3, 1988.

Rich, Bruce. "World Bank/IMF: Fifty Years Is Enough." In *Fifty Years Is Enough: The Case Against the World Bank and the International Monetary Fund,* edited by Kevin Danaher. Boston: South End Press, 1994.

Ridgeway, James. "Looney Tune Terrorists." *Village Voice,* July 23, 1985.

Robertson, Ian. *Sociology.* 3d ed. New York: Worth, 1987.

Rodney, Walter. *How Europe Underdeveloped Africa.* Washington, D.C.: Howard University Press, 1994.

Roettinger, Philip C. "Reagan Is Repeating Eisenhower's Error." *Los Angeles Times,* March 26, 1986.

Rohter, Larry. "Remembering the Past; Repeating It Anyway." *New York Times,* July 24, 1994.

———. "Haiti Takes the Next Big Step." *New York Times,* December 17, 1995.

———. "Cables Show U.S. Deception on Haitian Violence." *New York Times,* February 6, 1996.

———. "Brazilians Find Political Cost for Help From I.M.F." *New York Times,* August 8, 2002.

Rones, Philip L., Randy E. Ilg, and Jennifer M. Gardner. "Trends in Hours of Work Since the Mid-1970's." *Monthly Labor Review* (April 1997).

Rose, Nancy E. *Put to Work: Relief Programs in the Great Depression.* New York: Monthly Review Press, 1994.

Rosenthal, A. M. "American Class Struggle." *New York Times,* March 21, 1995.

———. "The Secrets of the War." *New York Times,* April 23, 1999.

Ross, John. *Rebellion from the Roots.* Monroe, Maine: Common Courage Press, 1995.

———. *The Annexation of Mexico: From the Aztecs to the IMF.* Monroe, Maine: Common Courage Press, 1998.

Rostow, W. W. *The Stages of Economic Growth.* London: Cambridge University Press, 1964.

Rowse, Arthur E. "Gladio: The Secret U.S. War to Subvert Italian Democracy." *Covert Action Quarterly* (summer 1994).

Running Out of Time. Oregon Public Broadcasting, 1994.

Said, Edward. "Thoughts on a War: Ignorant Armies Clash by Night." In *Beyond the Storm,* edited by Phyllis Bennis and Michel Moushabeck. New York: Olive Branch Press, 1993.

Sampson, Anthony. *The Sovereign State of ITT.* Greenwich, Conn.: Fawcett Publications, 1974.

Sanger, David E. "Trade Group Orders U.S. to Alter Law for First Time." *New York Times,* January 18, 1996.

———. "U.S. to Alter Law for First Time." *New York Times,* April 30, 1996.

Sau, Ranjit. *Unequal Exchange, Imperialism and Underdevelopment.* Oxford, England: Oxford University Press, 1978.

Schaeffer, Robert K. *Understanding Globalization.* 2d ed. New York: Rowman and Littlefield, 2003.

Scher, Abby. "Habitual Offenders." *Dollars and Sense,* September–October 1999.

Schlesinger, Stephen, and Stephen Kinzer. *Bitter Fruit.* Garden City, N.Y.: Anchor/Doubleday, 1983.

Schmitt, Eric. "U.S. Army Buried Iraqi Soldiers Alive in Gulf War." *New York Times,* September 15, 1991.

———. "Clinton Devises New Guidelines on Arms Sales." *New York Times,* November 16, 1994.

———. "School for Assassins, or Aid to Latin Democracy?" *New York Times,* April 3, 1995.

Schor, Juliet B. *The Overworked American: The Unexpected Decline of Leisure.* New York: Basic Books, 1992.

Sclove, Richard E., Madeline L. Scammell, and Breena Holland. *Community-Based Research in the United States.* Amherst, Mass.: Loka Institute, 1998.

Scott, Anthony, and David Gordon. "The Russian Timber Rush." *Amicus Journal* (fall 1992).

Seguino, Stephanie. "Trade Secrets: Sexism and Export-led Growth in South Korea." *Dollars and Sense,* January–February 1995.

Sennot, Charles M. "The $150 Billion 'Welfare' Recipients: U.S. Corporations." *Boston Globe,* July 7, 1996.

Shalom, Stephen Rosskamm. "Capitalism Triumphant?" *Z Magazine,* April 1989.

———. *Imperial Alibis.* Boston: South End Press, 1993.

Sherman, Howard J. "The Concentration of Economic Power in the United States." In *Critical Perspectives in Sociology,* edited by Berch Berberoglu. Dubuque, Iowa: Kendall/Hunt, 1993.

Shiva, Vandana. "International Institutions Practicing Environmental Double Standards." In *Fifty Years Is Enough: The Case Against the World Bank and the International Monetary Fund,* edited by Kevin Danaher. Boston: South End Press, 1994.

Shniad, Sid. "Former UN Official on Human Cost of Iraq Policy." *Guardian,* January 28, 1999.

Shor, Fran. "One Person, One Vote—Seize the Time." *Common Dreams News Center* [online], www.commondreams.org/wiews/110900-102.htm [November 9, 2000].

Shortchanging Education: How U.S. Spending on Grades K–12 Lags Behind Other Industrial Nations. Washington, D.C.: Economic Policy Institute, 1990.

Shuman, Michael. *Going Local: Creating Self-Reliant Communities in the Global Age.* New York: Free Press, 1997.

———. "Going Local: Devolution for Progressives." *Nation,* October 12, 1998.

Sick, Gary. *October Surprise: America's Hostages in Iran and the Election of Ronald Reagan.* New York: Times Books, 1991.

Simpson, Christopher. *The Splendid Blonde Beast: Money, Law, and Genocide in the Twentieth Century.* Monroe, Maine: Common Courage Press, 1995.

Sims, Calvin. "Two in Chile Get Jail Terms In U.S. Killing." *New York Times,* May 31, 1995.

———. "Chilean Jail for Officers Is Gracious, But Still Jail." *New York Times,* November 24, 1995.

———. "In Peru, a Fight for Fresh Air." *New York Times,* December 12, 1995.

Singer, Daniel. "Letter From Europe: Ex-Communists and Rough Beasts." *Nation,* November 14, 1994.

Skolnick, Jerome H., and Elliot Currie. *Crisis in American Institutions.* 6th ed. Boston: Little, Brown and Company, 1985.

Sloyan, Patrick J. "Army Said to Plow Under Possibly Thousands of Iraqi Soldiers in Trenches." *Washington Post,* September 12, 1991.

Smart, Tim. "Count Corporate America Among NATO's Staunchest Allies." *Washington Post,* April 13, 1999.

Snell, Bradford. "GM and the Nazis." *Ramparts* (June 1974).

———. "American Ground Transport." In *Crisis in American Institutions.* 6th ed. Edited by Jerome H. Skolnick and Elliot Currie. Boston: Little, Brown and Company, 1988.

Snyder, Louis L. *The Making of Modern Man.* Princeton, N.J.: Van Nostrand Co., 1967.

Social Policy (summer 1992).

Solis, Dianne. "In Mexico, a New Kind of Rebel Emerges." *Wall Street Journal,* September 1, 1995.

Solomon, Norman. *False Hope.* Monroe, Maine: Common Courage Press, 1994.

Sommer, Jeff. "Shares Absorb a New Shock to the System." *New York Times,* June 30, 2002.

Specter, Michael. "Red Flag Aloft, a Russian City Defiantly Upholds Soviet Ways." *New York Times,* February 3, 1996.

Stack, Louise, and Don Morton. *Torment to Triumph in Southern Africa.* New York: Friendship Press, 1976.

Stanley, Alessandra. "The Americans Who Saved Yeltsin (Or Did They?)." *New York Times,* July 9, 1996.

Stavrianos, Leften S. *Global Rift.* New York: William Morrow, 1981.

Steele, Jonathan. *Eternal Russia.* Cambridge, Mass.: Harvard University Press, 1994.

Stein, Nancy, and Mike Klare. "Police Aid for Tyrants." In *The Trojan Horse: A Radical Look at Foreign Aid,* edited by Steve Weissman et al. San Francisco: Ramparts Press, 1974.

Sterngold, James. "Nafta Trade-Off: Some Jobs Lost, Others Gained." *New York Times,* October 9, 1995.

Stevenson, Richard, and Janet Elder. "Poll Finds Concerns That Bush Is Overly Influenced by Business." *New York Times,* July 18, 2002.

Stiglitz, Joseph E. *Globalization and Its Discontents.* New York: W. W. Norton, 2002.

Stockwell, John. *In Search of Enemies.* New York: W. W. Norton, 1978.

Stokes, Randall. *Introduction to Sociology.* Dubuque, Iowa: W. C. Brown, 1984.

Stork, Joe. "Dinosaur in the Tar Pit: The U.S. and the Middle East After the Gulf War." In *Altered States*, edited by Phyllis Bennis and Michel Moushabeck. New York: Olive Branch Press, 1993.

Sweezy, Paul. "What's New in the New World Order?" *Monthly Review* (June 1991).

Szymanski, Albert. *The Capitalist State and the Politics of Class.* Cambridge, Mass.: Winthrop Publishers, 1978.

———. *The Logic of Imperialism.* New York: Praeger, 1981.

Tagliabue, John. "As Multinationals Run the Taps, Anger Rises over Water for Profit." *New York Times,* August 26, 2002.

Tanzer, Michael. *The Sick Society.* New York: Holt, Rinehart, Winston, 1971.

———. "Globalizing the Economy." *Monthly Review* (September 1995).

Taylor, Jeffery. "Russia Is Finished." *Atlantic Monthly* [online], www.theatlantic monthly.com/issues/2001/05/taylor-pl.htm [May 2001].

Taylor, Stuart. "In Wake of Invasion, Much Official Misinformation by U.S. Comes to Light." *New York Times,* November 6, 1983.

Terry, Don. "Cuts in Public Jobs May Hurt Blacks Most." *New York Times,* December 10, 1991.

Thomas, Clive. *The Rise of the Authoritarian State in Peripheral Societies.* New York: Monthly Review, 1984.

Todd, Walker. "Bailing Out the Creditor Class." *Nation,* February 13, 1995.

Toner, Robin. "Casting Doubts: Economy Stinging Bush." *New York Times,* November 26, 1991.

"Understanding the Polish Revolt: An Interview with Daniel Singer and Marta Petrsewicz." *Radical America* (May–June 1981).

United for a Fair Economy. *Too Much* (summer 2001).

———. "Sometimes Failure Is an Option." *Too Much* (summer 2001).

———. "Here's What Enron Actually Did." *Too Much* (winter 2002).

Trainer, Ted. "What Is Development?" *Society and Nature* 3, no. 1 (1995).

Traster, Tina. "Passaic River Listed as 'Endangered.'" *Record,* April 7, 1998.

Tucker, Robert C., ed. *The Marx-Engels Reader.* New York: W. W. Norton, 1972.

Uchitelle, Louis. "As Output Gains, Wages Lag." *New York Times*, June 4, 1987.

———. "This Time, It's a Slow-Growth Economy, Stupid." *New York Times,* March 17, 1996.

———. "1995 Was Good for Companies, and Great for a Lot of C.E.O.'s." *New York Times,* March 29, 1996.

———. "Working Families Strain to Live Middle-Class Life." *New York Times,* September 10, 2000.

United Nations. *Demographic Yearbook, 1999.*

United Nations Association of the USA. "Policy Positions on Substantive Issues:

Resolution on the Western Hemisphere Institute for Security Cooperation" [online], www.unausa.org/ [2001].

United Nations Development Program. *Human Development Report, 1995.* New York: Oxford University Press, 1995.

———. *Human Development Report, 1999.* New York: Oxford University Press, 1999.

———. *Human Development Report, 2001.* New York: Oxford University Press, 2001.

———. *Human Development Report, 2002.* New York: Oxford University Press, 2002.

United Nations Population and Vital Statistics Report.

United Nations Press Release. GA/9979 [online], www.un.org/News/Press/docs/2001/ga9979.doc.htm.

United States Bureau of the Census. *Statistical Abstract of the United States,* Washington, D.C.: Government Printing Office (GPO), various years.

———. Current Population Reports, series P60, no. 176-RD, *Measuring the Effects of Benefits and Taxes on Income and Poverty: 1990.* Washington, D.C.: GPO, 1991.

———. Current Population Reports, series P60–188. *Income, Poverty, and Valuation of Noncash Benefits: 1993.* Washington, D.C.: GPO, 1995.

———. Current Population Reports, series P60–209. *Money Income in the United States: 1999.* Washington, D.C.: GPO, 2000.

———. Current Population Reports, series P60–214. *Poverty in the United States.* Washington, D.C.: GPO, 2001.

———. Current Population Reports, series P60–218. *Money Income in the United States: 2001.* Washington, D.C.: GPO, 2002.

———. Current Population Reports, series P60–219. *Poverty in the United States: 2001.* Washington, D.C.: GPO, 2002.

United States Congress, Congressional Budget Office. *The Changing Distribution of Federal Taxes: 1975–1990,* October 1987.

United States Department of Labor, Bureau of Labor Statistics, bull. 2240. July 1985.

"US Arms Sales." *Mother Jones* [online], www.mojones.com/arms/.

vanden Heuvel, Katrina. "Russia Versus Yeltsin." *Nation,* January 29, 1996.

Vaughan, Doug. "Too Good to Be True: Special Prosecutor's 'Final Report' on Iran-Contra." *Covert Action Quarterly* (spring 1994).

Vilas, Carlos M. "Neoliberal Social Policy: Managing Poverty (Somehow)." *NACLA Report on the Americas* (May–June 1996).

Village Voice, July 23, 1985.

Wallach, Lori, and Michelle Sforza. *Whose Trade Organization?* Washington, D.C.: Public Citizen, 1999.

Wallerstein, Immanuel. *The Capitalist World Economy.* Cambridge, England: Cambridge University Press, 1979.

Walsh, Mary Williams. "Reversing Decades-Long Trend, Americans Retiring Later in Life." *New York Times,* February 26, 2001.

Walters, Ronald. "The Reagan Revolution Sparked L.A.'s Rebellion." *Wall Street Journal,* May 7, 1992.

War Watch. Santa Cruz, Calif.: Out Now, no. 22 (February 1994).

———. Santa Cruz, Calif.: Out Now, no. 23 (May 1994).

Washburn, Jennifer. "Power Bloc: Turkey and Israel Lock Arms." *Progressive,* December 1998.

Wasserman, Harvey. *Harvey Wasserman's History of the United States.* New York: Harper and Row, 1972.

"We Arm the World: U.S. Is Number One Weapons Dealer." *Defense Monitor* 20, no. 4 (1991).

Weber, Max. "Class, Status, Party." In *From Max Weber: Essays in Sociology,* edited by Hans H. Gerth and C. Wright Mills. New York: Oxford University Press, 1946.

Webster, Andrew. *Introduction to the Sociology of Development.* 2d ed. Atlantic Highlands, N.J.: Humanities Press, 1991.

Weiner, Jon. "Capitalist Shock Therapy." *Nation* (June 25, 1990).

Weiner, Tim. "Key Haiti Leaders Said to Have Been in the C.I.A.'s Pay." *New York Times,* November 1, 1993.

———. "C.I.A. Formed Haitian Unit Later Tied to Narcotics Trade." *New York Times,* November 14, 1993.

———. "In 1990, U.S. Was Still Training Salvadoran Civilians Tied to Killings." *New York Times,* December 14, 1993.

———. "Guatemalan Agent of C.I.A. Tied to Killing of American." *New York Times,* March 23, 1995.

———. "Long Road to Truth About Killings in Guatemala." *New York Times,* March 24, 1995.

———. "Once Commandos for U.S., Vietnamese Are Now Barred." *New York Times,* April 14, 1995.

———. "Haitian Ex-Paramilitary Leader Confirms C.I.A. Relationship." *New York Times,* December 3, 1995.

———. "U.S. Plan to Change Iran Leaders Is an Open Secret Before It Begins." *New York Times,* January 26, 1996.

Weiner, Tim, with Sam Dillon. "In Guatemala's Dark Heart, C.I.A. Lent Succor to Death." *New York Times,* April 2, 1995.

Weiss, Lawrence D. "Excellent Benefits: Clinton Embraces the Private Health Insurance Industry." *Socialist Review* 23, no. 1 (1993).

Weissman, Steve, et al. *The Trojan Horse: A Radical Look at Foreign Aid.* San Francisco: Ramparts Press, 1974.

"What the Boss Makes." *Forbes,* June 15, 1987.

Whitt, J. Allen. "Toward a Class-Dialectical Model of Power: An Empirical

Assessment of Three Competing Models of Political Power." *American Sociological Review* (February 1979).

"Who Is Next?" *Nation,* November 12, 1983.

Wiener, Jon. "Capitalist Shock Therapy." *Nation,* June 25, 1990.

Wilkerson, Isabel. "Two Decades of Decline Chronicled by Kerner Follow-Up Report." *New York Times,* March 1, 1988.

Williams, Darol J. "IMF Lends $10 Billion to Russia." *Star Ledger,* February 23, 1996.

Williams, Ian. *The U.N. for Beginners.* New York: Writers and Readers Publishing, 1995.

Wilson, William Julius. *The Truly Disadvantaged.* Chicago: University of Chicago Press, 1987.

Wines, Michael. "Bush's Responses Come from Script." *New York Times,* November 26, 1991.

————. "An Ailing Russia Lives a Tough Life That's Getting Shorter." *New York Times,* December 5, 2000.

Wise, David. *The Politics of Lying.* New York: Vintage, 1973.

Wise, David, and Thomas B. Ross. *The Invisible Government.* New York: Vintage, 1974.

Wolfe, Alan. *The Seamy Side of Democracy.* 2d ed. New York: Longman, 1978.

Wolff, Edward N. *The Rich Get Increasingly Richer: Latest Data on Household Wealth During the 1980s.* Washington, D.C.: Economic Policy Institute, 1993.

————. "Trends in Household Wealth in the United States, 1962–83 and 1983–89." *Review of Income and Wealth,* series 40, no. 2 (June 1994).

World Almanac and Book of Facts, 1993. New York: Pharos Books, 1993.

World Book of Facts, 1996. New York: Pharos Books, 1996.

World Facts in Brief. New York: Rand McNally, 1986.

World Guide, 1997/1998. Oxford, England: New Internationalist Publications, 1998.

World Guide, 2000/2001. Oxford, England: New Internationalist Publications, 2001.

World Trade Organization [online], www.wto.org/english/thewto_e/thewto_e.htm.

Yates, Michael. *Longer Hours, Fewer Jobs.* New York: Monthly Review Press, 1994.

Youngers, Coletta. "US Entanglements in Columbia Continue." *NACLA Report on the Americas* (March–April 1998).

Zaidi, Sarah, and Mary C. Smith Fawzi. "Health of Baghdad's Children." *Lancet* (December 2, 1995).

Zepezauer, Mark, and Arthur Naiman. *Take the Rich off Welfare.* Tucson, Ariz.: Odonian Press, 1996.

Zinn, Howard. *A People's History of the United States.* New York: Harper and Row, 1980.

Zuger, Abigail. "Russia Has Few Weapons as Infectious Diseases Surge." *New York Times,* December 5, 2000.

INDEX

399